Knowledge Spillover-based Strategic Entrepreneurship

T0300086

This book is about the role of knowledge spillovers and strategic entrepreneurship in the management context. It focuses on how knowledge spillovers and strategic entrepreneurship are crucial to the process of creative destruction and construction.

The book aims to provide insights into and discussion on how firms combine entrepreneurial action that creates new opportunities for industries, regions and economies. This book is first of its kind to link knowledge management perspectives to strategic entrepreneurship to understand the co-creation process. Being interdisciplinary in nature, this book appeals to entrepreneurship and knowledge management scholars, students and practitioners.

João J. Ferreira is Associate Professor in Management at the University of Beira Interior and NECE Research Unit in Business Sciences, Portugal.

Leo-Paul Dana is Professor at Montpellier Business School, France.

Vanessa Ratten is Associate Professor of Entrepreneurship and Innovation at the Department of Management and Marketing, La Trobe University, Australia.

Routledge Frontiers of Business Management

Knowledge Spillover-based Strategic Entrepreneurship

Edited by João J. Ferreira, Leo-Paul Dana and Vanessa Ratten

LONDON AND NEW YORK

First published 2017 by Routledge

2 Park Square, Milton Park, Abingdon, Oxfordshire OX14 4RN
52 Vanderbilt Avenue, New York, NY 10017

Routledge is an imprint of the Taylor & Francis Group, an informa business

First issued in paperback 2019

British Library Cataloguing in Publication Data
A catalogue record for this book is available from the British Library

Library of Congress Cataloging-in-Publication Data
A catalog record for this book has been requested

ISBN: 978-1-138-95074-0 (hbk)
ISBN: 978-0-367-37045-9 (pbk)

Typeset in Galliard
by Apex CoVantage, LLC

Contents

Figures

Tables

Contributors

José Ricardo C. Andrade is Professor of Human Resources Management at Instituto Superior de Gestão e Administração, Leiria, Portugal.

Liliana Araújo is Master in Economics and Business Administration at Universidade do Porto, Portugal.

Ronald C. Beckett is Adjunct Research Professor at the Centre for Transformative Innovation, Swinburne University, Australia.

Gerard Berendsen is Chairman of the Board of Foundation, Our Common Future 2.0, and is coordinating Next Generation Business Model research initiatives.

Alexander Brem is Professor of Technology and Innovation Management and Head of SDU Innovation and Design Engineering at the University of Southern Denmark, Sønderborg.

Paul K. Couchman is Emeritus Professor at the Department of Management and Marketing of Deakin University, Australia.

Başak Dalgıç is Associate Professor of Economics at the Department of Public Finance, Hacettepe University, Turkey.

Léo-Paul Dana is Professor at Montpellier Business School, France.

Daniela Di Cagno is Full Professor of Microeconomics and Economics of Uncertainty and Information in Luiss "Guido Carli" University of Rome and Head of the Lab for Experimental Economics (CESARE).

Andrea Fabrizi is Official at the Italian Ministry of Economic Development, PhD at LUISS University (Rome, Italy) in History and Theory of Economic Development.

Burcu Fazlıoğlu is Assistant Professor of Economics at the Department of International Entrepreneurship, TOBB University of Economics and Technology, Turkey.

Sara Fernández-López is Associate Professor at the University of Santiago de Compostela, Spain and the Secretary of the Committee of PhD program in Economics and Business.

Fernando Ferreira is Professor at the University Institute of Lisbon (Portugal).

João J. Ferreira is Associate Professor in Management at the University of Beira Interior and NECE Research Unit in Business Sciences, Portugal.

Daniel Feser is Researcher at the Chair of Economic Policy and SME Research, University of Goettingen, Germany.

Dennis Lyth Frederiksen is an MSc. student at Aalborg University, Denmark.

Maribel Guerrero is Researcher at Department of Strategy, Deusto Business School, Spain.

Fernando Herrera is Associate Professor in Engineering and Science at Tecnológico de Monterrey, Campus León, México, and PhD Candidate in Business and Entrepreneurial Activity Management at Universidad de Cantabria, Spain.

Mei-Chih Hu is a Professor of Technology Management at the National Tsing Hua University, China.

Ian McLoughlin joined Monash University in 2008 and was Head of the Department of Management (2008–2013).

Valentina Meliciani is Full Professor of Industrial Economics at the Department of Business and Management at the University LUISS Guido Carli of Rome.

Manuela F. Neves is a PhD candidate in Management at the University of Beira Interior, Portugal.

Andrew O'Loughlin is MBA Director and Associate Professor of Innovation at La Trobe Business School, La Trobe University, Australia.

Till Proeger is Researcher at the Chair of Economic Policy and SME Research, University of Goettingen, Germany.

Vanessa Ratten is Associate Professor of Entrepreneurship and Innovation at the Department of Management and Marketing, La Trobe University, Australia.

David Rodeiro-Pazos is Associate Professor at the University of Santiago, Spain.

María Jesús Rodríguez-Gulías is substitute Professor in the University of A Coruña. She worked in the technology transfer office of University of Santiago de Compostel as technician.

Frank Shiu is Deputy Director of Strategic Planning Division at Display Technology Center of ITRI, Taiwan.

Sandra Tavares Silva is Assistant Professor in Economics at the Universidade do Porto and researcher at CEF.UP, Portugal.

Aurora A.C. Teixeira is Associate Professor in Economics at the Universidade do Porto and researcher at CEF.UP, INESC TEC and OBEGEF, Portugal.

David Urbano is Associate Professor of Entrepreneurship at the Department of Business, Universitat Autònoma de Barcelona, Spain.

Iris Wanzenböck is a PhD Student at the AIT Austrian Institute of Technology, Innovation Systems Department, Austria.

Connie Zheng is Senior Lecturer of Human Resource Management at Deakin Business School, Australia.

Foreword

A generation ago, entrepreneurship was barely on the radar screen of scholars and policy makers. In a world where scale and scope bestowed competitive advantage, there seemed to be little room for start-ups and small business. With the advent of globalization and the shift to knowledge and innovation as driving forces of competitiveness, the prospects for entrepreneurship seemed even more dismal. Scholars dating back to Joseph A. Schumpeter provided compelling reasons why the innovative advantage was inevitably in the domain of the large, incumbent enterprises.

However, sometimes even the experts are wrong. Investments in knowledge, creativity and new ideas are not automatically transformed into innovations. As has been shown time and again, it is one thing to create a new idea; it is another thing to act on that idea. What has become clear in the time elapsing between the previous and present generations is that entrepreneurs have emerged as the conduit for knowledge spillovers by taking ideas and knowledge created in one organizational context and transforming it into innovative activity in the context of a very different organization. Along with the emergence of The Entrepreneurial Society has come the recognition that it is with remarkable consistency the entrepreneurs who are willing to invest the requisite blood, sweat and tears to transform knowledge and ideas into new products and processes.

This book put together by three leading scholars of strategic entrepreneurship, João J. Ferreira, Léo-Paul Dana and Vanessa Ratten, takes knowledge spillovers seriously as a source of strategic entrepreneurship, just as it takes seriously strategic entrepreneurship as a conduit driving those knowledge spillovers, and with it the ensuing regional economic performance. The series of studies contained in these chapters build on a truism that may well prove to be the mantra for economic success in this new strategy – what is good for the entrepreneurs is also good for the place. As the editors share, these chapters provide 'insights and discussion about how firms combine entrepreneurial action that creates new opportunities for industries, regions and economies. This means linking the co-creative knowledge process with environmental dynamics that are strategic and entrepreneurial in nature'.

What emergences in this original, thoughtful and important book is a unity between place and entrepreneurship. The key to linking these two sides of the same coin – place and entrepreneurship – is strategy. What exactly those strategies are and how they transcend entrepreneurship into strategic entrepreneurship just as they transcend regional economies into the strategic management of place is the secret revealed in this inspiring book.

David B. Audretsch
Bloomington, Indiana

Preface

This edited research book is about the role of knowledge spillovers and strategic entrepreneurship. Increasing global attention is being paid to strategic action that generates an entrepreneurial competitive advantage in the marketplace. Knowledge spillovers and strategic entrepreneurship are important to the process of construction in which economies, regions and industries develop and change based on competitive dynamics.

A vast body of literature exists on the knowledge spillover theory of entrepreneurship. The large increase in interest in knowledge spillovers has coincided with the growth of the knowledge economy in the global marketplace.

The aim of the book is to provide insights and discussion about how firms combine entrepreneurial action that creates new opportunities for industries, regions and economies. This means linking the co-creative knowledge process with environmental dynamics that are strategic and entrepreneurial in nature. Part of this approach may be looking at new approaches to knowledge spillovers and strategic entrepreneurship from emerging perspectives such as open innovation, social capital or knowledge intensive business services. This book collects among the most recent developments about knowledge spillovers and strategic entrepreneurship, their determinants and effects to the process of creative destruction and construction in the international environment.

The first chapter, *Knowledge spillover-based strategic entrepreneurship* by V. Ratten, L-P. Dana and J. Ferreira focuses on knowledge spillovers and strategic entrepreneurship by giving a broad overview of the knowledge spillover theory of entrepreneurship and how it influences innovation and public policy decisions. As there is more interest in the role of strategy on entrepreneurial activities it is important to discuss how the research is changing.

Chapter 2, undertaken by L. Araújo, S. Silva and A. Teixeira, *Knowledge spillovers and economic performance of firms located in depressed areas: does geographical proximity matter?*, focuses on the role knowledge spillovers have on the economic performance of firms in depressed areas. This is an interesting approach to take on knowledge spillovers as much of the existing literature focuses on the technology sector, which has a continual flow of knowledge. The chapter discusses the role of geographic proximity to knowledge spillovers but from the perspective of less industrialized areas.

Chapter 3, *The role of multinationals in creating export spillovers as an additional process to productivity spillovers: evidence from Turkey*, by B. Dalgıç and B. Fazlıoğlu, explains the different roles played by the government, university and individual entrepreneurs to foster strategic knowledge creation and diffusion, and commercialization of research outputs in order to build a high-tech-oriented city that would help facilitate the creation and development of many new enterprises to come for future.

Chapter 4 by D. Di Cagno, A. Fabrizi, V. Meliciani and I. Wanzenböck, *Relational spillovers and knowledge creation across European regions: are there differences across R&D institutional sectors?*, identifies the impact of relational spillovers utilizing a European approach, which integrates regional strategy with growth of knowledge-based industries. The chapter suggests that joint research projects are important ways to facilitate knowledge spillovers as they offer a way to share knowledge that would otherwise be hard to access.

Chapter 5, *How to boost knowledge-spillover effects in disadvantaged regions?* by M. Neves, J. Ferreira and F. Ferreira, involves analysis of the means by which HEIs located in poorly industrialized regions, and therefore correspondingly disadvantaged as in the case of Centro, the central inland region of Portugal, might prove able, through specific strategies focusing upon their third *transfer of knowledge* mission, to boost and support the launch and future survival of new companies and thereby contributing towards the competitiveness and development of their host regions.

Chapter 6, *Institutional entrepreneurship: a new interconnectivity between government—university—enterprises in Wuhan future technology city of China*, by C. Zheng, discusses institutional entrepreneurship by examining the interconnectivity of government and university in China. As the world's largest economy China has increasingly become focused on knowledge intensive industries as way to increase their population's standard of living. This has meant that increased emphasis has been given to knowledge industries that have value-added benefits for industry. The chapter highlights how technology cities are emerging in parts of China from the knowledge spillovers that exist in these geographic areas.

Chapter 7 by S. Fernández-López, M. Rodríguez-Gulías and D. Rodeiro-Pazos, *The performance of the academic KIBS firms in a 'moderate innovators' country: a longitudinal analysis*, focuses on the performance of knowledge-intensive business services in a moderate innovators country. This chapter takes the interesting approach that knowledge and innovation are better understood using longitudinal data that focuses on the emerging context of industry settings. The role of academic depositories of knowledge spillovers is discussed in terms of its affect on innovation performance.

Chapter 8, *Ambidexterity revisited: the influence of structure and context and the dilemma exploration vs. exploitation*, by J. Andrade, J. Ferreira and V. Ratten, presents a systematic literature review regarding the influence of context and structure in the formation of organizational ambidexterity. The main mechanisms of structure and context with effects on organizational ambidexterity are presented in a holistic view of the main debates in the field.

Chapter 9, by R. C. Beckett and G. Berendsen, *Learning to compete: entrepreneurial roles exploiting knowledge spillovers*, aims to explore innovative opportunities and exploiting knowledge spillovers may give a competitive advantage to an established enterprise or may lead to the establishment of a new enterprise. In this chapter, the authors extend a representation of five generic internal and external innovation roles observed in more than 60 Australian and Dutch innovative SME projects to consider entrepreneurial and spillover influence, building on the combined work of others.

Chapter 10, *Interconnectivity between academic organizations and established firms for a strategic and knowledge fostering purpose: an exploratory study in an emerging economy*, by F. Herrera, M. Guerrero and D. Urbano, discusses the interconnectivity between academic and established firms using the knowledge spillover theory of entrepreneurship. Due to the significance of academic organizations in the knowledge economy, the chapter stresses how more firms need to use strategy as way of understanding regional innovation and global competitiveness. In addition, the chapter focuses on an emerging economy perspective, which is important due to the abundance of studies on developed countries. As more emerging economies are utilizing knowledge spillovers to increase their economic performance, the way innovation is used as a strategic necessity is crucial to the continued success of firms as part of their transition.

Chapter 11, *International knowledge transfer from Kodak to ITRI: a strategic alliance learning perspective*, by F. Shiu, C. Zheng and M-C. Hu, utilizes a case study approach to examine the role of knowledge spillovers in international business transactions. This means the changing nature of Kodak is evaluated in terms of knowledge transfers and strategic alliances. As coopetition is important in facilitating knowledge spillovers this chapter has crucial linkages to strategic decisions.

Chapter 12 by D. Feser and T. Proeger, *Heterogenous professional identities as an intra-sectoral knowledge filter*, stresses the role of intra-sectoral knowledge filters by focusing on heterogenous professional identities. This is represented by different types of knowledge spillovers that make the information dissemination process more complex.

Chapter 13, *From knowledge to innovation: a review on the evolution of the absorptive capacity concept*, by D. L. Frederiksen and A. Brem, explores the evolution of the absorptive capacity concept in knowledge management research. Absorptive capacity has been viewed as a key ingredient for knowledge spillovers, which lead to successful strategies for entrepreneurial ventures. As knowledge and innovation are interwoven concepts due to their applicability in management research, this chapter contributes to a better understanding of dynamic entrepreneurial processes based on knowledge spillovers.

Chapter 14 by P. K. Couchman, A. O'Loughlin, I. McLoughlin and V. Ratten, *Knowledge spillovers and innovation spaces in Australia*, seeks to put the 'political' back into the 'economy', and in so doing pursue a perspective which hitherto has been poorly developed in the study of innovation and its management. The authors argue that innovation and associated government policy is essentially political in so far as the actors so engaged 'exert control, influence, or power over each other' in order to pursue interests and achieve desired ends. They examine one element of contemporary innovation policy and practice, i.e. attempts at fostering innovation at sub-national levels in regions and localities through the designation of defined spaces – 'precincts' and 'corridors' – in terms of their presumed or prospective capacity to become locales of innovation.

The last chapter (Chapter 15), *Future research directions for knowledge spillovers and strategic entrepreneurship*, by V. Ratten, L-P. Dana and J. Ferreira, concludes the book by discussing future research directions for knowledge spillovers and strategic entrepreneurship. The conclusion chapter summarizes the research about the theory of knowledge spillovers by suggesting areas of interest for emerging research. This is important in helping future researchers continue to study the important area of knowledge spillovers and strategic entrepreneurship.

The Editors

João J. Ferreira, Léo-Paul Dana and Vanessa Ratten

Acknowledgements

I would like to thank my family.
   João Ferreira
   I thank my mum Kaye Ratten for her entrepreneurial spirit, support, fun and intelligence.
   Vanessa Ratten
   In memory of my parents gone with the Christchurch earthquakes.
   Léo-Paul Dana

Introduction

1 Knowledge spillover-based strategic entrepreneurship
An overview

Vanessa Ratten, Léo-Paul Dana
and *João J. Ferreira*

Introduction

A new linkage between the knowledge management and entrepreneurship literature has occurred with the emergence of the knowledge spillover theory of entrepreneurship (Ghio et al., 2015). This is due to knowledge being one of the main drivers of a regions' competitive advantage when it is combined with entrepreneurship (Caiazza et al., 2015). The term knowledge spillover gained ascendancy with the publication of David Audretsch's seminal book 'Innovation and Industry Evolution', which focused on the role of entrepreneurial and innovative firms in creating wealth-generating activities.

Despite the novelty of knowledge spillovers and entrepreneurship there is a lack of consensus in the definition of the theory (Ghio et al., 2015). This is due to the knowledge spillover theory of entrepreneurship still having some ambiguities due to the blurred links between knowledge management and strategic entrepreneurship (Qian and Acs, 2013). Caiazza et al. (2015:5) proposes that according to the knowledge spillover theory of entrepreneurship 'entrepreneurial opportunities created in a firm, but left in a latent form as a result of the uncertainty in knowledge, serve as a source of latent entrepreneurship that others can turn into an emergent form'. The latent part of the knowledge spillover theory of entrepreneurship is important as it acknowledges that there are undiscovered usages and elements of knowledge that can be found by others. Audretsch (1995) focused on the latent perspective by stating that there is a discrepancy between the creation of knowledge and its exploitation. By focusing on the opportunities created by knowledge then others can exploit it at a later stage.

Liao and Phan (2015) describe latent entrepreneurship as coming from entrepreneurial opportunities, which emerge from the identification of entrepreneurial capabilities. The undertaking of entrepreneurial activity means that firms, organizations and individuals can discover and act upon opportunities (Ratten, 2011; 2014). This means that it is important to utilize entrepreneurial opportunities to create new possibilities, as it enables creativity to emerge, which previously may have been missed. Entrepreneurial opportunities often lead to the concretization of knowledge that is later developed by other firms (Acs et al., 2009).

Knowledge spillovers are not directly observable due to the difficulty in describing and explaining how information is accumulated and transferred. A general overview of knowledge spillovers includes procedures about why things are done or the skills and competences that are part of a firms business activity. Cohen and Levinthal (1989:571) define knowledge spillovers as 'any original, valuable knowledge generated in the research process which becomes publicly accessible, whether it be knowledge fully characterizing an innovation, or knowledge of a more intermediate nature'. This means that the extent of knowledge spillovers is sometimes hard to articulate as it can be shared in a variety of different ways. Some firms collaborate by exchanging knowledge so it leaks rather than is directly transferred in a deliberate process.

A broader definition of knowledge spillovers is used by some researchers to include the elusive nature of knowledge as it is hard to capture. A recent definition is by Ko and Liu (2015:263) who define knowledge spillovers as 'the unintentional flow of knowledge from one network party to another'. This means that there are external benefits from the creation of knowledge when it is spilled over to other sources (Audretsch and Lehmann, 2006). Due to the importance of knowledge-generating activity, there is growing recognition of the knowledge spillover theory of entrepreneurship by business, academics and policy analysts (Ghio et al., 2015). In conjunction with this importance has been the focus for most research on the key research questions in the field of knowledge spillovers and entrepreneurship being: 'what is the role of knowledge spillovers to entrepreneurship?', and 'what impact does knowledge have in the entrepreneurial society?'.

Ghio et al. (2015) suggests that three conditions need to be met in order for the knowledge spillover theory of entrepreneurship to be met. First, there needs to be a curiosity about the role of knowledge in order for the development of entrepreneurship to occur. Second, there needs to be a serious commitment by the researchers to focus on knowledge spillovers using an entrepreneurship perspective. Third, there needs to be justification of the link between knowledge and entrepreneurship using appropriate theory and data collection. These conditions are important and provide the basis for this chapter in terms of linking knowledge spillovers to strategic entrepreneurship.

Despite the increased interest in knowledge spillovers there is still little understanding about the concept from a strategic entrepreneurship perspective (Ko and Liu, 2015). During the knowledge spillover process, firms can change the way they share knowledge depending on their strategies around entrepreneurship. In this chapter, we seek to develop a better understanding about the process of knowledge spillovers and strategic entrepreneurship. The central research question that motivates this chapter is: 'What is the role of knowledge spillovers to strategic entrepreneurship?' and 'How is knowledge being spilled over to enable entrepreneurial opportunities to develop?'.

In this chapter, we anticipate that knowledge spillovers will become increasingly important for entrepreneurial firms to develop their strategic direction. In addition, we expect that firms that focus on developing knowledge spillovers can become better strategic entrepreneurs. Therefore, we suggest the next step in developing the knowledge spillovers and strategic entrepreneurship fields includes three main areas of exploration. First, more research is needed on how international collaboration is impacting knowledge spillover in different sectors. Second, the type of knowledge spillover needs to have more light shed on them to develop potential new theories incorporating strategic entrepreneurship. Third, the ways policies and regulations can facilitate knowledge spillovers need to be investigated. These areas are highlighted in the next sections of the literature review, which focus on knowledge spillovers.

Literature review

Sometimes firms will see knowledge in a novel way so its value is differentiated depending on the circumstance. Knowledge due to its complex nature is subject to spillovers as it is not possible to exclude it from business transactions. Normally knowledge flows between firms that have similar inputs or outputs as part of their value creation process (Steen and Hansen, 2014). However, sometimes knowledge flows from one source to another without direct intervention and rather through association. This has led to knowledge playing a key role in economic, regional and social growth (Hulsbeck and Pickave, 2014).

Knowledge is a broad concept that has a variety of meanings depending on the context and situation under investigation. Steen and Hansen (2014:2033) define knowledge as 'including technological know-why, operational know-how, organizational capabilities, network relations (know-who) and as embedded in tools, equipment and infrastructure'. This definition is adopted in this chapter as it takes an open and inclusive approach to the meaning of knowledge.

The spillover part of knowledge is also difficult to conceptualize due to its elusive nature. This is due to spillovers taking a variety of forms depending on their applicability, composition and content (Cooke, 2012). Erlinghagen and Markard (2012) refer to spillover mechanisms as mostly entrepreneurial spin-offs that involve the development of innovative capabilities. Other types of spillovers include diversification into other sectors, social networking for business growth and mobility of technology for other usages.

Knowledge can take a variety of forms including useful new knowledge and existing knowledge that is spilled over and utilized in the formation of innovation (Acs et al., 2002). Steen and Hansen (2014: 2030) states 'knowledge spillovers are crucial to innovation, but it is largely unclear what knowledge spillovers are actually made of and how they happen'. When knowledge is transferred into a new context, development and commercialization opportunities often occur (Bathelt et al., 2011). Entrepreneurial spin-offs enable new knowledge to be produced by individuals employed by a firm (Karlsen, 2011).

Knowledge can be learned without much intention but needs to be transferred in order for it to have a spillover effect. Sometimes knowledge is also lost depending on the situation, which means that investing in the development of knowledge requires effort and time on behalf of the entities involved (Jensen et al., 2007). This has led to there being a growing recognition particularly amongst technology firms of the cognitive distance between new and old forces of knowledge (Desrochers and Leppala, 2011).

Knowledge is a resource that can help increase a firm's competitive advantage as it enables the generation of additional income. This results from knowledge affecting a firm's competitive strategies that impacts market position (Henderson and Cockburn, 1994). In order for firms to compete better they need to create, combine and transfer knowledge in a new way (Kogut and Zander, 1992). Knowledge can be improved when firms invest more in research and development (Peters, 2009). Sometimes firms invest by collaborating with other firms in their network in order to absorb and share knowledge (Carmeli and Waldman, 2010). This may involve absorptive capabilities when relational aspects between firms serve as a way to develop knowledge. Absorptive capabilities involve firms exploiting sources of knowledge to apply it to business purposes (Cohen and Levinthal, 1990). An important way to do this is by firms recognizing the value of new knowledge by incorporating it into their strategic direction.

Ko and Liu (2015) discuss how it is difficult to control knowledge as there is limited collaborative arrangements between the developer and receiver of knowledge. There can be a time delay in the receiver of knowledge absorbing it and then implementing it within an organizational context (Audretsch and Lehmann, 2006). Knowledge is received and shared in different ways depending on how, when and where it was developed (Argote and Ingram, 2000). Knowledge transfer can also occur by mutual consideration but is often the result of serendipity.

The absorption of knowledge needs to incorporate both collaborative and innovative capabilities in order for it to have success (Cozza and Zanfei, 2015). Part of this success involves firms being in proximity when transferring knowledge. This is due to firms absorbing knowledge when they collaborate with others (Audretsch, 1995). Part of this process involves firms accessing external spillovers, which can serve as investments in research and development. In order to facilitate the absorption of external knowledge it is helpful for firms to be in close proximity to individuals, firms and government entities that are originators of novel innovations (Audretsch and Lehmann, 2005).

The key difference in knowledge spillovers compared to knowledge transfer is that it is uncompensated or undercompensated when it occurs (Agarwal et al., 2010). The additional advantages of knowledge spillovers to other sources mean that it is different to knowledge transfer, which implies a compensation rather than positive association to both creator and recipient. Knowledge flows occur when knowledge is transferred from one context to another (Hansen, 2008). This means that knowledge differs from information as it is complex and hard to codify or explain (Fischer and Varga, 2003). Information that is factual can usually be transferred through oral or written communication and is more easily ascertainable than knowledge.

Knowledge-originating firms can be oblivious to the value of their knowledge until it is recognized by others. This lack of intelligence about how to realize the full potential of knowledge is an important strategic consideration for firms (Kotha, 2010). Ko and Liu (2015) assert that knowledge is only ascertained and valued when it is used in an appropriate manner. There has been an increased interest in the knowledge economy due to the emergence of technological innovations, which have changed society. Knowledge intensive industries have developed that have given rise to more entrepreneurial ventures that compete based on timely introduction of technological innovations.

Knowledge that is generated can be socially or commercially exploited by firms. The potential value of knowledge may be unrecognized by existing firms that are unable to utilize it effectively. This means there is an unwillingness to introduce new knowledge that changes the status quo of their firms. This results in knowledge to spill over from its origin to be acted upon by entrepreneurs that create a new venture. This has lead to knowledge being the primary source of entrepreneurship and resulting economic growth (Acs et al., 2013).

Knowledge spillovers

Knowledge spillovers involve a process, which assesses the transferring or diffusing of knowledge into a new context or domain (Steen and Hansen, 2014). Innovation needs knowledge spillovers as it enables knowledge to be applied in a different way. The process of knowledge spillovers has enabled business models and markets to combine knowledge in a new way. Despite the increased attention of knowledge spillovers in the literature, there is still limited information about how spillovers occur, the reasons why they happen and what they actually involve (Steen and Hansen, 2014).

Beaudry and Schiffauerova (2009) proposed that knowledge spillovers can have either agglomeration or urbanization effects. Agglomeration effects are the result of the co-location of similar firms in the same sector (Steen and Hansen, 2014). Sometimes agglomeration effects are discussed as Marshall–Arrow–Romer specialization externalities (Beaudry and Schiffauerova, 2009). This means that agglomeration effects often result in continuous incremental innovation due to firms in the same sector collaborating in a steady manner (Asheim et al., 2011). This incremental innovation means that strategic entrepreneurship results when knowledge spillovers occur to create new products, processes or technologies. Urbanization effects involve the co-location of different economic activities.

Sometimes referred to as Jacobs or diversity externalities, they are important in heterogenous economic entities combining knowledge in a new way. This means that as compared to agglomeration effects, urbanization effects often result in radical innovations (Asheim et al., 2011). Fischer and Varga (2003) propose that innovation involves the application and use of knowledge to solve practical problems. The knowledge utilized in innovation can be scientific or technical depending on its source and the way it is transformed and explained to others. The essential knowledge used in a spillover context can be specialized and in tacit rather than explicit form (Fischer and Varga, 2003). This means that knowledge when it is transferred needs to be easy to apply in order for it to be strategically utilized for entrepreneurial activities.

Most studies on knowledge spillovers focus on how it occurs rather than the ingredients of the process (Steen and Hansen, 2014). The three main generic knowledge spillover mechanisms are adaptation, application and collaboration

(Desrochers and Leppala, 2011). Knowledge can be disseminated in a variety of ways including by informal collaboration, information leakage and staff turnover (Pinch and Henry, 1999). Most knowledge spillovers come from the knowledge within individuals that is embedded as part of their experiences. The other ways knowledge can be spilled is from the processes and actors involved.

Steen and Hansen (2014) refer to knowledge spillovers as including people, patents, equipment, standards and business models. The uncertainty of knowledge spillovers means that there is some risk involved in the process. This has lead to investment being needed in developing partnerships that integrate new knowledge sources that can take time and money to develop (Steen and Hansen, 2014). In addition, when there are geographically distant sources of knowledge then there may be more risk involved in tapping into ways of using this knowledge (Nooteboom et al., 2007). Organizational diversity is increasingly being referred to as a way to access knowledge spillovers as individuals look at things in a new way (Schot and Geels, 2007). The diversity management literature suggests that individuals with different socio-economic backgrounds can cooperate in an entrepreneurial manner.

The production of new knowledge relies on this experiential aspect of learning that impacts knowledge spillovers. The cost of accessing knowledge spillovers is reduced when there is less geographical proximity making knowledge flows location-specific (Padmore and Gibson, 1998). The local nature of knowledge spillovers means that economic geography has been a key issue in the literature. Economic geography and strategy means that knowledge can be external to a firm but located in a close geographic location (Patton et al., 2009). Jaffe (1989) found that firms absorb knowledge more easily when it is technologically close to their existing sources of knowledge. Woerter (2012) suggests that the technological proximity of firms to other firms results in higher competitive performance due to better knowledge diffusion. This happens in public/private partnerships that exist between academia and technology firms that feed an innovation trajectory (Teece et al., 1997).

Firms usually find it easier to absorb and recognize useful knowledge when other firms are in close geographic or industry proximity. The sharing of knowledge between firms in close geographic proximity enables better understanding about the context of the knowledge (Brown and Duguid, 2001). The meaning of knowledge changes when it is shared amongst participants.

The flow of knowledge is influenced by a number of factors, including environmental context (Ko and Liu, 2015). More specifically, knowledge spillovers involve firms collecting leaked knowledge and transforming it into strategic action (Ko and Liu, 2015). The flow of knowledge is sometimes difficult to control as it can be unintentional and unknown until it is recognized by individuals. This means that there are different ways firms can strategically capture and process knowledge that has spilled over from different sources.

Knowledge spillovers are different to other theories about entrepreneurship as it focuses on sources of innovation from unintended circumstances. There can be more knowledge spillovers resulting from research organizations that create

and Grigoroudis, 2014). Ways to do this might be through both informal and formal regulatory behavior. Informal knowledge creation can be supported by policies aimed at making it easier to start and retain businesses that are innovating. This could include informal networking events that are sponsored by governments, which encourage free thinking and creativity. This would enable new ways of looking at knowledge without the constraining environments of traditional workplaces. Informal policies can focus more on culture and social capabilities needed for knowledge creation and sharing (Caiazza et al., 2015). Cultures that encourage new ways of doing things through open innovation can affect entrepreneurship policies. Social behavior is also part of informal mechanisms that enable knowledge to be linked to business creation. A way to do this might be to implement policies aimed at emphasizing social innovations or collaboration that provides strategic benefits to society. This might include medical or technology innovations that help us lead better lives.

The facilitation of inter-firm collaboration by sharing knowledge is a crucial part of the way policy can impact society in a positive manner. Formal policies can include emphasizing better regulatory frameworks for encouraging the emergence of specific industries. This might include the reduction in tax rates needed for knowledge creation, especially those linking public and private institutions. Policies are often determined based on regional differences and the way government interacts with business and educational providers. Regions have different levels of competitiveness that depend on political support of knowledge creation, dissemination and exploitation, which impacts entrepreneurial activity (Levie and Autio, 2011). A region's competitiveness will be based on their investment in knowledge that results in the creation and transfer of strategic entrepreneurial outcomes.

Conclusion

In this chapter we have discussed the emergence of the knowledge spillover theory of entrepreneurship. We have integrated the role of knowledge spillovers with strategic entrepreneurship, which is the focus of this book. We indicated that it is important for firms' and regions' competitiveness that knowledge spillovers are utilized for strategic entrepreneurship reasons. This is due to the knowledge effects on entrepreneurial capabilities that can serve as a means for reinforcing global competitive advantage. We provided an explanation for the importance of knowledge spillovers and strategic entrepreneurship by revealing the crucial role information plays in society. For researchers, this chapter is useful in synthesizing the knowledge spillover theory of entrepreneurship and how it has evolved to focus more on strategic objectives of our global society. For managers, our chapter suggests that knowledge dissemination and commercialization is important for a firm's strategic growth. For policy planners, our chapter has discussed the importance of knowledge being developed and supported at a local, regional and international level. Overall, this chapter serves as good starting point for the other chapters that follow in this book.

References

Acs, Z.J., Anselin, L. and Varga, A. (2002) 'Patents and innovation counts as measures of regional production of new knowledge', *Research Policy*, 31(7): 1069–85.

Acs, Z.J., Audretsch, D.B., Braunerhjelm, P. and Carlsson, B. (2004) *The missing link: The knowledge filter and endogenous growth* (Discussion paper), Center for Business and Policy Studies, Stockholm.

Acs, Z.J., Audretsch, D.B. and Lehmann, E.E. (2013) 'The knowledge spillover theory of entrepreneurship', *Small Business Economics*, 41(4): 757–74.

Acs, Z., Braunerhjelm, P., Audretsch, D.B. and Carlsson, B. (2009) 'The knowledge spillover theory of entrepreneurship', *Small Business Economics*, 32(1): 15–30.

Agarwal, R., Audretsch, D.B. and Sarkar, M.B. (2010) 'Knowledge spillovers and strategic entrepreneurship', *Strategic Entrepreneurship Journal*, 4(4): 271–83.

Argote, L. and Ingram, P. (2000) 'Knowledge transfer: A basis for competitive advantage in firms', *Organizational Behavior and Human Decision Processes*, 82(1): 150–69.

Armington, C. and Acs, Z.J. (2002) 'The determinants of regional variation in new firm formation', *Regional Studies*, 36(1): 33–45.

Asheim, B.T., Boschma, R. and Cooke, P. (2011) 'Constructing regional advantage: Platform policies based on related variety and differentiated knowledge bases', *Regional Studies*, 45(7): 893–905.

Audretsch, D.B. (1995) *Innovation and industry evolution*, MIT Press, Cambridge, MA.

Audretsch, D.B. and Keilbach, M. (2007) 'The theory of knowledge spillover entrepreneurship', *Journal of Management Studies*, 44(7): 1242–54.

Audretsch, D.B., Keilbach, M. and Lehmann, E.E. (2006) *Entrepreneurship and economic growth*, Oxford University Press, New York.

Audretsch, D.B. and Lehmann, E.E. (2005) 'Does the knowledge spillover theory of entrepreneurship hold for regions?', *Research Policy*, 34(8): 1191–1202.

Audretsch, D.B. and Lehmann, F. (2006) 'Entrepreneurial access and absorption of knowledge spillovers: Strategic board and managerial composition for competitive advantage', *Journal of Small Business Management*, 44(2): 155–66.

Audretsch, D.B. and Thurik, A.R. (2001) 'What's new about the new economy? Sources of growth in the managed and entrepreneurial economies', *Industrial and Corporate Change*, 10(1): 267–315.

Bathelt, H., Feldman, M. and Kogler, D.F. (2011) 'Territorial and relational dynamics in knowledge creation and innovation: An introduction', In H. Bathelt, M. Feldman and D.F. Kogler (Eds) *Beyond Territory*, p 1–17, Abingdon, Routledge.

Baumol, W.J. (2002) 'Entrepreneurship, innovation and growth: The David-Goliath symbiosis', *The Journal of Entrepreneurial Finance*, 7(2): 1–10.

Beaudry, C. and Schiffauerova, A. (2009) 'Who's right, Marshall or Jacobs? The localization versus urbanization debate', *Research Policy*, 38(2): 318–37.

Boschma, R. and Frenken, K. (2011) 'The emerging empirics of evolutionary economic geography', *Journal of Economic Geography*, 11(2): 295–307.

Brown, J.S. and Duguid, P. (2001) 'Knowledge and organization: A social-practice perspective', *Organization Science*, 12(2): 198–213.

Caiazza, R., Richarson, A. and Audretsch, D. (2015) 'Knowledge effects on competitiveness: From firms to regional advantage', *Journal of Technology Transfer*, 40(6): 899–909.

Carayannis, E. and Grigoroudis, E. (2014) 'Linking innovation, productivity, and competitiveness: Implications for policy and practice', *Journal of Technology Transfer*, 39(2): 199–218.

Carmeli, A. and Waldman, D.A. (2010) 'Leadership, behavioral context, and the performance of work groups in a knowledge-intensive setting', *Journal of Technology Transfer*, 35(4): 384–400.

Cohen, W.M. and Levinthal, D.A. (1989) 'Innovation and learning. The two faces of R&D', *Economic Journal*, 99: 569–96.

Cohen, W.M. and Levinthal, D.A. (1990) 'Absorptive capacity: A new perspective on learning and innovation', *Administrative Science Quarterly*, 35(1): 128–52.

Cooke, P. (2012) 'Transversality and regional innovation platforms', In P. Cooke, B.T. Asheim, R. Boschma, R. Martin, D. Schwartz and F. Todling (Eds) *Handbook of Regional Innovation and Growth*, pp 303–14, Cheltenham, Edward Elgar.

Cozza, C. and Zanfei, A. (2015) 'Firm heterogeneity, absorptive capacity and technical linkages with external parties in Italy', *Journal of Technology Transfer*, 41(4): 1–19.

Desrochers, P. and Leppala, S. (2011) 'Opening up the "Jacobs spillovers" black box: Local diversity, creativity and the processes underlying new combinations', *Journal of Economic Geography*, 11(5): 843–63.

Dicken, P. (2011) *Global shift, mapping the changing contours of the world economy*, The Guilford Press, New York.

Erlinghagen, S. and Markard, J. (2012) 'Smart grids and the transformation of the electricity sector: ICT firms as potential catalysts for sectoral change', *Energy Policy*, 51: 895–906.

Fischer, M.M. and Varga, A. (2003) 'Spatial knowledge spillovers and university research: Evidence from Austria', *The Annals of Regional Science*, 37: 303–22.

Ghio, N., Guerini, M., Lehmann, E. and Rossi-Lamastra, C. (2015) 'The emergence of the knowledge spillover theory of entrepreneurship', *Small Business Economics*, 44: 1–18.

Hansen, G.H. (2008) 'The far side of international business: Local initiatives in the global workshop', *Journal of Economic Geography*, 8(1): 1–19.

Henderson, R. and Cockburn, I. (1994) 'Measuring competence? Exploring firm effects in pharmaceutical research', *Strategic Management Journal*, 15: 63–84.

Hulsbeck, M. and Pickave, E.N. (2014) 'Regional knowledge production as determinant of high-technology entrepreneurship: Empirical evidence for Germany', *International Entrepreneurship and Management Journal*, 10: 121–38.

Jaffe, A.B. (1989) 'Real effects of academic research', *American Economic Review*, 79(5): 957–70.

Jaffe, A.B., Trajtenberg, M. and Henderson, R. (1993) 'Geographic localization of knowledge spillover as evidenced by patent citations', *Quarterly Journal of Economics*, 63(3): 577–98.

Jensen, M.B., Johnson, B., Lorenz, E. and Lundvall, B.Å. (2007) 'Forms of knowledge and modes of innovation', *Research Policy*, 36(5): 680–93.

Karlsen, A. (2011) 'Cluster creation by reconfiguring communities of practice', *European Planning Studies*, 19(5): 753–74.

Klepper, S. (1996) 'Entry, exit, growth, and innovation over the product life cycle', *The American Economic Review*, 86: 562–83.

Ko, W.W. and Liu, G. (2015) 'Understanding the process of knowledge spillovers: Learning to become social enterprises', *Strategic Entrepreneurship Journal*, 9: 263–85.

Kogut, B. and Zander, U. (1992) 'Knowledge of the firm, combinative capabilities, and the replication of technology', *Organization Science*, 3(3): 383–97.

Kotha, S. (2010) 'Spillovers, spill-ins, and strategic entrepreneurship: America's first commercial jet airplane and Boeing's ascendancy in commercial aviation', *Strategic Entrepreneurship Journal*, 4(4): 284–306.

Levie, J. and Autio, E. (2011) 'Regulatory burden, rule of law, and entry of strategic entrepreneurs: An international panel study', *Journal of Management Studies*, 48(6): 1392–419.

Liao, Y.C. and Phan, P.H. (2015) 'Internal capabilities, external structural holes network positions, and knowledge creation', *Journal of Technology Transfer*, First Online 30 April 2015, 1–20.

Mella, P. (2006) 'Spatial co-localisation of firms and entrepreneurial dynamics', *International Entrepreneurship and Management Journal*, 2(3): 391–412.

Nooteboom, B., Van Haverbeke, W., Duysters, G., Gilsing, V. and Van Den Oord, A. (2007) 'Optimal cognitive distance and absorptive capacity', *Research Policy*, 36(7): 1016–34.

Padmore, T. and Gibson, H. (1998) 'Marketing systems of innovation: II. A framework for industrial cluster analysis in regions', *Research Policy*, 26(6): 625–41.

Patton, D., Warren, L. and Bream, D. (2009) 'Elements that underpin high-tech business incubation processes', *Journal of Technology Transfer*, 34(6): 621–36.

Peters, B. (2009) 'Persistence of innovation: Stylised facts and panel data evidence', *Journal of Technology Transfer*, 34(2): 226–43.

Pinch, S. and Henry, N. (1999) 'Paul Krugman's geographical economics, industrial clustering and the British motor sport industry', *Regional Studies*, 33(9): 815–27.

Qian, H. and Acs, Z.J. (2013) 'An absorptive capacity theory of knowledge spillover entrepreneurship', *Small Business Economics*, 40(2): 185–97.

Ratten, V. (2011) Ethics, entrepreneurship and the adoption of e-book devices. *International journal of innovation and learning*, 10(3): 310–325.

Ratten, V. (2014) Encouraging collaborative entrepreneurship in developing countries: the current challenges and a research agenda. *Journal of Entrepreneurship in Emerging Economies*, 6(3): 298–308.

Schot, J. and Geels, F. (2007) 'Niches in evolutionary theories of technical change', *Journal of Evolutionary Economics*, 17(5): 605–22.

Steen, M. and Hansen, G.H. (2014) 'Same sea. Different ponds: Cross-sectorial knowledge spillovers in the North Sea', *European Planning Studies*, 22(10): 2030–49.

Teece, D.J., Pisano, G. and Shuen, A. (1997) 'Dynamic capabilities and strategic management', *Strategic Management Journal*, 18(7): 509–33.

Varga, A. (2000) 'Local academic knowledge transfers and the concentration of economic activity', *Journal of Regional Science*, 40(2): 289–309.

Woerter, M. (2012) 'Knowledge-based spinoff in technology transfer: The case of autodoc. Inc', *Journal of Technology Transfer*, 21(1–2): 70–6.

Part I

Knowledge spillovers in multiple contexts

2 Knowledge spillovers and economic performance of firms located in depressed areas

Does geographical proximity matter?

Liliana Araújo, Sandra Tavares Silva and *Aurora A.C. Teixeira*

Introduction

Knowledge is defined by several authors, in line with Polanyi (1958), as a learning process that involves cognitive structures and the assimilation of different types of information. A new concept emerges from the diffusion of knowledge: knowledge spillovers, which correspond to a transmission mechanism by which firms benefit from the knowledge produced by other organizations (Sena, 2004). Specifically, knowledge spillovers enable firms to use a greater range of external knowledge, which influences their ability to innovate (Webster, 2004; Yang et al., 2010; LeSage and Fischer, 2012; Song, 2015).

Relating knowledge spillovers with innovation activities is crucial and the evolutionary approach to economic geography appears as essential to frame this relationship as it focuses on the importance of organizational routines within the firm on innovation processes (Boschma and Frenken, 2006).

The importance of knowledge spillovers has been the focus of a significant number of studies that intend to assess, among other aspects, their contribution to regional growth and to explain the differences in economic performance of firms located in distinct regions (Funke and Niebuhr, 2005; Döring and Schnellenbach, 2006; Rodriguez-Pose and Crescenzi, 2008; Autant-Bernard et al., 2013; Kalapouti and Varsakelis, 2014). These studies emphasize, in particular, the positive impact that knowledge spillovers – from the same region or neighbouring regions – have on the regions' growth (Rodriguez-Pose and Crescenzi, 2008). The analysis of the geographical reach of knowledge spillovers is central to a large part of these studies. For some (e.g., Bode, 2004; Verspagen and Schoenmakers, 2004), knowledge diffuses only over short distances, while others (e.g., Bathelt et al., 2004, Teixeira et al., 2008) show that geography is not as relevant in terms of proximity, meaning the transmission of knowledge can occur over long distances.

Notwithstanding the valuable contributions to the literature, most studies on knowledge spillovers refer to countries and regions with relatively high levels of development – USA (e.g., Jaffe, 1986), or, in the European context, Germany (e.g., Beise and Stahl, 1999; Bode, 2004; Funke and Niebuhr, 2005), Sweden (Andersson and Karlsson, 2007) and Italy (Caragliu and Del Bo, 2011).

The peripheral regions have been relatively neglected in this regard (López-Fernández et al., 2012; Grillitsch and Nilsson, 2015). Moreover, they use innovation variables such as patents to measure knowledge spillovers, which correspond to only a part of the innovation process of organizations, especially those larger in size and resources, mostly located in relatively dynamic and developed areas. The few studies (e.g., Fitjar and Rodríguez-Pose, 2011) that have measured knowledge spillovers employing other variables, such as product and process innovation within firms, and that recognize the importance of using different sources of knowledge more related to the routines of firms in innovation processes, have also focused on more developed countries.

More peripheral countries, such as Portugal, have only very recently become the object of interest in terms of research. In particular, Faria and Lima (2012) and Natário et al. (2012) address the specific case of Portugal and Portuguese firms. Using data from the Third Community Innovation Survey (CIS III), Faria and Lima (2012) explicitly analysed the issue of knowledge spillovers, having found positive spillovers of innovation on firm value added and that process innovation spillovers were more prevalent than product innovation spillovers. However, despite the interesting analysis performed, these authors did not tackle the issue of knowledge spillovers in firms located in depressed regions. Natário et al. (2012), in turn, did analyse firms located in depressed/laggard regions, more specifically small and medium enterprises (SMEs) located in Guarda and Azores, concluding that firms in these regions innovate more in marketing and organizational aspects, but did not explicitly address the issue of knowledge spillovers.

The present chapter seeks to fill in this gap by analysing the knowledge spillovers and economic performance of firms located in depressed areas and assessing the extent to which geographical proximity matters. While external knowledge can be acquired on different spatial scales, there are strong theoretical arguments as to why geographical proximity is important for knowledge transfer, particularly in less developed areas (see Grillitsch and Nilsson, 2015). Being that innovation is essentially a collective process where firm-internal knowledge is combined with firm-external knowledge, local knowledge spillovers play a potential important role to access firm-external knowledge.

Thus, the present study, using the concept of depressed areas (PRASD, 2004), analyses the importance and mechanisms of knowledge spillovers to the economic dynamics of firms located in these areas (in this case, the *Vale do Ave*, a region of northern Portugal) in a relatively peripheral country such as Portugal (Fontes, 2005).

The chapter is organized as follows. Section 2 presents a literature review that systematizes the main contributions produced on the concept of knowledge spillovers, within the framework of economic geography and, more specifically, the Evolutionary Economic Geography research line. An overview of the empirical studies that have been submitted in this field is also presented. Section 3 describes the methodology adopted in this study and the empirical results are detailed in Section 4. Finally, we present the conclusions and the main lines for future research.

Importance of knowledge spillovers for the economic performance of firms

Knowledge is seen as a major factor explaining the growth differences between regions (Döring and Schnellenbach, 2006), particularly the differences that exist in terms of corporate performance (Faria and Lima, 2012). In this context, the productivity of a firm tends to depend on knowledge spillovers, including the knowledge that such a firm can absorb (Ornaghi, 2006). In the evolutionary economics framework (e.g., Dosi, 1988), knowledge is considered as intrinsically dynamic; it has a cumulative and path dependence nature, and is not transmitted automatically.

A key question that emerges from the analysis of knowledge spillovers is their link with innovation. In fact, knowledge spillovers influence the innovativeness of firms, because they can draw on a wider range of external knowledge to conduct innovative activities (Yang et al., 2010). The knowledge diffuses from a source firm to another, when the receptor firm uses this knowledge in innovation activities (Griliches, 1992). Webster (2004) confirms this link between knowledge spillovers and innovation. Through an analysis of large Australian firms, the author measures the reasons that lead firms to engage in innovation activities. The results indicate that the routines common to all industries and knowledge spillovers influence the innovative capacity of firms. Thus, knowledge spillovers seem to be a critical part of the activity and innovative capacity of firms (Czarnitzki and Kraft, 2012).

Most studies about the importance of knowledge spillovers for the dynamics of firms and regions are focused on their impact on the following indicators: (i) economic performance of firms and regions, for example the GDP per capita growth rate of the region (e.g., Rodriguez-Pose and Crescenzi, 2008); and (ii) innovation, for example the number of innovations introduced through public research (Beise and Stahl, 1999) or the number of patents granted (Bode, 2004). Also, these studies propose indicators such as patents of neighbouring regions (Bode, 2004), R&D (Rodriguez-Pose and Crescenzi, 2008) or accessibility (Andersson and Karlsson, 2007) to account for knowledge spillovers.

Focusing on the US, Jaffe (1986) measured the spillovers through proximity between firms and expenditure on R&D from other firms and found that there was a positive impact of spillovers on these firms' patenting activity. The study by Beise and Stahl (1999), aimed at determining whether spillovers have an impact on the number of innovations introduced by firms through access to public research, also include variables such as R&D and proximity; in this case, to research at public institutions. They consider the following measures of the spillovers: spending on R&D, firm size and proximity to public research institutions as identified by firms. The authors conclude that, in the case of Germany, firm size and expenditure on R&D have a positive impact, but no significant impact is derived from the proximity of businesses to public research institutions, contrarily to findings from other studies on intra-regional accessibility to R&D in universities, for example, Andersson and Karlsson (2007). This latter study examines another type of spillover, the intra-municipal, using three measures of knowledge, business R&D, R&D in universities and patents, where accessibility to knowledge is measured between areas belonging to each municipality. As in the case of intra-regional spillovers, intra-municipal accessibility emerges as statistically significant and positive in the three types of knowledge, so its effect on municipality growth is positive, measured by the variation in the added value per employee of the municipality.

In summary, these studies show the importance of knowledge spillovers as determinants of economic performance (e.g., Rodriguez-Pose and Crescenzi, 2008) and innovation (Beise and Stahl, 1999).

The analysed studies employ variables that reflect the formal part of business innovation, embodied in indicators such as patents or R&D. Such activities, however, have little expression in less developed regions, particularly in depressed regions. In this context, Fitjar and Rodríguez-Pose (2011) analysed 436 firms in a peripheral region of southwest Norway, using the innovation capacity of firms as the dependent variable, measured through the development of new or significantly improved products or by the fact that the innovation is new to the firm or the market. These authors conclude that the development of innovations is positively and significantly influenced by the diversity of information sources used by businesses. They also conclude that sources used by regional and national firms do not significantly influence the development of innovations. In contrast, international sources emerge as significantly and positively related to innovation. In this study, geographical proximity does not seem to be relevant, whereas other types of proximity, such as cognitive and organizational proximity, seem crucial. This result is to some extent challenged by Natário et al. (2012), who conclude, by analysing the innovation process of small and medium enterprises (SMEs) located in the peripheral areas of *Guarda, São Miguel* and *Santa Maria* in Azores, that the level of cooperation between firms and knowledge sources is higher in innovative firms, presenting a more local, regional or national scope of activity rather than international.[1]

The knowledge sources are also important in Bönte (2008). This author analyses the dissemination of knowledge and geographical proximity (for a maximum driving time of two hours) on the level of trust in customer–supplier relationships in 179 aeronautical firms in Germany. Therefore, as in previous studies, this study analyses the importance of access to external knowledge (customers and suppliers) for the achievement of product and process innovations. The appropriability of knowledge is also analyzed, understood as the risk of generated knowledge in the firm to move on to other firms. The level of trust in firms tends to be higher when partners have been important sources of external knowledge in the past.

Moreover, trust is hampered when firms are not able to protect their innovations. Bönte (2008) also concludes that geographical proximity has a positive impact on cooperation and confidence level.

Referring to the different types of innovation, Czarnitzki and Kraft (2012) employ a sample of 920 innovative firms in Germany, with explanatory variables of firm performance, measured by profit margin, related to knowledge flows that were essential to the development of a product or process, in particular from competitors, customers, suppliers and research institutions. The authors conclude that spillovers from competitors have a positive impact on profits, unlike spillovers from customers, suppliers or research institutions which did not reveal any effect on the firms' performance. In the case of Faria and Lima (2012) and Ornaghi (2006), despite having concluded that innovation and spillovers are positively related to business performance, the impact of externalities differ in the type of innovation – for the first authors, firms assimilate more knowledge from process innovations than product innovations (although the difference is small), whereas for Ornaghi (2006), product innovations have a relatively higher technological diffusion than process innovations.

Methodology

The selection of the depressed municipalities of Vale do Ave

Vale do Ave is located in the *Minho* region of northern Portugal and is composed of eight municipalities: *Fafe, Guimarães, Póvoa de Lanhoso, Santo Tirso, Trofa, Vieira do Minho, Vila Nova de Famalicão* and *Vizela*. This area is classified as depressed (according to *Resolução do Conselho de Ministros* n°11/2004), based on its local Purchasing Power Index, lower than 75 percent of the national Purchasing Power Index. The municipalities of *Vila Nova de Famalicão, Santo Tirso, Guimarães* and *Trofa* have a Purchasing Power Index of, respectively, 82.4 percent, 80.4 percent, 79.8 percent and 79.5 percent, exceeding the national average of 75 percent, so they are not considered depressed municipalities. In contrast, the municipalities of *Vizela, Fafe, Póvoa de Lanhoso* and *Vieira do Minho* (with a Purchasing Power Index of 65.6 percent, 64.8 percent, 58.4 percent and 55.4 percent, respectively), are considered depressed, and businesses located in these municipalities are the target of our analysis (Figure 2.1).[2]

According to the division of firms by sector of activity (cf. data from INE, 2011b), retail and wholesale is the sector with the greatest number of firms in the municipalities of *Vale do Ave* in general (27.4 percent) and in the depressed municipalities in particular. Manufacturing is also very relevant in terms of number of firms (16.2 percent), particularly in the municipalities of *Fafe* (18.9 percent) and *Vizela* (20.3 percent), emerging with the second highest weight after the trade sector.

For a country of intermediate development and its less developed regions, the manufacturing industry is often considered as to encompass productive activities that enrich its knowledge capabilities as well as increase the potential of knowledge transfer (Bournakis, 2014). Thus, we decided, in line with several recent studies (e.g., Saito and Gopinath, 2011; Poldahl, 2012; Lööf and Nabavi, 2015; Song, 2015), to restrict our analysis of knowledge spillovers to the manufacturing sector.

Data collection and sample representativeness

The process of data collection was based on a survey applied to firms in the depressed municipalities of *Vale do Ave*.[3] The survey is divided into three parts. In the first part (part A), firm data for the years 2009–2011 was requested in order to characterize the sample in terms of economic activity, the municipality to which the firm belongs, sales, Gross Value Added and total number of employees, as well as their disaggregation by Undergraduate, Master and PhD qualifications. The second part of the survey (part B) intended to assess the types of innovation (product and process) implemented by firms, including the collaborations that

Figure 2.1 Purchasing Power Index by municipality in *Vale do Ave*, 2009

Source: Authors' compilation based on data from INE (Portuguese Statistics Institute) (2011a).

they perform in terms of introducing these innovations. In order to measure the activities related to obtaining and producing new knowledge, some questions for the year 2008 were made about the amounts spent on R&D activities, acquisition of machinery, equipment and software and other external knowledge. The last part of the survey (part C) aimed to assess the contacts that firms establish with different sources of knowledge (e.g., customers, suppliers, universities) in terms of their importance to the firm and their location.

The addresses of the firms in the municipalities under analysis were collected between 12th and 20th March 2012. We started by gathering the information about firms' addresses on the Internet. Since in certain cases it was not possible to obtain email addresses, we have contacted some firms by phone. We have also used some contacts provided by the *Associação Têxtil e Vestuário de Portugal* (ATP) and by the *Associação Industrial do Minho* (AIM). In order to infer the viability of the survey questions, pilot tests were conducted in that same week, with three firms in the *Vale do Ave* region, not included in the municipalities under analysis. Given the success of these tests, the application of the survey began on 21st March 2012. The questionnaire was sent as a Word file to firms in the municipalities under analysis from an address created exclusively for the purposes of this research. Given that some firms did not have access to email, the survey was also sent by fax. The implementation of the survey was closed on 21st May 2012, although several direct contacts with the firms[4] were required over this period.

Based upon the distribution of firms by sector in manufacturing industries, a simple quota sampling was established, in order to ensure the sample's representativeness not only by municipality, but also by sector. The initial goal was to obtain a representative sample of 300 firms in the four municipalities under review, which corresponds to 20.6 percent of the total manufacturing enterprises in these municipalities, distributed as follows (see Table 2.A1 in Appendix): 165, 50, 10 and 75 for the municipalities of *Fafe, Póvoa de Lanhoso, Vieira do Minho* and *Vizela*, respectively.

In the end of the survey process, we were able to gather 259 responses from firms located in the municipalities considered (average response rate of 86.3 percent), which were distributed by municipality in number (response rate) as: 132 (80.0 percent) in *Fafe*, 45 (90.0 percent) in *Póvoa de Lanhoso*, 8 (80.0 percent) in *Vieira do Minho* and 74 (98.7 percent) in *Vizela*.

The specification of theoretical model

Based on the literature review developed in Section 2, the theoretical relationship between the economic performance of firms and knowledge spillovers, controlling for a set of factors/determinants that, according to this same literature, will tend to influence performance, is put forward as follows:

$$
\text{Performance of the company}_i = f \left(
\begin{array}{c}
\text{Location of knowledge sources} \\
\text{(municipality, } \textit{Vale do Ave} \text{ except municipality, outside} \\
\textit{Vale do Ave} \text{, outside the country), Companies that} \\
\text{innovate in product or process by industry in } \textit{Vale do Ave} \\
\hline
\text{Knowledge spillovers} \\
\text{Importance of contacts with knowledge} \\
\text{sources : Universities, suppliers, consultants} \\
\text{and private institutions of R\&D} \\
\hline
\text{Contacts} \\
\text{Innovation index (implementation of} \\
\text{product and process innovations)} \\
\hline
\text{Implementation of innovation activities} \\
\text{Collaborations in the activities of} \\
\text{product and process innovation} \\
\hline
\text{Collaborations} \\
\text{Internal and external R\&D, acquisition of machinery,} \\
\text{equipment and software and other external knowledge} \\
\hline
\text{Obtaining and production of knowledge} \\
\text{Industry, total number of employees, human capital} \\
\hline
\text{Company characteristics} \\
\hline
\text{Purchasing Power Index} \\
\hline
\text{Municipality characteristic}
\end{array}
\right)
$$

The first group of determinants corresponds to knowledge spillovers. The location of knowledge sources (e.g., suppliers, universities) was used as a proxy for knowledge spillovers, based on Fitjar and Rodríguez-Pose (2011) and Natário et al. (2012). We developed an index that corresponds to the number of sources that the firm has from each location (municipality, *Vale do Ave* except the municipality, outside *Vale do Ave* and outside the country) in order to assess the importance of proximity of knowledge sources for corporate performance. In addition to knowledge sources, we used another variable as a proxy for knowledge spillovers, the intra-industry pool of knowledge and innovation, which corresponds to the ratio of firms that innovate in product or process by sector in *Vale do Ave*, based on data from 2006 to 2008 from CIS. This variable is in line with the procedures followed in Faria and Lima (2012).

The group of contacts corresponds to the level of importance attributed to information and knowledge sources (Bönte, 2008; Fitjar and Rodríguez-Pose, 2011, Czamitzki and Kraft, 2012). We recoded those variables in order to obtain an index of contacts with universities, suppliers, consultants and private R&D institutions, which includes the use and importance attributed to a particular source.

Our model also incorporates the implementation of innovation activities, particularly product and process, in line with Ornaghi (2006) and Faria and Lima (2012). Regarding the implementation of product and process innovations, we developed an index, an Innovation Index, which is the sum of the different types of innovations implemented by firms (e.g., new or improved goods, new or improved services). Moreover, at the level of collaboration in the development of product and process innovations (Fitjar and Rodríguez-Pose, 2011), we recoded the variables in order to determine whether these have an impact on corporate performance.

The activities of producing and obtaining knowledge (Ornaghi, 2006; Czamitzki and Kraft, 2012), in particular internal R&D, external R&D, acquisition of machinery, equipment and software, and other external knowledge, have been relativized by the sales value.

Finally, we added control variables for the characteristics of firms and municipalities. The group of firm characteristics includes those related with the industry/sector to which the firm belongs and human capital, including the weight of employees with Undergraduate, Master or PhD qualifications in the total number of employees, intended to measure whether the education level of employees influences the performance of firms. We also added a variable to our model that corresponds to a characteristic of the municipalities, the local Purchasing Power Index, which indicates each municipality's level of economic development.

In Table 2.1 a systematization of the variables introduced in the econometric model is provided.

Empirical results

Descriptive analysis

There is a concentration of firms around relatively low values of sales per employee, with an average of 50,801 euros/year. The same applies to Gross Value Added

Table 2.1 Systematization of the variables included in the econometric model

Group of variables	Variables	Proxies	Papers
Performance	Firm performance (average for the period 2009–2011)	Gross Value Added per worker in ln	Faria and Lima (2012)
Knowledge spillovers	Location of knowledge sources: municipality, *Vale do Ave* except the municipality, outside the country outside *Vale do Ave*	Number of sources from each location – Index from 0 to 8 in ln	Fitjar and Rodríguez-Pose (2011), Natário et al. (2012)
	Pool of knowledge and innovation	Intra-industry innovation in *Vale do Ave*	Ratio of firms that innovate in product or process by industry in *Vale do Ave*	Faria and Lima (2012)
Contacts	Importance of contacts with knowledge sources: universities, suppliers, consultants and private R&D institutions	Construction of a composite variable based on the following variables: - Use (dummy variable: 0 if no, 1 if yes) - Importance (0 if none, 1 if low/average, 2 if high) Importance Index from 0 to 2 (Use x Importance) in ln	Bönte (2008), Fitjar and Rodríguez-Pose (2011), Czamitzki and Kraft (2012)
Implementation of innovation activities	Innovation Index: implementation of product and process innovations (goods and services, production processes, logistic methods, deliver and distribution, support activities)	Innovation Index (in ln) – sum of innovations implemented by the firm – index from 0 to 5 (0 means zero innovations and 5 means that the firm implements all distinct types of innovation)	Ornaghi(2006), Faria and Lima (2012)

(*Continued*)

Table 2.1 (Continued)

Group of variables	Variables	Proxies	Papers
Collaborations	Collaborations in innovation activities (product and process)	Collaborations in product innovation in ln (0 if zero, 1 if it is mainly the firm or group, 2 if it is the firm in collaboration or other firms/institutions) Collaborations in process innovation in ln (0 if zero, 1 if it is mainly the firm or group, 2 if it is the firm in collaboration or other firms/institutions)	Fitjar and Rodríguez-Pose (2011)
Obtaining and production of knowledge	Internal R&D External R&D Acquisition of machinery, equipment and software Acquisition of other external knowledge	Ratio of internal R&D by sales Ratio of external R&D by sales Ratio of acquisition of machinery, equipment and software by sales Ratio of acquisition of other external knowledge by sales	Ornaghi (2006), Czamitzki and Kraft (2012)
Firm characteristics	Industry	Industry: dummy variable (0 if other industries, 1 if clothing and textile industries)	Natário et al. (2012)
	Dimension	Total number of employees in ln (average for the period 2009–2011)	Fitjar e Rodríguez-Pose (2011)
	Human Capital	Ratio of the number of employees with higher education in the total number of employees (average for the period 2009–2011)	Faria and Lima (2012)
Municipality characteristic	Development level	Purchasing Power Index in ln	Rodriguez-Pose and Crescenzi (2008)

per employee, a measure of firm performance used in our econometric model, whose average value stands at 10,604 euros/year.

The clothing and textile industries have a high weight in the municipalities under analysis, so we joined these two categories into a single industry, while the remaining cases are treated together (other industries). In the total of the four municipalities, 64.5 percent of the firms belong to the clothing and textile industries. In the municipalities of *Fafe* and *Vizela*, the percentage of firms in this industry is high (72.7 percent and 63.5 percent, respectively). The importance of this industry is much lower in *Vieira do Minho* ('only' 25.0 percent), when compared to the other municipalities.

Regarding the human capital of firms located in the municipalities studied, we found that the percentage of employees with higher education (Undergraduate, Master or PhD) is relatively low – on average, only 3.2 percent of employees in enterprises located in these municipalities has an undergraduate degree or higher, being particularly low in *Vieira do Minho* (1.1 percent). The weight of employees engaged in R&D is even lower for the municipalities as a whole (0.8 percent).

In relation to types of innovations, we found that approximately half (51.0 percent) of the firms stated they have implemented innovations to support process activities, where innovation in manufacture or production methods is the most significant (47.9 percent). On average, only 19.3 percent of the firms innovate in logistics, delivery or distribution.

Concerning the collaboration of firms by type of innovation, we classified the five types of innovation mentioned above into two major groups: product innovation and process innovation. In all the municipalities, there is a small percentage of firms that collaborate with other firms or institutions, where the implementation of innovations is carried out primarily by the firm or the group to which it belongs. In fact, in the four municipalities, the development of product innovations is mainly conducted by the firm or the group to which it belongs (83.4 percent) and a low percentage by the firm in cooperation with other firms or institutions (16.0 percent), with only 0.6 percent occurring in other enterprises or institutions. The same is true for the development of process innovations, because only 13.2 percent of the firms cooperate with other firms or institutions, whereas 5.4 percent of the firms indicate that these innovations are mainly developed by other firms or institutions.

Finally, it appears that firms in all the municipalities spend more on the purchase of machinery, equipment and software. In fact, the weight of this spending in sales is 5.7 percent for all municipalities, although *Fafe* and *Póvoa de Lanhoso* present a slightly higher figure (6.6 percent). In contrast, the acquisition of other external knowledge has little or no relevance in these municipalities.

The main information and knowledge sources for innovation activities used by firms in these municipalities are: the firm itself, customers and suppliers. In contrast, the least used information sources are universities or other higher education institutions and state laboratories or other public organizations with R&D activities. Specifically, about 70 percent of the surveyed firms use their own firm (or group of firms) and customers to obtain information/knowledge, and in these cases, more than 80 percent consider these sources as highly relevant to their activities – these two groups shared a pole position on the most relevant source of information for the surveyed firms.

The external sources of information that require some pro-activity and organizational complexity by firms – e.g., universities and other higher education institutions – are barely used (only 4.6 percent of the surveyed firms admit to their use, and from these, only half consider this source as very important for the development of their activities, with only 8.3 percent regarding it as the most important source).

In addition to resources and importance of knowledge sources, it is critical to assess the respective location, especially if they belong to the municipality in analysis or to *Vale do Ave* except the municipality, outside *Vale do Ave* or outside the country. This feature allows us to assess the potential existence of geographical knowledge spillovers.

According to the data collected, almost all the firms and groups of firms that constitute an information and knowledge source relevant to the firm's innovation activities during the period 2006–2008 are located in the same municipality of the reference firm (the surveyed firm). Similarly, but to a lesser extent, competitors or other firms in the same industry are located near the firm of reference – or in the municipality or in other municipalities of *Vale do Ave*. Customers, suppliers and professional and business associations seen as relevant to the firm's innovation activities are located primarily in *Vale do Ave* (except the municipality where the firm is located) or outside *Vale do Ave*.

Universities or other higher education institutions and state laboratories or other public institutions with R&D activities that are relevant to the activities of the analyzed firms are located mainly outside *Vale do Ave*, but inside the country. Foreign entities seem to be considered important only for a minority of firms, involving clients/consumers (36.5 percent), equipment suppliers and related (16.9 percent), consultants, laboratories or private R&D institutions (10.0 percent) and competitors or other firms in the same industry (6.1 percent).

These data seem to indicate that the surveyed firms generally fail to perform prospection and to use information and knowledge sources for innovation outside their restricted scope of location and/or action.

Based on a correlation analysis (Table 2.A2 in Appendix), in terms of knowledge spillovers, sources located at greater geographical distance from the firm (outside *Vale do Ave* and outside the country), reveal a closer relation with the firm's economic performance. In other words, on average, firms that recognize that the most critical information and knowledge sources for their innovation activities are located outside *Vale do Ave* and especially outside the country, are those that have higher levels of productivity. Still regarding spillovers, the importance of firms in the same sector of activity that innovate in product or process in *Vale do Ave* also seems to be related to the highest economic benefits for the firms themselves; in particular, we found that a larger number of firms in the same industry in *Vale do Ave* that innovate tend, on average, to be correlated with better firm performance.

Furthermore, the use of universities and other higher education institutions and suppliers as sources of knowledge for innovation activities emerge as positively associated with better performance in firms of these depressed municipalities of *Vale do Ave*.

We also found that innovation (in its different dimensions) appears associated with good economic performance. Thus, a higher number of different types of innovation (e.g., new goods, new services) are associated with higher economic performance, measured by Gross Value Added per worker. Additionally, collaboration with other firms or institutions in the development of product and process innovations appears correlated with firms that have higher productivity.

In relation to firm characteristics, we observed a negative correlation of Gross Value Added per worker with industry. This means that firms belonging to the textile and clothing industry have, on average, lower productivity than their counterparts in other industries. We also concluded that firm size (total number of employees) and, in particular, the respective human capital (weight of employees with higher education in total number of employees) is positively correlated with firm performance, showing that larger firms with higher levels of qualification/education are more productive.

Finally, regarding correlations between independent variables, it is crucial to note that there is a strong correlation between the Innovation Index and collaboration in terms of the development of product and process innovations, such as between the location of sources in the municipality itself and *Vale do Ave* (except the municipality itself). Also, there is a high correlation between the industry dummy variable and the ratio of firms that innovate in product or process by industry in *Vale do Ave*.[5]

Results of the econometric estimation

Given the strong correlation between the Innovation Index and the proxy variables of collaboration in the development of product and process innovations, as well as between the location of sources of knowledge and information for innovation activities from the firm's municipality and in *Vale do Ave* except the municipality, we decided it would be appropriate to estimate four different models (see Table 2.2). Thus, Model 1 includes collaborations in terms of product and process innovations and Model 2 considers the innovation index. These two models comprise the knowledge sources located in *Vale do Ave* except the municipality. Models 3 and 4 are similar to Models 1 and 2 but include knowledge sources located in the firm's municipality rather than in *Vale do Ave* except the municipality. The dependent variable in all estimated models corresponds to a measure of each firm performance: the Gross Value Added per worker in ln (average for the period 2009–2011).

The estimation (via method of ordinary least squares) of the four models, produced similar results, with an acceptable quality of adjustment (cf. adjusted R^2).

Taking into account standard significance levels (1 percent, 5 percent and 10 percent), we found that knowledge spillovers associated with geography, measured in this study by the location of sources of knowledge, emerge with huge importance. Thus, knowledge sources located in the firm's municipality (Models 3 and 4) and located in *Vale do Ave* except the municipality are statistically significant and negative. Firms that have a greater number of sources

Table 2.2 Results of the econometric estimation

Group of variables	Proxies	Model 1	Model 2	Model 3	Model 4
Knowledge Spillovers — Number of knowledge sources (in ln) located	in the municipality			−0.464**	−0.435**
	in *Vale do Ave* except the municipality	−0.572***	−0.531***		
	outside *Vale do Ave*	0.332*	0.359*	0.315	0.342*
	outside the country	0.410*	0.441*	0.463**	0.491**
Pool of knowledge and innovation	Ratio of firms that innovate in product or process by industry in *Vale do Ave*	1.255*	1.340**	1.093*	1.187*
Contacts (index in ln)	Importance of universities	0.178	0.194	0.134	0.153
	Importance of suppliers	0.176	0.169	0.111	0.11
	Importance of consultants and private R&D institutions	−0.122	−0.117	−0.145	−0.14
Implementation of innovation activities	Innovation Index (in ln)	0.423***		0.379***	
	in product innovation (in ln)		0.164		0.163
	in process innovation (in ln)		0.343		0.271
Obtaining and production of knowledge	Ratio of internal R&D by sales	−0.145	0.255	−0.164	0.225
	Ratio of external R&D by sales	10.186	15.483	0.673	6.285
	Ratio of acquisition of machinery, equipment and software by sales	−0.649	−0.535	−0.654	−0.542
	Ratio of acquisition of other external knowledge by sales	10.072	12.491	7.559	9.967
Firm characteristics	Dimension (total number of employees in ln)	0.216***	0.237***	0.207***	0.226***

Group of variables	Proxies	Model 1	Model 2	Model 3	Model 4
	Human Capital (ratio of the number of employees with higher education in the total number of employees)	3.154**	2.984**	3.449***	3.305***
Municipality characteristic	Development level (Purchasing Power Index in ln)	−0.08	−0.061	0.183	0.201
	Constant	7.168	7.114	6.177	6.127
	N	257	257	257	257
	Adjusted R²	0.203	0.185	0.192	0.175

Note: statistically significant at: * $p < 0.1$, ** $p < 0.05$, *** $p < 0.01$.

of knowledge for innovation activities located in their municipality or *Vale do Ave* except their municipality tend to observe, *ceteris paribus*, a lower level of productivity. In contrast, firms with a greater number of knowledge sources for innovation activities outside *Vale do Ave*, and especially abroad, emerge as, *ceteris paribus*, more productive.

In this context, inter-regional knowledge spillovers and particularly international ones emerge as crucial for firms located in depressed regions, in particular, those located in the relatively underdeveloped municipalities of *Vale do Ave*. Still on the spillovers proxy, associated with the pool of knowledge and innovation of firms in the region belonging to the same industry, it emerges as a key determinant of productivity. In other words, the intra-industry innovation environment associated with firms located in the *Vale do Ave* region influences positively and significantly the firm's performance. To that extent, the presence of innovative firms in the same industry seems to be critical for firms located in depressed areas – it is here that the importance of intra-industry spillovers resides.

Notwithstanding, the most innovative firms (cf. Models 1 and 3) present, *ceteris paribus*, higher levels of productivity. Firms that show higher levels of collaboration for innovation (product and process) did not emerge as significantly different from other firms. This result is most probably associated with the fact that the main key issue here is not so much the collaboration type, as we measured, but its frequency.

We concluded, finally, that firm size (total number of employees) and the respective human capital (weight of employees with higher education) are positive and statistically significant variables in the four models. Thus, *ceteris paribus*, on average, larger firms and with higher levels of human capital emerge as more productive (with higher levels of Gross Value Added per worker).

Conclusions

This study analyzed the importance of knowledge spillovers for the economic performance of firms in a region in northern Portugal, *Vale do Ave*, focusing particularly on four municipalities in the region – *Fafe*, *Póvoa de Lanhoso*, *Vieira do Minho* and *Vizela* – identified as economically depressed areas.

We concluded that geographical proximity does not seem to be an important aspect for the performance of firms in these municipalities. According to the results, municipal and intra-regional knowledge spillovers lead to lower performance levels in the firms of these municipalities. In contrast, contacts with knowledge sources outside *Vale do Ave* (inter-regional spillovers) and outside the country (international spillovers) appeared as significant for the performance of these firms, having a positive and significant effect. This finding seems to contrast with the results conveyed by the studies that focus on more developed areas, including regions of Germany (Funke and Niebuhr, 2005) and the EU (Rodríguez-Pose and Crescenzi, 2008), which concluded that the effects of spillovers on the growth of these regions diminish with distance.

Regarding the studies on firms located in peripheral areas, Natário et al. (2012) concluded, contrary to our study, that the scope of activity of these firms is local, regional or national, rather than international. However, Fitjar and Rodríguez-Pose (2011), who analyzed firms in peripheral areas of Norway, show that international sources play a key role in the innovation performance of firms. In this latter case, geographical proximity does not emerge as particularly important, being the organizational and cognitive proximity critical to business innovation. In the same line, Amin and Cohendat (2000) reported that relative proximity to organizational routines is more important than geographical proximity.

Our study, concluding that inter-regional and international spillovers are crucial for firms in these depressed municipalities of *Vale do Ave*, seems to show, in line with recent studies, that geographical proximity is not the critical dimension of the firms' economic performance. This result suggests that other types of proximity beyond the geographical are more important for these firms, such as routines in organizational innovation, as Boschma (2005) pointed out.

Still in relation to knowledge spillovers, the innovations developed by other firms also emerged as relevant to the performance of a given firm. We found that the intra-industry innovative environment in *Vale do Ave*, identified by the pool of knowledge and innovation (measured by the relative weight of firms that innovate in product or process in *Vale do Ave* by industry), significantly influences the economic performance of a particular firm in these municipalities. These results are in line with Faria and Lima (2012), who demonstrated that, also for a number of Portuguese firms, the percentage of firms involved in innovation activities influences the performance of other firms.

In relation to aspects associated with innovation, the most innovative firms, which implement different types of product and process innovation, are also associated with a higher performance.

With respect to the characteristics of firms, the results show that the employees' qualifications are also important, and that firms with a higher percentage of skilled employees have a better performance. Additionally, innovation activities developed in these firms, as well as the contacts made with inter-regional and international sources of knowledge in the years from 2006 to 2008, were found to positively influence the firm's performance, as measured by Gross Value Added per employee in the triennium from 2009 to 2011. This evidence confirms the relevance of the phenomenon of path dependency, as supported by evolutionary economic geography (Boschma and Frenken, 2006).

In terms of economic policy, the results highlight that it is crucial to promote policies that encourage businesses, particularly in depressed areas, to develop innovations, but especially given the positive effect of inter-regional and international spillovers, to establish contacts with sources from other regions, particularly at the international level. These international contacts are relevant to the economic performance of a firm, in particular the contacts established with clients, suppliers of equipment, materials, components or software and consultants, laboratories or private R&D institutions, which correspond to the most used knowledge and information sources for innovation activities at international level by the firms in these depressed areas.

Further research on this matter is in order. Our study has one main limitation which results from its implementation in just four depressed Portuguese regions. This limitation offers future research possibilities such as the implementation of our survey to other depressed regions of Portugal. Another interesting research approach could be the comparison of our results with the outcome that would emerge in the municipalities of *Vale do Ave* that are not categorized as depressed areas. This last approach is important to verify if the geographical scope of spillovers remains more important at the inter-regional and international levels.

Appendix

Table 2.A1 The sample representativeness

	Population								Answers							
Manufacturing	Fafe		Póvoa de Lanhoso		Vieira do Minho		Vizela		Fafe	Póvoa de Lanhoso	Vieira do Minho	Vizela Vizela	Fafe	Póvoa de Lanhoso	Vieira do Minho	Vizela Vizela
	Nr	%	Nr	%	Nr	%	Nr	%	Nr	Nr	Nr	Nr	Nr	Nr	Nr	Nr
Food products	24	3.0	20	8.3	4	8.0	12	3.3	5	4	1	2	1	4	1	2
Beverages	8	1.0	4	1.7	1	2.0	2	0.5	2	1	0	0	1	1	0	0
Textiles	101	12.6	14	5.8	1	2.0	109	29.9	21	3	0	22	18	3	0	22
Wearing	469	58.6	92	38.2	16	32.0	123	33.7	97	19	3	25	78	19	2	25
Leather and related products	24	3.0	2	0.8	0	0.0	41	11.2	5	0	0	8	5	0	0	9
Wood and products of wood and cork, except furniture; articles of straw and plaiting materials	37	4.6	23	9.5	6	12.0	8	2.2	8	5	1	2	7	3	2	2
Paper and paper products	5	0.6	1	0.4	0	0.0	12	3.3	1	0	0	2	1	0	0	2
Printing and reproduction of recorded media	7	0.9	9	3.7	0	0.0	10	2.7	1	2	0	2	2	2	0	2
Chemicals and chemical products, except pharmaceuticals	4	0.5	4	1.7	0	0.0	2	0.5	1	1	0	0	1	1	0	0
Rubber and plastic products	0	0.0	1	0.4	1	2.0	1	0.3	0	0	0	0	0	0	0	0
Other non-metallic mineral products	21	2.6	8	3.3	2	4.0	8	2.2	4	2	0	2	4	2	0	3
Basic metals	3	0.4	2	0.8	0	0.0	0	0.0	1	0	0	0	2	0	0	0
Fabricated metal products, except machinery and equipment	61	7.6	28	11.6	18	36.0	22	6.0	13	6	4	5	6	6	3	5
Computer, electronic and optical products	1	0.1	0	0.0	0	0.0	0	0.0	0	0	0	0	0	0	0	0
Machinery and equipment, n.e.c.	11	1.4	1	0.4	0	0.0	1	0.3	2	0	0	1	3	0	0	0
Furniture	9	1.1	5	2.1	0	0.0	5	1.4	2	1	0	0	2	1	0	1
Other manufacturing	10	1.2	27	11.2	1	2.0	2	0.5	2	6	0	0	0	3	0	0
Repair and installation of machinery and equipment	6	0.7	0	0.0	0	0.0	7	1.9	1	0	0	1	1	0	0	1

Table 2.A2 Correlations between relevant variables in the model

Group of variables	Proxies	1.	2.	3.	4.	5.	6.	7.	8.	9.	10.	11.	12.	13.	14.	15.	16.	17.	18.	19.	20.
Performance	1. Productivity (ratio of Gross Value Added per worker in ln)	1	0.040	0.035	0.228**	0.254**	0.171**	0.160*	0.131*	0.002	0.277**	0.163**	0.217**	0.089	0.079	0.062	0.055	0.200**	0.289**	0.269**	0.018
Knowledge Spillovers	Number of knowledge sources (in ln) located																				
	2. in the municipality		1	0.615**	0.486**	0.122	-0.061	0.109	0.464**	0.262**	0.257**	0.297**	0.132*	0.068	0.061	0.155*	0.044	0.044	0.034	0.052	0.030
	3. in Vale do Ave except the municipality			1	0.494**	0.103	0.027	0.127*	0.495**	0.260**	0.335**	0.322**	0.229**	0.080	0.141*	0.128*	0.099	0.077	0.083	0.029	-0.019
	4. outside Vale do Ave				1	0.287**	0.049	0.289**	0.494**	0.156*	0.352**	0.304**	0.265**	0.125*	0.201**	0.077	0.048	-0.123*	0.238**	0.184**	0.019
	5. outside the country					1	-0.008	0.120	0.228**	0.194**	0.244**	0.170*	0.191**	0.094	0.143*	0.032	-0.041	0.013	0.336**	0.087	-0.007
Pool of knowledge and innovation	6. Ratio of firms that innovate in product or process by industry in Vale do Ave						1	0.012	0.071	-0.096	0.123*	0.119	0.129	0.050	0.050	-0.007	-0.045	-0.630**	-0.073	0.237**	-0.135*

(Continued)

Table 2.A2 (Continued)

Group of variables	Proxies	1.	2.	3.	4.	5.	6.	7.	8.	9.	10.	11.	12.	13.	14.	15.	16.	17.	18.	19.	20.
Contacts (index in ln)	7. Importance of universities							1	0.087	0.012	0.177**	0.180**	0.169**	0.120	0.036	0.045	-0.013	-0.068	0.132*	0.327**	-0.094
	8. Importance of suppliers								1	0.024	0.221**	0.181**	0.166**	0.096	0.078	0.058	0.077	-0.108	0.128*	0.086	0.026
	9. Importance of consultants and private institutions of R&D									1	0.178**	0.198**	0.110	0.085	0.184**	-0.017	0.073	0.140*	0.172*	-0.064	0.012
Implementation of innovation activities	10. Innovation Index (in ln)										1	0.779**	0.751**	0.135*	0.155*	0.100	0.101	-0.053	0.232**	0.142*	0.000
Collaborations	11. Collaborations in product innovation (in ln)											1	0.454**	0.088	0.103	0.029	0.053	-0.061	0.164**	0.113	-0.041
	12. Collaborations in process innovation (in ln)												1	0.110	0.099	0.087	0.056	-0.054	0.132*	0.222**	0.014

Learning and production of knowledge	13. Ratio of internal R&D by sales	1	-0.029	0.026	-0.056	0.079	0.020	-0.051
	14. Ratio of external R&D by sales		1	-0.032	-0.007	-0.124*	0.037	-0.039
	15. Ratio of acquisition of machinery, equipment and software by sales			1				
	16. Ratio of acquisition of other external knowledge by sales				1	0.056	0.011	0.076	0.032
Firm characteristics	17. Industry (0 if is other industries, 1 if is clothing and textile industries)					1	0.138*	-0.214**	0.200**

(*Continued*)

Table 2.A2 (Continued)

Group of variables	Proxies	1.	2.	3.	4.	5.	6.	7.	8.	9.	10.	11.	12.	13.	14.	15.	16.	17.	18.	19.	20.
Munici-pality charac-teristic	18. Dimen-sion (total num-ber of employ-ees in ln)																		1	0.070	0.048
	19. Human Capital (ratio of the num-ber of employ-ees with higher educa-tion in the total num-ber of employ-ees)																			1	−0.098
	20. Devel-opment level (Index of Pur-chasing Power in ln)																				1

Note: statistically significant at: *p < 0.05, **p< 0.01. N=257.

Notes

1 Similarly to Fitjar and Rodríguez-Pose (2011), aspects related to innovation and spillovers are captured through the number of employees involved in innovation activities, the level of collaboration (low, medium or high) and the scope of activity (local, regional, national or international).

2 Purchasing Power Index is computed by INE (Portugal's official Statistical Body) and translates the purchasing power manifested daily, in per capita terms, in the different municipalities or regions, with reference to the national value (Portugal = 100). It is computed using the gross income declared for the purposes of personal income tax per capita.

3 To define the survey questions, we tried to follow as closely as possible the templates of the Community Innovation Survey (CIS). Although it is possible, by protocol, to access data from CIS 2008, this latest document is not representative at the municipal level, or even NUTS III, including a very small number of firms from the municipalities considered. Thus, there was no alternative but to survey directly the firms located in these municipalities.

4 Many telephone contacts were not valid, so it was not possible to contact those firms. Moreover, some of the firms were already insolvent and others were not willing to respond to our survey. Others also had to be excluded from the analysis because they did not have activity for the period under study. These firms were replaced by others in order to maintain the sample representativeness by sector in each municipality.

5 Therefore, due to a potential problem of multicollinearity, it is not advisable to put these two variables in the same model. We decided to exclude the industry dummy variable from the results presented in the main text and keep the variable used as a proxy for spillovers in our econometric estimation. The results of econometric estimation without the variable pool of knowledge and innovation and with the industry variable can be provided on demand to the corresponding author.

References

Amin, A. and Cohendat, P. (2000) 'Organisational learning and governance through embedded practices', *Journal of Management and Governance*, 4: 93–116.

Andersson, M. and Karlsson, C. (2007) 'Knowledge in regional economic growth – The role of knowledge accessibility', *Industry and Innovation*, 14: 129–49.

Autant-Bernard, C., Fadairo, M. and Massard, N. (2013) 'Knowledge diffusion and innovation policies within the European regions: Challenges based on recent empirical evidence', *Research Policy*, 42(1): 196–210.

Bathelt, H., Malmberg, A. and Maskell, P. (2004) 'Clusters and knowledge: Local buzz, global pipelines and the process of knowledge creation', *Progress in Human Geography*, 28: 31–56.

Beise, M. and Stahl, H. (1999) 'Public research and industrial innovations in Germany', *Research Policy*, 28: 397–422.

Bode, E. (2004) 'The spatial pattern of localized R&D spillovers: An empirical investigation for Germany', *Journal of Economic Geography*, 4: 43–64.

Bönte, W. (2008) 'Inter-firm trust in buyer–supplier relations: Are knowledge spillovers and geographical proximity relevant?', *Journal of Economic Behavior & Organization*, 67: 855–70.

Boschma, R. (2005) 'Proximity and innovation: A critical assessment', *Regional Studies*, 39: 61–74.

Boschma, R. and Frenken, K. (2006) 'Why is economic geography not an evolutionary science? Towards an evolutionary economic geography', *Journal of Economic Geography*, 6: 273–302.

Bournakis, I. (2014) 'Costs, knowledge and market structure: Understanding the puzzle of international competitiveness with Greek export data', *International Review of Applied Economics*, 28(2): 240–69.

Caragliu, A. and Del Bo, C. (2011) 'Determinants of spatial knowledge spillovers in Italian provinces', *Socio-Economic Planning Sciences*, 45: 28–37.

Czarnitzki, D. and Kraft, K. (2012) 'Spillovers of innovation activities and their profitability', *Oxford Economic Papers*, 64: 302–22.

Döring, T. and Schnellenbach, J. (2006) 'What do we know about geographical knowledge spillovers and regional growth? A survey of the literature', *Regional Studies*, 40(3): 375–95.

Dosi, G. (1988) 'Sources, procedures, and microeconomic effects of innovation', *Journal of Economic Literature*, 26: 1120–71.

Faria, P. and Lima, F. (2012) 'Interdependence and spillovers: Is firm performance affected by others' innovation activities?', *Applied Economics*, 44: 4765–75.

Fitjar, R. and Rodríguez-Pose, A. (2011) 'Innovating in the periphery: Firms, values and innovation in Southwest Norway', *European Planning Studies*, 19: 555–74.

Fontes, M. (2005) 'Distant networking: The knowledge acquisition strategies of "out-cluster" biotechnology firms', *European Planning Studies*, 13: 899–920.

Funke, M. and Niebuhr, A. (2005) 'Regional geographic research and development spillovers and economic growth: Evidence from West Germany', *Regional Studies*, 39: 143–53.

Griliches, Z. (1992) 'The search for R&D spillovers', *Scandinavian Journal of Economics*, 94: 29–47.

Grillitsch, M. and Nilsson, M. (2015) 'Innovation in peripheral regions: Do collaborations compensate for a lack of local knowledge spillovers?', *Annals of Regional Science*, 54(1): 299–321.

INE (2011a) Estudo sobre o Poder de Compra Concelhio 2009, Instituto Nacional de Estatística, I.P. (editor).

INE (2011b) Anuário Estatístico da Região Norte 2010, Instituto Nacional de Estatística, I.P. (editor).

Jaffe, A. (1986) 'Technological opportunity and spillovers of R&D: Evidence from firms' patents, profits and market value', *American Economic Review*, 76: 984–1001.

Kalapouti, K. and Varsakelis, N.C. (2014) 'Intra and inter: Regional knowledge spillovers in European Union', *Journal of Technology Transfer*, 40 (5): 760–81.

LeSage, J.P. and Fischer, M.M. (2012) 'Estimates of the impact of static and dynamic knowledge spillovers on regional factor productivity', *International Regional Science Review*, 35(1): 103–27.

Lööf, H. and Nabavi, P. (2015) 'Knowledge spillovers, productivity and patent', *Annals of Regional Science*, 55(1): 249–63.

López-Fernández, C., Serrano-Bedia, A.M. and García-Piqueres, G. (2012) 'Innovative capacity in European peripheral regions: Determinants and empirical evidence', 18th International Conference on Engineering, Technology and Innovation, ICE 2012 – Conference Proceedings, Art. no. 6297652.

Natário, M., Couto, J. and Sousa, M. (2012) 'Innovation processes of SMEs in less favoured municipalities of Portugal', *Investigaciones Regionales*, 22: 81–103.

Ornaghi, C. (2006) 'Spillovers in product and process innovation: Evidence from manufacturing firms', *International Journal of Industrial Organization*, 24: 349–80.

Polanyi, M. (1958) *Personal knowledge: Towards a post-critical philosophy*, Routledge & Kegan Paul, London.

Poldahl, A. (2012) 'The two faces of R&D: Does firm absorptive capacity matter?', *Journal of Industry, Competition and Trade*, 12: 221–37.

Programa de Recuperação de áreas e sectores deprimidos (PRASD) (2004), http://www.cedintec.pt/images/PRASD1.pdf, accessed October 20, 2011.

Resolução do Conselho de Ministros n° 11/2004, Diário da República – I Série – B, N.° 40, 17.02.2004, http://www.iapmei.pt/resources/download/RCM_11_2004.pdf, accessed October 22, 2011.

Rodríguez-Pose, A. and Crescenzi, R. (2008) 'Research and development, spillovers, innovation systems, and the genesis of regional growth in Europe', *Regional Studies*, 42(1): 51–67.

Saito, H. and Gopinath, M. (2011) 'Knowledge spillovers, absorptive capacity, and skill intensity of Chilean manufacturing plants', *Journal of Regional Science*, 51: 83–101.

Sena, V. (2004) 'Total factor productivity and the spillover hypothesis: Some new evidence', *International Journal of Production Economics*, 92: 31–42.

Song, B. (2015) 'Location proximity and productivity spillovers: The case of Korean manufacturing plants', *Asian Economic Papers*, 14(1): 104–18.

Teixeira, A., Santos, P. and Brochado, A. (2008) 'International R&D cooperation between low-tech SMEs: The role of cultural and geographical proximity', *European Planning Studies*, 16: 785–810.

Verspagen, B. and Schoenmakers, W. (2004) 'The spatial dimension of patenting by multinational firms in Europe', *Journal of Economic Geography*, 4: 23–42.

Webster, E. (2004) 'Firms' decisions to innovate and innovation routines', *Economics of Innovation and New Technology*, 13(8): 733–45.

Yang, H., Phelps, C. and Steensma, H. (2010) 'Learning from what others have learned from you: The effects of knowledge spillovers on originating firms', *Academy of Management Journal*, 53: 371–89.

3 The role of multinationals in creating export spillovers as an additional process to productivity spillovers

Evidence from Turkey

Başak Dalgıç and *Burcu Fazlıoğlu*

Introduction

Foreign direct investment impacts on the economic performance of host countries directly and indirectly by contributing to capital savings, increasing production capacity and bringing along technology diffusion and management skills. Indirect benefits from multinational firms are usually referred to as spillover effects of foreign direct investment. Spillover effects result from a number of sources, including the linkages formed between domestic and foreign owned firms, namely multinationals, and increased competition in the domestic market. A recent literature review suggests that the interaction of domestic firms with multinationals can also affect the export decision and performance of domestic firms i.e. create export spillovers (Görg and Greenaway, 2004; Greenaway and Kneller, 2004; Ruane and Sutherland, 2004; Kneller and Pisu, 2007; Wagner, 2007; Bajgar and Javorcik, 2013). Compared to the vast literature which investigates the impact of foreign direct investment on productivity (i.e. productivity spillovers),[1] relatively little effort has been spent on export spillovers. This is despite the fact that firms' involvement in international markets might reduce the costs of entering into these markets for non-exporting firms i.e. non-exporting firms gain the opportunity to learn to export from other firms' export experience which is a phenomenon termed as export spillovers by Aitken et al. (1997).

The existing literature on export spillovers suggest that foreign direct investment has an impact on the export decision and export performance of firms in host countries through horizontal (intra-industry) and vertical (inter-industry) linkages. According to this literature, foreign presence might affect exporting behavior of firms mainly by three channels: (i) leading to knowledge acquisition about foreign markets (information externalities on foreign markets); (ii) improving technological capacity of domestic firms and (iii) through increased competition (Rodriguez-Clare, 1996; Aitken et al., 1997; Greenaway et al., 2004). Just as these channels are defined separately, it is not possible to distinguish between them. For instance, it is difficult to identify the type of knowledge transferred between foreign and domestic firms, whether it is the knowledge about international markets or technological knowledge. The latter could help firms increase their productivity and hence their probability of being able to export. On the other hand, competition channel may also work in the same way. Thus, productivity spillovers might act as a side-product and/or outcome of competition and technological knowledge channels raised by foreign direct investments. In other words, technological knowledge transfer and competitive pressure are likely to result in higher productivity and therefore a higher chance of exporting. In order to assess whether export spillovers act as an additional process to productivity spillovers, in this paper we are particularly interested in export spillovers stemming from knowledge externalities raised by multinationals.

The extent of export spillovers generated by foreign direct investment differs subject to whether there exist horizontal or vertical linkages between domestic and multinational firms. The studies that have considered the impact of multinationals on export behavior have essentially focused on horizontal linkages where domestic firms benefit from multinational firms that are operating within the domestic firms' own industry. Horizontal linkages may positively affect exporting behavior of domestically owned firms through increased competition, however they may also constrain exporting activity of these firms by hurting their profitability through decreased market shares and restrained access to a skilled labor force (Blalock and Gertler, 2008).[2] Foreign presence can also create export spillovers via vertical linkages. As mentioned above, supplying multinationals in downstream and outsourcing from multinationals in upstream industries can positively affect firms' decision of starting to export. Foreign affiliated firms require local firms to catch up with international standards in terms of quality, variety, managerial know-how and level of technology used in production processes. In general, horizontal linkages yield to export spillovers mainly through the competition channel while other channels are more pronounced for vertical spillovers.

Against this background, this study focuses on the existence of export spillovers that arise from foreign direct investments through horizontal and vertical linkages between domestic and multinational firms in Turkey. Even if we show the existence of export spillovers, it could still remain unclear whether they constitute a separate spillover mechanism from foreign direct investment or they are rather a side-product of productivity spillovers. We specifically attest whether export spillovers act as an additional channel to knowledge spillovers in Turkish manufacturing industry. We use a comprehensive and recent firm level panel covering the period 2003–2012. We construct our horizontal and vertical (backward and forward) foreign direct investment generated linkage variables utilizing Turkish input–output matrix and our firm level panel. In order to avoid selection bias arose by firms' export decision, we employ Heckman's two-step procedure.

The case of Turkey is interesting since over the last decade it has witnessed a remarkable inflow of foreign direct investments and a rapid rise in exports. In fact Turkey has integrated into the globalized world, while transforming into one of the major recipients of foreign direct investment in its region. Alongside with this striking foreign investment performance Turkey has experienced a dramatic export boom after 2002. Over the period 2002–2012 Turkey's exports have increased by 325 percent. To the best of our knowledge this study is the first attempt to investigate the export spillovers that arise from foreign direct investment (FDI) for Turkey. Focusing on a developing country is important since the potential for benefiting from export spillovers is higher than that of developed countries.

The rest of the study is structured as follows: Section two briefly reviews the existing literature. Section three introduces the data and presents some descriptive evidence. Section four presents the methodology and results of the empirical investigation. Section five concludes.

Background literature

Pioneering studies of Romer (1990) and Aghion and Howitt (1992) attributed a key role to knowledge yielding to an increased interest in the international linkages as channels to reach accumulated knowledge of the frontier economies. Among the knowledge diffusion channels FDI has received special attention as it brings several benefits to host economies. The direct benefits of FDI stem from the fact that the presence of multinational companies brings additional capital to the host country as well as increasing demand for labor and leading to increased R&D efforts by putting competitive pressure on domestic firms. In terms of knowledge transfer multinational firms provide access to frontier technologies, as domestic firms are able to observe their production and management skills. Among the impacts of FDI a noticeable research effort has been paid on the productivity gains of domestic firms indirectly through interacting with multinational firms (Görg and Greenaway, 2004).

The related literature mainly concentrates on two different linkages through which foreign firms create productivity gains for domestic firms, namely productivity spillovers from FDI. The earlier literature focuses on horizontal linkages searching for the existence of spillovers from multinationals located in the same industry. A more recent literature investigates vertical linkages analyzing the effects of FDI in upstream or downstream industries that foreign firms interact with. The micro evidence[3] on horizontal productivity spillovers is mixed, presenting negative and insignificant effects of horizontal linkages on domestic firms (see, among others, Aitken and Harrison, 1999; Javorcik, 2004; Javorcik and Spatareanu, 2008, 2011; Fons-Rosen et al., 2013) along with the positive effects (see, among others, Konings, 2001; Keller and Yeaple, 2009). Empirical evidence is stronger in explaining positive spillovers created by vertical linkages (see, among others, Mucchielli and Jabbour, 2004; Javorcik, 2004; Mervelede and Schoors, 2005; Blalock and Gertler, 2008; Javorcik and Spatareanu, 2008, 2011). Thus far, while the literature on the benefits of FDI mainly focuses on productivity gains (namely productivity spillovers), little effort has been put on other indirect benefits such as those related to exporting activity of the firms.

Expecting export-related benefits from FDI is motivated by some stylized facts provided by the new international trade literature (see Aw and Hwang 1995; Bernard and Jensen, 1995; Roberts and Tybout, 1997; Melitz, 2003; Bernard et al., 2003). Regarding the exporting activity of firms, the international trade literature has witnessed a substantial progress over the past eighteen years where the firm heterogeneity has become a core topic.[4] With the availability of firm level datasets a vast empirical literature has conveyed that internationalized firms show superior performance to the firms who serve only to the domestic markets[5] as more productive firms self-select into exporting.[6] The self-selection of more productive firms into export markets stems from the existence of sunk costs. Through increasing competition or creating technological knowledge spillovers, presence of multinationals reduces sunk costs of exporting and hence facilitates export market participation (Kneller and Pisu, 2007).

There are three channels affecting the export market participation of firms stemming from multinationals, namely creating export spillovers. The first channel is about gathering information about foreign markets (e.g. regulations in foreign markets, taste and preference of foreign consumers, competitive pressure in foreign markets, etc.) i.e. information externalities. Multinational firms in host countries usually possess knowledge about foreign markets via their parent firms. In the pre-entry stages of exporting this knowledge accumulation about foreign markets plays an important role in reducing the sunk costs of exporting. Such accumulated knowledge stock facilitates the post-entry benefits of exporting as well. The second channel emphasizes the role of technology brought by multinationals. Domestic firms benefit from the more advanced technologies employed by multinational firms through demonstration and imitation effects (Greenaway et al., 2004). The third channel stems from the competition effect. Entry of multinationals into an industry creates higher competition. While this may initially affect domestic firms negatively, the increased competitive pressure force them to become more productive, in turn reducing the sunk costs and increasing their probability of selecting into export markets.

There are a handful of empirical studies assessing the effect of multinational firms on exporting. Among them Aitken et al. (1997) highlight the role of information externalities created by multinationals within an industry on export decision of firms. They state that sunk costs of exporting are lower for foreign affiliated firms who are already part of international production networks. Using plant-level data on the Mexican manufacturing industry, their study reveals that firms are more likely to export when there is a higher concentration of exporting activity by multinationals in the same industry and region. Kneller and Pisu (2007) also focuses on information externalities and shows that foreign affiliated firms are more likely to export and export more intensively. Considering the trade openness of the Uruguay economy, Kokko et el. (2001) show that the probability of exporting increases with the presence of foreign firms established after 1973 (a more outward-oriented period), whereas the likelihood of exporting is not affected by the presence of foreign firms established before 1972 (Uruguay's inward-oriented period). Greenaway et al. (2004) show that the intensity of foreign firms' R&D expenditure, the relative importance of multinational firms' production and their export activities have a positive impact on the probability of exporting for firms located in the United Kingdom. Among them the level of foreign production in an industry is the most influential one. In terms of export propensity, a positive impact associated with foreign affiliation is evident. While they verify the effects of knowledge transfer and competition channels on export propensity, they cannot find any support for information externalities. Utilizing firm-level data for Ireland and following the theoretical approach of Aitken et al. (1997) and empirical methodology of Greenaway et al. (2004), Ruane and Sutherland (2005) analyze the effects of concentration of multinationals in the host country and the export share of multinationals on export decisions and export intensities of domestic firms. Examining the effect of spillovers resulting from the concentration of multinationals they find positive effects for both the export decision of domestic firms and export intensity of those firms once they export. Whereas they find negative effects for the latter in terms of both decision to export and the export intensity of domestic firms.

Using a dataset of British manufacturing firms, Kneller and Pisu (2007) not only assess the extent of horizontal but also vertical spillovers from foreign affiliated firms towards domestic companies. Their results indicate diverse effects of foreign presence on export behavior of domestic firms. Accordingly, export decision of domestic firms is found to be affected by FDI only through backward linkages, whereas horizontal or forward linkages do not have any effect on export participation of domestic firms.

Bajgar and Javorcik (2013) assert that, with the exception of Aitken et al.'s (1997) study, the regarding literature only focuses on developed countries. They contribute to the literature by investigating the presence of horizontal and vertical spillovers from multinationals on different margins of domestic-firm exporting and on the quality of exports by domestic firms for a developing country, Romania. Their results convey that the presence of multinationals in downstream sectors is positively associated with the probability of starting to export, the number of products exported and export destinations (i.e. extensive margins of exporting), whereas foreign presence in firms' own sector has a negative effect. Besides, they do not find solid evidence on the impact of foreign presence in downstream sectors on the quality of firms' exports proxied by unit values.

Data and descriptive evidence

A key feature of the Turkish economy over the last decade has been the robust economic growth with an average annual rate of 5 percent. This remarkable performance of growth together with prudent fiscal policies and major structural reforms has integrated the Turkish economy into the globalized world, while transforming Turkey into one of the major recipients of FDI in its region. Turkey has become the 13th most attractive FDI destination in the world by $123 billion of FDI in the past decade (FDI Confidence Index; Kearney, 2012). FDI inflows to Turkey have had an upward trend particularly since 2005 and reached $22 billion in 2007, with its highest level ever recorded (See Figure 3.1). Over this period the increase in FDI inflows into Turkey is significantly higher than that of countries in the same income group. However, as most of the emerging economies, Turkey was hit by the global crisis in 2008 and affected by the global decline in capital flows leading it to a fluctuating course of FDI since 2009.

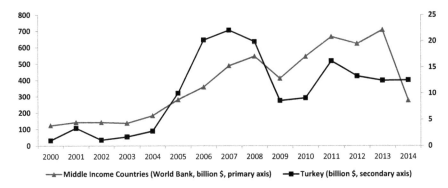

Figure 3.1 FDI flows into Turkey and middle income countries (2000–2014)
Source: World Bank.

Alongside with this striking economic performance Turkey experienced a dramatic export boom after 2002. Turkey's total trade volume increased from $88 billion in 2002 to $389 billion in 2012, an increase of 342 percent in a decade's time. Turkey's exports increased by 325 percent (to $153 billion from $36 billion) over the same period. This compares to the average export performance of its peers in the same income group (Brazil, China, Mexico, and South Africa) whose exports grew by 212 percent in the same period. While Turkey has undergone a structural transformation process both in terms of production and trade patterns along with sectoral and geographical diversification,[7] its integration into global value chains increased substantially in the meantime.

Considering this notable performance in terms of FDI inflows and exports we try to understand to what extent FDI leads to export spillovers in Turkey. For this purpose we use a recent and comprehensive dataset on Turkish manufacturing firms over the period 2003–2012. Over that period the share of Turkish manufacturing industry in GDP was 23.5 percent on average. While manufacturing industry constituted 13.5 percent of overall employment in Turkey, it generated 93.5 percent of the total export volume. With such a large share the characteristics of the manufacturing industry play an important role in determining Turkish export performance and telling about possible export spillovers taking place. Besides, the manufacturing industry accounts for the 43.3 percent of total FDI inflows in 2012.

Our unbalanced panel relies on two different sources of data collected by Turkish State Institute of Statistics (TURKSTAT). The first one is 'The Annual Industry and Service Statistics' and the second one is 'Annual Trade Statistics'.[8] In order to conduct our analyses we merged two datasets. The Annual Industry and Service Statistics is a census for the firms with more than 19 employees and a representative survey for firms with less than 20 employees. In this dataset, firms are classified according to their main activity, as identified by EUROSTAT's NACE Rev.1.1 standard codes for sectoral classification. It provides detailed information on a number of structural variables which are mainly seen on a firm's balance sheet, such as revenues, value added, intermediate inputs cost, tangible and intangible investment costs information on geographical location, the number of employees as well as foreign ownership information. We select the whole population of private Turkish manufacturing firms with 20 employees or more, where firms with 20 and more than 20 employees account for a large share of Turkish manufacturing industry.

The second data we utilize are firm level foreign trade flows, which are sourced from customs declarations. The import and export flows are collected for the whole universe of imports and exports at 12-digit GTIP (Customs Tariff Statistics Position) classification, the first 8 digits of whom correspond to CN classification whereas the last 4 digits are national.

Before conducting the analyses, we calculate capital stock series of firms applying the perpetual inventory methodology using the data on investment cost series for machinery and equipment, building and structure, transportation equipment and computer and programming. We estimate total factor productivity (TFP) of firms using Levinsohn-Petrin's (2003) semi-parametric methodology.

The information on foreign affiliation enables us to distinguish between purely domestic firms, mixed ownership status and purely foreign ownership. We define firms as multinationals if the share of foreign ownership is positive. Table 3.1 presents total number of firms, number of exporter firms and number of multinational firms in each year over the analysis period.[9] In Table 3.2, some summary statistics are shown for domestic and multinational firms. It is clear that

Table 3.1 Number of firms, multinationals and exporters (2003–2012)

Year	Number of firms	Number of multinationals	Number of exporters
2003	14,785	473	6,803
2004	16,443	583	7,850
2005	18,462	638	9,381
2006	19,532	729	9,728
2007	18,481	682	9,294
2008	17,924	742	9,148
2009	15,480	695	8,432
2010	21,076	832	10,477
2011	22,351	860	10,538
2012	24,465	834	11,530

Table 3.2 Firm performance with respect to ownership status (2003–2012)

	Number of employees	Log of sales	TFP	Capital intensity	Export intensity
Domestic Firms	88.857	14.903	7.612	10.530	0.001
Multinational Firms	317.905	16.772	7.988	11.307	0.007

multinationals show superior performance with respect to domestic firms in terms of each indicator.

We construct our horizontal and vertical linkage variables using our firm level panel and Turkish input–output table for 2002 prepared by TURKSTAT. In this table, Turkish Liras at current prices are used as units and NACE Rev.1.1. Industrial classification, where each manufacturing industry corresponds to one or several two-digit industries in terms of NACE including 59 sectors, is employed. We match the firm data with the input–output table concentrating only on the manufacturing sectors.

Our horizontal linkage measure is originated from Aitken and Harrison (1999) and represents the foreign presence within an industry in which firms operate (own industry). It is calculated as follows:

$$FDI\_Own_{Jt} = \frac{\sum_{j \in J} f_{jt} * \Upsilon_{jt}}{\sum_{j \in J} \Upsilon_{jt}}$$

where j denotes each firm in each two-digit manufacturing sector J, f_{jt} is the foreign capital share of the firm j and Υ_{jt} is the total output of the firm j. Accordingly, an increase in this horizontal linkage proxy indicates that the output of the foreign affiliated firms in one sector is expanding faster than that of the domestic firms in the same sector.

We determine two vertical linkage measures i.e. vertical spillover effects can be classified into two categories: vertical backward (FDI_Back_{Jt}) and vertical forward (FDI_For_{Jt}). The degree of spillovers stemming from backward linkages for sector J outsourcing from other sectors is computed as follows where α_{KJt} are weights defined as the share of inputs purchased by industry J from industry K in total inputs sourced by J.

$$FDI\_Back_{Jt} = \sum_{\forall K \neq J} \propto_{KJt} * FDI\_Own_{Kt}$$

Accordingly, as the backward spillover measure gets larger, the higher is the proportion of foreign affiliated firms' output in industry K and, the greater is the share of inputs from industry K in total inputs used by industry J. The second vertical linkage variable stemming from forward linkages for sector J providing inputs to other sectors is calculated as follows where γ_{KJt} are weights defined as shares of the total output of industry J supplied as inputs to each downstream industry K, where they sum to less than 1.[10] Thereby, this forward spillover measure gets larger the higher is the proportion of foreign affiliated firms' output in industry K and, the greater is the share of output supplied as inputs to industry K in total output produced by industry J.

$$FDI\_For_{Jt} = \sum_{\forall K \neq J} \gamma_{KJt} * FDI\_Own_{Kt}$$

Table 3.3 Linkage measures with respect to two-digit NACE sectors

NACE	Sector	FDI_Own	FDI_Back	FDI_For
15	Food and Beverages	0.127	3.421	6.858
17	Textiles	0.025	0.437	0.115
18	Apparel	0.033	0.438	0.127
19	Leather	0.003	3.392	6.815
20	Wood	0.006	0.172	0.011
21	Paper	0.212	2.914	15.163
22	Printing	0.023	0.018	0.031
24	Chemical	0.345	7.058	0.155
25	Rubber	0.197	11.180	2.150
26	Non-Metalic Minerals	0.085	0.286	1.157
27	Basic Metal	0.045	0.282	1.130
28	Metal Products	0.137	11.402	2.235
29	Machinery & Equipment	0.174	0.098	1.907
31	Electrical Machinery	0.352	3.004	20.800
32	Radio TV	0.326	6.974	0.275
33	Medical & Optical Instruments	0.073	0.165	0.131
34	Motor Vehicles	0.467	10.073	6.153
35	Other Transports	0.074	0.009	0.385
36	Furniture	0.130	3.341	34.289

Table 3.3 provides the average values of the linkage measures for manufacturing industries at the two-digit level. One can observe from the table that spillover variables are characterized by significant variation across industries. In general, the motor vehicles industry has the highest values in terms of all linkage variables. The lowest values of linkage variables are observed in wood, printing and other transport industries.

Empirical strategy and results

Studies in the existing literature assert that the presence of foreign firms can promote domestic firms' export performance through reducing export costs via creating information externalities about foreign markets, providing technological knowledge transfer and increasing competitive pressure. In line with this literature we aim to test for the existence of export spillovers that arise from foreign direct investment generated linkages between domestic and foreign firms. In order to test for the presence of spillover effects arising from the presence of foreign firms in the Turkish manufacturing industry, we employ an empirical model, which is based on the studies of Aitken et al. (1997), Greenaway et al. (2004) and Kneller and Pisu (2007). This model allows us to analyze whether the linkages with multinationals impacts on the decision of domestic firms to export and whether the presence of multinationals affects the export intensity of domestic firms, which is a fundamental measure of a firm reflecting its export performance. According to the firm heterogeneity framework in the presence of sunk costs, export market entry can be thought of as a two-stage decision process whereby firms first decide whether to export or not, and second how much to export. To account for both stages we use the Heckman's (1979) selection model that avoids selection bias.[11]

The implementation of this model requires identifying exogenous independent variables from the first stage equation of export decision, which can be validly excluded from the set of independent variables in the second stage regression (Little, 1985). The estimated equations are as follows:[12]

$$Export\_Decision_{ijt} = f\left(Export\_Decision_{ijt-1}, FDI\_Own_{jt-1},\right.$$
$$\left. FDI\_Back_{jt-1}, FDI\_For_{jt-1}, Controls_{ijt-1}, u_{ijt}\right)$$

$$Export\_Intensity_{ijt} = g(FDI\_Own_{jt-1}, FDI\_Back_{jt-1}, FDI\_For_{jt-1},$$
$$Controls_{ijt-1}, FDI\_Own_{jt-1}, FDI\_Back_{jt-1},$$
$$FDI\_For_{jt-1}, Controls_{ijt-1}, {}_{ijt})$$

where *Export_Decision*$_{ijt}$ is a binary variable that takes the value of 1 if firm *i* in industry *j* exports in year *t* and 0 otherwise. *Export_Intensity*$_{ijt}$ is the share of firm *i*'s exports in its total sales, u_{ijt} and μ_{ijt} are random variables that capture the effect of omitted variables. In the *Controls* vector we include firm specific variables, hence we are able to control for other factors that may affect the correlation of the linkage measures with the export behavior of Turkish firms. These firm level variables are as follows and they are included in the regressions in their lagged values: number of employees to account for firm size, wage per employee as a proxy for skill intensity of workers, tangible and intangible investment dummies and import dummy indicating whether the firm is an importer or not. We also include capital intensity and Herfindahl index computed as a four-digit sectoral level to capture changes to the competitiveness across time of each industry as well as region and four-digit sector dummies. Note that to avoid endogeneity between exporting behavior and spillover variables they enter into the regressions in their one-year lagged values. Hereafter all the regressions apply only to the sample of domestically owned exporters.

The estimated results from the first- and second-stage equations are summarized in Table 3.4. For the first model, column 1 reports the results of the export decision equation and column 2 gives the results from export intensity equation. The significant and positive coefficient of the lagged dependent variable in the first equation indicates hysteresis in the export behavior of firms. This suggests the existence of sunk costs for exporting (Bernard and Wagner, 1997; Roberts and Tybout, 1997; Bernard and Jensen, 2004). The firm-level characteristics have the expected sign and support previous findings in other studies (Girma et al., 2001; Bernard and Jensen, 1995; Bernard and Wagner, 1997). The other firm-level variables indicate that both the probability of exporting and export intensity are increasing in the size of the firm and skill intensity of the workers.

Table 3.4 Heckman Selection Model

Variables	Export decision	Export intensity	Export decision	Export intensity
Export Dummy (t – 1)	2.0746***		2.0457***	
	(0.000)		(0.000)	
FDI_Own (t – 1)	0.0846***	0.0078***	0.0655***	0.0067***
	(0.000)	(0.000)	(0.000)	(0.000)
FDI_Back (t – 1)	0.0067	0.0009***	0.0037	0.0003***
	(0.100)	(0.000)	(0.114)	(0.000)
FDI_For (t – 1)	0.0007***	0.0001*	0.0005***	0.0001***
	(0.000)	(0.074)	(0.000)	(0.000)
TFP (t – 1)			0.0273***	0.0070***
			(0.000)	(0.000)
Employee (t – 1)	0.0039***	0.0821***	0.0043***	0.0882***
	(0.001)	(0.000)	(0.000)	(0.000)
Wage per Employee (t – 1)	0.0127***	0.1012***	0.0076***	0.0982***
	(0.000)	(0.000)	(0.002)	(0.000)
Tangible Investment (t – 1)	-0.0094***	0.1163***	-0.0038	0.0341**
	(0.000)	(0.000)	(0.161)	(0.011)
Intangible Investment (t – 1)	-0.0102***	0.1144***	-0.0106***	0.1050***
	(0.000)	(0.000)	(0.000)	(0.000)
Herfindal Index (t – 1)	-0.0222	0.2662***	-0.0189	0.1870***
	(0.252)	(0.000)	(0.345)	(0.001)
Sectoral Capital Intensity (t – 1)	0.0021	0.0630***	0.0024	0.0515***
	(0.668)	(0.000)	(0.621)	(0.000)
Import Status Dummy (t – 1)	0.0206***	0.5190***	0.0230***	0.4682***
	(0.000)	(0.000)	(0.000)	(0.000)
Four-Digit Industry Dummies	X	X	X	X
Region Dummies	X	X	X	X
Lambda	-0.1092***		-0.1131***	
	(0.000)		(0.000)	
Observations	126513	126513	112852	112852

Notes: Robust standard errors in parentheses below the coefficients. Asterisks denote significance levels ***p < 0.01, **p < 0.05, *p < 0.1. Lambda provides the estimated coefficient on the inverse Mills ratio. Significance of this variable indicates the presence of a sample selection bias.

The coefficient of the dummies, indicating whether the firm made tangible and/ or intangible investments in the previous year, is positive in the export intensity equation whereas it turns to be negative in the decision equation. Since investment decision incurs additional financial burdens on a firm it may create an obstacle for entry into export markets which already require sunk costs. On the other hand, once the sunk costs are internalized these investments bear pay-offs and promotes the firm's exporting intensity. Finally, in line with the firm heterogeneity literature, previous import status of the firm positively affects both the export decision and export intensity. Note that the sectoral control variables, sectoral capital intensity and Herfindahl index (both of which can show the extent of competition within an industry), has no significant effect on the probability of exporting, while they are found to increase export intensity. These positive effects suggest that higher degree of industry concentration creates economies of scale conditions and leads to higher export intensity.

The coefficients on the horizontal linkage variables are positively significant for both equations. This suggests that domestic firms are more likely to enter the export markets and they are likely to export more of their output if they operate in a sector where the presence of foreign firms is stronger. This result is in line with the view that increased competitive pressure forces domestic firms within the same industry to operate more efficiently and in turn reduce their sunk costs and increase their probability of selecting into export markets. The results concerning the backward linkage variable tell a different story in export decision and export intensity equations. Foreign multinationals operating in the upstream sectors appear to create export spillovers towards domestic firms in terms of their export intensity while they have no significant effect on their export decision behavior. This might be interpreted in terms of the presence of high sunk costs of exporting discouraging entry into export markets. Put differently, with regards to backward spillovers domestic firms can gain access to new, improved or less costly intermediate inputs produced by foreign firms and can improve their export performance once they decide to export. The coefficients on spillover variables associated with forward linkages between foreign and domestic firms are positive and statistically significant. This finding on this vertical linkage variable supports the view that supplying multinationals in downstream industries creates export spillovers, improving domestic firms' performance in terms of their export value.[13]

These findings so far suggest that there are important export spillovers stemming from horizontal and vertical linkages between multinationals and domestic firms. Yet it is still unclear whether export spillovers from foreign direct investment constitutes an additional spillover mechanism benefiting domestic firms apart from productivity spillovers. Put differently, if more productive firms self-select into exporting, it is possible that multinationals help to improve productivity of domestic firms and this in turn may allow them to cover the fixed costs of entry into export markets. Thus, picking over productivity effects raised by foreign firms would enable us to shed light on whether the channel of knowledge accumulation about international markets is at work, apart from the technological knowledge accumulation and competition channels which lead to productivity increases as a side-product of creating export spillovers. As productivity is positively associated with exporting, failing to control for productivity of firms might create an obstacle on identifying export spillovers correctly. Thus in order to eliminate the productivity improving channels, as a first approach, we control for productivity in the regressions to get cleaner results. Regarding regression results are shown in columns 3 and 4 of Table 2.4. When we control for total factor productivity the coefficients of both horizontal and vertical linkage variables are reduced but still significant. This suggests that the export spillovers are indeed an additional spillover process through which contact with multinationals benefits domestic firms.

As an alternative approach, to eliminate productivity spillovers and have a clearer understanding of export spillovers taking place, we reran the regressions over samples of firms, which are constructed upon their place in the productivity distribution of the whole sample. In the presence of heterogeneous firms in terms of productivity, it is appropriate to examine the export spillover dynamics at different points of the distribution rather than examining the issue at conditional means. Thus, we define four sub-samples with respect to percentiles of productivity distribution. Results of Heckman regressions over these samples are presented in Table 3.5. Previous control variables apply to the estimation model as well as total factor productivity. The first two columns show the estimation results for the firms at the bottom of the productivity distribution (1st quartile), while last two columns show results for the firms at the top. Overall, across quartiles there exists significant heterogeneity both in terms of statistical significance and magnitudes of the coefficients for linkage variables. Namely, foreign direct investment linked export spillovers through horizontal and vertical linkages between multinationals and domestic firms vary considerably with the level of their productivity.

To start with, the impact of horizontal linkages on the decision to export and export intensity is significantly positive for all parts of the productivity distribution except the first quartile. Further, among the rest, there exists a hierarchical structure in the extent of export spillovers that are taking place through horizontal linkages. The firms with low levels of productivity are least likely to benefit from horizontal linkages whereas higher levels of firm productivity indicates higher benefits. This finding suggests that only as the firms improve their productivity beyond a threshold value are they able to benefit from horizontal linkages, which then outweigh the possible adverse effects of competitive pressure.

As far as the impact of vertical linkages is considered, a U-shaped relationship between productivity and backward linkage benefits is observed. That is, the estimated coefficients are negatively significant for the low productivity groups, whereas they are found to be positively significant for the upper quartiles. This suggests that Turkish firms with low levels of productivity gain no benefit from the presence of foreign firms through backward linkages due to the high sunk costs of exporting. As information externality and technological knowledge channels are more pronounced for vertical linkages and productivity spillovers may act as an outcome of technological knowledge channel, this finding indicates that export spillovers stemming from knowledge externalities raised by multinationals are in fact at work as an additional process for high productivity firms. The results presented in Table 3.5 further suggest that the impact of horizontal linkages on the decision to export and export intensity is significantly positive for all parts of the productivity distribution. This finding indicates that, irrespective of the level of firm productivity, supplying to multinationals inspires domestic firms to enter the export markets and increase their export performance in terms of export intensity. These positive spillover effects via forward linkages are more pronounced for firms operating with higher productivity.

Next, in order to provide more robust evidence for the fact that export spillovers from multinationals are indeed at work as an additional spillover process to

Variables	First Quartile Exp. decision	First Quartile Exp. intensity	Second Quartile Exp. decision	Second Quartile Exp. intensity	Third Quartile Exp. decision	Third Quartile Exp. intensity	Fourth Quartile Exp. decision	Fourth Quartile Exp. intensity
Export Dummy (t − 1)	2.1177*** (0.000)		2.0326*** (0.000)		1.9955*** (0.000)		1.9855*** (0.000)	
FDI_Own (t − 1)	0.0355*** (0.000)	0.0011 (0.380)	0.0445*** (0.000)	0.0031*** (0.000)	0.0646*** (0.000)	0.0053*** (0.000)	0.0818*** (0.000)	0.0065*** (0.000)
FDI_Back (t − 1)	-0.0295*** (0.000)	-0.0002*** (0.000)	-0.0189** (0.015)	-0.0007*** (0.000)	0.0059** (0.018)	0.0015* (0.009)	0.0036*** (0.000)	0.0027*** (0.002)
FDI_For (t − 1)	0.0001*** (0.000)	0.0001*** (0.000)	0.0003*** (0.000)	0.0001*** (0.000)	0.0007*** (0.000)	0.0001*** (0.000)	0.0006*** (0.000)	0.0003*** (0.000)
TFP (t − 1)	0.0186*** (0.000)	0.0022*** (0.000)	0.0203*** (0.000)	0.0057** (0.024)	0.0299*** (0.000)	0.0072*** (0.000)	0.0276*** (0.000)	0.0094*** (0.000)
Employee (t − 1)	0.0045*** (0.000)	0.0782*** (0.000)	0.0036*** (0.000)	0.0820*** (0.000)	0.0056*** (0.000)	0.0826*** (0.000)	0.0831*** (0.000)	0.0854*** (0.000)
Wage per Employee (t − 1)	0.0061 (0.131)	0.0778 (0.166)	0.0043*** (0.000)	0.073 (0.555)	0.0053*** (0.000)	0.0851*** (0.000)	0.0079*** (0.002)	0.08134*** (0.008)
Tangible Inv (t − 1)	-0.0068 (0.811)	0.0384 (0.148)	-0.0047 (0.068)	0.0327 (0.584)	-0.0041 (0.130)	0.0318*** (0.000)	-0.0035 (0.211)	0.0304*** (0.000)
Intangible Inv (t − 1)	-0.0104** (0.018)	0.1459*** (0.000)	-0.0083** (0.032)	0.0946*** (0.000)	-0.0087** (0.024)	0.0835*** (0.000)	-0.0177*** (0.000)	0.0701*** (0.002)
Herfindal Index (t − 1)	-0.0147 (0.212)	0.1691 (0.809)	-0.0146 (0.105)	0.1638 (0.235)	-0.0137 (0.759)	0.1850*** (0.000)	-0.01328 (0.038)	0.1873*** (0.000)
Sectoral Capital Intensity (t − 1)	0.0021 (0.085)	-0.0149 (0.842)	0.0027 (0.070)	-0.3592*** (0.000)	-0.003 (0.807)	0.0501 (0.407)	-0.0086 (0.297)	0.0536** (0.020)
Import Status (t − 1)	0.0318*** (0.000)	0.4693*** (0.000)	0.0100* (0.037)	0.4527*** (0.000)	0.0081* (0.100)	0.4551*** (0.000)	0.0394*** (0.000)	0.4138*** (0.000)
4-Digit Industry	X	X	X	X	X	X	X	X
Region	X	X	X	X	X	X	X	X
Lambda	-0.1012*** (0.000)		-0.1087*** (0.000)		-0.1117*** (0.000)		-0.1431*** (0.000)	
Observations	26408	26408	27495	27495	27026	27026	27869	27869

Notes: Robust standard errors in parentheses below the coefficients. Asterisks denote significance levels ***p < 0.01, **p < 0.05, *p < 0.1. Lambda provides the estimated coefficient on the inverse Mills ratio. Significance of this variable indicates the presence of a sample selection bias.

productivity spillovers, we incorporate the concept of technological gap between domestic and foreign firms. Within the context of productivity spillovers, in an early theoretical paper, Findlay (1978) emphasizes domestic firms' speed of adoption of newly available technologies i.e. spillover benefits stemming from multinational firms. Accordingly, the greater the technological distance between multinationals and domestic firms the faster the adaption of domestic firms. Namely, the productivity spillovers are more pronounced if the technological gap is larger. With a counterfactual argument, the technological gap between domestic and multinational firms can be interpreted as an indicator of absorptive capacity of host country firms which is defined as the ability to absorb and utilize the knowledge available from multinationals (Glass and Saggi,1998). According to this view, the larger the technological gap is the less likely are the existence of the productivity spillovers.

Following these discussions,[14] we utilize the concept of technology gap defined in terms of productivity differentials between foreign and domestic firms. Specifically, it is measured as the distance of a firm's TFP from technology frontier at four-digit industry level, where technology frontier is defined as the mean productivity of foreign firms within the borders of an industry. The technological gap variable and its interaction with our horizontal and vertical linkage variables are added into the Heckman specification with the usual controls as well as productivity. Results from these regressions are presented in Table 3.6. In line with the baseline results in Table 3.4, we find significant export spillover effects. The coefficient of our technology gap variable is negatively significant, indicating that this variable acts as an indicator of absorptive capacity in our case as opposed to the convergence effect. Looking at the interaction terms we find further evidence for the fact that export spillovers operate as an additional spillover mechanism. Specifically, as the technology gap narrows down, the benefits from horizontal and vertical linkages become more and more pronounced.

Table 3.6 Heckman Selection Model and technology gap

Variables	Export decision	Export intensity
Export Dummy (t − 1)	2.0470***	
	(0.000)	
FDI_Own (t − 1)	0.0426***	0.0058***
	(0.000)	(0.000)
FDI_Back (t − 1)	0.0033	0.0001***
	(0.103)	(0.000)
FDI_For (t − 1)	0.0006***	0.0001***
	(0.000)	(0.000)
TFP (t − 1)	0.0307***	0.0064***
	(0.000)	(0.000)
Employee (t − 1)	0.0023***	0.0601***
	(0.000)	(0.000)
Wage per Employee (t − 1)	0.0080***	0.0996***
	(0.000)	(0.000)

Variables	Export decision	Export intensity
Tangible Investment (t - 1)	-0.0044	0.0216
	(0.132)	(0.111)
Intangible Investment (t - 1)	-0.0107***	0.0961***
	(0.000)	(0.000)
Herfindal Index (t - 1)	-0.0140	0.1697***
	(0.303)	(0.000)
Sectoral Capital Intensity (t - 1)	0.0004	0.0269
	(0.389)	(0.125)
Import Status Dummy (t - 1)	0.0231***	0.4587***
	(0.000)	(0.000)
Technology Gap (t - 1)	-0.0313***	-0.0095***
	(0.000)	(0.000)
HOR* Technology Gap (t - 1)	-0.0078***	-0.0024***
	(0.000)	(0.0003)
BACK* Technology Gap (t - 1)	-0.0012*	-0.0004***
	(0.0007)	(0.000)
FORW* Technology Gap (t - 1)	-0.0001***	-0.0001***
	(0.000)	(0.000)
Lambda	-0.1140***	
	(0.000)	
Observations	108571	108571

Notes: Robust standard errors in parentheses below the coefficients. Asterisks denote significance levels ***$p<0.01$, **$p<0.05$, *$p<0.1$. Lambda provides the estimated coefficient on the inverse Mills ratio. Significance of this variable indicates the presence of a sample selection bias.

Conclusion

Recently Turkey has shown a significant performance in increasing the extent of its international exposure, both in terms of increased inward flows of foreign direct investment and exporting activity. Since the interaction of domestic firms with foreign-owned firms can affect the export decision and performance of domestic firms, in this paper we explore the extent to which foreign direct investment has affected exporting behavior of Turkish firms, namely export spillovers raised by multinational firms. Just as the exporting activity is carried by firms and not all firms are able to export, understanding what determines exporting behavior of firms is crucial to any design of adequate policies aimed at stimulating export capacity of an emerging economy like Turkey. Thus, in this study, by making use of a recent firm level dataset over the period 2003–2012, we investigate the existence of export spillovers from foreign direct investment generated by horizontal and vertical linkages between domestic and multinational firms in Turkey. We specifically attest whether export spillovers act as an additional process to productivity spillovers in Turkish manufacturing industry.

The results of the study suggest that significant spillover effects arise from domestic firms' interaction with multinational firms through horizontal and vertical linkages even after controlling for productivity. Still, foreign direct investment linked export spillovers through horizontal and vertical linkages vary considerably with the level of firms' productivity. We find positive and significant effects with regard to horizontal linkages. This finding underlines that increased competition within an industry puts pressure on domestic firms to operate more efficiently. In turn, domestic firms increase their probability of entering into export markets and export intensity. Nevertheless, the firms operating with low levels of productivity are least likely to benefit from horizontal linkages. This finding suggests that only as the firms improve their productivity beyond a threshold value are they able to benefit from horizontal linkages, which then outweigh the possible adverse effects of competitive pressure.

Multinationals operating in the upstream sectors create export spillovers towards domestic firms in terms of their export intensity while they have no significant effect on their export decision behavior. This may suggest that domestic firms can gain access to new, improved or less costly intermediate inputs produced by foreign firms and can improve their export performance once they decide to export. Looking at this issue among different quartiles sheds further light on this finding. The results reveal a U-shaped relationship between productivity and backward linkage benefits suggesting that Turkish firms with low level of productivity gain no benefit from the presence of foreign firms through backward linkages due to the high sunk costs of exports. Findings on the vertical linkage variable support the view that supplying multinationals in downstream industries create export spillovers. Irrespective of the level of firm productivity, supplying to multinationals inspires domestic firms to enter the export markets and increase their export performance in terms of export intensity. These positive spillover effects via forward linkages are more pronounced for firms operating with higher productivity.

The results are reinforced when we control for technology gap between domestic firms and multinationals. Specifically, as the technology gap narrows down the benefits from horizontal and vertical linkages become more and more pronounced. As a result, we conclude that export spillovers stemming from knowledge externalities raised by multinationals are indeed at work as an additional process to productivity spillovers.

Notes

1 See, among others, Blomström, 1986; Aitken and Harrison, 1999; Blomström and Kokko, 2001; Javorcik, 2004; Keller and Yeaple, 2009; Blalock and Gertler, 2008; Mucchielli and Jabbour, 2004; Mervelede and Schoors, 2005; Javorcik and Spatareanu, 2011.
2 Empirical evidence in the regarding literature is mixed. While some studies provide evidence on the positive impact of horizontal linkages i.e. export spillovers via horizontal linkages (see among others Kokko et al., 2001; Kneller and Pisu, 2007; Alvarez and Lopez, 2008), some of them finds zero or negative impact (see among others Aitken and Harrison, 1999; Djankov and Hoekman, 2000; Greenaway et al., 2004).
3 Macroeconomic studies that focus explicitly on the productivity spillover effect of FDI are scarce (see, among others, Van Pottelsberghe de la Potterie and Lichtenberg, 2001).

4 While the micro-econometrics of firms' engagement in international trade was pioneered by Bernard and Jensen (1999), Aw and Hwang (1995) and Roberts and Tybout (1997), the theoretical framework has been largely stimulated by the seminal works of Melitz (2003) and Bernard et al. (2003).

5 See Greenaway and Kneller (2007), Wagner (2007) and Wagner (2012) for a survey of the empirical evidence.

6 There is a vast empirical evidence supporting the self-selection hypothesis (see among others Roberts and Tybout, 1997; Bernard and Jensen, 1999; Aw et al., 2000; Bernard and Wagner, 1997; Isgut, 2001)

7 The 2002–2012 period witnesses a structural shift away from traditional export sectors of textiles and clothing towards machinery and metals. A transition across destination markets occurs where the EU and EFTA lose ground towards new markets in the MENA as well as in Europe and Central Asia.

8 These datasets are available under a confidential agreement by which all the elaborations can only be conducted at the Microdata Research Centre of TURK-STAT under the respect of the law on the statistic secret and the personal data protection.

9 The original sample size in the merged dataset was slightly larger but we applied a cleaning procedure which is largely inspired by Hall and Mairesse (1995). We threw out the abnormal observations (zero/negative) for the main variables such as output, intermediate inputs, labor cost etc. Then, we excluded observations where main variables and ratios (e.g. employee, value added per employee, capital per employee) displays extraordinary jumps and drops over one year. Finally, we excluded firms in NACE sectors 16 (Manufacture of tobacco products), 23 (Manufacture of coke, refined petroleum products and nuclear fuel), 30 (Manufacture of office, accounting and computing machinery), 37 (Recycling) since they include small number of firms.

10 We give more weight to upstream industries which supply a larger share of their output as inputs to downstream industries rather than selling it for final consumption.

11 Selection occurs when observations are non-randomly sorted into discrete groups, resulting in the potential for coefficient bias in estimation procedures such as ordinary least squares (Maddala, 1991). Heckman (1979) develops a standard approach to control for this bias, which is referred to as the selection model. In our case the non-random sample of exporters could lead to selection bias if the determinants of being an exporter are correlated with the error term.

12 This two-step methodology involves estimating first the probability of the export decision (i.e. selection equation), computing the inverse of the Mills ratio and inserting it as regressor in the second regression.

13 As a robustness check we replicate these and the remaining regressions excluding horizontal linkage variable. This exclusion does not significantly alter the results. They are available upon request.

14 See Kokko (1994), Kokko et al. (1996), Girma et al. (2001), Kinoshita (2001), Barrios and Strobl (2002).

References

Aghion, P. and Howitt, P. (1992) 'A model of growth through creative destruction', *Econometrica*, 60(2): 323–51.

Aitken, B., Gordon H.H. and Harrison, A.E. (1997) 'Spillovers, foreign investment, and export behavior', *Journal of International Economics*, 431(2): 103–32.

Aitken, B.J. and Harrison, A.E. (1999) 'Do domestic firms benefit from direct foreign investment? Evidence from Venezuela', *American Economic Review*, 89(3): 605–18.

Alvarez, R. and Lopez, R.A. (2008) 'Is exporting a source of productivity spillovers?', *Review of World Economics*, 144(4): 723–49.

Aw, B.Y., Chung, S. and Roberts, M.J. (2000) 'Productivity and turnover in the export market: Micro-level evidence from the Republic of Korea and Taiwan, China', *The World Bank Economic Review*, 14(1): 65–90.

Aw, B.Y. and Hwang, A. (1995) 'Productivity and the export market: A firm-level analysis', *Journal of Development Economics*, 47(2): 313–32.

Bajgar, M. and Javorcik, B.S. (2013) Exporters' stargate: Supplying multinationals and entry into new markets. CESifo-Delphi Conference proceedings. Unpublished manuscript.

Barrios, S. and Strobl, E. (2002) 'Foreign direct investment and productivity spillovers: Evidence from the Spanish experience', *Weltwirtschaftliches Archiv*, 138(3): 459–81.

Bernard, A., Eaton, J., Jensen J.B. and Kortum, S.S. (2003) 'Plants and productivity in international trade', *American Economic Review*, 93(4): 1268–90.

Bernard, A. and Jensen, B. (1999) 'Exceptional exporter performance: Cause, effect, or both?', *Journal of International Economics*, 47(1): 1–25.

Bernard, A. and Jensen, B. (2004) 'Why some firms export', *The Review of Economics and Statistics*, 86(2): 561–69.

Bernard, A. and Wagner, J. (1997) 'Exports and success in German manufacturing', *Weltwirtschaftliches Archiv*, 133(1): 134–57.

Bernard, A.B. and Jensen, J.B. (1995) 'Exporters, jobs, and wages in US manufacturing: 1976–1987', *Brookings Papers on Economic Activity. Microeconomics*, 1995(1995): 67–119.

Blalock, G. and Gertler, P.J. (2008) 'Welfare gains from foreign direct investment through technology transfer to local suppliers', *Journal of International Economics*, 74(2): 402–21.

Blomström, M. (1986) 'Foreign investment and productive efficiency: The case of Mexico', *Journal of Industrial Economics*, 35(1): 97–112.

Blomström, M. and Kokko, A. (2001) 'Foreign direct investment and spillovers of technology', *International Journal of Technology Management*, 22(5–6): 435–54.

Djankov, S. and Hoekman, B. (2000) 'Foreign investment and productivity growth in Czech enterprises', *World Bank Economic Review*, 14(1): 49–64.

Findlay, R. (1978) 'Relative backwardness, direct foreign investment, and the transfer of technology: A simple dynamic model', *Quarterly Journal of Economics*, 92(1): 1–16.

Fons-Rosen, C., Kalemli-Ozcan, S., Sørensen, B.E., Villegas-Sanchez, C. and Volosovych, V. (2013) Quantifying productivity gains from Foreign investment. NBER Working Paper 18920.

Girma, S., Greenaway, D and Wakelin, K. (2001) 'Who benefits from foreign direct investment in the UK?', *Scottish Journal of Political Economy*, 48(2): 119–33.

Glass, A.J. and Saggi, K. (1998) 'International technology transfer and the technology gap', *Journal of Development Economics*, 55(2): 369–98.

Görg, H. and Greenaway, D. (2004) 'Much ado about nothing? Do domestic firms really benefit from foreign direct investment?', *The World Bank Research Observer*, 19(2): 171–97.

Greenaway, D. and Kneller, R. (2004) 'Exporting productivity in the United Kingdom', *Oxford Review of Economic Policy*, 20(3): 358–71.

Greenaway, D and Kneller, R. (2007) 'Firm heterogeneity, exporting and foreign direct investment', *Economic Journal*, 117(517): 134–61.

Greenaway, D., Sousa, N. and Wakelin, K. (2004) 'Do domestic firms learn to export from multinationals?', *European Journal of Political Economy*, 20(4): 1027–43.

Hall, B.H. and Mairesse, J. (1995) 'Exploring the relationship between R&D and productivity in French manufacturing firms', *Journal of Econometrics*, 65(1): 263–93.

Heckman, J. (1979) 'Sample selection bias as a specification error', *Econometrica*, 47(1): 153–61.

Isgut, A. (2001) 'What's different about exporters?. Evidence from Colombian manufacturing', *Journal of Development Studies*, 37(5): 57–82.

Javorcik, B.S. (2004) 'Does foreign direct investment increase the productivity of domestic firms? in search of spillovers through backward linkages', *American Economic Review*, 94(3): 605–27.

Javorcik, B.S. and Spatareanu, M. (2008) 'To share or not to share: Does local participation matter for spillovers from foreign direct investment?', *Journal of Development Economics*, 85(1–2): 194–217.

Javorcik, B.S. and Spatareanu, M. (2011) 'Does it matter where you come from? Vertical spillovers from foreign direct investment and the origin of investors', *Journal of Development Economics*, 96(1): 126–38.

Kearney, A.T. (2012) Cautious investors feed a tentative recovery. Foreign Direct Investment (FDI) Confidence Index. Online: http://www. atkearney. com/ documents/10192/fdaa84a5-a30a-4e4e-bc36-453375d6596fb (30.04. 2013).

Keller, W. and Yeaple, S.R. (2009) 'Multinational enterprises, international trade, and productivity growth: Firm-level evidence from the United States', *The Review of Economics and Statistics*, 91(4): 821–31.

Kinoshita, Y. (2001) R&D and technology spillovers through FDI: Innovation and absorptive capacity. CEPR Discussion Paper 2775.

Kneller, R. and Pisu, M. (2007) 'Industrial linkages and export spillovers from FDI', *The World Economy*, 30(1): 105–34.

Kokko, A. (1994) 'Technology, market characteristics, and spillovers', *Journal of Development Economics*, 43(2): 279–93.

Kokko, A., Tansini, R. and Zejan, M.C. (1996) 'Local technological capability and productivity spillovers from FDI in the Uruguayan manufacturing sector', *Journal of Development Studies*, 32(4): 602–11.

Kokko, A., Tansini, R. and Zejan, M.C. (2001) 'Trade regimes and spillover effects of FDI: Evidence from Uruguay', *Weltwirtschaftliches Archiv*, 137(1): 124–49.

Konings, J. (2001) 'The effects of foreign direct investment on domestic firms', *Economics of Transition*, 9(3); 619–33.

Levinsohn, J. and Petrin, A. (2003) 'Estimating production functions using inputs to control for unobservables', *Review of Economic Studies*, 70(2): 317–42.

Little, R. (1985) 'A note about models for selectivity bias', *Econometrica*, 53(6): 1469–74.

Maddala, G.S. (1991) 'A perspective on the use of limited-dependent and qualitative variables models in accounting research', *The Accounting Review*, 66(4): 788–807.

Melitz, M.J. (2003) 'The impact of trade on intra-industry reallocations and aggregate industry productivity', *Econometrica*, 71(6): 1695–725.

Merlevede, B. and Schoors, K. (2005) Conditional Spillovers from FDI within and between sectors: Evidence from Romania. Mimeo.

Mucchielli, J.L. and Jabbour, L. (2004) Technology transfer through backward link ages: The case of the Spanish manufacturing industry. Unpublished manuscript.

Roberts, M. and Tybout, J. (1997) 'The decision to export in Colombia: An empirical model of entry with sunk costs', *American Economic Review*, 87(4): 545–64.

Rodriguez-Clare, A. (1996) 'Multinationals, linkages and economic development', *American Economic Review*, 84(4): 852–73.

Romer, P. (1990) 'Endogenous technological change', *Journal of Political Economy*, 98(5): 71–102.

Ruane, F. and Sutherland, J. (2004) Ownership and export characteristics of Irish manufacturing performance. International Institute of Integration Studies IIIS. Discussion Paper No. 32. Trinity College, Dublin.

Ruane, F. and Sutherland, J. (2005) 'Export performance and destination characteristics of Irish manufacturing industry', *Review of World Economics*, 141(3): 442–59.

Van Pottelsberghe de la Potterie, B. and Lichtenberg, F. (2001) 'Does foreign direct investment transfer technology across borders?', *Review of Economics and Statistics*, 83(3): 490–97.

Wagner, J. (2007) 'Exports and productivity: A survey of the evidence from firm level data', *The World Economy*, 30(1): 60–82.

Wagner, J. (2012) 'International trade and export performance: A survey of empirical studies since 2006', *Review of World Economics / Weltwirtschaftliches Archiv*, 148(2): 235–68.

4 Relational spillovers and knowledge creation across European regions

Are there differences across R&D institutional sectors?

Daniela Di Cagno, Andrea Fabrizi, Valentina Meliciani and *Iris Wanzenböck*

Introduction

Recently several papers have investigated the role of geographical spillovers for regional growth (Bottazzi and Peri 2003; Peri, 2004; Moreno et al., 2005; Rodriguez-Pose and Crescenzi, 2008; Crescenzi and Rodriguez-Pose, 2011), mainly finding that spillovers are very localized and exist only within short distances.[1]

However, the special role of geographical distance with respect to other types of distances has been questioned by a seminal paper of Boschma (2005), claiming that geographical proximity per se is neither a necessary nor a sufficient condition for learning to take place. Cognitive, organizational, social and institutional distances may be equally relevant, although they may be strengthened by geographical proximity.[2]

The aim of this chapter is to assess the role of relational and geographical R&D spillovers arising from participation in European Framework Programmes (FP) on knowledge creation across European regions. It also investigates whether the impact of such spillovers differs across R&D performed in different institutional sectors. European Framework Programmes have specific characteristics, making them an appropriate source of data to measure relational spillovers. In fact, participation in EU funded projects creates supranational networks potentially able to give rise to international knowledge transfers based on 'relational' distance, going beyond geographical proximity. If geographical proximity is important for exchanging knowledge since it favours personal interactions, participation in international research programmes can be a way of reconciling the need of 'face to face' contacts (through the mobility of researchers during and after the project) with knowledge exchange via interactions over long distances.

Differently from other cooperative initiatives that originate spontaneously from the decision of private or public agents,[3] FP are public initiatives where the European Union is investing a relevant and increasing amount of resources on the assumption that they should have a positive impact on knowledge generation, diffusion, economic growth and convergence. Consequently, it is important to assess whether and to what extent participation in FP creates relational knowledge spillovers in addition to geographical spillovers.

Another interesting feature of FP is that they facilitate the cooperation between private companies, public research centres and universities within and across different countries/regions. Therefore, data on participation to these programmes can also be used to assess the extent of geographical and relational spillovers arising from R&D performed in different institutional sectors.[4]

Only few papers have looked at the impact of participation in EU framework programmes on knowledge transfers between regions (Maggioni et al., 2007; Hoekman et al., 2013; Di Cagno et al., 2015) or countries (Di Cagno et al., 2014).[5] Differently from previous studies, our contribution is on the additional effect of relational spillovers with respect to geographical spillovers and on assessing which kind of linking structure (if any) are more effective in generating spillovers. Moreover, we are interested to analyse whether relational and geographical spillovers differ across R&D sectors (namely private sector, public sector and higher education sector), an issue that has been neglected in previous studies but which has important policy implications.

The chapter is organised as follows: the next Section presents the conceptual framework and introduces our research hypotheses and econometric methodology; Section 3 describes the data and presents descriptive statistics on EU regional innovation networks based on collaborations in FP; Section 4 presents the results of the econometric estimations while Section 5 concludes and draws policy implications.

Conceptual framework, research hypotheses and econometric methodology

Recent contributions have used data from EU framework programmes to estimate the impact of relational distance on knowledge creation at the regional level (Maggioni et al., 2007; Hoekman et al., 2013). In particular, Maggioni et al. (2007) investigate the role of both geographical and relational distance, finding that spatial proximity and geographical centrality are always significant in determining the co-patenting activity whereas joint collaborations also appear as another important factor. They also estimate a knowledge production function using two spatial error models based respectively on geographical and relational (co-participation to EU projects) distance matrixes. They find that relational networks influence the behaviour of regional innovation systems, but that spatial proximity plays a more relevant role in determining their performance.

Hoekman et al. (2013), using a regionalised dataset of joint FP participations and joint co-publication activities, study whether the acquisition and effect of FP funding is disproportionally concentrated in the leading research regions. They show that the returns to FP funding are highest when involving scientifically lagging regions concluding that the current FP policy is in line with the EU cohesion policy.

Our paper, similarly to Maggioni et al. (2007), looks at the respective role of geographical and relational proximity for knowledge creation, however, it adopts a spatial lag of X (R&D) model (SLX) (Lesage, 2014) of the knowledge production function including, at the same time, R&D weighted by two different distance matrices, one based on geographical distance across regions and the second based on relational distance. This allows disentangling the additional effect of R&D relational spillovers over geographical ones.

This is in line with the reasoning that R&D spillovers follow the routes of distinct knowledge transmission mechanisms, established for example in the form knowledge networks (e.g. Owen-Smith and Powell, 2004). Typically, joint R&D projects involve activities related to sharing or pooling knowledge or resources. The linkages cover longer geographical distance, not bounded to distinct geographical surroundings. A number of studies provide strikingly coherent evidence that factors like technological similarities, joint membership in multi-national cooperations or relations in global value chains even outweigh the importance of a mutual geographical embedding (Knoben and Oerlemans, 2006; Hoekman et al., 2009; Scherngell and Barber, 2009). Hence, our main hypothesis is that i) *relational spillovers matter for knowledge creation and have an additional effect with respect to geographical ones.*

As discussed in the previous section, Framework Programmes involve the interaction between different actors such as private companies, public research centres and universities. These actors have heterogeneous capabilities, thus helping create new knowledge especially as a result of the complementarities of their skills. However, their interaction may involve difficulties due to the different types of knowledge and objectives inherent to private firms, research centres (private and public) and universities (Foray and Lissoni, 2010). Most notably, the diversity between university and industry plays a key role. In terms of the nature of research activity, the former mainly develops basic research and promotes knowledge diffusion; the latter aims at exploiting the appropriability of knowledge for the commercialisation of the results of the research activity. In terms of the reasons to collaborate, universities mainly collaborate to find resources and ideas for future research resulting in scientific publications, while private companies interact to obtain advantages in terms of industrial applications and patents (De Fuentes and Dutrenit, 2011). This leads to our second hypothesis: ii) *the type and the extent of knowledge spillovers is likely to differ across R&D sectors.* In particular, according to the characteristics of sectors and the nature of their cooperation above mentioned, universities seem to have an international cooperation propensity greater than that of the business sector (Scherngell and Barber, 2011). Therefore, we might expect relational spillovers to matter more in the higher education sector with respect to the private sector, while this is not necessarily the case when looking at geographical spillovers. These hypotheses are tested by estimating the impact of R&D (geographical and relational) spillovers on patents separately for the three main R&D sectors (business enterprises, government and higher education).

The empirical framework is that of a knowledge production function at the regional level allowing for both geographical and relational R&D spillovers. Our basic equation, in logarithm terms, is the following:

$$PAT_t = RD_{t-s}\beta_1 + Wgeo_{t-s}RD_{t-s}\beta_2 + Wrel_{t-s}RD_{t-s}\beta_3 + HC_{t-s}\beta_4 + PD_{t-s}\beta_5 + \lambda_t e_N + v_t;$$ (1)

where PAT_t denotes an Nx1 vector of patent applications to the EPO divided by population (consisting of one observation for every region in period t); RD denotes R&D expenditures divided by GDP (an Nx1 vector consisting of one observation for every region in period $t - s$, where s denotes the time lag between the dependent and the explanatory variables); HC are human resources in science and technology divided by population; PD is population divided by the region's area;[6] W_{t-s} is an NxN non-negative row standardized spatial weights matrix, specified in terms of geographical ($Wgeo$) or relational ($Wrel$) distance, diagonal elements are all equal to zero, for period $t - s$; β_1, β_2, β_3, β_4 are response parameters; λ_t denotes a time specific effect, which is multiplied by an Nx1 vector of units elements and v_t is an Nx1 vector of residuals for every spatial unit with zero mean and variance σ^2. We also distinguish R&D (and R&D spillovers) by sector of performance (business enterprise R&D, government R&D and higher education R&D).

Due to the variability of data over time, patents are computed as averages over the periods 1997–2000, 2001–2004, 2005–2008 and 2009–2010. Since there exists a time lag between inputs and outputs in the production of new knowledge all explanatory variables (including the relational matrix) are computed as averages over the periods 1995–1998, 1999–2002, 2003–2006 and 2007–2010.[7] Overall we have a panel of 257 regions over four time periods.

Our specification only takes into account 'local' R&D spillovers by estimating a spatial lag of X (R&D) model (SLX) (Lesage, 2014). This means assuming that the outcome (patents) of each region i is affected by the R&D expenditures only of regions cooperating in the same network, ruling out higher order effects possibly arising from the indirect impact of the R&D of regions cooperating with regions with whom region i cooperates (neighbours to the neighbours indirect effects). In this respect our chapter follows Di Cagno et al. (2015) and differs from Maggioni et al. (2007) estimating a spatial error model and from Marrocu et al. (2013) estimating a spatial lag model. Our choice is dictated by different reasons described in a recent paper by Vega and Elhorst (2013) and already discussed in Gibbons and Overman (2012). First, the SLX model is the simplest among the spatial models used to take into account local spatial spillover effects. Moreover, the SLX overcomes some identification problems of an alternative model, such as the spatial Durbin model (SDM) which contains both a spatially lagged endogenous variable and spatially lagged exogenous variables.[8] Finally, the spatial autoregressive model (SAR) and the spatial error model (SEM) do not allow disentangling which variables are responsible for spillovers.

Data

Data from regional collaborations in EU FPs are extracted from the EUPRO database that contains information on organisations participating in FP funded projects.[9] FPs are the context under which research and technological development EU policies are implemented. Due to the FPs rules, projects submitted by applicants and approved by the European Commission has multilateral nature: it involves more actors (firms and/or universities and/or research centres) from different regions. A project, therefore, creates links among the participants, or differently, links among regions where the actors involved operate. Considering all projects funded, we can construct a collaborative, or relational, matrix, one for each FP.

To obtain our relational weight matrices, we follow Scherngell and Barber (2009) and construct region-by-region collaboration matrices containing the FP collaboration intensities between all regional pairs for each year over the period of observation.[10] The entries of the matrices give information on the number of links between two regions in a specific year, i.e. collaborative R&D projects between organisations located in these regions. Table 4.1 shows, for each FP, the annual average of collaborations created and the number of participating regions.[11] We can observe that the number of both regions participating in EU funded projects and inter-regional FP collaborations increase considerably over the period of observation. This may be traced back to the fact that the amount of EU financial resource allocated under FPs has risen from 3,408.9, in the 2000 budget, to 6,471.3 million EUR in the 2008 budget.[12] Table 4.1 shows also the annual average number of participants by R&D for institutional sector (in brackets the percentage value on total). We can observe that the participation of both BES and HES sectors has an opposite trend: for the first descending, whereas the second growing up to become the primary sector. For the other two sectors, the participation is broadly stable.

Furthermore, Figure 4.1 shows the role of regions in the FPs based on their average collaboration intensity per capita (and the average number of linkages a region has with other regions, over the period 1995–2010). We see that FP projects are highly concentrated on a set of strongly interlinked core – mainly capital – regions across Europe. The transparency of the lines represents the number of

Table 4.1 FPs collaborations

FPs Nr.	collabo- rations	Regions (NUTS-2)	BES	GOV	HES	PNP	Total
4	132,947	222	6,434 *(40%)*	3,823 *(24%)*	4,787 *(30%)*	1,115 *(7%)*	16,159
5	208,426	238	5,883 *(30%)*	5,610 *(29%)*	6,106 *(31%)*	1,975 *(10%)*	19,574
6	370,675	239	2,867 *(19%)*	3,984 *(27%)*	5,280 *(35%)*	2,817 *(19%)*	14,948
7	374,126	246	3,068 *(25%)*	3,133 *(25%)*	4,479 *(36%)*	1,668 *(14%)*	12,348

Source: EUPRO database and Annual Reports of the European Commission

Figure 4.1 R&D collaboration in the EU Framework Programmes across European NUTS-2 regions

Notes: Average values for the period 1995–2010 are used. Node size corresponds to a region's total number of collaborations (p.c.), line transparency corresponds to the number of joint FP projects between two regions.

Source: EUPRO database

collaboration between two regions, indicating that Île de France is the most central region with the highest number of linkages to other regions. Related to their regional population, however, we can further see on the size of the nodes that the regions Bruxelles-Capitale, Helsinki-Uusimaa, Prov. Brabant Wallon, Inner London and Wien (in order of rank) have the highest embeddedness in the inter-regional network of FP collaborations.

In Table 4.2, we summarize the descriptive statistics for the main variables of the knowledge production function (KPF), as described in Section 2. As explained above, data are computed at NUTS-2 level[13] and as average over a four year period, due to the variability of data over time.

For patents per million population, the (global) mean is 90.84, with values greater than 600 observed in two regions: Stuttgart Oberbayern (Germany) and

Table 4.2 Descriptive statistics

Variable	Mean	Std. Dev.	Min	Max	Observations
Patent (per million population)	90.8447	113.0128	0.0788	705.7323	N = 1028
R&D/GDP, %	1.3762	1.2113	0.0901	8.0806	N = 1028
Business R&D/GDP, %	0.8695	0.9971	0.0103	7.5747	N = 1028
Government R&D/GDP, %	0.1812	0.2353	0	2.0299	N = 1028
HES R&D/GDP, %	0.3260	0.2632	0.0008	1.6340	N = 1028
HRST/POPULATION, %	17.5017	6.2321	3.3414	44.1581	N = 1028

Source: EUROSTAT

Noord-Brabant (Netherlands). Low patenting activity (less than one patent per capita) is found in some regions of southern Europe (Spain, Greece, Portugal and South of Italy) and in a large part of Eastern European regions. If we have a look at the evolution over time, we will find out relevant improvements in Eastern countries in the recent years (see also Figure 4.3).

For the R&D expenditure over GDP, a standard input of KPF, the average R&D intensity in Europe is 1.37 percent with a minimum of 0.09 percent in Notio Aigaio (Greece) and a maximum of 8.08 percent in Brabant Wallon (Belgium). In this case, once again, the spatial distribution in Europe appears quite dispersed. R&D intensity can be decomposed at a sectorial level: first, the business sector (BES, mean value is 0.86 percent); second, the government spending on R&D (GOV, mean value is 0.32 percent), and finally, the higher education sector (HES, mean value is 0.18 percent). At a country level, the HES R&D expenditure along with the government spending on R&D count more than business R&D expenditure in Eastern countries and Italy as well (characterized by a lower level in these variables and other ones, compared to the other large countries).

We also take into account the availability of human capital as an additional input, supposed to influence the process of knowledge production at the local level. We measure human capital with a ratio between human resources in science and technology and the total population.[14] This variable has lower dispersion across the European regions compared to other variables, and it shows a clearly identifiable national pattern. A high endowment of human capital characterizes the Scandinavian countries, the UK, and Germany, while lower values are generally detected in the Eastern countries (except for Baltic countries), France and Italy. In the last period, some regions have recorded particularly high values (over 36 percent): Praha, Helsinki-Uusimaa, Stockholm, East Anglia and Inner London.

The chapter analyses the influence of space and relational distance on knowledge creation. At the basis of the analysis, we have a matrix indicating the strength of links among regions. Then, we use this matrix to estimate R&D spillovers. For each period FP_t, the spillovers are computed as a product of row-standardized weight matrices W, relational *(rel)* or geographical *(geo)*, and an R&D intensity vector: accordingly, the matrix product Wx is an R&D intensity spatial (relational) lag variable.

In order to visualize these links we use spatial tools, in particular Moran's statistics (Moran's I) and local indicators of spatial association, or LISA (Anselin, 1995; Pisati, 2001). The former measure is an index of global spatial (relational) autocorrelation: in presence of either positive or negative values, the spatial distribution of the variable of interest x shows a systematic pattern, meaning that the value taken on by x at each location i tends to be similar to the values taken on by x at (spatially or relationally) contiguous locations. The latter is an estimate of local spatial (relational) autocorrelation.

In Figures 4.2 (two Moran scatterplots[15]) and 4.3 (two LISA maps) we draw Moran's statistics in the FP6, the latest framework programme for which we have full data. The left plots are based on matrix *rel*, the right ones are based on matrix *geo*. By comparing the two plots, we can infer whether spatial and relational R&D correlations have substantial differences. Moreover, the figures also help us to identify differences in the underlying matrixes: as noted by Pace et al.

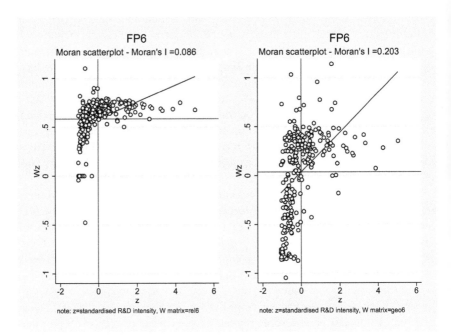

Figure 4.2 Moran scatterplot (relational and space matrixes)

LISA

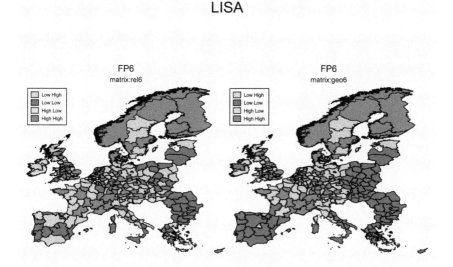

Figure 4.3 Relational and geographical LISA

(2013), it is useful to survey the resulting spatial lag variable (*Wx*), whereas it is not possible to directly compare two or more weight matrices. We can observe that R&D spatial correlation is higher than relational correlation. This means that, while regions with similar levels of R&D expenditure tend to be spatially clustered, collaborations in FP might involve also regions with different levels of R&D expenditure (the number of regions located in quadrants with negative correlation is higher when using relational distance).

More broadly, as highlighted also in Di Cagno et al. (2015) for both matrixes, spatial (relational) correlation in R&D declines over time. This is partly due to the behaviour of some Eastern European regions that have performed remarkably well over time, so that some of them presenting low values of R&D at the beginning (with low R&D spatial/relational neighbours) have moved to high values at the end of the period (Figure 4.3). The decline in relational correlation in R&D is consistent with the increasing effort of the European Commission to stimulate the creation of networks involving also laggard regions.

The impact of geographical and relational spillovers on patent creation: differences across R&D sectors

Table 4.3 reports the results of the estimation of equation (1) with three different R&D sectoral specifications. Results are based on GLS estimations of a spatial lag

Table 4.3 Relational spillovers and knowledge creation: GLS results

	(1)	(2)	(3)
	Patents	*Patents*	*Patents*
Business enterprise R&D intensity BERD	0.483***		
	(52.56)		
Relational spillovers BERD	0.167**		
	(2.59)		
Geographical spillovers BERD	0.801***		
	(24.22)		
Government R&D intensity GERD		0.0176***	
		(5.46)	
Relational spillovers GERD		−0.0840	
		(−1.20)	
Geographical spillovers GERD		0.775***	
		(14.40)	
Higher education R&D intensity HERD			0.00570
			(0.79)
Relational spillovers HERD			0.918***
			(7.05)
Geographical spillovers HERD			0.528***
			(7.94)
Human capital	0.410***	1.205***	1.061***
	(10.05)	(19.87)	(18.61)
Population density	0.119***	0.152***	0.183***
	(12.68)	(15.10)	(19.02)
FP5	−0.0156	0.0399	−0.0980***
	(−0.98)	(1.95)	(−4.17)
FP6	0.0435*	0.0328	−0.165***
	(2.41)	(1.40)	(−5.31)
FP7	−0.394***	−0.418***	−0.749***
	(−18.47)	(−16.37)	(−15.33)
Constant	−1.904***	−2.807***	0.431
	(−6.10)	(−5.27)	(0.46)
Country dummies	YES	YES	YES
chi2	60191.730	52520.486	1.40e+05
Rho-squared	0.911	0.851	0.850
N	970	970	970
Groups	252	252	252
Time	4	4	4

Note: rho-squared are the square of correlation coefficient between the patents and their predicted values.

t statistics in parentheses
Coefficients are heteroskedasticity-consistent
*$p < 0.05$, **$p < 0.01$, ***$p < 0.001$

of X (R&D) model (SLX) (Lesage, 2014). In all models, the dependent variable is the regional number of patents per million population. In the first column we introduce Business Enterprise R&D intensity (BERD) relational spillovers into a knowledge production function controlling for regional BERD, human capital, population density and BERD geographical spillovers, with time and countries dummies. In the other columns, we have the same model for the government and higher education R&D sectors.

The results show that relational spillovers are always positive and significant, except for the sector GOV, while the geographical spillovers are positive and significant in all models. The explanatory power of relational spillovers with respect to geographical spillovers confirms our first hypothesis: cooperation in FPs creates knowledge flows that add to the usual spillovers based on geographical distance. This evidence is also consistent with previous studies finding that participation in FPs increases R&D spillovers (Maggioni et al., 2007; Hoekman et al., 2013; Di Cagno et al., 2014). The regression results also show that patents increase with R&D expenditure, human capital and population density: in order to reap benefits from international collaboration countries/sectors have to invest in the domestic research community. Finally, the impact of geographical R&D spillovers is large and highly significant, indicating that physical proximity is still very important for knowledge transmission.

The estimation results show interesting differences across R&D performed in different sectors, thus providing support to our second hypothesis on the heterogeneity of the mechanisms and incentives of knowledge generation in private companies, public research centres and universities. First, we can observe that the business sector fits very well equation 1 (better than the government and higher education sectors), with both R&D and R&D spillovers having a positive and significant impact on patent generation. This is not too surprising considering that firms compose the largest sector and they have a higher attention with respect to universities or public research centres for intellectual property rights and knowledge commercialization. Second, it appears that while R&D performed in universities is not significant on patents, R&D spillovers accruing from participation in FP are very important for patent generation in the higher education sector. This may indicate that universities co-operating in FP may be pushed to give more attention to the applicability and commercialization of research activity. It is also worth observing that the main generators of relational spillovers are universities, with a coefficient (elasticity) much higher than in the other sectors (0.918). The positive relational spillovers/knowledge transfers associated with higher education R&D are in line with the strong participation of universities in European FP.

Finally, in the case of the government sector the impact of R&D on patents is much smaller than in the private sector. This result is consistent with the finding of Maggioni at al. (2007) who provide as a possible explanation the fact that publicly funded R&D primarily addresses basic research which rarely produces patentable (or patented) results. More surprising is the evidence that only geographical spillovers are significant in the government sector, while relational spillovers do not seem to matter.

Overall, our findings confirm that the production pattern of innovation is shaped not only by spatial proximities but also by the presence of relational proximity, which emerges through participation in research networks. Marrocu et al. (2013) argue that the simultaneous presence of different proximity dimensions implies that spillovers may have a dual nature: one unintended and one intended. Our results show that in the business and higher education R&D sector both types of spillovers occur, while in the government sector unintended spillovers (or, more properly, knowledge transfer) based on agents and institutions which exchange ideas on a non-voluntary basis prevail.

Conclusions

This chapter has investigated whether the impact of geographical and relational spillovers differ across R&D sectors. We find that there are strong differences across sectors in the importance of the two sources of spillovers. This result adds to the existing literature by showing that, in order to evaluate the size of R&D spillovers, it is important to distinguish between R&D performed in different institutional sectors since the mechanisms of knowledge creation and diffusion might differ.

In particular, the results show how the main enablers, in terms of patenting activity, of participation in FP are universities. This suggests that co-operation makes universities more concerned about the appropriability and possible commercialization of inventions. Since, in most European countries, the main problem still appears to be the low propensity of academic institutions to collaborate with firms and to transform new knowledge into new processes and products, the results of this study are encouraging for one of the purposes of private-public collaborations, namely that of stimulating the applicability of new ideas to the commercial sphere.

The finding that private R&D appears to create less spillovers from knowledge partnerships than R&D performed in universities raises the question of whether firms lack the necessary managerial capabilities. In particular, the significant complementarity between innovation (R&D) and absorptive capacity (human capital) supports the hypothesis that knowledge management practices might help firms' innovation performance by improving the efficiency of collective learning (Autant-Bernard et al., 2013). At the same time, firms should invest in human capital in order to increase the level of absorptive capacity that favours effective management practises allowing recognising, assimilating and implementing external knowledge by governing the exchange of knowledge flows among co-operating agents (Dunphy et al., 1997; Vega-Jurado et al., 2008).

Finally, the differing impact of public and private R&D and their associated spillovers on patents' generation, emerging from the empirical analysis, raises the question of whether networks with a different composition of private and public participants are more or less efficient in creating knowledge spillovers. Future research with more detailed data on the composition of FP would allow shedding more light on this issue that deserves further investigation.

Notes

1 This argument is also supported by other studies in the field of the geography of innovation stating that geography matters because it enhances interpersonal relationships and face-to-face contacts, thus making easier to transfer tacit knowledge (Zucker et al. 1998; Almeida and Kogut 1999; Singh 2005; Balconi et al. 2004; Breschi and Lissoni 2009; Mairesse and Turner 2006).

2 Similarly Autant-Bernard et al. (2007a) and Maggioni and Uberti (2009; 2011) argue that the proper impact of the geographical dimension cannot be assessed in isolation but has to be considered in relation to other types of proximity. In this context Singh (2005) finds that geographical proximity (being in the same region or firm) has little additional effect on the probability of knowledge flow among inventors who already have close network ties (past collaborations). Similar results are also found by Marrocu et al. (2013), Ponds et al. (2007), D'Este et al. (2013), and Crescenzi et al. (2014).

3 For a discussion of the game theoretic literature on the private incentives to cooperate in R&D see Cassiman and Veugelers (2002).

4 By institutional sectors, or R&D institutional sectors, we refer to the four institutional sectors of performance of R&D activities: business enterprise (BES), government (GOV), higher education (HES), and the private non-profit (PNP), that are the overall actors involved in innovative activity.

5 Several studies look at the structure of the FP research networks and at the factors facilitating their formation (Breschi and Cusmano, 2004; Maggioni et al., 2007, 2011; Autant-Bernard et al., 2007b, Scherngell and Barber, 2009; Ortega and Aguillo, 2010; Scherngell and Barber, 2011; Hoekman et al. 2013; Wanzenbock et al. (2015).

6 Source data on patent applications to the European Patents Office (EPO), R&D expenditure, GDP, human resources in science and technology (HRST), population and geographical: Eurostat, sub-national section (NUTS 2 level). We use the terms regions and NUTS2 (Nomenclature des Unitès Territoriales Statistiques) as synonymous.

7 We call the four periods, 1995–1998, 1999–2002, 2003–2006 and 2007–2010, FP4, FP5, FP6 and FP7, respectively, in accordance with EU Framework Programmes nomenclature and their temporal extension. The same structure can be applied to patents for their reference point.

8 Gibbons and Overman (2012) point out that in the SDM it is difficult to disentangle endogenous and exogenous interactions effects.

9 EUPRO is constructed and maintained by AIT (Austrian Institute of Technology). It provides systematic information on funded projects, such as project name, project objectives and achievements, etc., as well as on participating organisations including the full name, type of organisation, the full address and the assignment of each organisation to specific NUTS regions of Europe. To relate FP participations to the respective NUTS-2 level, we use – if available – the location of the participating department. In this way, bias towards headquarters of large organisations can be reduced.

10 In the estimations we use averages over the four time periods 1995–1998, 1999–2002, 2003–2006 and 2007–2010.

11 The data include all FP projects recorded until March 2010. The number of participants for the last available year (2010) of the FPs is estimated as the average of the previous three years.

12 Source: EU budget 2008 – Financial Report.

13 For some countries, the smaller ones (Cyprus, Latvia, Lithuania, Luxembourg, Malta and Estonia), and others (Denmark, Norway, Slovenia and Switzerland), the regional breakdown is not available either in Eurostat or in EUPRO database.

In this case we have considered the country level (NUTS-0). We have chosen this approach because we would consider the widest possible coverage of the European territory (EU27 plus Switzerland and Norway). In addition, we use all information (data at NUTS-1 level and NUTS-0 level) to fill the gap in the missing values in our dataset, so that we can obtain a balanced panel.

14 In the human resources in science and technology *(HRST)* statistics are persons with the tertiary level of education or employed in a science and technology occupation for which a high qualification is normally required and the innovation potential is high, according to the *Canberra Manual* (OECD and Eurostat, 1995).

15 The Moran scatterplot is a plot of spatial lag variable, *Wx*, versus *x*, where *x* denotes, in our case, standardized R&D intensity. The oblique line represents the linear regression line obtained by regressing *Wx* on *x*, and its slope equals Moran's I.

References

Almeida, P. and Kogut, B. (1999) 'Localization of knowledge and the mobility of engineers', *Management Science*, 45: 905–17.

Anselin, L. (1995) 'Local indicators of spatial association – LISA', *Geographical Analysis*, 27(2): 93–115.

Autant-Bernard, C., Billand, P., Frachisse, D. and Massard, N. (2007a) 'Social distance versus spatial distance in R&D cooperation: Empirical evidence from European collaboration choices in micro and nanotechnologies', *Papers in Regional Science*, 86(3): 495–519.

Autant-Bernard, C., Fadairo, M. and Massard, N. (2013) 'Knowledge diffusion and innovation policies within the European regions: Challenges based on recent empirical evidence', *Research Policy*, 42: 196–210.

Autant-Bernard, C., Mairesse, J. and Massard, N. (2007b) 'Spatial knowledge diffusion through collaborative networks', *Papers in Regional Science*, 86(3): 341–50.

Balconi, M., Breschi, S. and Lissoni, F. (2004) 'Networks of investors and the role of academia: An exploration of Italian patent data', *Research Policy*, 33: 127–45.

Boschma, R. (2005) 'Proximity and innovation: A critical assessment', *Regional Studies*, 39(1): 61–74.

Bottazzi, L. and Peri, G. (2003) 'Innovation and spillovers in regions: Evidence from European patent data', *European Economic Review*, 47: 687–710.

Breschi, S. and Cusmano, L. (2004) 'Unveiling the texture of a European Research Area: Emergence of oligarchic networks under EU Framework Programmes', *International Journal of Technology Management*, 27(8): 747–72.

Breschi, S. and Lissoni, F. (2009) 'Mobility of skilled workers and co-invention networks: An anatomy of localized knowledge flows', *Journal of Economic Geography*, 9(4): 439–68.

Cassiman, B. and Veugelers, R. (2002) 'Spillovers and R&D cooperation: Some empirical evidence from Belgium', *American Economic Review*, 92: 1169–84.

Crescenzi *et al.* (2016) and Crescenzi R., Nathan, M., Rodríguez-Pose, A. (2016) "Do inventors talk to strangers? On proximity and collaborative knowledge creation", *Research Policy*, 45(1): 177–94.

Crescenzi, R. and Rodriguez-Pose, A. (2011) Innovation and regional growth in the European Union, Advances in spatial science. Springer, Berlin, Germany. ISBN 9783642177606.

D'Este, P., Guy, F. and Iammarino, S. (2013) 'Shaping the formation of university-industry research collaborations: What type of proximity does really matter?', *Journal of Economic Geography*, 13(4): 537–58.

De Fuentes, C. and Dutrénit, G. (2011) 'SMEs´ absorptive capacities and large firms´ knowledge spillovers: Micro evidence from Mexico', *Papers in Innovation Studies*, Lund University, Center for Innovation, Research and Competences in the Learning Economy.

Di Cagno, D., Fabrizi, A. and Meliciani, V. (2014) 'The impact of participation in European Joint Research projects on knowledge creation and economic growth', *Journal of Technology Transfer*, 39: 836–58.

Di Cagno *et al.* (2016) and Di Cagno, D., Fabrizi, A., Valentina Meliciani, V., Wanzenböck, I. (2016) "The impact of relational spillovers from joint research projects on knowledge creation across European regions" *Technological Forecasting and Social Change*, Volume 108: 83–94.

Dunphy, D., Turner, D. and Crawford, M. (1997) 'Organisational learning as the creation of corporate competencies', *Journal of Management Development*, 16(4): 232–44.

Foray, D. and Lissoni, F. (2010) 'University research and public–private interaction', In *Handbook of the Economics of Innovation*, Vol. 1, Chapter 6, Elsevier, BV.

Gibbons, S. and Overman, H.G. (2012) 'Mostly pointless special econometrics', *Journal of Regional Science*, 52(2): 172–91.

Hoekman, J., Frenken, K. and van Oort, F. (2009) 'The geography of collaborative knowledge production in Europe', *Annals of Regional Science*, 43: 721–38.

Hoekman, J., Scherngell, T., Frenken, K. and Tijssen, R. (2013) 'Acquisition of European research funds and its effect on international scientific collaboration', *Journal of Economic Geography*, 13: 23–52.

Knoben, J. and Oerlemans, L A G. (2006) 'Proximity and inter-organizational collaboration: A literature review', *International Journal of Management Reviews*, 8: 71–89.

Lesage, James P. (2014) What regional scientists need to know about spatial econometrics, doi.org/10.2139/ssrn.2420725.

Maggioni, M.A., Nosvelli, M. and Uberti, T.E. (2007) 'Space versus networks in the geography of innovation: A European analysis', *Papers in Regional Science*, 86(3): 271–93.

Maggioni, M. and Uberti, T.E. (2009) 'Knowledge networks across Europe: Which distance matters?', *The Annals of Regional Science*, 43: 691–720.

Maggioni, M. and Uberti, T. (2011) "Networks and geography in the economics of knowledge flows," *Quality & Quantity*, vol. 45(5): 1031–51.

Mairesse, J. and Turner, L. (2006) 'Measurement and explanation of the intensity of co-publication in scientific research: An analysis at the laboratory level', In C. Antonelli, D. Foray, B.H. Hall and E. Steinmueller (Eds) *New Frontiers in the Economics of Innovation and New Technology: Essays in Honour of Paul David*, pp 255–95, Edward Elgar Publishing, United Kingdom.

Marrocu, E., Paci, R. and Usai, S. (2013) 'Proximity, networking and knowledge production in Europe: What lessons for innovation policy?', *Technological Forecasting and Social Change*, 80: 1484–98.

Moreno, R., Paci, R. and Usai, S. (2005) 'Spatial spillovers and innovation activity in European regions', *Environment and Planning*, 37(10): 1793–812.

OECD/EU/Eurostat, G.D. (1995) The Measurement of Human Resources Devoted to S&T – *Canberra Manual*.

Ortega, J.L. and Aguillo, I.F. (2010) 'Shaping the European research collaboration in the 6th Framework Programme health thematic area through network analysis', *Scientometrics*, 85(1): 377–86.

Owen-Smith, J. and Powell, W.W. (2004) 'Knowledge networks as channels and conduits: The effects of spillovers in the Boston biotechnology community', *Organization Science*, 15: 5–21.

Pace, R.K., Lesage, J.P. and Shuang, Z. (2013) 'Interpretation and computation of estimates from regression models using spatial filtering', *Spatial Economic Analysis*, 8(3): 352–69.

Peri, G. (2004) 'Knowledge flows and productivity', *Rivista di Politica Economica*, 94(2): 21–59.

Pisati, M. (2001) 'Tools for spatial data analysis', *Stata Technical Bulletin*, 60: 21–37.

Ponds, R., van Oort, F. and Koen, F. (2007) 'The geographical and institutional proximity of research collaboration', *Papers in Regional Science*, 86(3): 423–43.

Rodriguez-Pose, A. and Crescenzi, R. (2008) 'Research and development spillovers, innovation system, and genesis of regional growth in Europe', *Regional Studies*, 42(1): 51–67.

Scherngell, T. and Barber, M. J. (2009) 'Spatial interaction modelling of cross-region R&D collaborations: Empirical evidence from the 5th EU framework programme', *Papers in Regional Science*, 88(3): 531–46.

Scherngell, T. and Barber, M. J. (2011) 'Distinct spatial characteristics of industrial and public research collaborations: Evidence from the fifth EU Framework Programme', *The Annals of Regional Science*, 46(2): 247–66.

Singh, J. (2005) 'Collaborative networks as determinants of knowledge diffusion patterns', *Management Science*, 51(5): 756–70.

Vega, S.H. and Elhorst, P. (2013) On spatial econometric models, spillover effects, and W, *ERSA conference papers*. No. ersa13p222, European Regional Science Association.

Vega-Jurado, J., Gutiérrez-Gracia, A., Fernández-de-Lucio, I. and Manjarrés-Henríquez, L. (2008) 'Analyzing the determinants of firm's absorptive capacity: Beyond R&D', *R&D Management*, 38(4): 392–405.

Wanzenböck, I., Scherngella, T. and Lata, R. (2015) 'Embeddedness of European regions in European Union-funded research and development (R&D) networks: A spatial econometric perspective', *Regional Studies*, 49(10): 1685–1705.

Zucker, L.G., Darby, M. and Armstrong, J. (1998) 'Intellectual capital and the firm: The technology of geographically localized knowledge spillovers', *Economic Inquiry*, 36: 65–86.

5 How to boost knowledge-Spillover effects in disadvantaged regions?

Manuela F. Neves, João J. Ferreira and
Fernando Ferreira

Introduction

Over the past two decades or so, there has been considerable progress in the theory of knowledge spillover, which is also rooted on the foundations of entrepreneurship theory (Ghio, Guerini, Lehmann and Rossi-Lamastra, 2014). In this chapter, we seek to relate the phenomenon of knowledge spillover with the *transfer of knowledge*, generally considered the third component of Higher Education Institutions' (HEIs) mission. First, HEIs have to obtain the competences necessary to *transfer* knowledge. Subsequently, in a second phase, the economic actors (EAs) have to deploy the capability to *absorb* the knowledge created, enabling the generation of innovative and marketable ideas that, when boosted by a favourable local context, can contribute towards regional development.

As pointed out by Acs, Audretsch and Lehmann (2013), the creation of a new company can frequently represent a local response to knowledge creation that is not yet commercially exploited. According to Ghio et al. (2014), knowledge, whether tacit, explicit or codified, 'releases itself' or 'breaks free' of its source (and thus 'spills over') and is absorbed by the EAs (entrepreneurs) that set up new companies. Following these authors, this means that the creation of new knowledge generates *new ideas*, whilst entrepreneurial activities constitute the ways and the means to *commercialise* these new ideas. Within this framework, the creation of academic *spin-offs* occurs to generate revenues for the research ongoing at HEIs (Karnani, 2012). The launch of a new *venture*, through a *spin-off*, represents the development of knowledge created at the HEI and not rewarded through royalties, licences or patents (Audretsch and Lehmann, 2005). Furthermore, as Koo and Cho (2011) describe, the mobility of workers among companies boosts both the learning process and the establishing of new *ventures*. Hence, HEIs alongside research institutions and the companies located in a specific region are identified as the main source of knowledge spillovers. In this regard, Acs, Braunerhjelm, Audretsch and Carlsson (2009) state that, even in underdeveloped economies, the contribution made by local knowledge towards economic growth depends on the propensity of the respective region to create new companies. In turn, Audretsch and Lehmann (2005) conclude that the number of businesses located within the vicinity of HEIs is positively influenced by the regional capability for knowledge and the knowledge-based outputs from HEIs. Nevertheless, in inland regions, with low levels of industrialisation, economies based upon public services and where the locally prevailing context does not prove favourable, there are difficulties in advancing with new companies as these, due to globalisation, prefer to cluster in the large urban centres where they gain access to more resources (Koo, 2005).

In accordance with the limitations identified by Ghio, Guerini, Lehmann, and Rossi-Lamastra (2014), as regards the need to analyse the launching of new companies as a source of economic growth when large companies and corporations otherwise fail to register any presence and HEIs prove the main sources of spillovers of knowledge, the general objective of this study involves analysis of the means by which HEIs located in poorly industrialised regions, and therefore correspondingly disadvantaged as in the case of Centro, the central inland region of Portugal, might prove able, through specific strategies focusing upon their third *transfer of knowledge* mission, to boost and support the launch and future survival of new companies and, thereby, contributing towards the competitiveness and development of their host regions.

The literature review set out in the following section focuses upon the importance of HEIs as generators of the research and development (R&D) that serves as a strategic resource for company innovation and competitiveness and, alongside the consequences of the *spillover*, impact on regional development. Subsequently, there is a description of Portugal's Centro region in economic terms, detailing the existing knowledge infrastructures and, based upon the inferences and conclusions resulting from these research findings and the conceptual models published in the literature, we then propose a theoretical model for the interconnections between researchers and EAs whilst also identifying the core competences to any service attempting to deepen the interrelationship between research communities and EAs in support of the founding and running of new companies.

Literature review

HEIs and EAs: partners or rivals?

In addition to 'teaching' and 'research', there is now a third component to the HEI mission: the 'transfer of knowledge', which influences the economic development of the HEI host region as well as its surrounding society in overall terms (Kronberga, 2013). HEIs are considered as one of the main actors responsible for sustaining the development of their surrounding economies (Gunasekara, 2006; Etzkowitz, 2011; Fromhold-Eisebith and Werker, 2013; Kronberga, 2013). In Portugal, HEIs have taken on a dominant role as drivers of regional development (Marques, Caraça and Diz, 2006).

As pointed out by Wright and Dana (2003), we now find ourselves in a paradigm in which companies apply all of their resources to their core businesses and correspondingly opting in favour of outsourcing rather than undertaking certain activities internally. Indeed, as Cowan and Zinovyeva (2013) maintain, due to the investment and financial burdens incurred by R&D, HEIs tend to help offset the lack of R&D infrastructures in their host regions. These authors furthermore conclude in favour of a positive correlation between the presence of HEIs and innovative activities ongoing in regions before stating the role of HEIs inherently involves overcoming this lack of R&D infrastructures (see also Etzkowitz, 2011; Fromhold-Eisebith and Werker, 2013). Additionally, Fernandes and Ferreira (2013) identify geographic proximity as a factor influencing the levels of cooperation prevailing. However, there is a major difference between the knowledge generated by HEIs and that which undergoes effective application in commercial terms. This difference gets designated the 'knowledge filter' (Acs, Plummer and Sutter, 2009). Hence, both academics and users prove unanimous in concluding how such transfers require encouragement not only to foster the creation of value for societies (Becheikh, 2010; Etzkowitz, 2011, 2013; Fromhold-Eisebith and Werker, 2013) but also to ensure the sustainability of the HEIs themselves as, without financial resources, these would be unable to proceed with their knowledge generating activities (Zack, 1999).

From the 1980s onwards, in the wake of the Cold War, major American corporations leveraged their competitiveness through R&D-based investment strategies (Etzkowitz, 1998; Lécuyer, 2005; Vallas and Kleinman, 2007). Far from some mere coincidence, in this same decade, HEIs received a new component to their mission: the 'transfer of knowledge' (Fernandes and Ferreira, 2013; Kronberga, 2013). Irrespective of their scale, companies should evaluate, just as they do with any other strategic resource, whether they retain the knowledge necessary for the performance of their functions. Correspondingly, managers need to perceive whether their organisations are 'creators' of knowledge or 'users' of knowledge (Grant and Baden-Fuller, 2004). In the latter case, this inherently requires recourse to external acquisition (Grant and Baden-Fuller, 2004; Greiner *et al.*, 2007), through alliances (Grant Baden-Fuller, 2004; Franco and Haase, 2011;Jiang et al., 2013), networking with other organisations or even to the extent of internalising knowledge sources into their own respective structures (Djellal, Gallouj and Miles, 2013; Zack, 1999). Franco and Haase (2011: 34) define 'cooperation agreements' as 'a strategic decision adopted by two or more independent companies (national or foreign) with the purpose of exchanging or sharing resources in order to seek out opportunities in the market and attain mutual benefits', hence foreseeing the productive specialisation of each participant in their respective area of action (CCDR-Centro, 2011). Nevertheless, stemming from a change to the prevailing paradigm of international business management, companies made HEIs their preferred partner for cooperation in the transfer of knowledge through R&D for innovation (CCDRC, 2008; CCDR-Centro, 2011). As such, they opted to abandon formal control and the internalisation of certain competences and tended to apply all of their resources to their '*core business*' (Wright and Dana, 2003). In fact, due to the investments and financial burdens incurred by companies whenever engaging in R&D, HEIs have tended to offset the lack of R&D infrastructures in the respective host region (Cowan and Zinovyeva, 2013). The establishing of collaborative networks between companies and HEIs designed to generate intensive knowledge proves important for the former to remain updated whilst not expending high resource levels on the internalisation of intensive knowledge services (Amesse and Cohendet, 2001).

In light of this reasoning, HEIs seek out contacts with industry in order to apply and commercialise the results of their research and take advantage of the learning resulting from the different means of interpreting information (Laukkanen, 2003; Metcalfe, 2006). In addition, companies also duly recognise universities as sources of knowledge (Lundvall and Borrás, 1997; Hertog, 2000; Tornatzky, 2001; Silva, 2003; Metcalfe, 2006; Alves, 2010; Becheikh, 2010; Cohen, Nelson and Walsh, 2002; Etzkowitz, 2011; Wilkesmann and Wilkesmann, 2011; Smith and Bagchi-Sen, 2012; Forti, Franzoni and Sobrero, 2013). Greiner *et al.* (2007) conclude that the most successful knowledge management projects derive from those incorporating market needs and where the objectives consist of adding value to companies. In practice, an entrepreneurial HEI is an institution that transforms not only the problems in their local contexts but also the academic outputs susceptible to generating economic activities (Etzkowitz and Klofsten, 2005). To a greater or lesser extent, this also contributes to sustaining their own knowledge creation activities, as the *"exploration of knowledge without any benefits is not economically sustainable"* (Zack, 1999: 137).

Academic spin-offs: the founding of new companies

The technological transfer of commercial knowledge from HEIs to industry has taken place through licensing agreements, research joint ventures and through start-ups (Siegel, Waldman, Atwater and Link, 2003). According to Wilson (2012), the most suitable system involves employers agreeing to finance student college fees that, allied with the government authorities disseminating the needs and results of employment, then encourages HEIs to boost the support for students within a context of employability and their own transitions to the labour market. In this way, public sector financing will decline as a proportion of overall HEI funding due to the contributions made by employers.

Laukkanen (2003), Siegel, Waldman and Link (2003) and Meyer (2006), among others, approach the variables influencing levels of HEI-company cooperation, finding that gender, age and faculty shape the propensity of academic staff to cooperate with the business sector and broadly concluding that the fields of engineering are those most propitious to applied research. Furthermore, Rothaermel, Agung and Jiang (2007) identify the following series of factors as impacting on the launch and performance of university spin-offs: incentive systems, university statutes, location, culture, intermediary entities, experience and university objectives. Beyond these, the literature also identifies certain other factors as able to shape the incidence of spin-offs, such as: (1) industrial revenues going into research (Lockett and Wright, 2005; O'Shea, Allen, Chevalier and Roche, 2005; Powers and McDougall, 2005); (2) the presence and experience of a Knowledge Transfer Office (KTO) (Lockett and Wright, 2005; Powers and McDougall, 2005; O'Shea, Chugh and Allen, 2007); (3) experience in and the frequency of transfer activities (Lockett and Wright, 2005; Powers and McDougall, 2005); (4) the quality of the respective HEI, generally measured according to scientific publications and citations (Powers and McDougall, 2005; O'Shea et al., 2007); and (5) the contextual characteristics measured primarily through the level of innovation (Lockett and Wright, 2005; Powers and McDougall, 2005).

In their meta-analysis, Rothaermel et al. (2007) put forward four factors determining the success of newly founded companies: (1) *intellectual property*: the HEI strategic policy as regards intellectual property as well as the conditions prevailing for seed and equity capital investment related to high levels of spin-offs (see also Gregorio and Shane, 2003; Lockett, Wright and Franklin, 2003); (2) *spin-off networking activities*: exploring the impact and the intentions of spin-off founders within the terms of their networking connections as well as the frequency of interactions with external partners (*e.g.* companies, research institutions and public bodies) for the success of new ventures (Grandi and Grimaldi, 2003), establishing links with the HEI holding in order to obtain infrastructures and experience (Grandi and Grimaldi, 2003; Johansson, Jacob and Hellstro, 2005), and connections with venture capital firms to obtain financing and reduce the risk of failure (Shane and Stuart, 2002); (3) *resources*: prior requisites to research success are human resource qualities (thus, both the founding faculty team and the KTO staff members), donating the university's technology and financing, industry and venture capital firms (Shane and Stuart, 2002; Link and Scott, 2005; O'Shea et al., 2005; Powers and McDougall, 2005); and (4) *the total involvement of the university as a core factor of success for processes leading to the founding of new companies*: spanning university policies, incubator models and the prevailing research ambience. Sidharta, Arai, Putro and Morimoto (2014) further maintain that academic spin-offs also open up employment opportunities which cannot otherwise be met by companies. Furthermore, also requiring good management, these academic spin-offs may grow and expand into major businesses. Hence, public policies have also sought to drive and incentivise the creation of knowledge with commercial value as an alternative to the lack of public financing, a fact that has shaped and shifted researcher labour behaviours in recent years: *i.e.* more focused on seeking out research funding and collaboration with industry (Franco, Haase and Fernandes, 2014).

It is worth noting, however, that there are barriers to the transfer of the knowledge built up by HEI researchers to companies in need of such inputs (Lundvall and Borrás, 1997; Bank, 2002; Nations, 2005; Becheikh, 2010; Fromhold-Eisebith and Werker, 2013; Sedlacek, 2013). As such, to the gain of countries counting on their respective contributions, attention should focus on the utilisation and application of knowledge by companies to the benefit of all of society (Lundvall and Borrás, 1997; Siegel, Waldman, Atwarter and Link, 2003; Silva, 2003; Augusto Mateus and Associados, 2012). Still, the incidence of efficient organisations exploiting the knowledge generated by other organisations remains scarce (Zack, 1999; Laukkanen, 2003). Thus, the relevance of the role of an HEI within its host region stems from the extent of its capabilities to cooperate with other actors in the transfer of the knowledge generated internally through the activities of their researchers (Etzkowitz, 2011; Cowan and Zinovyeva, 2013). In truth, this proves a form of symbiosis: on the one hand, HEIs seek out contacts with industry to apply their research results, leveraging the learning processes arising out of the different means of interpreting the information (Laukkanen, 2003; Metcalfe, 2006); whilst, on the other hand, companies do provide appropriate recognition to universities as sources of knowledge (Cohen *et al.*, 2002; Figlioli and Porto, 2006; Etzkowitz, 2011).

Regional development: the spillover effect and the transfer of knowledge

In any given region, actors should be willing and available to interact and cooperate in order to maximise the gains to each individual participant so that they all mutually benefit in overall terms. According to Fromhold-Eisebith and Werker (2013), there are three causes driving failure in the transfer of knowledge at the regional level: (1) the lack of actors or actors performing badly; (2) shortcomings and poor performances in the relationships ongoing between actors; and (3) the lack of institutions or inappropriate institutions (Woolthuis *et al.*, 2005; Metcalfe, 2006). Hence, in this study, we aim to analyse the ways in which the HEI knowledge transfer strategy may focus on the founding of new companies in an inland region in Portugal otherwise characterised by its lack of industry and an economy based upon the provision of public services. The spillover theory encapsulates the idea that both tacit and explicit knowledge expands to foster new knowledge. This recognises that HEIs and scientific institutions perform the role of catalysers and disseminators of knowledge that, in turn, gain the designation of knowledge spillovers (Ghio *et al.*, 2014). As pointed out by Acs *et al.* (2009), this theory corresponds to endogenously created knowledge that then results in the dissemination of knowledge.

The transfer of tacit knowledge as explicit knowledge requires a great deal of personal contact and trust (Tornatzky, 2001; Alves, 2010; Wilkesmann and Wilkesmann, 2011). The building of trust enables and fosters cooperative behaviours (Hertog, 2000; Tornatzky, 2001; Metcalfe, 2006; Becheikh, 2010; Smith and Bagchi-Sen, 2012; Wilkesmann and Wilkesmann, 2011). Therefore, the tacit knowledge transfer process by researchers through to the effective application of the research results in processes generating value to societies involves close collaborative processes characterised by trust and mutual confidence (Tornatzky, 2001; Alves, 2010; Forti *et al.*, 2013; Wilkesmann and Wilkesmann, 2011). The difficulty in codifying tacit knowledge thus gets overcome through personal interaction and hence the spatial-geographic relationship between the creator and the user of this tacit knowledge impacts on the actual knowledge transfer process (Agrawal, 2001).

After the 1980s, in parallel with the 'transfer of knowledge' becoming a component to the HEI mission, in Europe, the United States and Asia, there appeared the HEI supported science and technology parks designed to strengthen the interconnections with regional development (Varga, 2000; Fernandes and Ferreira, 2013). In a study on the interactions between companies located in such science and technology parks and HEIs, Monck *et al.* (1988) conclude that the most commonly referenced relationship type was that of '*informal contract*', followed by '*access to equipment*' and, finally, '*formal relationships*' with HEIs. These, according to Figlioli and Porto (2006), serve to facilitate the conversion of basic HEI research into commercially viable innovations. Thus, the geographic clustering of innovative companies, HEIs, research centres and technological service companies represents a key determinant of regional development (Zucker *et al.*, 1994; Feldmann and Desrochers, 2003; Koo, 2005). In turn, the results of a study by Koo (2005) state that the agglomeration (of companies) and spillovers are endogenously related and mutually self-reinforcing.

The innovative capability of small and medium-sized enterprises (SMEs) to a large extent results from the knowledge generated but not commercialised at HEIs (Acs *et al.*, 2009). Audretsch and Feldman (2007) and Koo and Cho (2011), in their analysis of the interrelationship between industry and innovative activities, both conclude in favour of a trend towards forming spatial clusters in which economic knowledge plays a more relevant role, which, in turn, tends to spatially determine the location of production and consequently of innovation. Therefore, political decisions about the allocation of funding interrelate with this regional 'absorption capability', and thus with the existence of knowledge spillovers able to drive innovation and development. Jaffe (1989) put forward the first study of knowledge in geographic terms and duly concludes that more patents get registered in states where more public and private knowledge gets created. Other studies, such as those by Agrawal and Cockburn (2002), Agrawal and Henderson (2002) and Agrawal (2000, 2006), based on analysis of patents and citations of researchers connected with patents, furthermore confirm that geographic proximity to HEI generates effective implications as the patent location in the same region significantly impacts on the probability of there being citations (a probability that fades over distance as measured in kilometres). Similarly, the incidence of scientific article citations proves positively associated with 'quality' inventions with the spillovers of knowledge rendering private inventions better (Jaffe, 1989; Jaffe, Trajtenberg, and Henderson, 1993; Branstetter, 2003; Rocha *et al.*, 2013). Agrawal (2000), analysing the importance of geographic distance and direct interactions between researchers, inventors and company researchers to the success of transfers and the commercialisation of patents, finds that geographic distance, as measured in kilometres, between the Massachusetts Institute of Technology (MIT) and license holding companies generates a negative impact on the commercial success of the license. These effects, furthermore, prove statistically insignificant whenever including a variable for scientific interaction measured in terms of number of hours. In another preliminary study, Agrawal and Cockburn (2002), even while not reporting evidence of either agglomerations of university research or of agglomerations of commercial activities, do report evidence as to the co-localisation of these upstream–downstream activities, identifying the existence of companies underpinned by the State and by their field of research as a feasible explanation for the variations in research-for-commercialisation productivity. Agrawal (2006), in turn, finds that the geographic distance between the HEI and the industry returns a negative impact on the commercialisation of products, even while the direct interaction between inventors and industry, measured in hours, results in a positive impact on such commercialisation. Audretsch and Feldman (2007) also find in favour of a greater propensity for innovative activities to be geographically based with R&D, research and specialist labour (*i.e.* knowledge spillovers), representing important regional level inputs.

Smith and Bagchi-Sem (2012) consider that factors facilitating change and inducing its impact on the region are: (1) the HEI strategy; (2) the research reputation; (3) the national context; (4) financing and capitalisation facilities; (5) technological change; and (6) regional characteristics. Correspondingly, Fernandes and Ferreira (2013) point to geographic proximity as a factor influencing and shaping cooperation. Therefore, the transfer of knowledge to regions contributes to their development through the capability to innovate, launch new products onto the market and boost the ability to generate economic growth in accordance with the levels of competitiveness prevailing within the regional context. Gunasekara (2006) highlights the advantages from physical and social proximity to HEIs with local partners contributing to structuring the relationships within regional networks and strengthening the competitiveness of the respective territories (Franco and Belo, 2013). Lendel (2010) furthermore affirms that the impact of HEIs on regional economies proves strong in periods of expansion, but with only those HEIs with strong commitments to research returning a positive impact in periods of economic decline through maintaining financing for research, the wages of the academic participants and stable student flows. Fuller and Rothaermel (2012) consider how "star" researchers–founders are able to overcome geographic distance from risk capital firms as well as the disadvantages of not being in any alliance with a university research institute. Hence, in accordance with the literature review, we may group the facilitating characteristics as set out in Table 5.1.

Florida (2002) proposes the concept of "Creative Regions" in defending how regions only attain competitiveness when *creative* and only the presence of HEIs is able to leverage this creativity. Furthermore, Smith and Bagchi-Sem (2012) describe the "Scientific Cities" initiatives held in the United Kingdom in 2005 with their objective of fostering deep ties between science and the market and attempting to ensure that science, technology and innovation become the motor of economic growth. Etzkowitz and Klofsten (2005) state that the necessary conditions for any innovative region, beyond mechanisms for the transfer of knowledge, include the existence of an HEI with a broad scope for research alongside an entity serving as the intermediary between HEIs and those EAs undertaking entrepreneurial roles. Smith and Bagchi-Sem (2012), in turn, identify five factors out of the seven defined by Lendel (2010) that enable HEIs to nurture competitive advantage in their host regions: (1) the capability for local absorption; (2) competitive infrastructures; (3) the professional and technological labour markets; (4) culture and entrepreneurial activities; and (5) quality of life. Boucher

Table 5.1 Factors facilitating regional development

	Regional development facilitators	Authors
HEI	Incentive systems	Rothaermel *et al.* (2007); Wilson (2012)
	University statutes	Rothaermel *et al.* (2007); Wilson (2012)
	University objectives: - (intellectual property/equity); - Research applied industry earnings; - Larger number of spin-offs; - HEI involvement in the founding of new companies	Agrawal & Cockburn (2002); Agrawal (2001); Gregorio and Shane (2003); Lockett *et al.* (2003); Rothaermel *et al.* (2007); Wilson (2012)
	HEI strategies	Franco and Belo (2013); Gunasekara (2006)
	HEI quality: - Research reputation; - Scientific publications and number of citations	O'Shea *et al.* (2007); Powers and McDougall (2005); Smith and Bagchi-Sen (2012) Smith and Bagchi-Sen (2012)
EA	Professional and technological labour markets	
	Access to equipment – competitive infrastructures	
	Establishing bonds with the HEI holding to obtain infrastructures and experience	Grandi and Grimaldi (2003); Johansson *et al.* (2005)
	Ease of accessing financing and capital investments: ties with venture capital firms to offset risks of failure	Shane and Stuart (2002); Smith and Bagchi-Sen (2012)
	Highly qualified human resources	Link and Scott (2005); O'Shea *et al.* (2005); Powers and McDougall (2005); Shane and Stuart (2002)
	Donation of technology (HEI); HEI financing; industry and companies	
GEO. PROX.	Location: geographic proximity	Branstetter (2003); Fernandes and Ferreira (2013); Jaffe *et al.* (1993); Jaffe (1989); Rocha *et al.* (2013)
	Public policy incentives for creating knowledge with commercial value as an alternative to state financing of HEIs	Wilson (2012)
	Contextual characteristics: - National context Regional characteristics: - Level of innovation; - Levels of regional competitiveness; - Local capacity of absorption; - Quality of life	Lockett and Wright (2005); Powers and McDougall (2005); Smith and Bagchi-Sen (2012)
	Spatial cluster: relationships ongoing in the regional network (strengthening regional competitiveness)	Audretsch and Feldman (2007); Koo and Cho (2011)

(*Continued*)

Table 5.1 (Continued)

Regional development facilitators	Authors
EA & HEI	Culture and entrepreneurial activities Intermediary actors (technology transfer offices, etc.)	Meyer (2006); Wilson (2012) Gunasekara (2006); Lockett and Wright (2005); O'Shea *et al.* (2007); Powers and McDougall (2005); Rothaermel *et al.* (2007)
	Experience and frequency of transfers	Rothaermel *et al.* (2007); Wilson (2012)
	Academic spin-off networking (networking connections established by the founder and the frequency of interactions among external partners) to the success of ventures	Gómez Gras et al. (2007); Grandi and Grimaldi (2003); Johansson *et al.* (2005); Lockett *et al.* (2003); O'Shea *et al.* (2005)
	Direct interactions between HEI researchers and companies	Link and Scott (2005); O'Shea *et al.* (2005); Powers and McDougall (2005); Shane and Stuart (2002)

et al. (2003) highlight how the existence of HEIs in a region fosters an ambience of learning, skill and competence development along with the resources necessary to competitiveness and social cohesion.

The Centro (inland) region

The socioeconomic situation of the Centro Region (CR) of Portugal experienced a period of convergence with European and national averages running from Portugal's late 1980s accession to the then European Economic Community throughout the 1990s. However, in the following decade, this process stagnated both in relationship to the national average and to the European averages (CCDR-Centro, 2011).

Through to 1990, there was a perception of the CR as '*a hinge-mosaic between North and South*', an area with very different characteristics constituted by a multiplicity of small territories with their own particular identities (Gaspar, 1993). According to the 1991 *Census*, the CR contained a total of 10 NUT III and 78 councils corresponding to a surface of 23,665 Km² and a population of 1,721,541 inhabitants (INE, 1991). The differentiation prevailing in the region immediately becomes visible through contrasting the coastal and the inland zones (Jacinto, 1993). Since the 1960s, the CR has been shedding population, though the rate slowed in the 1970s due to the convergence of three factors: (1) the return of emigrants from Europe; (2) the arrival of a substantial number of Portuguese citizens from the former colonies who took up residence there; and (3) a fall in the flows of emigration resulting from the international recession (Alexandre, 1991). The region's natural heritage proved rich in surface and subterranean hydro resources (natural mineral waters, springs and thermals), non-metallic mineral resources (clays and kaolin), forestry with major potential in the production of renewable energies, and forestry sourced biomass, wave or geothermal power (Jacinto, 1993; CRER 2020, 2014). The industrial sector and the history of the industrialisation process encapsulate the prevalence of SMEs, high levels of sectorial diversification, the lack of inter-sectorial technical relationships, specialisation in a certain number of non-metallic mineral sectors, light metal working, transport equipment, chemical, textiles, cellulose and wood (Alexandre, 1991; Jacinto, 1993). The deficiency in services interrelates with the lack of a regional metropolis given that Coimbra has proven unable to take on such a role with the resulting shortcomings met by recourse to Lisbon, Oporto or internationally (Alexandre, 1991). The role of strategic coordination might have fallen to the universities and polytechnic institutions that set themselves up as fundamental links to this network in such crucial specialist/complementary fields as teaching, training and R&D (Alexandre, 1991; Jacinto, 1993).

Through to 2010, the CR displayed a low level of population density stemming from the existence of intra-regional asymmetries characterised by the desertification of inland settlements in contrast with the more populous and urbanised coastal region (CCDR-Centro, 2011). Despite the region featuring a multi-pole level of city organisation, well distributed in territorial terms, the medium-sized urban centres have prevailed, placing the region in a lower position in terms of the proportion of the population residing in predominantly urban areas (Alexandre, 1991; INE, 1991, 2002; CRER 2020, 2014). Furthermore, alongside desertification, the region hosts an ageing population, recording in 2008 the second highest rate of ageing and the lowest gross birth rate when compared with other Portuguese regions (Alexandre, 1991; Gaspar, 1993; Jacinto, 1993; INE, 2002; CCDRC, 2010; CRER 2020, 2014). On the contrary, indicators of a more social nature, spanning fields such as education, healthcare and social or environmental protection return figures far closer to the national averages. In the education field, the region hosts a strong presence in the higher education sector. According to CCDR-Centro (2011), in the business sphere, there is a large percentage of companies per inhabitant, positioning the region very close to the national average, above all in the micro-company category, which then reflects in how the region registered one of the lowest indices for employees per company in 2007. Traditionally, the region's economic activities incorporate a diversified productive structure in which areas of traditional specialisation (*e.g.* ceramics, non-metallic minerals such as the production of cement, forestry and its by-products such as pulp and paper) coexist alongside economic activities, including metal working, moulds and knowledge-intensive activities. Nevertheless, investment has mostly targeted poorly developed and labour-intensive branches of technology and on natural resources (a regional asset) in a factor generally contributing towards the regionally prevailing low level of productivity (Alexandre, 1991; Gaspar, 1993; Jacinto, 1993; INE, 2002; CCDRC, 2010; CRER 2020, 2014).

Currently, the structure of the Portuguese territory, in accordance with the new NUTS (this organisational structure of Portuguese regions for statistical purposes was enacted by the EU Commission Regulation no. 868/2014, dated 8th

August 2014), contains 3 NUTS I (mainland Portugal, the Autonomous Region of the Azores and the Autonomous Region of Madeira); 7 NUTS II (equivalents to the Norte, Centro, Metropolitan Area of Lisbon, Alentejo, Algarve, Azores and Madeira 'regions') and 25 NUTS III (23 mainland inter-municipal entities and 2 autonomous regions equivalent to 'sub-regions') (AICEP, 2013). Alongside the NUTS, Portugal divides into 18 mainland districts (Aveiro, Beja, Braga, Bragança, Castelo Branco, Coimbra, Évora, Faro, Guarda, Leiria, Lisbon, Oporto, Portalegre, Santarém, Setúbal, Viana do Castelo, Vila Real and Viseu) (CCDRC, 2010; AICEP, 2013; CRER 2020, 2014). The geographic centrality of the CR, as in the past, endows a strategic positioning across three levels: (1) the interrelationship between the national territory and its urban system; (2) national access to the north and centre of Europe; and (3) the potential of its extensive Atlantic frontage spanning 275 Km with medium-sized ports (Aveiro, Figueira da Foz and Peniche) (CCDR-Centro, 2011). Internally, the region breaks down into two urban territorial systems and five sub-systems generally made up of a core, medium-sized city and a rural hinterland inhabited by around 75 percent of the resident population (CCDR-Centro, 2011): (1) the region's coastal zone integrates three urban systems: i) the Baixo Vouga urban system (around the poles of Aveiro/Águeda, including Ílhavo/Estarreja/Albergaria-a-Velha/Oliveira-do-Bairro/Ovar); ii) the Baixo Mondego urban system (structured around the poles of Coimbra/Figueira da Foz, along with Lousã/Miranda do Corvo/Condeixa-a-Velha/Penela/Montemor-o-Velho/Soure/Cantanhede/Mealhada); and iii) the Pinhal Litoral urban system (around the poles of Leiria/Marinha Grande, including Batalha and Pombal); and (2) in the inland region, with a further two urban systems: i) the Dão-Lafões urban system centred on Viseu, and including Mangualde/Nelas/S. Pedro do Sul/Tondela; and ii) the longitudinal axis of Guarda/Covilhã/Fundão/Castelo Branco (CCDR-Centro, 2011).

Despite the balanced distribution of these medium-sized cities across the territory, there is only an incipient level of mutual articulation between the coastal urban systems and those of the inland zone. This situations fails to leverage the potential of either technological cooperation or of strategic alliances between companies and hinders, for reasons of economies of scale, the provision of specialist technical services (*e.g.* R&D, information, training, logistics, industrial waste management), not only capable of generating positive externalities for these places but also guaranteeing the conditions necessary to industrial development and competitiveness (Alexandre, 1991; Gaspar, 1993; Jacinto, 1993; INE, 2002; CCDRC, 2010; CRER 2020, 2014).

The region's Gross Domestic Product (GDP) *per capita* (€10,200) comes in below the national average (€12,500), with the same reflected in working productivity (€19,100 and €22,500, respectively). All the sub-regions report figures below the national average for both of these two indicators (INE, 2002; CCDR-Centro, 2011; CRER 2020, 2014). The CR, in comparison with the other Portuguese regions, features a highly diversified productive structure and territorially heterogeneous, with differing and spatially well-defined productive systems also displaying dynamics in terms of the generation of earnings and growth that prove very different between the different sub-regions. The region's primary sector accounts for 5.3 percent of the Gross Added Value (GAV) and 23 percent of employment, the secondary sector 33.8 percent and 30.4 percent, and the tertiary sector 60.9 percent and 46.6 percent respectively. The specialist profile focuses upon the exploration of 'natural resources', processing above all the initial segments of the value chain in which the scope for value creation proves more limited, whilst the specialist profile targeting 'low cost labour' involves intensive and non-qualified labour in an aspect worsened by ageing and lower level of population rejuvenation, which contributes to explaining the low level of regional productivity (Alexandre, 1991; Gaspar, 1993; Jacinto, 1993; INE, 2002; CCDRC, 2010; CRER 2020, 2014).

Micro-companies (with fewer than nine employees), lacking critical mass, whether in terms of human or financial resources, for investing in innovation, prove dominant and make up over 70 percent of the productive sector in the CR. This facet has also been on the rise since the 1990s, especially due to industrial restructuring processes that led to the closure of a large number of large scale companies (CRER 2020, 2014). Despite the positive trends seen in recent years at the national level, the regional productive system remains characterised by low levels of technological and innovation intensity that places strong constraints on both economic growth and regional competitiveness (CCDRC, 2008, 2015). As regards the provision of technological services, the CR proves fairly well served whether in terms of quantity or quality on science and technology supply (CCDR-Centro, 2011) (Table 5.2).

Taking into account the supply and demand for technological services, we may report that the level of technology incorporated into regional productive outputs falls below the opportunities existing, as regional companies do not stimulate

Table 5.2 The regional supply of science and technology

Higher education institutions	There are three state universities in Aveiro, Coimbra and Covilhã, and seven state polytechnic institutions located in Aveiro, with a branch in Águeda, Coimbra, with a branch in Oliveira do Hospital, Leiria, with a branch in Peniche, Guarda, Castelo Branco, Viseu and Tomar. There are also three private universities located in Viseu, Coimbra and Figueira da Foz along with various higher education institutes.
Technological centres	There are four technological centres associated with the traditional economic sectors: CITEVE (the Technological Centre of Textiles and Clothing), with a branch in Covilhã, CENTIMFE (the Technological Centre of Moulds and Special Tools and Plastics) in Marinha Grande, CTCV (the Technological Centre of Ceramics and Glass) in Coimbra, and CTIC (the Technological Centre of the Leather Industries), located in Alcanena.

(*Continued*)

Table 5.2 (Continued)

Research units	Beyond the R&D centres integrated into the universities, there are other centres of this type that we would highlight here for their adaptation to regional productive specialist fields: PT Inovação in Aveiro (telecommunications); CBE (Centre of Biomass for Energy) in Miranda do Corvo; RAIZ (Forestry and paper industries) in Aveiro; IBILI (Biomedical Institute of Light and Image) in Coimbra.
Incubators and technology transfer centres	There are two knowledge and technology interface units at the universities of Coimbra and Aveiro, the Pedro Nunes Institute and GrupUnave, 7 incubators located in Coimbra, Aveiro, Mira, Figueira da Foz, Leiria, Marinha Grande, and Covilhã, and a biotechnology technology transfer centre, BIOCANT, located in Cantanhede.

Source: CCDR-Centro (2011).

any growth in the regional availability of technological services by R&D centres (CCDR-Centro, 2011). The State remains by far the greatest investor, through both State-funded laboratories and HEIs, which together amount to 57 percent of total R&D expenditure taking place at the regional level in a rate of investment greater than the national average (55 percent). In turn, the technological centres account for 11 percent and companies 32 percent of expenditure, one percentage point below the average of private sector R&D undertaken nationally (CCDRC, 2008).

The capability for CR private sector initiative constitutes a reference benchmark even while highly localised around the traditional poles of Marinha Grande/Leiria (Pinhal Litoral) and Águeda/Aveiro (Baixo Vouga), which, since the 19th century, have seen the peculiar phenomenon of substantial industrial dynamism through the founding of locally based family type firms (that also occurred with the textile industry in Serra de Estrela (Covilhã, Seia and Serra da Lousã, Castanheira de Pêra) (Alexandre, 1991; CCDRC, 2010; CCDR-Centro, 2011). As for company support services, there are currently over 200 business, commercial, retail, industrial and mixed associations providing information and technical support services to firms and businesses in the CR. In some cases, these serve as intermediaries in the management of state SME financial support schemes, specifically through the Centro Business Council (CEC), an associative institution with the status of a Chamber of Commerce and Industry that brings together around 40 business associations from across the region (CCDRC, 2008; CCDR-Centro, 2011).

Establishing an investment favourable environment depends on minimising the contextual costs that hinder company activities. Hence, in addition to bureaucracy or the shortcomings in capital market common to the country as a whole, the CR also displays a lack of market-focused qualifications, rigid costs in the productive structure, and failings in the industrial, transport and logistics infrastructures. Table 5.3 below presents the SWOT analysis drafted in 2011 by CCDR-Centro (2011).

The forms of governance existing should encourage inter-sectorial relationships and the participation of interested parties in the design of public policies,

Table 5.3 SWOT analysis of the Centro regions

Strengths	Weaknesses
- Geo-strategic positioning within the 'Atlantic' framework and the connections between Europe and the rest of the world; - Good integration into trans-European and national territorial networks; - Diversified natural heritage with landscape quality and environmental values and good soil and climate conditions; - Natural resources: Atlantic ocean (275 km of coastline), endowed with hydro, thermal, geological and forestry (47% of the territory is forested, representing 32% of Portugal's forested area), and non-metallic mineral resources; - Potential for renewable energy production across various fields: hydro, mini-hydro, wind, solar, biofuels, wave energy, geothermal, forest biomass and biogas; - Relevant historical and architectonic heritage, cultural identity and regional products with tradition and quality; - Multi-core organisation of urban systems based on a balanced network of medium sized cities; - Diversified regional productive structure with traditional specialist fields distributed in a balanced fashion across the territory; - Scientific and technological system with quality outputs: HEIs, state laboratories, university research centres, technological centres and transfers of technology;	- Shortcomings in the connections between the region and its surrounding areas: roads and above all rail and ports; - Lack of logistics infrastructures; - Deep and high asymmetries in intra-regional development; - High levels of hydro resource pollution across the majority of the regional hydrographic network due to urban and industrial pressures with negative impacts on the coastal waters; - Ageing population and with only a poor capacity for rejuvenation; - Poor intra-regional means of access: isolation of inland regions; - Low ICT utilisation rates at the regional level in comparison with the national average and low access rates to broadband Internet; - Structural problems ensuring difficulties in implementing the sustainable management of forests and the profitability of this resource; - Severe structural weaknesses in terms of the productive structure: private sector made up of small scale units (70% are micro-firms), with low intensity technology and innovation and lacking in export capabilities (only 12% of companies export); - Severe structural weaknesses in terms of human capital: low qualifications (70% of human resources only have basic schooling) reflecting in low levels of labour productivity; - Precarious location of industrial infrastructures in terms of planning, the environment, technological and logistics services;

(Continued)

Table 5.3 (Continued)

Strengths	Weaknesses
- Regional areas of excellence in the fields of healthcare and life sciences, biotechnology and the ICTs (IT and telecommunications).	- Environmental issues stemming from delays in the selective collection and recycling of urban solid wastes and resolving problems associated with regionally produced household and industrial waste; - Shortage in population and functional scale and the poor level of competitiveness of urban centres.

Opportunities	Threats
- Establishing integrated inter-modal platforms and advanced logistics services in conjunction with Iberian and European logistics networks; -Strengthening the competitiveness of regional ports within the framework of Short Distance Maritime Transport; - Enhancing natural, heritage and cultural resources for the development of tourism, diversifying the regional economy and boosting the core local economic; - Fostering the competitiveness of cities through requalification and structuring and strengthening their urban networks; - Installation of telecommunications network systems, boosting broadband Internet access and general ICT utilisation rates; - Consolidating and upgrading urban territorial systems through implementing the PRN 2000 and providing multi-functional services at the supra-municipal level; - Implementing an integrated RIB management network aligned with the respective industrial clusters; - Support for technical teaching and the interrelationships between teaching and professional training systems; - Investing in professional requalification strategies and the social reintegration of the long term unemployed in proximity services and in social economy related fields;	- Model of development based on labour intensive activities and with low unit labour costs and over time compromising the economic competitiveness of the region within an open economy context; - Profile of specialisation fundamentally based on natural resources and low labour costs; - Climate changes leading to situations of extreme drought and raising the risks of fires and flooding; - Lack of coordination among state institutions across both the vertical and horizontal levels; - Poor presence of international investment capital in the region; - Lack of a culture of evaluation for public policies and difficulties in obtaining details on the results of their respective implementation; - Excess of regulation and great complexity in its interpretation and application; - Imbalance between the supply and demand for qualifications; - Structural unemployment in more disadvantaged geographic areas brought about by the decline in the primary sector and the traditional industrial sector; - Deficit in the cooperation ongoing between the public and private sectors: organisational failings, an individualist business culture and a closed academic culture.

Strengths	Weaknesses
- Clustering economic activities, broadening and densifying, through the incorporation of innovation and technology, the traditional sector chain of value with export potential; - Exploring the energy potential and other regional productive fields of excellence.	

Source: CCDR-Centro (2011).

fostering an integrated approach to problems and their solutions in order to bring about resource efficiency gains and improve intervention effectiveness.

Connecting actors

As Fernandes and Ferreira (2013) describe, the transfer of knowledge in inland regions contributes to their development through the capability to innovate, launch new products onto the market and manage economic growth in accordance with the respective levels of economic competitiveness prevailing within the regional context. Etzkowitz (2011, 2013) and Figlioli and Porto (2006) argue that the main actors making up national systems of creativity and of knowledge appropriation are companies, universities and the government.

The literature refers to the importance of establishing strong interlinkages between HEIs, industry and political power within a spirit of collaboration in order to attain good levels of scientific performance (Balconi and Laboranti, 2006; Wilson, 2012). In this regard, as stated by Kohengkul, Wongwanich, and Wiratchai (2009), 'collaboration' means cooperation between working groups or teams both at the organisational level and at the individual level with the objective of producing useful innovation to achieving the respective collectively established objectives. Thus, actors have to get involved and work together as a team throughout every stage of the process, from the setting of objectives through to the planning, working on the resolution of different problems. This includes investing and sharing information and responsibilities, as well as knowledge and experiences. To ensure the conditions for cooperation, the role of the 'intermediary connecting actors' proves crucial and, according to Becheikh (2010), may include any specialist interested in research, educational advisers to the academic system or professional managers involved in knowledge transfer activities. These agents are commonly designated 'correctors' of knowledge, 'expanders of frontiers', 'guardians' or 'translators', and engage in contacts with researchers, enabling a greater level of interaction between knowledge transfer agents (Smith and Bagchi-Sen, 2012).

Other authors perceive that this role may be played by science and technology parks. However, the passive role of *infrastructure supplier* requires replacing with a dynamic role focused on networked interactions that enable learning processes rather than simply attempting to connect scientific innovation and regional development (Hansson, Husted, and Vestergaard, 2005). Monck *et al.* (1988), in their study of interactions ongoing between companies (located in science and technology parks) and HEIs, conclude that the relationships most commonly referenced were, first, the 'informal contract' followed by 'access to equipment' and, finally, 'formal relationships' with HEI professionals. In turn, Figlioli and Porto (2006) identify several actions necessary for the transfer of knowledge from HEIs to companies located in science and technology parks, namely: the identification of knowledge created by the university and then seeking out projects that may deploy them, establishing IT networks, encouraging the founding of university spin-offs, transferring staff between academia and companies and attracting research sponsors or partners, among others. The report entitled *Review of Technology Transfer Arrangements* (1994) recommends HEIs regulating their intellectual property in order to capitalise on the benefits resulting from the founding of spin-offs (set up whether by academics, technical specialists or students). Furthermore, Graf (2007), in a study on the 'guardians' of knowledge, to the contrary of Bessant and Rush (1995), who prescribe outsourcing, state that universities best undertake the role of the bridging point in the transfer of knowledge to society before concluding that the size of the organisation does not impact on its capability to serve as a gatekeeper and that the core characteristics derive from the capability for absorption (*i.e.* proving able to absorb external knowledge and spreading this through the local system). In addition, this same author maintains that public organisations serve more as 'guardians' than do entities in the private sector. Smith and Bagchi-Sem (2012) also propose that companies prefer to make recourse to services connecting them to HEIs with good research rankings. These services focus upon networking and, on the one hand, enable researchers to make their time profitable and, on the other hand, enable entrepreneurs and business managers to seek out experts within HEIs.

The response, therefore, encapsulates the strategic association of entities/firms with HEIs in collective development strategies (Franco and Belo, 2013) as the latter constitute guardians that transfer regional *inter* and *intra* internal knowledge through the business sector (Graf, 2007). According to Etzkowitz (2011), the key to fostering innovative regions involves creating human capital and R&D infrastructures characterised by permeable borders between industry and government and with interactive helices. However, Siegel *et al.* (2003) recognises the difficulties (*i.e.* applied research) posed to public HEIs that push the direction of science towards commercial ends. However, cooperation, due to differences not only in expectations but also in the structures and objectives of each organisation, proves no easy task. Thus, there are institutionalised mechanisms for university–company interaction involving cooperative research centres, science and technology parks, technological hubs and technology company incubators (Figlioli and Porto, 2006). Following this, Godin and Doré (2005) suggest that there is considerable room for the definition of a theoretical model enabling the understanding of the interconnections between knowledge and socioeconomic progress, as well as establishing a forum for representatives of both the HEIs and the EA on an equal basis. Indeed, the underlying objective of such a theoretical model involves attaining the capability to establish partnerships with companies operating in sectors of relevance to the universities and that enable the ongoing development of their research (Wilson, 2012).

In light of this reasoning, a conceptual model that incorporates cooperation between HEIs and EAs, within the scope of the spillover effects of HEIs, is presented in the next section. Because the model proposed is associated with an overflow of knowledge absorption by EAs in disadvantaged regions, it aims to contribute to their regional development.

Conceptual model

As conveyed by the literature review, EAs turn to HEIs to minimise the costs of R&D investment. In effect, in such cases, and not as 'creators' but rather as 'users' of knowledge as Grant and Baden-Fuller (2004) maintain, the EAs make external recourse to HEIs through alliances, networks or other forms of coop-eration such as licensing, joint ventures and start-ups to obtain the R&D results necessary to carrying out their entrepreneurial role as the provider of innovative services for the real problems of society (markets) (Siegel *et al.*, 2003; Greiner *et al.*, 2007; Franco and Haase, 2011; Jiang *et al.*, 2013). However, how are HEIs able to contribute through their own strategies towards boosting the com-petitive advantages of their respective hosts regions? The proposed answer to this question is set out in the conceptual model featured in Figure 5.1.

An entrepreneurial HEI thus transforms the problems existing within its local context and renders them as academic outputs susceptible to generating eco-nomic activities. Nevertheless, whilst HEIs do not engage in mutually favour-able contacts with EAs, they tend to undertake theoretical research with findings that are only applicable to reality and the resolution of real problems with great difficulty, representing a prerequisite to encouraging regional economic growth (the knowledge filter as designated by Acs *et al.* (2009)). Within such a con-text, it seems certain that the relevance of the HEI role in the region derives from its greater or lesser capability to cooperate with other actors in the transfer of the knowledge generated internally by the ongoing activities of its research-ers (Etzkowitz and Klofsten, 2005; Etzkowitz, 2011; Cowan and Zinovyeva, 2013). Hence, taking into consideration that the tacit knowledge built up in HEI requires a lot of personal contact and trust to be effectively transferred, and that such proximate relationships foster cooperative behaviours (Hertog, 2000; Tornatzky, 2001; Metcalfe, 2006; Alves, 2010; Becheikh, 2010; Wilkesmann and Wilkesmann, 2011; Smith and Bagchi-Sen, 2012), there is thus a greater propensity for innovative activities whenever the geographic location brings together R&D, researchers and labour experts (Zucker *et al.*, 1994; Agrawal, 2001; Feldmann and Desrochers, 2003; Koo, 2005; Audretsch and Feldman,

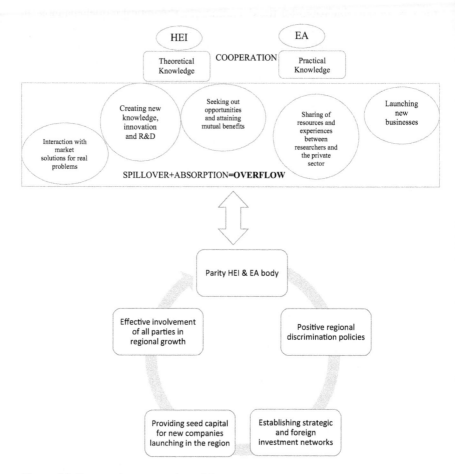

Figure 5.1 Proposed conceptual model

2007; Acs *et al.*, 2009; Koo and Cho, 2011). Nevertheless, as Smith and Bagchi-Sen, (2012) note, for an HEI to foster competitive advantages for its host region, there has to be: (1) the capability for local absorption; (2) a competitive infrastructure; (3) professional and technologically specialised labour markets; (4) an entrepreneurial culture and ongoing activities and; and (5) quality of life.

Final remarks

It is widely acknowledged that the existence of HEIs fosters an ambience of learning in their respective regions, developing the competences and resources necessary for competitiveness and social cohesion (Boucher *et al.*, 2003). However, even while the HEI strategy focuses on regional cooperation and development, overcoming the barriers to interactions with EAs through the setting up of an internal body or committee on which representatives from both the HEI and the EAs sit on an equal basis, requires a concerted approach by public intervention. This intervention allows positive discrimination among regional actors to be fostered, deepening the interrelationship between companies and R&D centres and boosting the level of ongoing collaboration over scientific and technological research practices and the absorption capability of the private sector (CCDR-Centro, 2011). This, in turn, ensures that new knowledge flows to the society (*i.e.* overflow). What Jacinto (1993: 39) stated over two decades ago correspondingly remains very contemporary; *i.e.* regional policy holds 'vital importance to economic and territorial cohesion, which deeply demands greater levels of effectiveness and persistence in the actions engaged in. They have to be, above all, more active, persistent and cooperative'.

In light of this reasoning, this study presented a theoretical model that delineates the inferences and conclusions resulting from the extant literature. In addition, it also incorporated the findings, discoveries and experiences of the technical team that drafted a SWOT analysis regarding the context faced by the Portuguese CR. Within this same logic, the model proposed still requires both adaptation and experimental testing to discuss and extrapolate the results obtained. This should allow for the construction of a more robust model for the transfer of knowledge arising from the research results produced by HEIs for their users (EAs), in a spillover effect, to the benefit of this disadvantaged region.

Bibliography

Acs, Z., Audretsch, D. and Lehmann, E. (2013) 'The knowledge spillover theory of entrepreurneuship', Small Business Economics, 41(4): 757–74.

Acs, Z., Braunerhjelm, P., Audretsch, D. and Carlsson, B. (2009) 'The knowledge spillover theory of entrepreurneuship', In Z. Acs (Ed) *The Knowledge Spillover Theory of Entrepreurneuship* (The Intern., pp 510–25), Northampton, UK, Edward Elgar Publishing Limited.

Acs, Z., Plummer, L. and Sutter, R. (2009) 'Penetrating the knowledge filter in 'rust belt' economies', *Annals of Regional Science*, 43(4): 989–1012.

Agrawal, A. (2000) Importing scientific inventions: Direct interaction, geography, and economic performance. *Mimeo.*

Agrawal, A. (2001) 'University-to-industry knowledge transfer: Literature review and unanswered questions', *International Journal of Management Review*, 3(4): 285–302.

Agrawal, A. (2006) 'Engaging the inventor: Exploring licensing strategies for university inventions and the role of latent knowledge', *Strategic Management Journal*, 27: 63–79.

Agrawal, A. and Cockburn, I. (2002) *University research, technology commercialization, and the anchor tenant hypothesis*, Roundtable on Engineering Entrepreneurship Research, Georgia Institute of Technology, Atlanta, Georgia, March, 21–23.

Agrawal, A. and Henderson, R. (2002) 'Putting patents in context: Exploring knowledge transfer from MIT', *Management Science*, 48(1): 44–60.

AICEP (2013) *As Regiões de Portugal*, http://www.portugalglobal.pt/PT/Investir Portugal/RegioesMultifacetadas/Paginas/RegioesMultifacetadas.aspx, accessed January 28, 2016.

Alexandre, J. (1991) *A especialização funcional na região centro (Portugal). Monogra-fias.* Coimbra, http://br.monografias.com/trabalhos2/regiao-centro-portugal/regiao-centro-portugal2.shtml

Alves, L. (2010) *Transferência de tecnologia para spin-offs universitárias: estudo de casos,* Universidade do Minho.

Amesse, F. and Cohendet, P. (2001) 'Technology transfer revisited from the perspective of the knowledge-based economy', *Research Policy,* 30(9): 1459–78.

Audretsch, D. and Feldman, M. (2007) 'R & D spillovers and the geography of innovation and production', *The American Economic Review,* 86(3): 630–40.

Audretsch, D. and Lehmann, E. (2005) 'Does the knowledge spillover theory of entrepreneurship hold for regions?', *Research Policy,* 34(8): 1191–202.

Augusto Mateus and Associados (2012) *Plano de Desenvolvimento Estratégico para a Universidade da Beira Interior 2012–2020,* Covilhã.

Balconi, M. and Laboranti, A. (2006) 'University–industry interactions in applied research: The case of microelectronics', *Research Policy,* 35(10): 1616–630.

Bank, T. (2002) *Constructing knowledge societies: New challenges for tertiary education.* (The World Bank, Ed.), The World Bank, Washington, DC.

Becheikh, N. (2010) 'How to improve knowledge transfer strategies and practices in education? Answers from a systematic literature review', *Research in Higher Education Journal,* 7: 1–21.

Bessant, J. and Rush, H. (1995) 'Building bridges for innovation: The role of consultants in technology transfer', *Research Policy,* 24(18): 97–114.

Boucher, G., Conway, C., Meer, E. Van Der and Meer, E. (2003) 'Tiers of engagement by universities in their region's development', *Regional Studies,* 37(9): 887–97.

Branstetter, L. (2005) 'Exploring the link between academic science and industrial innovation', *Annales d'Economie et de Statistique,* 1: 119–42.

CCDR (2011) *Mais Centro Programa Operacional Regional do Centro de Portugal (2007–2013),* Coimbra, http://www.ccdrc.pt/

CCDRC (2008) *Dinâmicas regionais na região centro: sistema científico e tecnológico.* Coimbra, http://www.ccdrc.pt/

CCDRC (2010) *Boletim Trimestral – Dinâmicas Regionais na Região Centro,* Coimbra, Boletim Trimestral – CCDRC, http://www.ccdrc.pt/index.php?option=com_content&view=article&id=348&Itemid=253&lang=pt

CCDRC (2015) *Barómetro Centro de Portugal. Direção de serviços de Desenvolvimento Regional,* http://datacentro.ccdrc.pt

Cohen, W., Nelson, R. and Walsh, J. (2002) 'Links and impacts: The influence of public research on industrial R & D', *Management Science,* 48(1): 1.

Cowan, R. and Zinovyeva, N. (2013) 'University effects on regional innovation', *Research Policy,* 42(3): 788–800.

CRER 2020 (2014) *Centro de Portugal: competitividade responsável, estruturante e resiliente,* Coimbra.

Djellal, F., Gallouj, F. and Miles, I. (2013) 'Two decades of research on innovation in services: Which place for public services?', *Structural Change and Economic Dynamics,* 27(December 2013): 98–117.

Etzkowitz, H. (1998) The norms of entrepreneurial science: Cognitive effects of the new university–industry linkages', *Research Policy,* 27(8): 823–33.

Etzkowitz, H. (2011) Silicon valley: The sustainability of an innovative region. *First Science City Conference, York, U.K. Oct. 2005 to the conference on 'Cluster Policies' at the Institute for Entrepreneurship,* Audencia Nantes School of Management, Nantes,

France, Oct. 2009 and the 'Commercialising University Research Workshop', Univ. Edinburgh.

Etzkowitz, H. (2013) 'Anatomy of the entrepreneurial university', *Social Science Information*, 52(3): 486–511.

Etzkowitz, H. and Klofsten, M. (2005) 'The innovating region: Toward a theory of knowledge-based regional development', *R&D Management*, 35(3): 243–55.

Feldmann, M. and Desrochers, P. (2003) 'Research universities and local economic development: Lessons from the history of Johns Hopkins University', *Industry and Innovation*, 10(1): 5.

Fernandes, C. and Ferreira, J.J. (2013) 'Knowledge spillovers: Cooperation between universities and KIBS', *R&D Management*, 43(5): 461–72.

Figlioli, A. and Porto, G.S. (2006) 'XXIV Simpósio de Gestão da Inovação Tecnológica', In ANPAD (Ed) *Mecanismos de transferência de tecnologia entre universidades e parques tecnológicos*, pp 1–11.

Florida, R. (2002) *The rise of the creative class: And how it's transforming work, leisure, community, and everyday life.* (B. Book, Ed.) Basic Book, New York.

Forti, E., Franzoni, C. and Sobrero, M. (2013) 'Bridges or isolates? Investigating the social networks of academic inventors', *Research Policy*, 42(8): 1378–88.

Franco, M. and Belo, M. (2013) 'Cooperation networks as a mechanism for strengthening territorial competitiveness: The case of the Qualifica Association. World Review of Entrepreneurship', *Management and Sust. Development*, 9(4): 421–43.

Franco, M. and Haase, H. (2011) 'Network embeddedness: A qualitative study of small technology-based firms', *International Journal Management and Enterprise Development*, 11(1): 34–51.

Franco, M., Haase, H. and Fernandes, A. (2014) 'The influence of academic staff's personal and professional characteristics on the decision to cooperate with industry', *European J. International Management*, 8(3): 293–309.

Fromhold-Eisebith, M. and Werker, C. (2013) 'Universities' functions in knowledge transfer: A geographical perspective', *The Annals of Regional Science*, 51(3): 621–43.

Fuller, A. and Rothaermel, F. (2012) 'When stars shine: The effects of faculty founders on new technology ventures', *Strategic Entrepreneurship Journal*, 6(3): 220–35.

Gaspar, J. (1993) *Reordenamento Urbano em Portugal, Serviços e Desenvolvimento numa Região em Mudança*, Coimbra.

Ghio, N., Guerini, M., Lehmann, E. and Rossi-Lamastra, C. (2014) 'The emergence of the knowledge spillover theory of entrepreneurship', *Small Business Economics*, 44(1): 1–18.

Godin, B. and Doré, C. (2005) 'Measuring the impacts of science; beyond the economic dimension', INRS Urbanisation, Culture et Société. HIST Lecture, Helsinki Institute for Science and Technology Studies, Helsinki, Finland. Available at: http://www.csiic.

Graf, H. (20011) 'Gatekeepers in regional networks of innovators', *Cambridge Journal of Economics*, 35(1): 173–98.

Grandi, A. and Grimaldi, R. (2003) 'Exploring the networking characteristics of new venture founding teams', *Small Business Economics*, 4(21): 329–41.

Grant, R. and Baden-Fuller, C. (2004) 'A knowledge accessing theory of strategic alliances', *Journal of Management Studies*, 41(1): 1–24.

Gregorio, D. and Shane, S. (2003) 'Why do some universities generate more start-ups than others?', *Research Policy*, 32(2): 209–27.

Greiner, M., Böhmann, T. and Krcmar, H. (2007) 'A strategy for knowledge management', *Journal of Knowledge Management*, 11(6): 3–15.

Gunasekara, C. (2006) 'Reframing the role of universities in the development of regional innovation system', *Journal of Technology Transfer*, 31(1): 101–13.

Hansson, F., Husted, K. and Vestergaard, J. (2005) 'Second generation science parks: From structural holes jockeys to social capital catalysts of the knowledge society', *Technovation*, 25(9): 1039–49.

Hertog, P. Den. (2000) 'Knowledge-intensive business services as co-producers of innovation', *International Journal of Innovation Management*, 4(4): 491–528.

INE. (1991) *Census 1991 Resultados Definitivos*, Lisbon.

INE. (2002) *CENSOS 2001, Resultados Definitivos.* Censos 2001, 1–34. http://scholar.google.com/scholar?hl=en&btnG=Search&q=intitle:CENSOS+2001+RESULTADOS+DEFINITIVOS+Lisboa#0

Jacinto, R. (1993) 'As regiões portuguesas, a política regional e a reestruturação do território', *Cadernos de Geografia*, 12: 1–15.

Jaffe, A. (1989) 'Real effects of academic research', *The American Economic Review*, 79(5): 957.

Jaffe, A., Trajtenberg, M. and Henderson, R. (1993) 'Geographic localization of knowledge spillovers as evidenced by patent citations', *The Quarterly Journal of Economics*, 108(3): 577–98.

Jiang, X., Li, M., Gao, S., Bao, Y. and Jiang, F. (2013) 'Managing knowledge leakage in strategic alliances: The effects of trust and formal contracts', *Industrial Marketing Management*, 42(6): 983–91.

Johansson, M., Jacob, M. and Hellstro, T. (2005) 'The strength of strong ties: University spin-offs and the significance of historical relations', *Journal of Technology Transfer*, 30: 271–86.

Karnani, F. (2012) 'The university's unknown knowledge: Tacit knowledge, technology transfer and university spin-offs findings from an empirical study based on the theory of knowledge', *The Journal of Technology Transfer*, 38(3): 235–50.

Kohengkul, S., Wongwanich, S. and Wiratchai, N. (2009) 'Influences of strategies, knowledge sharing and knowledge transfer on the success of university-school collaboration in research and development', *Research in Higher* ..., 1–15. http://www.aabri.com/manuscripts/09267.pdf

Koo, J. (2005) 'Agglomeration and spillovers in a simultaneous framework', *The Annals of Regional Science*, 39(1): 35–47.

Koo, J. and Cho, K.R. (2011) 'New firm formation and industry clusters: A case of the drugs industry in the U.S', *Growth and Change*, 42(2): 179–99.

Kronberga, G. (2010) 'Latvian regional universities as agents of science and practice', In *An Enterprise Odyssey. International Conference Proceedings* (p. 460). University of Zagreb, Faculty of Economics and Business.

Laukkanen, M. (2003) 'Exploring academic entrepreneurship: Drivers and tensions of university-based business', *Journal of Small Business and Enterprise Development*, 10(4): 372–82.

Lécuyer, C. (2005) 'What do universities really owe industry? The case of solid state electronics at sanford', *Minerva*, 43(1): 51–71.

Lendel, I. (2010) 'The impact of research universities on regional economies: The concept of university products', *Economic Development Quarterly* 24(3): 210–30.

Link, A. and Scott, J. (2005) 'Universities as partners in U.S. research joint ventures', *Research Policy*, 34(3): 385–93.

Lockett, A. and Wright, M. (2005) 'Resources, capabilities, risk capital and the creation of university spin-out companies', *Research Policy*, 34(7): 1043–57.

Lockett, A., Wright, M. and Franklin, S. (2003) 'Technology transfer and universities' Spin-out strategies', *Small Business Economics*, 20: 185–200.

Lundvall, B. and Borrás, S. (1997) *The globalising learning economy: Implications for innovation policy*, Brussels: Office for Official Publications of the European Communities.

Marques, J., Caraça, J. and Diz, H. (2006) 'How can university–industry–government interactions change the innovation scenario in Portugal? – the case of the University of Coimbra', *Technovation*, 26(4): 534–42.

Metcalfe, J. (2006) '2 systems failure and the case for innovation policy', In P. Llerena and M. Matt (Eds) *Innovation Policy in a Knowledge-Based Economy: Theory and Practice* (ESRC. pp 47–74), Springer, Manchester.

Meyer, M. (2006) 'Academic inventiveness and entrepreneurship: On the importance of start-up companies in commercializing academic patents', *The Journal of Technology Transfer*, 31(4): 501–10.

Monck, S., Porter, R., Quintas, P., Storey, D. and Wynarczyk, P. (1988) *Science parks and the growth of high technology firms*. (C. Helm, Ed.) (Prometheus), Croom Helm, London.

Nations, U. (2005) *Understanding knowledge societies: In twenty questions and answers with the index of knowledge societies (United Nat.)*, Department of Economic and Social Affairs of the United Nations, New York.

O'Shea, R., Allen, T., Chevalier, A. and Roche, F. (2005) 'Entrepreneurial orientation, technology transfer and spinoff performance of U.S. universities', *Research Policy*, 34(7): 994–1009.

O'Shea, R., Chugh, H. and Allen, T. (2007) 'Determinants and consequences of university spinoff activity: A conceptual framework', *The Journal of Technology Transfer*, 33(6): 653–66.

Powers, J. and McDougall, P. (2005) 'University start-up formation and technology licensing with firms that go public: A resource-based view of academic entrepreneurship', *Journal of Business Venturing*, 20(3): 291–311.

Rocha, A., Águia, C., Chaves, D., Pinho, E., Queirós, H., Aguilar, J., . . . Vilela, T. (2013) *Manual para a Protecção Gestão e Valorização da Propriedade Intelectual.* (E. P. e I. N. da P. I. (INPI), Ed.) (1a ed.). Lisbon: COTEC PORTUGAL e INPI.

Rothaermel, F., Agung, S. and Jiang, L. (2007) 'University entrepreneurship: A taxonomy of the literature', *Industrial and Corporate Change*, 16(4): 691–791.

Sedlacek, S. (2013) 'The role of universities in fostering sustainable development at the regional level', *Journal of Cleaner Production*, 48(2013): 74–84.

Shane, S. and Stuart, T. (2002) 'Organizational endowments and the performance of university start-ups', *Management Science*, 48(1): 154–70.

Sidharta, M., Arai, T., Putro, U. and Morimoto, H. (2014) Modeling spin-off creation in university technology transfer with system dynamics, Proceedings of the 32nd International Conference of the System Dynamics Society, Delft, Netherlands, July 20–24.

Siegel, D., Waldman, D. and Link, A. (2003) 'Assessing the impact of organizational practices on the relative productivity of university technology transfer offices: An exploratory study', *Research Policy*, 32(1): 27–48.

Siegel, D., Waldman, D., Atwarter, L. and Link, A. (2003) Commercial knowledge transferes from universities to firms: Improving the effectiveness of university-industry collaboration', *Journal of High Technology Management Research*, 14(1): 111–33.

Silva, M. (2003) *Capacidade inovadora empresarial: estudo dos factores impulsionadores e limitadores nas empresas industriais portuguesas,* Universidade da Beira Interior.

Smith, H. and Bagchi-Sen, S. (2012) 'The research university, entrepreneurship and regional development: Research propositions and current evidence', *Entrepreneurship & Regional Development,* 24(5–6): 383–404.

Tornatzky, L. (2001) 'Benchmarking university-industry technology transfer: A six year retrospective', *Journal of Technology Transfer,* 26(3): 269–77.

Vallas, S. and Kleinman, D. (2007) 'Contradiction, convergence and the knowledge economy : The confluence of academic and commercial biotechnology', *Socio-Economic Review,* 6(2): 1–29.

Varga, A. (2000) 'Local academic knowledge spillovers and the concentration of economic activity', *Journal of Regional Science,* 40(2): 289–309.

Wilkesmann, M. and Wilkesmann, U. (2011) 'Knowledge transfer as interaction between experts and novices supported by technology', *Vine,* 41(2): 96–112.

Wilson, T. (2012) *A review of business – university collaboration,* London. Retrieved from www.nationalarchives.gov.uk/doc/open-government-licence

Woolthuis, R., Lankhuizen, M. and Gilsing, V. (2005) 'A system failure framework for innovation policy design', *Technovation,* 25(6): 609–19.

Wright, R. and Dana, L. (2003) 'Changing paradigms of international entrepreneurship strategy', *Journal of International Entrepreneurship,* 1(1): 135–52.

Zack, M. (1999) 'Developing a knowledge strategy', *California Management Review,* 41(3): 125–45.

Zucker, L., Darby, M. and Brewer, M. (1994) *Intellectual capital and the birth of U.S. biotechnology enterprises* (No. 4653), Cambridge University Press, Cambridge.

Part II
Strategic entrepreneurship and knowledge

6 Institutional entrepreneurship

A new interconnectivity between government–university–enterprises in Wuhan future technology city of China

Connie Zheng

Introduction

In an economy geared towards innovation and competitiveness in research and development activities, interrelationship between the university, private enterprise and government are of considerable interest to academics and practitioners alike. China, in its 12th five-year plan (2011–2015), clearly states its ambition to move from being 'the world factory' to becoming 'an innovation house' (KPMG, 2011; Cendrowski, 2015). Thus, considerable effort has been made by the government to encourage the cooperation between university research institutes and industries to generate the growth of high-tech and human-capital-intensive entrepreneurial firms that will help sustain the nation's dream of achieving the long lasting economic growth rate.

For the past 30 years, China's economic growth rate has maintained double digits until the 2008 Global Financial Crisis. The crisis hit badly the earlier-recognised Chinese globally competitive manufacturing sector, causing an alarm to the governing Communist Party. The Party subsequently determined to revise its export-oriented industry policy to implement a new industry policy that focuses on science, technology and innovation as a future developmental path (Cendrowski, 2015).

Seven pillar industries (i.e. new energy, new materials, nanotechnology, environmental protection, automobile, new medicine and ICT) have been mapped out as the industry developmental blueprint in the 12th five-year plan. To develop these strategic industries, the government has since allocated considerable amount of resources to establish additional three geographically-spread Science & Technology (S&T) parks. Following the first in Beijing Zhongguancun that was started in 1988, Shanghai Zhangjiang S&T Park; Wuhan East Lake S&T Park; and Chengdu S&T Park have been subsequently built and expanded with both domestic and global high-tech firms registered to operate inside the parks, especially since 2012 (Nan, 2015). The government also aims to acquire intellectual and human capitals worldwide using the 'Yantze Scholars' scheme and 'Sea Turtle' (i.e. Chinese words *Haigui* means returning Chinese scholars and professionals from overseas) attraction programs. Of course all universities and research institutes are encouraged, or literally commanded by the Party, to participate in transforming the nation's economic structure from the earlier agriculture-focused, manufacturing-oriented sectors to rapidly developing the service sector that would contain research and development (R&D) and high-tech components (KPMG, 2011; Cendrowski, 2015)

In this chapter, we aim to take one of such university research institutes – China University of Geosciences (CUG)'s Industry Technology Research Institute of Geo-Resources and Environment Co. Ltd.(IGE) (subsequently shortened with an acronym CUG-IGE) – as a window to look into the phenomenal development of Wuhan Future Technology City as a part of Wuhan East Lake S&T Park. We intend to explain the different roles played by the government, university and individual entrepreneurs to foster strategic knowledge creation and diffusion, and to commercise research outputs in order to build a high-tech-oriented city that would help facilitate the creation and development of many new enterprises to come for future.

Wuhan CUG-IGE (consistent with its name used under its own website http://ige-live.com.cn/), though registered as an independent and publically-owned company, was initially established by China University of Geosciences (CUG), with the support of a developmental fund of RMB¥200 million (US$35 million) by Wuhan Municipality Government in June 2013. Up to July 2015, the company has helped incubate 21 enterprises in total.

Because of the specific context of China, we see the operation of CUG-IGE as a unique type of strategic entrepreneurial activity that is in line with the concept of 'institutional entrepreneurship', defined by Eisenstadt (1980) as either individual or collective actors who engage in entrepreneurial activities, serve as catalysts for structural change, and take the lead in being the impetus for, and giving direction to, change. DiMaggio (1988) builds on Eisenstadt (1980) and introduces the notion of institutional entrepreneurship in institutional analysis to characterise organised actors with sufficient resources to contribute to the genesis of new institutions in which they see 'an opportunity to realise interest that they value highly'. Here, 'the interest' in the context of China is to develop an innovative nation or society as guided by the controlling Communist Party.

Using this theoretical framework of 'institutional entrepreneurship', our aim is to analyse and discuss the unique nature of government–university–enterprise link (also called Triple-Helix model) in the context of China's S&T park. The process of co-creating knowledge and commercialising research outputs as a part of knowledge spillover from university to enterprise will be examined.

China presents a different phenomenon with different institutional settings, whereby institutional entrepreneurship may account for relevant actors' institutional embeddedness (Battilana et al., 2009). The institutions' role as both enablers of and constraints on actions should be acknowledged. Therefore, taking the example of CUG-IGE and its 21 incubated companies as a case study, we will evaluate and critique the role of these institutional entrepreneurs to maintain and sustain the growth of enterprises and strategic industries inside the S&T park, as well as their subsequent contribution to the regional economic development of Wuhan, Hubei Province in China.

The rest of the chapter is organised as follows. Section 2 provides a brief discussion on the concept of 'institutional entrepreneurship' and its relevance and legitimacy to build a new government–university–industry link in the context of Wuhan Future Technology City. Section 3 discusses several forms of the Triple-Helix model, and their relevance to the case investigated. Different to the conclusion derived from the earlier studies on the government–university–enterprise link, which tend to treat universities as knowledge brokers, our study sees the current Chinese university's research institute – albeit CUG-IGE established as a company, not only as a knowledge broker, but also as an entrepreneur to build its own company as well as help incubate a total of 21 associated companies. Section 4 will profile CUG-IGE and its incubators as a way to outline the process to which knowledge spillover-based strategic entrepreneurship has taken place, with a strong institutional support from both the central and municipal government. Section 5 contains our critique on Chinese characteristics of institutional entrepreneurship and evaluation of the effectiveness of government–university–industry (GUI) partnership. Concluding marks are made in Section 6.

Institutional entrepreneurship

As argued by Marguis and Raynard (2015), emerging markets, such as China, are largely characterised by 'weak capital market and regulatory infrastructures and fast-paced turbulent change' (p. 291). When navigating in an increasingly complex and integrated global economy, Chinese organisations likely face a different set of opportunities and challenges. To survive and grow, organisations not only need to conform to various institutional mechanisms under which they are operating, they themselves have also become institutional entrepreneurs, acting as human agents to advocate and advance institutional change (Battilana, 2004, 2006; Battilana et al., 2009).

Institutional entrepreneurs are defined as 'actors who initiate changes that contribute to transforming existing, or creating new institutions' (Battilana et al., 2009, p. 66). Institutional entrepreneurs can be either individuals and/or organisations. Based on Battilana (2006), individuals' behaviours are determined by the need for them to be regarded as legitimate in their institutional environment. Organisations are made of individuals, thus patterns of individual action and organisational behaviour are likely shaped by institutions, under which individuals and organisations always tend to comply with their pressures to conform. Nevertheless, in recent times, an undue debate has centred on the transformational roles played by individuals and organisations to implement institutional change (Leca et al., 2010). The process of incorporating the role of individual actors and organisational interests into explaining the institutional change under the established overarching institutional theory is regarded as 'institutional entrepreneurship' (Eisenstadt, 1980; DiMaggio, 1988; Battilana, 2006; Leca et al., 2010).

Eisenstadt (1980) first used the term 'institutional entrepreneurship' to characterise actors who serve as catalysts for structural change and take the lead in being the impetus for, and giving direction to change. DiMaggio (1988) built on Eisenstadt (1980) and introduced the notion of institutional entrepreneurship in institutional analysis to characterise organised actors with sufficient resources to contribute to the genesis of new institutions in which they see 'an opportunity to realise interest that they value highly'. We see here that the 'interest' in the context of the Chinese current developmental path is referenced to develop an innovative nation or society as guided by its strong and controlling institution – the Communist Party (Cendrowski, 2015; Nan, 2015). Institutional entrepreneurs involved in developing an innovative China are represented by key *human agents* such as government administrators, research scientists, university professors and academic staff and students, who have entered into forming and 'institutionalising a new organisational form' (Battilana et al., 2009, p. 68), albeit via establishing one or more university-affiliated proprietary company(ies), or by taking a role of helping and/or creating new industrial enterprises. This complementary role shift is completely different from conventional university roles as knowledge creators and disseminators to teach and train students, without a clear aim to generate profit as a business enterprise.

The concept of human agents as 'knowledgeable' and 'enabled' entities implies that these agents are capable of putting their structurally formed capacities to work in creative or innovative ways (Sewell, 1992, p. 4; cited in Battilana, 2006, p. 14). Precisely in the words of Hsu (2006), who examined the case of for-profit ventures started by Chinese state organizations in the 1990s, Chinese institutional entrepreneurs tend to craft new organizational forms under unstable conditions, especially when all of the relevant organizational models have serious liabilities in terms of legitimacy. Thus, Chinese universities and their embedded constituents (such as professors and students) that have emerged as institutional entrepreneurs would need to deliberately increase ambiguity about the organization's central characteristics and its underlying moral logic. Similarly, state and government agents and their constituents lend the embedded institutional support to legitimise the operation of new organisations created by the university – one of the embedded agents within the institutional entrepreneurship framework (Etzkowitz, 2003; Battilana, 2006; Leca et al., 2010). This strategy makes it possible for new organizations to solve the problems of resources, competency and legitimacy by simultaneously adopting (and adapting) contradictory organizational elements. Contradictory to the central characteristics of conventional university as an educational and research entity, Chinese universities are now allowed to operate as a commercial business entity, financially supported by the central and local governments.

This idea of universities as entrepreneurs (see Fayolle and Redford, 2014) is not unique to China. It is believed that universities should now be responsible not only for social development but also to assist enterprises in promoting economic development of a nation (Fernández-Lopez et al., 2009). Thus, a strategic partnership of three parties, government, university and enterprise, is presented as a unique organisational form designed to integrate disparate pools of social and intellectual capitals, with participants in the partnership bringing to the table very different assets, skills, capabilities and organisational contexts (Fernández-Lopez et al., 2009; Fayolle and Redford, 2014; Carayannis et al., 2015). The key aim of such strategic alliance in the context of China is to quickly transfer research outputs generated from universities and commercialise them via industrial entities, and develop or 'evolve a shared community of innovation' (Carayannis et al., 2014, p. 611). This intention of close government–university–industry (GUI) partnership is to build national innovation system. The model well-known for such partnership is also called the Triple-Helix model, which emphasises the importance of flows and linkages between firms and external source of knowledge generated by university and state agencies. GUI partnerships are a mechanism for facilitating revolutionary innovation through knowledge infusion and diffusion (Dosi et al., 1988; Etzkowitz and Leydesdorff, 2000). This will be discussed further in the next section.

Government–university–industry (GUI) partnership

The idea of GUI partnership was initially generated from the desire to promote economic development as a result of technical and technological change, leading to building an innovative and knowledge-based economy (Dosi et al., 1988). The national innovation system is essential to compete in the knowledge-based world economy. Thus universities, where frontier research and development of science, technology and communication often take place, are believed to play an enhanced role in innovation in increasingly knowledge-based societies, especially for those transitional economies, such as China (Etzkowitz and Leydesdorff, 2000; Leydesdorff and Park, 2014). However, the underlying GUI partnership, also called the Triple-Helix model, is analytically different from the national systems of innovation approach, which considers the firm as having the leading role in innovation, and state is privileged to govern the transformational process in building the innovation system (Leydesdorff and Etzkowitz, 1998). The Triple-Helix model focuses on the network overlay of communications and expectations that shape and 'reshape the institutional arrangements among universities, industries, and governmental agencies' (Etzkowitz and Leydesdorff, 2000, p. 109). The case study recently conducted by Farinha et al. (2016) also came to conclude the importance of adopting Triple Helix networks in order to develop research, development and innovation (RDI) initiatives. Through RDI cooperation networks and the consequent commercialization of new tradable products, positive consequences are expected to be generated to contribute to regional competitiveness and national economic growth (Farinha et al., 2016, p. 259).

There are three main forms of the Triple-Helix model that have been identified by Leydesdorff and Etzkowitz (1998), and the latest one that integrates the global innovation system, with concerns on the contemporary issues of building civil society, environmental sustainability, and knowledge democracy, was claimed by Leydesdorff (2012), Carayannis et al. (2012), and Leydesdorff and Park (2014), which complemented the earlier forms.

In Triple-Helix I, university, industry and government are three helices institutionally defined. The interactions across three parties are defended with clear boundaries, and often mediated by organisational industrial liaison, technology transfer and contract offices (Leydesdorff and Etzkowitz, 1998). The Engineering Research Centres (ERC) Program administered by the US National Science Foundation (NSF) may represent this type of form, whereby each party has clearly defined boundary roles, with ERC assuming to focus more on fundamental research of broad interest to industry, rather than on joint development of specific products for individual firms or setting up a company of its own. And the partnerships among NSF, 26 ERCs and multiple industrial firms are managed by industrial liaison and contract offices (Carayannis et al., 2015). As such, institutional entrepreneurship may not be clearly present in this model, with perhaps only industrial firms being engaged in entrepreneurial activities.

In Triple-Helix II, three spheres are defined as different communication systems consisting of the operation of markets, technological innovations and control at the interfaces. The interfaces among three parties operate in a distributed mode that produces potentially new forms of communication as in a sustained technology transfer interface or in the case of patent legislation (Leydesdorff and Etzkowitz, 1998). The example of such a form would be University of California's (UC) Industry-University Cooperative Research Program, established in 1996, and supported by the joint investment of US$20 million per year by the State of California and UC, and matched dollar for dollar with funds from a California-based R&D firm. The aim of the Program was to expand industry access to the university and increase discovery research that could form the foundation for entirely new technologies and products, at the same time leverage industry, state and federal R&D investments (Edmondson et al., 2012). Here, different parties may perform the role of entrepreneurs. Different and complex communication systems are used to facilitate university-industry collaboration, technology transfer and joint product creation. However, the boundary roles of each party are still clearly defined, and operation of each party is controlled at the interfaces. There is no assuming role of the others taken by each party. Thus, university as an institutional entrepreneur is neither well-presented in this model, nor in Triple-Helix I.

In contrast to Triple-Helix II, the form of Triple-Helix III shows that each of the institutional spheres of university, industry and government, in addition to performing their traditional functions, has now assumed the roles of the others – that is the embedded role of institutional entrepreneur explained by Battilana (2004). In the context of CUG-IGE, the university helped create an industrial penumbra and perform a quasi-governmental role as a regional or local innovation organiser. Wuhan East-Lake S&T Park can be considered as an example of the internalisation of such organisational complexity. An intermediate level of agencies and small enterprises incubated within CUG-IGE is typical of the institutionally arranged research system that facilitates the development of more enterprises in the S&T Park. Leaders and managers of those incubated firms could also be brought in to perform teaching and research duties as they might as well be originally sourced from professors and academic staff from CUG. A similar case was illustrated in the collaboration between Microsoft-Cisco-Intel and University of Melbourne, and Aalto University (Finland) (see Edmondson et al., 2012), though these two cases have no strong involvement of government, as it would be the case with CUG-IGE in China.

Leydesdorff (2012) argued that a systemic innovation pattern can be expected to remain in transition because integration among the functions of wealth creation, knowledge production and normative control take place at the interfaces of government, university and industry, while exchanges on the market, scholarly communication in knowledge production, and political discourse tend to differentiate globally (p. 25). Carayannis et al. (2012) extended the concept of Triple Helix to 'Quadruple Helix', which places the emphasis on knowledge production and innovation within the emerging global knowledge economy. The authors believed that the sustainable development of a knowledge economy requires a coevolution with the knowledge society (Carayannis et al., 2012). In addition, it is likely that the Quintuple Helix also exists to stress the necessary socio-ecological transition of society and economy in the twenty-first century, with potential to allow the natural environments of society and the economy to act as drivers for further knowledge production and innovation, therefore defining opportunities for the knowledge economy (Carayannis et al., 2012, p. 1).

Later, Leydesdorff and Park (2014) extended the original linear Triple-Helix model to encompass the overall global innovation system. They developed a Triple Helix indicator of synergy as reduction of uncertainty in niches that can be shaped among three or more sets of relations. The synergies cover the distributions of firms/organisations over geographical addresses, technological classes and industrial-size classes for a number of nations in order to balance dynamic innovation between globalised and localised knowledge, while avoiding potential too much synergy locally that can be considered as lock-in (Leydesdorff and Park, 2014:1). The Microelectronics Developing for European Applications (MEDEA) initiative, based in Paris, is the case in point to explain the fourth form of Triple-Helix model, which has involved multiple firms, universities and research institutions across a number of European nations such as Germany, France, The Netherlands, Italy, Belgium and Austria to facilitate the wide diffusion of new innovations (Leydesdorff and Park, 2014; Carayannis et al., 2015). This is also the case with the operation inside the Wuhan Future Technology City, whereby the Wuhan City Municipality's encouragement of overseas investment, international collaboration of universities, joint-ventured enterprises and building sister-cities with those in foreign countries is a strong indicator to globalise the GUI partnership (Leydesdorff, 2012), and serves as a springboard for a latecomer country such as China to catch up with latest development of environmental and clean technology as suggested by Carayannis et al. (2012).

We now turn to analyse how 21 enterprises were established and incubated via the strategy of GUI partnership, with a particular reference to the third and fourth forms of the Triple-Helix model as discussed above.

Analysis of incubated enterprises

The data collected for this study was largely sourced from various Chinese web-sites, and two presentations made by CUG-IGE staff were recorded and used to support the analyses. Since its establishment as a proprietary company in 2013, CUG-IGE has helped incubate a total of 21 enterprises to date. Based on the Triple-Helix model, it is evident that university (CUG) and government (Wuhan Municipality) were engaged in incubating 21 innovative enterprises as in line with the national innovation policy that emphasises building sever pillar industries such as new energy, new materials, nanotechnology, environmental protection, automobile, new medicine and ICT (Nan, 2015), because 21 enterprises have a wide spread of industries represented. Most, nonetheless, industries represented are in line with the strategic industries outlined in the China's 12th national developmental plan, which focus on energy, bio- and nano-technology, water and ecological environmental products and services, except those companies focusing on jewelry design accompanied with cultural tourism as a trademark represented by the special College of Treasure and Jewelry Design under the auspices of China University of Geosciences (CUG).

Both government and university in this context have acted as institutional entrepreneurs to contribute not only resources (i.e. initial registered capitals and human capabilities) but also role-plays as shareholders or enterprise managers appointed from a pool of university professors and researchers. Table 6.1 shows that the majority of the incubators (20) were established in 2014, precisely within the half year from April to November 2014 (see Table 6.1). The latest three enterprises are wholly-owned by CUG-IGE as its subsidiaries; seven are jointly ventured between CUG-IGE with partners in industry, five companies were led by CUG academic staff and three were created by its doctoral, masters and undergraduate students; three companies were established with private funding or patent/research funds received by CUG professors and researchers.

Among seven joint-ventured projects, three joint partners were from Beijing, one from Zhangjiagang in Jiangsu Province; the rest of the partners were sourced locally from Hubei Province. From assessing the development of CUG-IGE from June 2013 (see www.ige-live.com/gywm/lsyg/2014–08–14/171.html) until today, it is found that CUG-IGE has had international collaboration with individuals and organizations from Korea, Spain and Switzerland. Therefore, it appears that the fourth stage of the Triple-Helix model that incorporates geographic dispersion for innovative ideas may have applied to CUG-IGE in developing its global GUI partnership.

Registered capitals of enterprises range from the smallest RMB¥300,000 (US$47,000) to RMB¥60 million (US$9.5 million). With this variety of capital range, it is assumed that the size of each enterprise would be dissimilar accordingly. However, data collected indicated that all enterprises have a range of employees, from 150 to 500. We double-checked the CUG-IGE's webpage, where it is indicated that the number of CUG-IGE employees is about 301–500. It is unclear whether the size of each incubated enterprise is a projected number

Table 6.1 Nature and characteristics of 21 incubated companies under CUG (Wuhan) – IGE

#	Company name	Established date/year	Main products/ services	Employee #	Registered capital RMB ¥ (= US$) ~000	Estimated annual outputs in RMB ¥ in US$) ~000	Enterprise ownership & shareholders
1	Environmental Protection Resources Co. Ltd. (地大环保资源有限公司)*	16 July 2014	Sapogenin extraction; pollution clearance service	150–500	¥20,000 (= US$3,150)	¥30,000 (= US$4,730)	CUG-IGE holding 10% shares
2	Hubei Robotics Engineering Technology Co. Ltd. (湖北艾瑞博特机器人工程技术有限公司)	16 July 2014	Robotic handles, industry robotics, auto-production line	150–500	¥2,000 (= US$3,150) registered as ¥5,900 (US$929)	¥20,000 (= US$3,150)	CUG-IGE holding 30% shares
3	Geophysical and Remote Sensing Co. Ltd. (武汉地大物探遥感有限公司)	23 April 2014	Shallow seismic interpretation, remote monitoring geological hazards and stratigraphic wells CT imaging scanner	150–500	¥50,000 (= US$7,880) but registered as ¥5,000 (= US$788) – a big gap	X	Formed by CUG academic staff from Faculty of Earth Space Sciences
4	Waterstone Environmental Protection Technology Co. Ltd.(武汉中地水石环保科技有限公司) http:// whzdsshbkjyxgs. 21hubei.com/	28 April 2014	Water salinity & purification, air monitoring & treatment, drinking water equipment	150–500	¥5,000 (= US$788)	X	CUG doctoral students' project

(*Continued*)

Table 6.1 (Continued)

#	Company name	Established date/year	Main products/ services	Employee #	Registered capital RMB ¥ (= US$) ~000	Estimated annual outputs in RMB ¥ (= US$) ~000	Enterprise ownership & shareholders
5	Wuhan SunEn-Tech Co. Ltd. (武汉中地西能科技有限公司) http://www.whzdxn.com/	24 July 2014	Manganese additives; and new insulation materials for oil pipelines	150–500	¥5,000 (= US$788)	Daily production of 200 kilograms of manganese additives	Patent owned by Prof. Tian Xike from CUG's Chemistry Dept.
6	Earth Rejuvenation Engineering Co. Ltd. (武汉中地大地修复工程技术有限公司) http://www.zdlyjny.com/hezuo/201506/201552529.html	22 May 2014	Contaminated site investigation and evaluation, and environmental remediation technology consulting	150–500	¥5,000 (= US$788)	X	Formed by CUG academic staff (currently recruiting CEO from market)
7	Phosphorus Resources Co. Ltd. (武汉中地磷资源科技有限公司)	28 Apri 2014	Phosphorus-related internal processing technology and equipment research and development, open-cut mine repair & water treatment, etc.	150–500	¥1,000 (= US$157) registered capital stated as 2,000,000	X	Formed by CUG academic staff

No.	Company	Date	Business	150–500	Amount	X	Notes
8	Jiangsu Hydrogen Energy Co., Ltd. (江苏氢阴能源有限公司) –mentioned in this partner website: http://www.furuise.com/	24 July 2014	Research and development and manufacture of hydrogen energy storage, conversion, application materials, equipment and technology, sales	150–500	¥60,000 (= US$9,451)	X (patent by 7 academic staff from CUG)	Joint-venture between CUG and Zhangjiagang (Jiangsu) Special Equipment Holding Co. Ltd.
9	TresureValley Cultural Tourism Industry Research Co., Ltd. (武汉中地宝谷文化旅游产业研究院有限公司) http://www.whzgbg.com/bbx/1965150-1965150.html?pid=1533188	3 April 2014	Sales of jewelry design, cultural tourism and creative industries planning, cultural tourism park management	150–500	¥1,000 (= US$157)	X	Set up by academic staff from School of Economics and Management, CUG.
10	Nano Technology Co., Ltd.(武汉中地纳米科技有限公司)*	24 July 2014	Nano-zirconia powder, lanthanum zirconate powder, thermal spraying nanostructured spherical powder, high performance mineral fiber	150–500	¥5,000 (= US$788)	X	Patent by CUG academic staff

(Continued)

Table 6.1 (Continued)

#	Company name	Established date/year	Main products/services	Employee #	Registered capital RMB ¥ (= US$) ~000	Estimated annual outputs in RMB ¥ (= US$) ~000	Enterprise ownership & shareholders
11	Gui-Yuan-Tong Environmental Protection Technology Co., Ltd. (武汉贵元通环保科技有限公司)*	25 July 2014	Vehicle exhaust purification catalyst research and development, production and sales	150–500	¥20,000 (= US$3,150)	X already invested ¥200 million in the project from Gui-Yuan-Tong	Joint-venture between CUG staff and Shi-yan Gui-Yuan Tong
12	Geothermal Resources Exploration and Development Co., Ltd. (武汉中地地热资源勘探开发有限公司)	23 May 2014	Geothermal resources exploration, development, planning, water resources assessment, geothermal energy development and utilization	150–500	¥5,000 (= US$780)	X	Set up by CUG academic staff
13	Feng-da Geological Engineering Co. Ltd. (武汉中地丰达地质工程有限公司)+ http://yt.tmjob88.com/vvip/cm1360028567772/index.php?urlType=jianj	25 July 2014 Feng-da established in 2002 via CUG	Deep foundation pit dewatering and supporting design technology	150–500 Feng-Da employs about 40 people of its own	¥12,000** (= US$1,890)	X	Joint venture between CUG and Feng-Da Co., which was also initially set up by CUG academic staff

#	Company	Date	Business	150–500	Capital		Notes
14	Architectural Design & Research Co., Ltd.(武汉中地建筑勘测设计研究院有限公司)*	25 July 2014	Engineering survey and design, measurement and monitoring, industrial and civil construction, municipal pipe network, bridges, tunnels, geological disaster prevention and utilization of urban geothermal, protection of geotechnical heritage	150–500	¥10,000 (= US$1,580)	X	Also set up by academic staff from CUG
15	Nan-Wang-Jing-Seng Jewelry Co., Ltd. (武汉地大南望晶生珠宝有限公司*)http://whddnwjszbyxgs.21hubei.com/	9 May 2014	Cultural and creative jewellery, arts and crafts design and sales	150–500	¥1,500 (= US$236)	X (aimed for graduate 'chuangke'	Formed by 2 CUG Masters graduates & 7 undergraduate students

(Continued)

Table 6.1 (Continued)

#	Company name	Established date/year	Main products/ services	Employee #	Registered capital RMB ¥ (= US$) ~000	Estimated annual outputs in RMB ¥ (= US$) ~000	Enterprise ownership & shareholders
16	Ecological Environment Space Technology Co., Ltd. (武汉中地生态环境空间技术有限公司)	24 April 2014	Deformation Monitoring System for morphological changes in dams, bridges, landslide, railway construction and the like. Other monitoring programs to include GPS rainfall monitoring, laser ranging monitoring.	150–500	¥20,000 ++ (= US$3,150)	X	Joint-venture between CUG-IGE, Hubei Qualcomm Space Technology Co., Ltd., and Beijing Jiang-wei Time Technology Co., Ltd.
17	Da-Yu Environmental Technology Co., Ltd. (武汉中地大禹环境科技有限公司)	22 September 2014)	Water ecological and environmental monitoring instruments and equipments	150–500	¥8,000 (= US$1,260)	X	Joint-venture between CUG-IGE and Beijing Global Water Technology Co., Ltd.

	Name	Date	Business scope		Capital		Notes
18	View Cloud Science & Technology Co., Ltd.* (武汉中地视云科技有限公司) http://zdvision.corp.dav01.com/index.html	22 September 2014)	Multimedia video network system integration, and its software development, production, marketing, and sales	150–500	¥10,000 (= US$1,575)	X	CUG-IGE with two private persons' investment
19	Jewellery Cultural Tourism Industry Investment Co., Ltd. (武汉地大珠宝文化旅游产业投资有限公司)	24 October 2014	Jewellery & tourism project investment, culture and art exchange activities, and related business & trade management and consultation	150–500	¥10,000 (= US$1575)	X	Wholly-owned by CUG-IGE
20	Jewellery Cultural Tourism Industry Research Co., Ltd. (武汉地大珠宝文化旅游产业研究院有限公司)	14 November 2014	Planning and creative design, jewelry management and research, cultural tourism and related jewelry industrial park construction investment and operations.	150–500	¥10,000 (= US$1,575)	X	Wholly-owned by CUG-IGE

(*Continued*)

Table 6.1 (Continued)

#	Company name	Established date/year	Main products/ services	Employee #	Registered capital RMB ¥ ~000 (= US$)	Estimated annual outputs in RMB ¥ (= US$) ~000	Enterprise ownership & shareholders
21	Wuhan Wei-Gao Design & Planning Co., Ltd. (武汉维高设计策划有限公司)	16 April 2015	Brand logo design, book, packaging, display space design, business planning, publicity design, and printing and advertising	150–500	¥300 (=US$47)	X	Wholly-owned by CUG-IGE

of employees for developmental aspiration or staffing is directly sourced from the CUG-IGE central employee pool.

Further analyzing the CEO profile of each enterprise, it is found that majority of CEOs for 21 enterprises were appointed by CUG-IGE, or more precisely the CEO roles were taken by either university administrators who are also Communist Party members, or professors, research staff and students who started the business. These personnel largely still hold dual roles – administrative, research and teaching at CUG while leading and managing the enterprises they had started up.

Among the available data for estimated annual outputs, only three companies provided detailed information about their outputs. This suggests that majority of enterprises were still under development and have not fully operated to generate products and profits as normal enterprises would.

Evaluation of institutional entrepreneurship and GUI partnership for CUG-IGE

As argued by Battilana et al. (2009, p. 68), institutional entrepreneurs are change agents, but not all change agents are institutional entrepreneurs. Actors must fulfil two conditions to be regarded as institutional entrepreneurs: 1) initiate divergent change; and 2) actively participate in the implementation of these changes. Divergent change is referred to as those changes that break with the institutionalised template for organising within a given institutional context. By examining a final product – the company named CUG-IGE – as a result of GUI partnership, it is argued that actors (i.e. Wuhan City Municipality and its officer, university administrator, professor and researcher) have indeed broken away from their traditional boundary roles as governors and educators, and moved towards engaging in business and entrepreneurial activities (i.e. incubating 21 associated enterprises). This move has been greatly encouraged by the ruling Chinese Communist Party, which aims to build an innovative nation by implementing its 12th developmental plan.

It is yet clear whether the operation of CUG-IGE and its associated firms would be successful and sustainable, as they are still at the early stage of development. However, as commented by Battilana et al. (2009, p. 70) again, actors participating in implementing the divergent change do not have to be successful to be considered as institutional entrepreneurs. Instead, institutional entrepreneurs are the ones who introduce business models that diverge from the predominant model in the normative institutional environment; and who are able to 'develop a vision and mobilise people behind the vision and motivate them to achieve and sustain it' (Battilana et al., 2009, p. 78). The vision here is closely in line with 'the national interest' to develop an innovative society as directed by the key state agent – the Communist Party. Mobilisation of people includes acquiring financial, human and social resources to facilitate activities undertaken to gain support for and acceptance of new routines. Motivating others to achieve and sustain the vision consists of various activities undertaken to institutionalise change. One of the most prominent activities undertaken by CUG-IGE to mobilise people is to actively recruit the 'Yantze Scholars' globally with exclusive funding provided by the Central government, as well as to attract Chinese graduates from overseas universities (*Haigui* – Sea turtles) with incentive programs, such as tax benefits or provision of start-up capitals, to undertake business activities inside the Wuhan Future City. In order to achieve and sustain the vision for innovation, CUG-IGE also regularly conducts promotional seminars, inviting staff and students to attend so as to provide them with templates of successful business ventures and encourage them to start up their own high-tech companies. This is complemented by national media and various new venture fairs that encourage and promote high-tech entrepreneurship among university staff and students. Notwithstanding, only a small percentage of university staff and student population (including doctoral and postgraduate students) are capable of starting a new business while undertaking normal research and teaching work for staff, and curriculum study for students. However, the vision has been instilled, as many university staff and students show support for those colleagues and classmates who are able to establish their own businesses, and treat these types of entrepreneurial activities as heroic actions, or to a large extent, a norm.

In addition, key determinants of successful institutional entrepreneurs appear to possess four attributes: effective use of discourse, formal authority, social capital and adopting discursive strategies in the institutionalised fields (Battilana et al., 2009). In the context of CUG-IGE, several Communist Party members as embedded institutional entrepreneurs serve also as administrators, professors and research scientists in newly created enterprises. They are commissioned by the central government to use the current development path discourse and endeavour to convince different constituencies embedded in the existing institutions of the need to develop an innovative nation, thus the change of conventional educational role to graft the entrepreneurial paradigm into academic structures (Dooley and Kirk, 2007). Formal authority was given to university professors and administrators by the state via appointment of formal positions as enterprise CEOs, who also have access to a web of social relations with both human and social capitals to gain information and political support. Marquis and Raynard (2015) suggested that discursive institutional strategies were likely adopted by organisations in emerging markets to address competitive challenges. Use of rhetorical strategies to exploit the general fascination with novelty was also commonly favoured by institutional entrepreneurs (Zimmerman and Zeitz, 2002; Battilana et al., 2009, p. 85). For instance, setting up a College of Gem and Jewelry Design within CUG appears to be 'revolutionary', but discursive. Its associated four jewelry-related tourism firms would, at surface, not be considered as high-tech companies. However, tourism-related activities are indeed considered to be discursive for it is related to one of the strategic industries under the auspices of the twelfth national development plan, which focuses on environmental protection. Therefore, rhetoric discourses with discursive strategies appear to work hand-in-hand to facilitate the operation of GUI partnership inside the case of CUG-IGE.

In discussing the success factors for university–industry collaboration, Edmondson et al. (2012) provide three recommendations. First, the state needs to 'keep the ship steady' by providing ongoing financial support for long-term strategic partnership between university and industry. This might be the key concern for emerging economies such as China. As commented by Moeliodihardjo et al. (2012) in their study of GUI partnerships in Indonesia, a strong state commitment to provide sufficient resources is the key to developing the knowledge, consensus and innovation space in developing nations. Second, there is a greater need to give universities autonomy to form partnerships. Whilst this might be a general trend for some European universities as reported in Edmondson et al. (2012), research and development activities of Chinese universities are still largely controlled by the state. We see the majority of CEOs with Party memberships appointed by the state. These personnel are more or less required to follow the developmental direction of the Party, rather than react to demand, problems and opportunities presented by the market. Third, the state needs to appropriately reward collaborative individuals and universities and help them to strive for excellence. Companies want to work with the best individuals and organisations, they can't afford to do otherwise. However, current university personnel arrangement in China is that individual researchers belong to their specific designated university. In Wuhan alone, there are 48 universities in total, and each has its own agenda to develop S&T entrepreneurial program in order to gain more funding support from the central and provincial government. Therefore, there is relatively less collaborative effort made by individuals across different universities. This would present a big issue. Even though China currently has more financial resources to back up innovative activities, as compared to Indonesia (Moeliodihardjo et al., 2012) and other Asian or European countries, it would likely sacrifice the opportunity to advance the frontier of science and technology development, without proper collaboration and coordination. It is the collaboration and coordination that help best and most effectively use limited resources.

With the rise of a global knowledge economy, there is indeed a greater need for strategic partnerships of government–university–industry. In particular, world-class research universities are at the forefront of pioneering such partnerships, playing a greater role in advancing the national innovation system (Edmondson et al., 2012). However, as argued by Dooley and Kirk (2007), whilst the GUI partnership would result in increased knowledge creation and contribution to economic development, it has a recursive effect on the university norms. Nezu (2005) also comments on the complexity to balance the 'exogenous' (i.e. curiosity-driven invention) and 'endogenous' (i.e. market-driven innovation) component of the academic research community. In the context of China, there is another important institutional factor – The Party's guideline, which directs the research activities of universities to centre on the commercial gains and economic development. All Chinese universities are called upon to make full contributions towards the increased production in China, and student entrepreneurs are also much encouraged. Such emphasis on the eventual commercial relevance of basic research may create fear amongst certain academics that their scope for academic freedom may be impinged, and that key educational missions may be lost. In addition, students, who look for venture opportunities especially at the undergraduate level, may not focus on basic training and education in their specific field of expertise. This drawback could be overcome by an effective GUI partnership that helps create an impact on teaching and learning and modernise curricula to address a growing skills gap and fierce competition for global talent (Edmondson et al., 2012). Until then, it is generally believed that universities should not give way to the pressure to contribute to commercial gains at the expense of its academic missions (Nezu, 2005).

Conclusion

This chapter outlines the operation of one university-run company CUG-IGE and its associated 21 enterprises under the microscope of 'institutional entrepreneurship'. The strategic partnership of government–university–industry is seen as necessary to help legitimise universities as the important embedded agent under the existing institutionalised field (Battilana et al., 2009) to mobilise China's national vision of building an innovative country for the 21st century. It appears that Chinese universities also play a key role in frontier knowledge development, technology transfer and exploitation both locally and globally. Nonetheless, different to the former analysis of GUI partnership, that treat universities as knowledge brokers (Edmondson et al., 2012), CUG-IGE has built its own companies, acting as a unique institutional entrepreneur to graft the entrepreneurial paradigm onto academic structure (Dooley and Kirk, 2007).

The extensive reliance of CUG-IGE on the state financial support and developmental direction may limit its autonomy to respond to the changing market conditions. There is also a need for CUG-IGE to have joint inter-university collaboration and coordination to mobilise resources for effective exploration and exploitation of new research outputs. As CUG-IGE is still in its early stage of development, there are other hindrance and success factors that should be further investigated.

The limitation of the current study is to focus on only one university and one company. There are thousands of universities in China, and many would have engaged in GUI partnerships in S&T parks in Beijing, Shanghai and other cities. Future studies should enlarge the scope of the study to test the theory of institutional entrepreneurship on a range of universities to examine how embedded actors could shape the changing role of institutions, especially the university's role in promoting economic growth, innovation and entrepreneurship among the modern society.

China is still an engine for economic growth. With the state's determination to make the country into an innovative nation, likely the role of universities would experience a dramatic paradigm shift. The concern to some academics would be how much academic freedom should be compromised by the pressure to attend to commercial relevance. Should universities belong to the educational space or succumb to become an entrepreneurial sphere? Or should they be both? The answers to these questions would be inconclusive, and largely depend on the institutionalised field, on which individuals set their feet, searching for moral answers.

Acknowledgement

Thanks to the School of Economics and Management of China University of Geosciences for inviting me to spend three weeks of my academic study leave in Wuhan that enabled me to collect data. Professor Bai-xuan Wang's organization of site visits to Wuhan Future Technology City and many discussions with me during my visit in September 2015, which helped formulate the initial ideas of writing this chapter, is highly appreciated. All errors remain with the author.

Notes

1 CUG=China University of Geosciences (CUG) (Wuhan); IGE = Institute of Geo-Environment's Industry Technology Research (see http://ige-live.com. cn/gywm/gyyjj/2015-10-12/443.html). Currency exchange rate was set on 1 November 2015.
2 Size of CUG-IGE is in the range of 301–500 according to one of the China HR websites (http://www.chinahr.com/job/ffc3ae84cdb9d95428dfac63j.html), and is stated as a state-owned enterprise.
3 All 21 companies can be searched using Chinese names via the Wuhan Business Registration Website (http://wuhan.abisou.com), but none of them have their own separate websites (except where website addresses were shown), except the ones found under CUG-IGE website.
4 *These companies were not registered or can be found under Wuhan Business Registration Website.
5 After two years' establishment, CUG-IGE has a total of outputs valued at RMB¥30 Million accessed on 2 Nov. 2015 via http://voice.cug.edu.cn/news Details.shtml?newskindid=200907132000186709ikrueqHur73k&newsinfoid=20 151010095154312kD07diKfyUYRK).
6 Wuhan Feng-Da is part of 武汉中地大资产经营有限公司, which was registered under the Wuhan Business Registration Website with capitals of RMB¥48,900,000(=US$7.7 million).

References

Battilana, J. (2004) 'Foundations for a theory of institutional entrepreneurship: Solving the paradox of embedded agency', *INSEAD Working Paper Series*, 2004/61/OB, http://www.insead.edu/facultyresearch/research/details_papers. cfm?id=13978, accessed September 20, 2015.
Battilana, J. (2006) 'Agency and institutions: The enabling role of individuals' social position', *Organization*, 13(5): 653–76.
Battilana, J., Leca, B. and Boxenbaum, E. (2009) 'How actors change institutions: Towards a theory of institutional entrepreneurship', *The Academy of Management Annals*, 3(1): 65–107.
Carayannis, E.G., Alexander, J. and Hausler, D. (2014) 'Managing the intellectual capital within government-university-industry R&D partnerships: A framework for the engineering research centres', *Journal of Intellectual Capital*, 15(4): 611–30.
Carayannis, E.G., Alexander, J. and Hausler, D. (2015) Government-university-industry partnership, http://www.referenceforbusiness.com/management/Ex-Gov/Government-University-Industry-Partnerships.html#ixzz3qxiqfJ7R, accessed November 9, 2015.

Carayannis, E.G., Barth, T.D. and Campbell, D.F.J. (2012) 'The Quintuple Helix innovation model: Global warming as a challenge and driver for innovation', *Journal of Innovation and Entrepreneurship*, 1(2): 1–12.

Cendrowski, S. (2015) China's new 5-year plan is about growth, http://fortune.com/2015/10/30/chinas-new-5-year-plan-is-about-growth/, accessed December 22, 2015

DiMaggio, P.J. 1988. 'Interest and agency in institutional theory', In L. Zucker (Ed) *Institutional Patterns and Organisation*, pp 3–22, Cambridge, MA, Ballinger.

Dooley, L. and Kirk, D. (2007) 'University-industry collaboration: Grafting the entrepreneurial paradigm onto academic structures', *European Journal of Innovation Management*, 10(3): 316–32.

Dosi, G. (1988) 'Sources, procedures, and microeconomic effects of innovation', *Journal of Economic Literature*, 26(3): 1120–71.

Edmondson, G., Valigra, L., Kenward, M., Hudson, R.L. and Belfield, H. (2012) *Making Industry-University Partnership Work: Lessons from Successful Collaborations*, Science/Business Innovation Board, http://www.sciencebusiness.net/Assets/94fe6d15–5432–4cf9-a656–633248e63541.pdf, accessed November 3, 2015

Eisenstadt, S.N. (1980) 'Cultural orientations, institutional entrepreneurs, and social change: Comparative analysis of traditional civilisation', *American Journal of Sociology*, 85(4): 840–69.

Etzkowitz, H. (2003) 'Innovation in innovation: The triple helix of university-industry-government relations', *Social Science Information*, 42(3): 293–337.

Etzkowitz, H. and Leydesdorff, L. (2000) 'The dynamics of innovation: From National Systems and "Mode 2" to a Triple Helix of university–industry–government relations', *Research Policy*, 29: 109–23.

Farinha, L., Ferreira, J. and Gouveia, B. (2016) 'Networks of innovation and competitiveness: A Triple Helix case study', *Journal of Knowledge Economy*, 7(1): 259–75.

Fayolle, A. and Redford, D. (eds). (2014) *Handbook of entrepreneurial university*, Edward Elgar, Cheltenham.

Fernández-Lopez, S., Otero, L., Rodeiro, D. and Rodriguez (2009) 'Entrepreneurial university, transfer technology and funding: An empirical analysis', *Journal of Enterprising Culture*, 17(2): 147–79

Hsu, C.L. (2006) 'Market ventures moral logics, and ambiguity: Crafting a new Institutional patterns and organizations', *The Sociological Quarterly*, 47: 69–92.

KPMG (2011) China's 12th Five Year Plan: Overview, http://www.kpmg.com/CN/en/IssuesAndInsights/ArticlesPublications/Publicationseries/5-years-plan/Documents/China-12th-Five-Year-Plan-Overview-201104.pdf, accessed December 22, 2015.

Leca, B., Battilana, J. and Boxenbaum, E. (2010) 'Agency and institutions: A review of institutional entrepreneurship', *Working Paper series*, http://citeseerx.ist.psu.edu/viewdoc/download?doi=10.1.1.461.6523&rep=rep1&type=pdf, accessed September 27, 2015

Leydesdorff, L. (2012) The Triple Helix of university-industry-government relations, http://eprints.rclis.org/16559/1/The%20Triple%20Helix%20of%20University-Industry-Government%20Relations.Jan12.pdf, accessed March 10, 2016

Leydesdorff, L. and Etzkowitz, H. (1998) 'The Triple Helix as a model for innovation studies', *Science and Public Policy*, 25(3): 109–203.

Leydesdorff, L. and Park, H.W. (2014) 'Can synergy in Triple-Helix relations be quantified? A review of the development of the Triple-Helix indicator', *Triple Helix*, 1(4): 1–18.

Marquis, C. and Raynard, M. (2015) 'Institutional strategies in emerging markets', *The Academy of Management Annals*, 9(1): 291–335.

Moeliodihardjo, B.Y., Soemardi, B.W., Brodjonegoro, S.S. and Hatakenaka, S. (2012) 'University, industry and government partnership: Its present and future challenges in Indonesia', *Social and Behaviour Sciences*, 52: 307–16.

Nan, H. (2015) 'Technology gains global spotlight', *China Daily*, http://www.chinadaily.com.cn/cndy/2015–09/10/content_21837039.htm, accessed December 22, 2015

Nezu, R. (2005) 'Technology transfer, intellectual property and effective university-industry partnerships: The experience of China, India, Japan, Philippines, The Republic of Korea, Singapore and Thailand', *Fujitsu Research Institute*, http://www.wipo.int/edocs/pubdocs/en/intproperty/928/wipo_pub_928.pdf, accessed November 10, 2015.

Zimmerman, M.A. and Zeitz, G.J. (2002) 'Beyond survival: Achieving new venture growth by building legitimacy', *Academy of Management Review*, 27(3): 414–31.

7 The performance of the academic KIBS firms in a 'moderate innovator' country

A longitudinal analysis

Sara Fernández-López, María Jesús Rodríguez-Gulías and *David Rodeiro-Pazos*

Introduction

In a knowledge-based economy, the Knowledge-Intensive Business Services (KIBS) firms are considered 'value drivers' given that they act as a catalyst for innovation systems (Castaldi 2009; Castellaci 2008; Fernandes and Ferreira 2013). They play a key role in the development and commercialisation of new products, processes and services (Muller and Doloreux 2009). KIBS firms are also a source of innovation for other firms (Den Hertog 2000; Muller and Doloreux 2009), partly due to the fact that they carry new ideas and practices from one firm to another (Smedlund and Toivonen 2007). As providers of knowledge-intensive services, the location of KIBS firms in a particular territory is often seen as a way to leverage regional competitiveness, even in non-KIBS firms in the surrounding region (Fernandes and Ferreira 2013).

Universities contribute substantially to the creation of these KIBS firms by spinning off new companies (university spin-offs or USOs) that apply research-developed knowledge to commercial ends. Over the period 2000–2010, the Spanish universities have particularly been active in the creation of KIBS firms; one out of four firms launched by them could be considered a KIBS firm. Moreover, while the number of professional KIBS firms (firms in legal activities, accountancy, registration and audit jobs, tax consultancy, market studies and publicity) remained residual, the share of technological KIBS firms (firms operating in information technologies research and development, engineering and architectural practices and consultancy, testing and analytical activities industries) in the USO activity stayed virtually constant over the decade, suggesting the considerable importance of this industry in the universities' activities of knowledge transfer (Calvo et al. 2016).

These academic KIBS firms can be seen as an instrument to simultaneously leverage strategic entrepreneurship and knowledge spillovers, both critical aspects to the process of constructing regional competitiveness (Agarwal et al. 2007; Fernandes et al. 2013). Being conscious of the universities' potential contribution to move towards an economic model based on knowledge and innovation, public governments have supported the creation of USOs in an effort to build the knowledge economy (Benneworth and Charles 2005). As a result, in many countries, a large amount of public funds have been invested in university-based entrepreneurship (Wright et al. 2008), which only makes sense if this entrepreneurship actually works as an effective way of setting up firms with growth potential. However, knowledge of the long-term performance of this kind of firm is limited (Löwegren and Bengtsson 2010).

The main goal of this chapter is to analyse the long-term performance of the KIBS firms launched by universities: if academic KIBS firms perform similarly to non-academic KIBS firms, the funding effort aimed at promoting the former would not make sense. Particularly, using a sample of 135 KIBS firms (academic and non-academic) over the period 2000–2010, we analysed whether academic KIBS firms grow more than non-academic KIBS firms. To the best of our knowledge, no study has explicitly focused on the analysis of the academic KIBS firms' growth. However, knowing what factors might influence the growth of this kind of firm could help policy makers to better design their supportive policies. On the basis of our results, we propose some policies to foster the growth of KIBS firms, which we consider the most significant contribution of this paper.

To achieve our goal, we have structured this work as follows. After this introduction, in the second section, we present the theoretical framework that allows us to establish the hypothesis investigated in this study. In the third section, the sample and the data are described. In the fourth section, the variables and the econometric models used are presented. Next, we provide the empirical results and conclude with the main findings and recommendations.

Theoretical framework

Over the last two decades, as the efforts geared towards promoting the university-based entrepreneurship increased, a stream of empirical literature on USOs began examining whether these firms grow more than other similar firms (non-USOs). According to the resource-based view theory (Penrose 1959; Wernerfelt 1984), a firm's success lies in the capacity to collect and deploy its resources, namely technological, human, social, financial, physical and organisational resources (Brush et al. 2001), leading to strong capabilities (Barney 1991). Drawing on the Resource Based View of the firm, different studies have tested if the resources and capabilities allow USOs to outgrow non-USOs but have led to inconsistent results (Cantner and Goethner 2011; Colombo and Piva 2005; Criaco et al. 2014; Enseley and Hmieleski 2005; George et al. 2002; Ortín and Vendrell 2010, 2014; Salvador 2010; Wennberg et al. 2011; Zahra et al. 2007; Zhang 2009).

To the best of our knowledge, none of these studies have focused on the academic KIBS firms, although they represent a significant share of the firms spun-off from universities (Calvo et al. 2016) and present common features that make them a homogenous group. Particularly, the activity of KIBS firms can be seen as connecting external knowledge sources (i.e., multinationals, research centres, universities, etc.) to the individual needs of customers (Scarso and Bolisani 2010).

Therefore, the KIBS firms' success strongly depends on their capability to manage knowledge flows among different players. Since knowledge is the major resource that KIBS firms handle, we analysed the growth of KIBS firms under the lens of the knowledge-based theory of a firm (Grant 1996), which may be understood as an extension of the RBV where knowledge has a dominant role over other resources.

According to Gallouj (2002), knowledge is not the only asset that KIBS use most intensively; it is also what they sell. Since academic KIBS firms are created in a university context, they are initially endowed with cutting-edge research knowledge, which may act as a source of the potential growth differences among academic KIBS firms and non-academic KIBS firms.

In addition, the highly-educated employees of the KIBS firms make up a significant part of the pool of their available knowledge (Castaldi et al. 2010). In KIBS firms, knowledge embedded in employees and in their relationships defines their organisational capabilities (Larsen 2001). In this sense, the technical skills and research experience of academic founders, as well as their permanent contact with the academic research context, may increase the quality and relevance of the knowledge transferred as a service (Colombo and Piva 2005; Rothaermel and Thursby 2005), benefitting academic KIBS firms. Moreover, KIBS firms usually create knowledge in a process of dynamic interactions with clients (Scarso and Bolisani 2010). Thus, expert knowledge of the KIBS firms needs to be continuously adapted to the requirements of clients in an interactive learning process (Muller and Zenker 2001). Academic entrepreneurs are actively engaged in their own learning in an interactive context, therefore they are more accustomed to interactive learning processes.

Finally, the links of academic KIBS firms with the parent universities can facilitate access to additional resources (financial resources, networks, physical resources, etc.), other than knowledge but equally necessary for the firms' success. Thus, universities may act as intermediaries between these firms and external stakeholders (i.e., clients, suppliers or investors) (Cantner and Goethner 2011; George et al. 2002). Another positive effect is the improved firm image as a result of its connectedness in the university. Furthermore, universities tend to provide academic KIBS firms with business support services as business incubators, business consultancy and training, and even financial resources (Calvo et al. 2013).

In sum, drawing on the knowledge-based theory of firms, we argue that the initial resources endowment of academic KIBS firms, namely cutting-edge research knowledge, founders with a research background and in the habit of interactive learning processes, and access to other conveniences are directly related to the quality and relevance of the knowledge transferred as a service. Therefore, we hypothesised that the academic KIBS firms would grow more than non-academic KIBS firms.

Academic KIBS firms in Spain: the sample and data

Traditionally, the studies on USOs have dealt with a paucity of data thus limiting research in the field (Zhang 2009). This is primarily due to the lack of a common definition of a USO (Aceytuno and Cáceres 2009). As we used the information provided by the Spanish Network of University of Technology Transfer Offices (Red OTRI) as the primary data source, we followed the definition established by Red OTRI in its reports: 'University spin-offs are companies generated to exploit the results from university research' (Red OTRI 2007).

USOs are a relatively recent phenomenon in the Spanish University System compared to other countries (e.g., the USA or the United Kingdom, among others). However, since 2001 there has been an incredible effort geared towards the creation of this kind of company (Figure 7.1). As a result, the number of USOs has increased significantly over the decade 2000–2010. Moreover, after 2006, the Spanish universities have annually created over 100 USOs. In spite of this significant growth, the spin-off activity has been concentrated in a few universities. Thus, around five to six universities are far more active than the rest, while half of all Spanish universities hardly create one spin-off annually (Barro and Fernández 2015).

As previously mentioned, Red OTRI provided us with a list of around 700 USOs established before January 1, 2011. In addition, we also used the database constructed by Rodeiro et al. (2008), which included 317 USOs mainly created before 2005. Once we unified both databases, any duplication was removed. Then, we managed to identify the USOs in the 'Sistema Anual de Balances Ibéricos' (SABI) database, which was used to obtain the firm-specific characteristics and the financial performance of USOs at the next stage. At the end of this process, the sample consisted of 547 USOs created between January 1, 1998 and December 31, 2010 (Figure 7.2).

Once the initial sample of USOs was defined, we looked for similar firms created in a non-university context. In so doing, we relied on quasi-experimental methods for estimating average treatment effects. Rosenbaum and Rubin (1983) proposed propensity score matching (PSM) as a method to reduce the bias in the estimation of treatment effects with observational (non-randomised) datasets. In our study, since it was impossible to simultaneously observe the

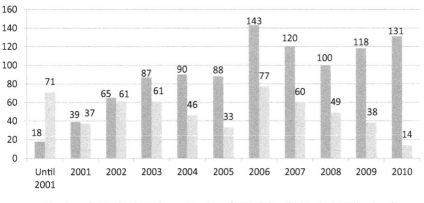

Figure 7.1 Number of university spin-offs

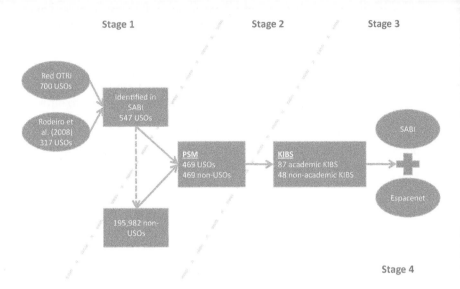

Figure 7.2 Preparation of the study sample

outcome of the same firm both under 'a university origin' and without 'a university origin', we used a matching procedure to identify a valid control group, which allows for outcome comparison between USOs and non-USOs (Caliendo and Kopeinig, 2005).

Hence, we created an initial sample of non-USOs by using SABI. Eligibility criteria required firms to have been created in the same period as USOs (i.e., between January 1, 1998 and December 31, 2010), and located in any of the autonomous communities where the USOs were also located, as well as having a sectorial code (NACE-2009) equal to any of the USOs in the sample. After applying these criteria, a total of 195,982 non-USOs were available.

Then, the PSM method was applied to reduce the selection bias of both comparable samples. As a result, we obtained two sub-samples consisting of 469 USOs and 469 non-USOs. To assess the matching quality, we tested whether the samples of USOs and non-USOs were significantly different in the mean values of the matching variables prior to matching and post-matching. The absence of statistically significant differences between samples after matching indicated that the process yielded good results.

In order to analyse the performance of the academic KIBS firms, similarly to Fernandes and Ferreira (2013), we identified two types of KIBS: (1) technological KIBS, involving information technologies research and development, engineering and architectural practices and consultancy, testing and analytical activities industries (NACE codes: 721, 722, 723, 724, 725, 729, 731, 732, 742, 743), and (2) professional KIBS, involving legal activities, accountancy, registration and audit jobs, tax consultancy, market studies and publicity (NACE codes: 741, 744, 745, 748).

Following this classification, the sample of 469 USOs included two professional KIBS firms (0.43 percent of the sample of USOs) and 85 technological KIBS companies (18.12 percent of the sample of USOs). In contrast, in the sample of non-USOs, four could be considered professional KIBS firms (0.85 percent of the sample), whereas 44 were technological KIBS (9.38 percent of the sample). Therefore, universities have been particularly active in the creation of KIBS companies, since more than one out of every six spin-offs launched by them could be considered a KIBS firm. Moreover, while the number of professional KIBS remained residual, the share of technological KIBS in the university spin-off activity has stayed virtually constant over the decade, suggesting the considerable importance of this industry in the universities' activities of knowledge transfer. Figure 7.3 depicts the distribution of KIBS firms in the sub-samples.

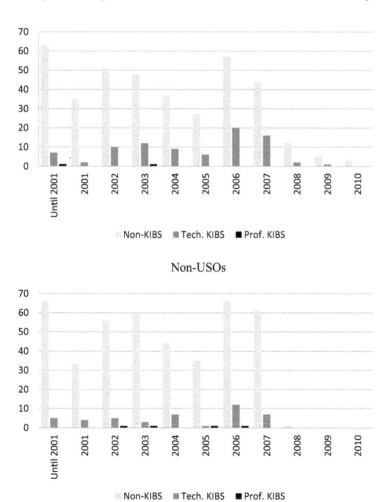

Figure 7.3 Distribution of KIBS firms in the sub-samples

Finally, we constructed a longitudinal dataset (2000–2010), combining data from two sources: SABI database to collect information regarding firm-specific characteristics and financial performance, and ESPACENET database to gather data on patent activity.

Methodology: definition of the variables and model specification

Growth is considered to be the most common indicator of performance in new firms, with employment and sales being widespread indicators (Wennberg et al. 2011). In particular, employment growth indicates the necessity of additional resources to fulfil clients' demands (Cantner and Goethner 2011) and seems to be an adequate measure when efforts are geared towards the creation of firms and employment (Ferguson and Olofsson 2004). However, employment growth may be artificially sustained by some agents that are willing to provide the firm with the resources to continue (Ferguson and Olofsson 2004), which can give rise to a phenomenon known as the 'living dead' (Hayter 2010). Furthermore, employment growth depends on the changes in workforce productivity caused by technological advances. Hence, a firm could grow without needing an increase in its staff.

To overcome these limitations of the 'employment growth' as an indicator in the analysis of firm growth, we also used the 'sales growth', even though it also has limitations. Thus, there is the possibility that a firm experiences growth before any sales at all. This is the case for most of the new firms that are technology intensive and need a long pre-commercial stage to develop technologies or proofs of concept before moving into the market maturity stage.

Therefore, we estimated separate models for employment growth and sales growth. Following Wennberg et al. (2011), we used the formula ln (size$_i$, t/size$i$, t − 1) to calculate the respective growth rates. The main independent variable, ACADKIBS, is a time-invariant dummy variable that takes the value 1 if the firm is an academic KIBS firm, and 0 otherwise. In addition, a number of independent variables were included, related to the firm-specific characteristics, firm financial performance and innovation characteristics (see Table 7.1).

Regarding firm-specific characteristics, firm size was measured as the natural logarithm of the firm assets (LN_ASSETS). Similarly, we also used the natural logarithm of the age of the firm (LN_AGE). In addition, we used the firm size and age squared to capture potential non-linearities. Age is closely related to firm size, and, in some cases, both variables are considered to represent the same phenomenon, and both have a direct influence on firms' growth (Coad 2009).

As proxies of firm financial performance, we used two financial ratios: the return on assets (ROA), i.e., net income divided by total assets, and the total asset turnover ratio (TOT_TUR), which measures sales relative to total assets. The evolutionary interpretation of the relationship between financial performance and firm growth indicates that firms face an ongoing fight to grow and only those with superior financial performance will be able to gain additional market share (Coad 2009).

Table 7.1 Definitions of independent variables and predictions

Variable	Measures	
Group 1: firm-specific characteristics		
Academic KIBS	*acadkibs (+)*	1 if the firm is an academic KIBS firm
Size	*ln_assets (+)*	Natural logarithm of the firm assets
	ln_assetssquar (–)	Natural logarithm of the firm assets squared
Age	*ln_age (+)*	Natural logarithm of the firm age
	ln_agesquar (–)	Natural logarithm of the firm age squared
Group 2: firm financial performance		
Return on assets	*roa (+)*	Net income divided by total assets
Total asset turnover	*tot_tur (+)*	Sales divided by total assets
Group 3: innovation characteristics		
Innovation	*npat_a (–)*	Number of the firm's patent applications annually filed
	npat_g (+)	Number of the firm's patent annually granted

Finally, patents were considered as proxies for the innovation activity of firms. Two patent measures were used: the number of the firm's patent applications annually filed at the Spanish Patent and Trademark Office, the European Patent Office (EPO), the US Patent and Trademark Office (USPTO) or submitted to a Patent Cooperation Treaty (NPAT_A), and the number of the patents annually granted by the Spanish Patent and Trademark Office, the EPO and the USPTO (NPAT_G). Despite endogenous growth models needing several filtering mechanisms for a significant relationship between innovation and economic growth to exist (March and Yagüe 2014), it is generally accepted that the higher the innovative capacity of firms, the higher their economic growth.

To analyse whether academic KIBS firms grow more than non-academic KIBS firms we used the panel data methodology, specifically carried out with GLS. Unlike cross-sectional analysis, panel data allow us to control for individual heterogeneity. This point is crucial in the analysis as the decision to be an academic firm is very closely related to firm specificity and, more importantly, the effect of being an academic firm on firm growth is strongly linked to the specificity of each firm. Therefore, to eliminate the risk of obtaining biased results, we controlled for this heterogeneity by modelling as an individual effect, α_i. Consequently, the basic specification of our model is as follows:

$$Growth_{it} = \beta_1 acadkibs + (\beta_2 ln\_age_{it} + \beta_3 ln\_agesquar_{it} + \beta_4 ln\_assets_{it} + \beta_5 ln\_assetssquar_{it}) + (\beta_6 roa_{it} + \beta_7 tot\_tur_{it}) + (\beta_8 npat\_a_{it} + \beta_9 npat\_g_{it}) + \alpha_i + \lambda_t + \varepsilon_{it}$$

where the error term has several components, besides the abovementioned individual or firm-specific effect (α_i): λ_t measures the time-specific effect using the time dummy variables, so that we can control for the effects of macroeconomic variables on firm growth and v_{it} is the random disturbance.

Since the main independent variable (*acadkibs*) is time-invariant, in the first stage of the strategy we used random effects models.

Empirical analysis

Univariate analysis

Table 7.2 shows the descriptive statistics of the dependent and independent variables. This information is displayed both for the global sample and for the two sub-samples (academic KIBS and non-academic KIBS firms). Table 7.2 also shows the difference in means for the variables used in the empirical analysis between academic KIBS firms and non-academic KIBS firms. The *t*-statistic was used to test the equality of means.

On average, the academic KIBS firms had higher sales growth rates (325.8 percent) than non-academic KIBS firms (43.3 percent), but the difference between sub-samples was not statistically significant. Similarly, the employment growth rates of the academic KIBS firms were also higher (55.3 percent than that of non-academic KIBS firms (17.0 percent), although in this case the difference was significant.

The KIBS firms in the sample had an average age of 4.2 years and were small and medium-sized enterprises (SMEs). In addition, the average ROA was negative in both the global sample (–14.2 percent) and sub-samples (–12 percent and –17.9 percent).

Nevertheless, the total asset turnover ratio showed significant differences between sub-samples. Hence, non-academic KIBS firms were shown to have a turnover asset ratio significantly higher (1.855) than academic KIBS firms (0.715), suggesting that the former are using assets to generate sales more efficiently than the latter. In fact, academic KIBS firms were significantly larger than non-academic KIBS firms in terms of assets. The previous descriptive results suggest that academic KIBS firms could have an amount of assets that are not being efficiently used to generate income.

The average number of patents filed and granted during the period of analysis was 0.273 and 0.062, respectively. The average values of both variables were significantly higher in the academic KIBS firms, indicating that academic KIBS are more innovative than non-academic KIBS, to some extent.

The correlation matrix of the independent continuous variables and the dependents variables are shown in Table 7.3.

Multivariate analysis

Table 7.4 presents random effects GLS models on sales growth and employment growth. To know whether academic KIBS firms grow more than non-academic KIBS firms, different empirical models were estimated. Model 1 considered the

Table 7.2 Descriptive statistics

Variable	Global sample		Academic KIBS		Non-academic KIBS		t-test	
	Mean	Std. Dev.	Mean	Std. Dev.	Mean	Std. Dev.	t	P>0
g_sales[1]	2.066	13.733	3.258	17.956	0.433	1.133	-2.204	0.986
g_emp[1]	0.400	1.103	0.553	1.262	0.170	0.753	-3.589***	0.000
age[1]	4.239	2.608	4.149	2.533	4.394	2.728	1.276	0.202
total assets[1]	993.718	2969.292	1432.363	3670.785	260.386	434.393	-5.115***	0.000
Roa	-0.142	2.321	-0.120	0.976	-0.179	3.557	-0.318	0.751
tot_tur	1.168	1.429	0.715	0.912	1.855	1.761	10.764***	0.000
npat_a	0.273	1.143	0.436	1.420	0.000	0.000	-5.251***	0.000
npat_g	0.062	0.349	0.098	0.438	0.000	0.000	-3.840***	0.000

Notes: [1] Variables are not in logs. * p < 0.1; ** p < 0.05; *** p < 0.01.

Table 7.3 Correlation matrix

	1	2	3	4	5	6	7	8	9	10
1 ln_g_sales	1									
2 ln_g_emp	0.2182*	1								
3 ln_age	-0.3267*	-0.3016*	1							
4 ln_agesquar	-0.2974*	-0.2862*	0.9505*	1						
5 ln_assets	0.0722	0.1958*	0.4271*	0.3931*	1					
6 ln_assetssquar	0.0737	0.1864*	0.4110*	0.3873*	0.9749*	1				
7 roa	0.0928*	0.1379*	0.002	0.0087	0.1407*	0.0946*	1			
8 tot_tur	-0.0308	-0.0805	-0.0118	-0.0317	-0.3983*	-0.3911*	-0.3917*	1		
9 npat_a	-0.0216	0.0438	0.0019	-0.0011	0.1747*	0.2072*	0.0011	-0.1370*	1	
10 npat_g	-0.0133	0.0265	-0.0291	-0.0337	0.0977*	0.1122*	-0.0053	-0.1202*	0.7073*	1

Notes: Table shows the Pearson correlation coefficients for the continuous variables considered in the empirical analysis. *$p < 0.05$; **$p < 0.01$; ***$p < 0.001$

Table 7.4 Panel regressions on sales growth and employment growth

	Sales growth				Employment growth			
	Model 1	Model 2	Model 3	Model 4	Model 1	Model 2	Model 3	Model 4
acadkibs	0.340***	0.309**	0.364***	0.358***	0.270***	0.176**	0.257***	0.259***
	(0.089)	(0.098)	(0.098)	(0.097)	(0.061)	(0.062)	(0.073)	(0.073)
yr2002c	0.418	0.011	0.016	0.058	0.454*	0.216	0.234	0.273
	(0.244)	(0.204)	(0.200)	(0.192)	(0.226)	(0.208)	(0.252)	(0.260)
yr2003c	1.066***	0.537	0.498	0.263	0.680***	0.393**	0.362*	0.295
	(0.305)	(0.316)	(0.316)	(0.215)	(0.144)	(0.152)	(0.171)	(0.161)
yr2004c	0.712**	0.304	0.284	0.247	0.387**	0.154	0.135	0.127
	(0.226)	(0.216)	(0.218)	(0.220)	(0.128)	(0.127)	(0.136)	(0.141)
yr2005c	0.596***	0.286	0.251	0.242	0.308***	0.105	0.054	0.057
	(0.162)	(0.158)	(0.158)	(0.162)	(0.093)	(0.116)	(0.111)	(0.114)
yr2006c	0.538***	0.329**	0.285*	0.278*	0.238**	0.089	0.049	0.069
	(0.124)	(0.124)	(0.125)	(0.127)	(0.086)	(0.098)	(0.101)	(0.103)
yr2007c	0.502***	0.236	0.184	0.171	0.283***	0.111	0.049	0.060
	(0.117)	(0.122)	(0.124)	(0.122)	(0.073)	(0.081)	(0.085)	(0.087)
yr2008c	0.483***	0.256*	0.201	0.205	0.312***	0.179*	0.141	0.152
	(0.117)	(0.118)	(0.121)	(0.124)	(0.084)	(0.087)	(0.091)	(0.094)
yr2009c	0.024	-0.074	-0.085	-0.097	0.062	-0.008	-0.021	-0.014
	(0.124)	(0.121)	(0.121)	(0.120)	(0.065)	(0.066)	(0.070)	(0.071)
ln_age		-2.631***	-2.687***	-2.959***		-1.028**	-1.008**	-1.041**
		(0.512)	(0.505)	(0.465)		(0.349)	(0.342)	(0.339)
ln_agesquar		0.667***	0.678***	0.769***		0.212*	0.205	0.216*
		(0.161)	(0.158)	(0.145)		(0.107)	(0.105)	(0.105)
ln_assets		0.340	0.503*	0.258		0.304*	0.395***	0.353**
		(0.217)	(0.249)	(0.160)		(0.119)	(0.106)	(0.117)
ln_assetssquar		-0.020	-0.031	-0.009		-0.017	-0.023**	-0.019*
		(0.019)	(0.020)	(0.013)		(0.009)	(0.008)	(0.009)

(Continued)

Table 7.4 (Continued)

	Sales growth				Employment growth			
	Model 1	Model 2	Model 3	Model 4	Model 1	Model 2	Model 3	Model 4
roa			0.022*	0.024*			0.033*	0.034*
			(0.011)	(0.011)			(0.013)	(0.013)
tot_tur			0.088*	0.083			0.094	0.094
			(0.044)	(0.047)			(0.051)	(0.051)
npat_a				-0.048				0.017
				(0.062)				(0.040)
npat_g				-0.056				-0.126
				(0.270)				(0.128)
_cons	-0.193*	1072	0.448	1.314*	-0.186***	-0.157	-0.611	-0.474
	(0.088)	(0.822)	(0.936)	(0.574)	(0.056)	(0.369)	(0.399)	(0.401)
Firm-year obs.	464	464	464	456	433	433	417	409
Unique firms	118	118	118	117	111	111	109	108
Wald χ^2	55.56***	126.11***	435.95***	416.76***	57.59***	152.81***	255.42***	261.05***

Notes: This table presents the results for random effects GLS models on sales growth and employment growth. Robust standard errors are in parenthesis. *p < 0.05; **p < 0.01; ***p < 0.001.

principal independent variable (*acadkibs*) and the dummy variables controlling for the time effect. In Models 2, 3 and 4 variables for the firm-specific characteristics, financial performance and innovation activity of firms were added.

In all the estimated models the independent variable for academic KIBS firms (*acadkibs*) was positively related with growth. These results supported the hypothesis that the academic KIBS firms grow more than the non-academic KIBS firms, suggesting that university origin is an advantage in the KIBS industry.

We also found a U-shaped relationship between age and KIBS firms' growth in terms of both sales and employment. The results suggest that during the early stage of firms, the growth capacity reduces over time, but, after reaching a given age, growth is positively correlated with the age of KIBS firms. In general, therefore, it seems that the experience gained in the market would help to leverage firm growth.

In the case of employment growth, the results also indicated the existence of non-linear effects of firm assets on KIBS firms' growth; larger KIBS firms showed higher employment rates, but beyond a certain size, the relation was reversed (negative). Regarding firm financial performance, the ROA was positively related to firm growth in terms of both sales and employment. A possible explanation for this might be that high ROA are a precondition for the generation of internal funding, which allows KIBS firms to grow organically funded. This way of funding firms' growth has been more and more important in the Spanish economy since 2007, when the bank credit availability, the traditional source of external funding for the Spanish firms, was drastically cut as a result of the economic downturn. This cutback strongly affected those firms whose main assets are intangible, which cannot be used as a guarantee of credits. This could be the case of KIBS firms, where their core assets are mainly knowledge (Miles et al. 1995).

Finally, neither firms' asset efficiency, measured by total asset turnover ratio, or innovation activity were shown to have effects on the KIBS firms' growth. Regarding innovation activity, these results may be due to the fact that patents are not a good proxy for innovation when the knowledge that firms commercialise is mostly tacit and uncodifiable, and, therefore, difficult to protect. This could be the case for a great share of the KIBS firms in the sample.

Conclusions and recommendations

The innovation system's capacity to be actually innovative depends on the creation of externalities through interactions between the actors within the system (firms, government, universities and liaison organisations). KIBS firms act as a catalyst in innovation systems and, in particular, academic KIBS firms are an instrument to leverage strategic entrepreneurship and knowledge spillovers by applying research-developed knowledge to commercial ends. In this study, using a sample of 135 KIBS firms (academic and non-academic) over the decade 2000–2010 we found that the academic KIBS firms grew more than the non-academic KIBS firms, suggesting that university origin is an advantage in the KIBS industry.

These results may indicate that the initial resource endowment of cutting-edge research knowledge and human resources with a research background is a competitive advantage for the academic KIBS firms. Similarly, the academic KIBS firms might be benefiting from other conveniences provided by the links with parent universities (established networks, positive image effects, incubation infrastructures and financial resources, among others).

The obtained evidence suggests the convenience of supporting university-based entrepreneurship by public administrations and by the universities, in so doing they are promoting economic growth and social development in their surroundings. These results also highlight the necessity of designing specific support policies for academic KIBS firms.

The employment and sales growth rates of the academic KIBS firms were higher than non-academic KIBS firms but the difference between sub-samples is only statistically significant for the employment. In this sense, academic KIBS could be hiring researchers of their university research groups. It could happen that a certain number of companies may be creating a university spin-off as a 'plan B' to externalize those projects that have not been developed within the university because of the difficulties currently faced by researchers in obtain public funds.

We also found a U-shaped relationship between age and KIBS firms' growth. Stemming from this result, we recommend establishing long-term programmes to support academic KIBS firms. Overall, the Spanish universities have developed mechanisms nearly exclusively focused on creating USOs. However, once academic KIBS firms have been launched, they face different constraints, challenges and needs (becoming global, financing growth . . .). Therefore, mentoring programs for USOs in the next stages of lifecycle are required.

Firm financial performance, measured as return of assets, was positively related to firm growth. As previously stated, the restriction of bank credit availability makes KIBS firms use financial resources internally generated for which having positive returns on assets is required. In this sense our proposal is to increase specific public funds dedicated to this kind of firms as they play a key role in innovation systems.

Finally, our results showed that academic KIBS are more innovative than non-academic. Therefore, university origin appears to contribute to create a firm culture that affects firm innovation. In this sense, authorities should support instruments to facilitate the transformation of this innovation in marketable product and technologies.

This study contributes to the research on the performance of the academic KIBS firms in a 'moderate innovator' country such as Spain. To the best of our knowledge, no study has explicitly focused on the analysis of the academic KIBS firms' growth. In addition, previous results showed some particularities of Spain which might be extended to other countries at a similar stage of experience in the creation of academic KIBS firms. On the basis of these results, we have proposed some general policies to foster the KIBS firms' growth. However, this paper also presents some limitations that could open the way for further research.

In particular, the lack of access to variables such as the founders' experience and managerial skills prevented a more thorough analysis over the long-term for these firms. Future research on this topic might benefit from collecting this kind of information.

References

Aceytuno, M. and Cáceres, F. (2009) 'Elementos para elaboración de un marco de análisis para el fenómeno de las spin-offs universitarias', *Revista de economía mundial*, 23: 23–52.

Agarwal, R., Audretsch, D. and Sarker, M.B. (2007) 'The process of creative construction: Knowledge spillovers, entrepreneurship and economic growth', *Strategic Entrepreneurship Journal*, 1(3–4): 263–86.

Barney, J.B. (1991) 'Firm resources and sustained competitive advantage', *Journal of Management*, 17(1): 99–120.

Barro, S. and Fernández, S. (2015) 'De la I+D al tejido productivo: luces y sombras', in *La transferencia de I+D, la innovación y el emprendimiento en las universidades. Educación Superior en Iberoamérica. Informe 2015. Ed. Barro, S.*, CINDA, Chile: 471–512.

Benneworth, P. and Charles, D. (2005) 'University spin-off policies and economic development in less successful regions: Learning from two decades of policy practice', *European Planning Studies*, 13(4): 537–57.

Brush, C.G., Greene, P.G. and Hart, M.M. (2001) 'From initial idea to unique advantage: The entrepreneurial challenge of constructing a resource base', *Academy of Management Executive*, 15(1): 64–78.

Caliendo, M. and Kopeining, S. (2005) 'Some practical guidance for the implementation of propensity score matching', IZA Discussion Paper n° 1588.

Calvo, N., Rodeiro-Pazos, D. and Fernández-Rodríguez, S. (2016) 'Science and Technology Parks (STPs) as accelerators of Knowledge-Intensive Business Services (KIBS). A case study', *International Journal of Business and Globalisation*, in press.

Calvo, N., Rodeiro-Pazos, D. and Soares, I. (2013) 'Are USOs more supported to compete than spin-offs not linked to universities? A dynamic overview and proposal of model of USOs support', *International Journal of Innovation and Learning*, 14(3/4): 271–88.

Cantner, U. and Goethner, M. (2011) 'Performance differences between academic spin-offs and non-academic star-ups: A comparative analysis using a non-parametric matching approach', *DIME Final Conference*, Maastricht, 6–8 April.

Castaldi, C. (2009) 'The relative weight of manufacturing and services in Europe: An innovation perspective', *Technological Forecasting and Social Change*, 76(6): 709–22.

Castaldi, C., Faber, J. and Kishna, M. (2010) 'Co-innovation by KIBS in environmental services: A resource-based view'. (ECIS working paper series; 2010.05). Eindhoven: Technische Universiteit Eindhoven.

Castellacci, F. (2008) 'Technological paradigms, regimes and trajectories: Manufacturing and service industries in a new taxonomy of sectoral patterns of innovation', *Research Policy*, 37: 978–94.

Coad, A. (2009) *The growth of firms – A survey of theories and empirical evidence, New perspectives on the modern corporation*, Edward Elgar, Cheltenham, Northampton.

Colombo, M.G. and Piva, E. (2005) 'Are academic start-ups different? A matched pair analysis'. IRIS Working Paper.

Criaco, G., Serarols, C., Minola, T. and Bhatiya, A. (2014) 'Companies spun out of universities: Different typologies for different performance patterns', In F. Therin (Ed) *Handbook of Research in Techno-Entrepreneurship*, pp 235–61, Cheltenham, UK, Edward Elgard.

Den Hertog, P. (2000) 'Knowledge-intensive business services as co-producers of innovation', *International Journal of Innovation Management*, 4(4): 491–528.

Ensley, M.D. and Hmieleski, K.M. (2005) 'A comparative study of new venture top management team composition, dynamics and performance between university-based and independent start-ups', *Research Policy*, 34: 1091–105.

Ferguson, R. and Olofsson, C. (2004) 'Science parks and the development of NTBFs: Location, survival and growth', *The Journal of Technology Transfer*, 29: 5–17.

Fernandes, C. and Ferreira, J. (2013) 'Knowledge spillovers: Cooperation between university and KIBS', *R&D Management*, 43(5): 461–72.

Fernandes, C., Ferreira, J. and Raposo, M. (2013) 'Drivers to firm innovation and their effects on performance: An international comparison', *International Entrepreneurship and Management Journal*, 43(5): 461–72.

Gallouj, F. (2002) 'Knowledge intensive business services: Processing knowledge and producing innovation', In J. Gadrey and F. Gallouj (Eds) *Productivity, Innovation and Knowledge in Services*, pp 256–84, Cheltenham, Northampton, Edward Elgar.

George, G., Zahra, S.A. and Wood, D.R. (2002) 'The effects of business – university alliances on innovative output and financial performance: A study of publicly traded biotechnology companies', *Journal of Business Venturing*, 17: 577–609.

Grant, R.M. (1996) 'Toward a knowledge-based theory of the firm', *Strategic Management Journal*, 17: 109–22.

Hayter, C.S. (2010) *The open innovation imperative: Perspectives on success from faculty entrepreuners*, George Washington University, Washington, DC.

Larsen, J.N. (2001) 'Knowledge, human resources and social practice: The knowledge-intensive business service firm as a distributed knowledge system', *The Service Industries Journal*, 21(1): 81–102.

Löwegren, M. and Bengtsson, L. (2010) 'University spin-offs in Sweden: A longitudinal study', *Industry & Higher Education*, 24(3): 219–25.

March, I. and Yagüe, R.M. (2014) 'Innovation and performance in Technology-based firms: A comparative analysis', INBAM Conference, Barcelona, June 24–27, 2014.

Miles, I., Kastrinos, N., Flanagan, K., Bilderbeek, R., Den Hertog, P., Hutink, W. and Bouman, M. (1995) 'Knowledge-intensive business services: Users, carriers and sources of innovation', DG13 SPRINT-EIMS, no. 15, Luxembourg: EC.

Muller, E. and Doloreux, D. (2009) 'What we should know about knowledge-intensive business services', *Technology in Society*, 31: 64–72.

Muller, E. and Zenker, A. (2001) 'Business services as actors of knowledge transformation: The role of KIBS in regional and national innovation systems', *Research Policy*, 30: 1501–16.

Ortin, P. and Vendrell, F. (2010) 'Why do university spin-offs attract more venture capitalists?', *Venture Capital*, 12(4): 285–306.

Ortín, P. and Vendrell, F. (2014) 'University spin-offs vs. other NTBFs: Total factor productivity differences at outset and evolution', *Technovation*, 34(2): 101–12.

Penrose, E.T. (1959) *The theory of the growth of the firm*, Basil Blackwell, Oxford.

Red OTRI de Universidades (2007) *Informe de la encuesta Red OTRI, 2007*, Conferencia de Rectores de las Universidades Españolas, CRUE, Madrid.

Rodeiro, D., Fernández, S., Rodríguez, A. and Otero, L. (2008) *La creación de empresas en el sistema universitario español*, Ed. Servizo publicacións Universidade de Santiago de Compostela, Santiago de Compostela.

Rosenbaum, P.R. and Rubin, D.B. (1983) 'The central role of the propensity score in observational studies for causal effects', *Biometrika*, 70(1): 41–59.

Rothaermel, F.T. and Thursby, M. (2005) 'Incubator firm failure or graduation?: The role of university linkages', *Research Policy*, 34(7): 1076–90.

Salvador, E. (2010) 'How effective are research spin-off firms in Italy?', *Revenue d'Économie Industrielle*, 133: 99–122.

Scarso, E. and Bolisani, E. (2010) 'Knowledge-based strategies for knowledge intensive business services: A multiple case-study of computer service companies', *Electronic Journal of Knowledge Management*, 8(1): 151–60.

Smedlund, A. and Toivonen, M. (2007) 'The role of KIBS in the IC development of regional clusters', *Journal of Intellectual Capital*, 8(1): 159–70.

Wennberg, K., Wiklund, J. and Wright, M. (2011) 'The effectiveness of university knowledge spillovers: Performance differences between university spinoffs and corporate spinoffs', *Research Policy*, 40: 1128–43.

Wernerfelt, B. (1984) 'A resource-based view of the firm', *Strategic Management Journal*, 5: 171–80.

Wright, M., Clarysse, B., Mustar, P. and Lockett, A. (2008) *Academic entrepreneurship in Europe*, Edward Elgar, Cheltenham.

Zahra, S A., Van de Velde, E. and Larrañeta, B. (2007) 'Knowledge conversion capability and the performance of corporate and university spin-off', *Industrial and Corporate Change*, 16(4): 569–608.

Zhang, J. (2009) 'The performance of university spin-offs: An exploratory analysis using venture capital data', *Journal of Technology Transfer*, 34: 255–85.

8 Ambidexterity revisited

The influence of structure and context and the dilemma exploration vs. exploitation

José Ricardo C. Andrade, João J. Ferreira and Vanessa Ratten

Introduction

The growing interest on organizational ambidexterity in recent years was reflected in multiple approaches, not having yet obtained a clear view of how organizational ambidexterity environments can be obtained. Evidence for this fact is revealed in a number of studies focusing on that goal (Turner, Swart and Maylor, 2013).

Also the literature has focused its attention on the elements that function as means to achieve organizational ambidexterity. Keeping this trend, this review attempts to critically address the mechanisms of structure and context with effects on organizational ambidexterity to provide a critical approach of the main debates in the field and report the main lines of future research (O'Cass, Heirati and Ngo, 2014; O'Reilly and Tushman, 2013; Rothaermel and Alexander, 2009; Sarkees, Hulland and Chatterjee, 2014; Turner and Lee-Kelley, 2012).

Thus, the concept of structure emerges in the literature about organizational ambidexterity mainly connected with firms' orientation towards exploitation and exploration activities. For instance, O'Reilly and Tushman (2008, 2013) consider that these activities are implemented through separate organizational units and also including a set of skills, work systems, specific incentives and culture aligned internally.

The concept of context is related to the conditions that enable the creation of functional relationships necessary for the specific processes within firms. For Ghoshal (1997), socialization, people management practices and teamwork promote shared values and coordination between all, facilitating sharing of information and ambidextrous action in firms. Lubatkin, Simsek, Ling and Veiga (2006) and Gibson and Birkinshaw (2004), report that an environment that fosters socialization processes and recognition, culture and interpersonal relations helps to encourage individual ambidexterity. Several scholars have pointed to this idea. Chang and Hughes (2012) have considered that contextual conditions can increase the quality of internal communication to develop and improve existing products and services. Andriopoulos and Lewis (2009) found that in small businesses, the enabling environment for the development of organizational ambidexterity environments could serve to support internal communication processes facilitating the disappearance of contradictory visions interpreted as impractical processes.

However, despite all the research on organizational ambidexterity in the last decade, scholars like Raisch, Birkinshaw, Probst and Tushman (2009) report that some of the elements related to the concept remain indistinct. They suggest that the literature has not been able to solve what has been termed as the 'central tensions' for organizational ambidexterity, stressing the need for more research. These tensions primarily reflect areas unexplored by most literature about how organizational ambidexterity can be developed in firms and the mechanisms that are associated with it.

The literature has also neglected an effective demonstration about the concept of organizational ambidexterity by failing to submit the management mechanisms that facilitate its development (Gibson and Birkinshaw, 2004).

For this study we used the typology presented by Raisch et al. (2009) to guide this review. From this typology derived the four balancing classifications used to support the explanation of how firms reach organizational ambidexterity and its relationship with context and structure. Each balancing has two dimensions that lead to organizational ambidexterity: differentiation and integration; individual and organizational; static and dynamic and, finally, external and internal. The literature identified to support this classification allowed: i) establish the relationship between the variables presented in the literature regarding the size in question and its main contribution to the study of organizational ambidexterity; and ii) build for each dimension and presented for context and structure an identification of the mechanisms for organizational ambidexterity and the main lines for future research.

In order to conduct this review and maintain the rating provided by Raisch et al. (2009), we used the database Scopus and ISI Web of Science. In these databases the search word was 'ambidexterity' both in terms of keywords and the title. The articles identified for this review were published between 2005 and 2015. According to Birkinshaw and Gupta (2013), these were the years of increased production related to the concept of organizational ambidexterity. The list of articles resulting from this first survey was analyzed and items that were not part of the social sciences, management sciences or behavioral sciences were removed. This search procedure, despite its reduction, generated a substantial list of items. ISI Web of Science left over 313 articles and Scopus, 279 articles. Each article was then classified and placed in one or more dimensions depending on its context, i.e., its framework at the level of balancing dimension: differentiation vs. integration, individual vs. organizational, static vs. dynamic or external vs. internal. This allocation was based on the relation between the mechanisms associated with each balancing.

Then, sorting criteria were defined to the main mechanism for structure and context and were grouped according to O'Reilly and Tushman (2013). These scholars reported the leadership, management of human resources practices, organizational culture, processes and separation of structural units as the elements with the largest representation in the study of organizational ambidexterity. We consider that with the grouping of mechanisms evidenced by literature in effect with organizational ambidexterity allowed for the reinterpretation of the relevance of the concept for the management and for integration into their common lexicon.

In fact, one of the main criticisms that are made to the concept of organizational ambidexterity is based on the idea that the concept does not have a clear correspondence in the management lexicon and for managers in general (Birkinshaw and Gupta, 2013). Based on this, we contribute to research on organizational ambidexterity in two ways: first, because it establishes a relationship between the different studies on organizational ambidexterity and balancing presented with relevance to structure and context as well as the mechanisms evidenced in the literature leading to organizational ambidexterity environments relevant to the management. Second, because this study presents an effective approach to make the organizational ambidexterity a closer concept of a common management language and not something academically far. Table 8.1 shows a set of mechanisms presented in the literature that contributes to the development of organizational ambidexterity environments.

Following the question from O'Reilly and Tushman (2013) 'how is ambidexterity achieved?' clues were sought in the literature to support an answer to it. For this purpose we used the guidelines referred to by those scholars to organize the mechanisms for context and structure associated with organizational ambidexterity.

To this end, this chapter is structured as follows. First, it shows organizational ambidexterity as a wide area of investigation in the management field and some of its main components with emphasis on the study. Then, the dilemma between exploration and exploitation is referred, identifying the main literature on each of its balancing based on the structure and context perspectives. Finally it is presented the main elements for context and structure and the main orientations for future research.

Literature review

The theoretical range of organizational ambidexterity

Perhaps one of the issues most frequently addressed in the literature is the extent to which the concept of organizational ambidexterity arises as a catalyst for research in management. Here, most of the evidence shows a clear pattern: the concept of ambidexterity arises related to leadership studies (Mihalache, Jansen, Van den Bosch and Volberda, 2014), networks and partnerships (Hill and Birkinshaw, 2012), organizational strategy (Benner and Tushman 2003; Ginsberg and Venkatraman, 1985; Harvey, Jas, Walshe and Skelcher, 2014; Hodgkinson, Ravishankar, Aitken and Fischer, 2014; O'Reilly and Tushman, 2011), social capital and human capital (Lehmann, Braun and Krispin, 2011; Li, Lin and Huang, 2014), knowledge and organizational learning (Blindenbach-Driessen and van den Ende, 2014; Groysberg and Lee, 2009; Jansen, Tempelaar,

Table 8.1 Main mechanisms identified in the literature for organizational ambidexterity

Leadership	Human Resource Practices	Management Organizational Culture	Process	Structural Units Separation
Top management behavior influences organizational ambidexterity (O'Reilly & Tushman, 2011).	Work environments that promote interaction and learning (Stadler, Rajwani & Karaba, 2014).	Creating organizational support environments (Güttel, Konlechner & Trede, 2015).	Standardization and monitoring work goals (Kim, Sting & Loch 2014).	Defined projects in different structural units (Gassmann, Widenmayer & Zeschky, 2012).
Transformational leadership style (Zacher, Robinson & Rosing, 2014).	Implementation of high performance work systems (Patel, Messersmith & Lepak, 2013).	Practices of alignment and adaptability (Gibson & Birkinshaw, 2004).	Development management designs so as to provide alignment (Pellegrinelli, Murray-Webster & Turner, 2014).	Inter-organizational alliances (Rothaermel & Deeds, 2004; Lavie & Rosenkopf, 2006)
Behavioral integration through sharing of information and communication, decision-making processes in team (Mihalache et al., 2014; Lubatkin, 2006; Yitzhack Halevi, Carmeli & Brueller, 2015)	Training, communication and information (Good & Michel, 2014)	Culture of flexibility and control (Patel et al., 2013).	Internal knowledge management (Mom, Van Den Bosch & Volberda, 2007; Nosella, 2014)	Formal integration mechanisms: departmentalization, formalization and standardization, strategic planning and control (Blindenbach-Driessen & van den Ende, 2014)
Development of collaboration environments (Good & Michel, 2014).	Knowledge management systems (Sirén, Kohtamäki & Kuckertz, 2012; Rothaermel & Alexandre, 2009)	Systematic assessment practices (Patel et al., 2013).	Software tools, innovative processes and product development (Hjelmgren & Dubois, 2013).	Definition of temporary teams, functional autonomy, integrated departments (Heinemeyer & Amnuayskul, 2014).

(Continued)

Table 8.1 (Continued)

Leadership	Human Resource Practices	Management Organizational Culture	Process	Structural Units Separation
Transactional and transformational leadership behaviors (Zacher et al., 2014).	Coordination of joint projects between departments (Chebbi, Yahiaoui, Vrontis & Thrassou, 2015)	Consolidation of internal lines for innovation strategies (Tan & Liu, 2014)	Promotion of organizational alliances (Rothaermel & Deeds, 2004)	Informal mechanisms such as socialization strategies, lateral relations and interdepartmental (Chen & Kannan-Narasimhan, 2014).
Feedback loop to promote strategic learning (Sirén et al., 2012)	Human resources management practices to the level of human capital and social capital (Syrigos, Konstantinos & Kostopoulos, 2013)	Creation of company culture indoctrination practices (Adler, Goldoftas & Levine, 1999).	Management of specific processes centered on work teams (O'Cass, Heirati & Ngo, 2014).	Segregation of duties and activities per unit and department (Tushman & O Reilly, 1996; Jansen et al., 2012)
Implementation of guidance processes to market (Voss & Voss, 2012)	Skills development and teamwork routines (Patel et al., 2013)	Dissemination of rules and procedures, values and attitudes (Prieto-Pastor & Martin-Perez, 2014).	Integration of knowledge exchange practices and skills (Puranam & Srikanth, 2007).	
Adjusting work processes and internal communication practice (Lubatkin, 2006).	Reward systems work team (Faisal Ahammad, Lee, Malul & Shoham, 2015)		Implementation of structural processes in relation to innovation (De Visser et al., 2010)	
Systems of coordination and monitoring of work teams (Alexiev, Jansen, Van den Bosch & Volberda, 2010)				

van den Bosch and Volberda, 2009; Lin and McDonough, 2014; Swart and Kinnie, 2010), organizational performance (Cao, Gedajlovic and Zhang, 2009) or innovation (Rothaermel and Alexander, 2009). In general the results of studies on organizational ambidexterity, using different measures of ambidexterity, variables, analysis of samples in different levels or types of organization are robust and contingent, relating to the environment where the firm operates (O'Reilly and Tushman, 2013).

The organizational ambidexterity is a critical process because it means a firm taking advantage of current market opportunities while creating and innovating to meet future challenges (Patel, Messersmith and Lepak, 2013). Thus, ambidextrous firms are able to simultaneously manage knowledge management processes, analyzing their portfolio of skills and exploring new areas with equal efficiency (Andriopoulos and Lewis, 2009). For this to happen, firms are adopting, according to the perspective of different scholars, a more exploitative orientation or a more explorative orientation (Birkinshaw, Hood and Jonsson, 1998; Chang and Hughes, 2012; Jansen et al., 2012; Raisch, Birkinshaw, Probst and Tushman, 2009). The first concerns with the activity involving skills, individual and collective knowledge and expertise. These, when combined and internalized allow incremental refinements to the technology level, marketing, product or service. It is an adaptive process at the level of existing technologies to better meet the needs of existing customers. The second orientation, explorative, emerges associated with the creation of innovative technologies, revolutionary new products and new markets.

However, as argued by Gibson and Birkinshaw (2004) and Lubatkin, Simsek, Ling and Veiga (2006), the orientation of ambidexterity, more explorative or more exploitative, comes balanced in the firm context and structure. Tasks and activities are developed according to the guidelines and management practices where flexibility in systems and organizational structures are often not compatible with the logic of efficient management of existing resources. So firms tend to follow certain guidelines of organizational ambidexterity depending on the access or not to certain features and the efficiency of the systems and organizational structures managing them. According to some scholars, the ability to innovate, develop and create is often contradictory with the logic of efficient management of these resources (Patel et al., 2013). This exploitative or exploratory orientation as well as the access to resources are the elements identified in the literature as being part of the role of organizational ambidexterity (Benner and Tushman, 2003; Gupta, Smith and Shalley, 2006; He and Wong, 2004; Hjelmgren and Dubois, 2013; Lavie and Rosenkopf, 2006).

The ambidexterity dilemma: the tension between exploration and exploitation

The literature has shown the existence of a dilemma about organizational ambidexterity in firms. On the one hand, a line of investigation states that it is not possible for firms to be simultaneously ambidextrous (Chang and Hughes, 2012;

Lubatkin, 2006). Another line of research refers to firms being ambidextrous, but upon the manifestation of certain conditionalities (Tushman and O'Reilly, 1996). The need for a balance between exploration and exploitation activities in organizational ambidexterity was initially presented by Tushman and O'Reilly (1996), for whom the ambidextrous organization must have the ability to compete in demanding markets through prospective processes, where cost factors, efficiency and incremental innovation are decisive, as well as through exploration processes, where speed of response and flexibility are critical success factors. However, other literature on exploration and exploitation notes that both concepts contain contradictory aspects in terms of knowledge processes (He and Wong, 2004; Hjelmgren and Dubois, 2013; Maletic, Maletic, Dahlgaard, Dahlgaard-Park and Gomišček, 2014).

Thus, a key element on firms' strategies is the respect of options to choose before different types of activities. While exploitation involves the use of knowledge, competence and efficiency and is associated with mechanistic structures in firms as routinization, control and bureaucracy, exploration appears as a response to the context trends that guide and establish the creation of new technologies, products and markets (Lubatkin, Simsek, Ling and Veiga, 2006). It is characterized by research, discovery, experimentation, risk taking and innovation (He and Wong, 2004). It appears associated to organic organizational structures, improvisation, autonomy and chaos, emerging technologies and markets. The dilemma is in how knowledge arises, especially on process management or administrative proceedings (He and Wong, 2004).

Exploitation involves the institutionalization of a process of top-down learning through routines and behaviors in order to refine the skills of organization. It involves mainly formalized interactions between hierarchical levels of management and connected process efficiency. Exploration involves learning new skills, knowledge and abilities triggered through changes in market factors or products (Lubatkin et al., 2006). It implies social interactions from the top management as well as the need for a different adaptability. These processes involving exploration and exploitation reflect ways of acting from the top management and from middle management levels, balanced between acting efficiently and acting in response to an external stimulus, usually linked to market needs or customers' needs.

According to He and Wong (2004), different studies indicate that both exploitation and exploration require structures, processes, strategies, cultures and resources with differentiated impact on the performance and capacity of adaptability of firms. Thus, in large companies, the internal processes that reflect new market trends or products tend to be slower, time-consuming in the existing organizational structure hierarchy. In small and medium-sized enterprises (SMEs) such aspects tend to be minimized since, being the organizational structures and hierarchies substantially smaller and shorter, individuals, either at an operational level or at an management level, are located much closer to operating core of the company. The ambidextrous organization orientation is strongly related to how the top management and its management team is integrated with the strategic vision of the company, more exploitative or more explorative.

Still, according to He and Wong (2004) the tension between exploitation and exploration is manifested by the systematic and continuous adaptation to environmental requirements of new market opportunities, product or customer demands and for the systematic testing of new alternatives, reducing the capacity to improve and to refine existing skills. Thus, an exploratory effort to a company cannot disturb the success routines in existing fields without there being any significant success in the new field to compensate for the loss of existing business.

Similarly, the focus on the internal capacity to improve processes and learnings makes it attractive when it is thought as a continuous refinement of existing abilities and skills but becomes rigid in terms of their core competencies, especially when checked at the level of contextual changes (Lubatkin et al., 2006).

Previously, Levinthal and March (1993) considered that firms divide their attention between resources for both types of ambidexterity orientation. For these scholars, firms must have the capability to ensure a sufficient dose of exploration to ensure this viability and to ensure a sufficient exploitation dose to ensure future viability. Excessive exploratory orientation can lead to the inability of many firms to achieve success in the market because of its tendency to constantly explore new products and unknown markets without allocating sufficient resources to explore their skills in a more familiar niche or narrower.

According to He and Wong (2004), companies instead of creating stability and balance should work disrupt their own competitive advantages by creating a set of temporary advantages, offsetting exploration and prospecting. In short, exploitation and exploration are fundamentally different logics that create tensions, competing for the scarce resources of the companies, resulting in the need for companies to manage the trade-offs as well as a synergistic effect between the two orientations.

Theories about the architecture of organizational ambidexterity, linked to the structures, suggest the existence of double structures and strategies in order to differentiate its efforts on more incremental or more radical innovation focus within firms. In contrast, the contextual ambidexterity emphasizes the social and behavioral significance of integrating exploration and exploitation (Gibson and Birkinshaw, 2004). As noted by these scholars, exploitation involves efficiency and convergent thinking to take advantage of existing capabilities and continuous improvement. Exploration, in contrast, aims to research, the variation and experimentation efforts to generate new knowledge combinations.

Tensions between exploitation and exploration represent tensions in innovation processes by creating vicious circles and ambiguous perspectives on one side of the exploitation-exploration dichotomy (Lubatkin et al., 2006). Firms advance towards homogeneity particularly with routines that support one of the types of innovation, scaling up their efforts in the preferred mode and neglecting the other (Raisch et al., 2009). However, the trend of the firm for exploitation may lead it to improve their level of skills and capabilities, enabling a reaction to the firm's needs translated in better performance. This, however, can lead to stagnation and the organization's vulnerability to the markets and technological change (Gibson and Birkinshaw, 2004). Moreover, firms that follow a more exploratory line assume a risk climbing and do not promote core competencies. The differentiation is achieved through the use of structure and strategy. Context uses behavioral and social means to integrate exploration and prospection activities.

This approach is common to the top-level management and is a more incisive approach. For Ghoshal (1997), the context acts as a set of stimuli and processes that influence and shape individual and collective behaviors towards organizational ambidexterity. To Gibson and Birkinshaw (2004), context can complement structures that promote exploration or exploitation activities and strategies by shared values and cooperation.

Balancing between differentiation and integration

The first balancing, concerns the distinction between differentiation and integration. According to Raisch et al. (2009), differentiation regards the distinction between exploration and exploitation activities in firms, and integration is related to mechanisms that firms have to exploit and to explore. Both are assumed to be complementary to the extent that they are effective mechanisms for firms to evolve into environments of organizational ambidexterity.

In the differentiation approach, an activity of exploration and exploitation occurs through tasks that are developed in exploitative or explorative contexts (Raisch et al., 2009). It can be considered as an organization structure approach, since, in these contexts, management processes are decentralized in small organizational units, adjusting their management processes in certain directions of innovation. The study by Blindenbach-Driessen and van den Ende (2014) on organizational ambidexterity and innovation in production and services found that separate units of innovation had a positive effect on the creation of ambidexterity environments on industries. However, the effect on improving operational activity, i.e., the level of exploration activities, is not clear. To Blindenbach-Driessen and van den Ende (2014) exploitation and exploration are two ends of a continuum and further exploration activities may result in an increased cost of exploitation activities These scholars reported that structurally separate units enhances the ability to develop exploration activities and also the development of organizational ambidexterity environments on industries. However, they found that these structurally separate units have a weaker positive effect on exploration activities and in the development of organizational environments ambidexterity on services companies. This finding, present in several studies (see Table 8.2) implies that the industrial and service companies can benefit from having innovation units separately, with the advantages of being bigger, this benefit, for industrial companies. Jansen, Tempelaar, Van den Bosch and Volberda (2009) consider that the structural differentiation can help ambidextrous firms maintain multiple contradictory activities. According to these authors, these different activities need to be mobilized, coordinated and integrated, suggesting formal and informal mechanisms.

Another approach, the study of Cao, Gedajlovic and Zhang (2009) shows that organizational ambidexterity is fostered by close inter-relationship between existing

Table 8.2 Balancing between differentiation and integration: relationship between variables presented and major contribution to the study of organizational ambidexterity

Study	Study variables	Main contribution	Elements for context and structure	Major research lines
Hodgkinson et al. (2014)	Effective implementation, organizational learning	The influence of middle management in the implementation of organizational ambidexterity environments.	• Differentiation and integration can be considered as complementary to one another • Tasks can contribute to exploration and exploitation • The decentralization of management can bring about changes in internal processes in an exploitation or exploratory way.	• To analyze the ability of mid-level managers to facilitate ambidextrous environments operating in different areas of industry and services.
Blindenbach-Driessen & van den Ende (2014)	Exploration, exploitation and performance	Exploitation and exploration activities benefit when working in differentiation.	• The ambidextrous performance of the company in exploration and prospecting may vary according to the size of it.	• Analyze the possible mediating variables that have an effect on the relationship between a separate innovation unit in terms of exploration and exploitation.
Cao, Gedajlovic & Zhang (2009)	Company performance, exploitation and exploration, the organization dimension	Managers in resource-limited settings can benefit from a focus on the management of exchanges between exploration and exploitation.	• The exploration and exploitation can be switched and combined to manage organizational ambidexterity. • In innovation processes companies can benefit from structural units separately, this effect felt in large firms.	• Analyze activities that do not justify the structural separation in firms.

(*Continued*)

Table 8.2 (Continued)

Study	Study variables	Main contribution	Elements for context and structure	Major research lines
Andriopoulos & Lewis (2009)	Differentiation, integration, strategic intent, customer orientation	Tactics integration and differentiation allow managing ambidexterity cycles.	• The social and human capital can be used to create ambidexterity environments. • Top management plays an important role in resource management and organizational skills	• Analyze what types of resources are needed in several practice areas. • Examine how SMEs can achieve innovation by exploratory route or via the complementary exploitation.
Taylor & Helfat (2009)	Organizational structure, social context, organizational cognition	The importance of middle managers in creating organizational ambidexterity connections in firms, key to the dynamic capabilities in technological transitions.		
O'Cass, Heirati & Ngo (2014)	Exploitative strategy and exploratory strategy	Integration of product innovation through exploration and prospecting is significant for the implementation of new capabilities in launching new products.		
Gilbert (2005)	Dependence on resources, perception of threats, structural differentiation	The structural autonomy helps to decouple the effects of cognition in different types of inertia structure and allows the perception of a threat to overcome the shortage of resources.		
Hill & Birkinshaw (2012)	Orientation for organizational ambidexterity	Ambidextrous firms seeks a favorable relational context defined by the strength of their relationships.		

Li, Lin & Huang (2014)	Domestic capital, foreign capital and environmental dynamism	Management relationships cause different types of innovation reflected the level of organizational ambidexterity.
Lubatkin et al. (2006)	Behavioral integration, orientation to ambidexterity	SMEs behaviorally integrated by top management have shown greater ambidextrous orientation capacity and achieve higher levels of performance
Jansen et al. (2009)	Ambidexterity, structural differentiation, formal and informal integration, connectivity, functional interface	The direct effect of structural differentiation in organizational ambidexterity operates by top management and formal organizational interfaces and integration mechanisms.
Chang & Hughes (2012)	Characteristics of leadership, contextual characteristics and structural characteristics	SMEs can achieve a balance between the activities of organizational ambidexterity by establishing differentiated organizational structures.

knowledge and new knowledge. For these scholars, the achieved synergy allows that the existing resources can be fully utilized for the acquisition of new skills and also allow that new knowledge can be fully integrated into all existing resources. Thus, the approaches of differentiation need to be combined with approaches of integration efforts to achieve the full potential of organizational ambidexterity. Andriopoulos and Lewis (2009) revealed that companies use a combination of integration and differentiation tactics to manage the dilemmas of exploration and exploitation in organizational ambidexterity environments that occur at different organizational levels. These dilemmas are described as the dilemma of strategic intent that operates at the enterprise level, the dilemma of customer orientation that affects efforts within projects, and the dilemma of the individual drivers of the individual knowledge workers. The study suggests that companies need to manage innovation dilemmas at various levels and interactions between the various levels in order to strengthen organizational ambidexterity practices.

Taylor and Helfat (2009) put forward a major contribution to the strain between differentiation and integration by recognizing the existence of organizational links between the new capabilities and potentially valuable pre-existing capabilities. For these authors organizational ambidexterity assumes that companies are able to exploit new knowledge, explore existing knowledge and coordinate these internal knowledge flows.

In turn, the study by O'Cass, Heirati and Ngo (2014) reinforces the organization's structural differentiation assumption to achieve ambidextrous environments which are considered fundamental prerequisites for the introduction of new products successfully. For them, these ambidextrous environments should not be limited to a single organizational level or a specific functional area. Companies become ambidextrous when exploration activities and exploitation strategies interact with each other at a corporate level and at an operational level in several functional areas matching each feature separately, allowing the implementation of specific strategies driving the introduction of new products on the market. This approach for differentiation strategies allows organizational structures to support specific skills in response to market requirements. To Gilbert (2005), the benefit of structural autonomy is more than to simply provide a separate environment for innovation. It is, above all, allowing that the structural autonomy escapes the routine of stiffness for new projects and products in response to market opportunities.

The approach for the integration refers to the behavioral mechanisms that allow individuals to go down by two types of activities, i.e., exploitation and exploration activities. Research has pointed towards firms developing exploration and prospecting activities by its employees. According to Hill and Birkinshaw (2012), to achieve ambidextrous environments it is necessary to feed a favorable relational context defined by the strength of their relationships. For Li, Lin and Huang (2014) internal social capital that can be used by top managers effectively to create innovation and can facilitate ambidexterity environments by balancing shared leadership processes in the company. In their study, Hodgkinson, Ravishankar and Aitken-Fischer (2014) refer to the human and organizational element as elements that can be mobilized by senior management and intermediate levels of leadership in incorporating activities oriented to alignment and adaptability. On the basis of these studies the work of Gibson and Birkinshaw (2004) describe how the organizational context allows the development of exploitation and exploration activities. Lubatkin et al. (2006) suggest that the top management team has an influential role in the results of firms through behavioral integration of essential management processes to achieve organizational ambidexterity. Jansen et al. (2009) go one step further suggesting that integration occurs, not only at top management level, but also between levels of formal departments.

However, for Raisch et al. (2009) is not clear how the processes of differentiation and integration should be combined since this involves managing the correct balance of each process in relation to the relative importance of their activities. Research on the topic has proposed structures and strategies to allow that combination of efforts, forcing management to build cycles of organizational ambidexterity (Raisch et al., 2009; Andriopoulos and Lewis, 2009; Benner and Tushman, 2003). Thus, both differentiation and integration are complementary and not alternative organizational mechanisms as a means of achieving organizational effectiveness. Thus, this balance varies depending on the type of activity and requires, to the management, a special attention to the process. Table 8.2 summarizes the main elements of context and structure for the balancing of differentiation and integration.

Balancing between the individual and organization

Literature has appointed a set of structural mechanisms enablers of organizational ambidexterity, but few studies have focused on the individual dimension of organizational ambidexterity. The study of Gibson and Burkinshaw (2004) considers that through the context can be acquired behavioral ability to demonstrate alignment and individual adaptability in the organization. The first one are the activities geared to enhance performance in the short term. It is achieved through goal-setting programs and incentive systems. The second are the activities geared to improve performance in the long term and it is achieved through a lesser degree of formalization within a firm. For them, organizational ambidexterity is influenced differently by the context or by structure, since is built on a set of processes or systems facilitators of individual behavior.

One of the issues that comes up with importance in the literature on organizational ambidexterity is to know how ambidexterity arises at the individual level (Groysberg and Lee, 2009; Harvey, Jas, Walshe and Skelcher, 2014; Hjelmgren and Dubois, 2013; Mom et al., 2007;. O'Reilly and Tushman, 2008, 2013; Raisch et al., 2009; Sears and Hoetker, 2014; Sirén et al., 2012; Sun, Aryee and Law, 2007). A series of studies states that the individual characteristics of leaders affects the ability to act ambidextrously, as well as organizational factors, such as socialization or practices of team working that lead individuals to act and to think ambidextrously.

Some scholars have suggested that the cognitive element can play an important role for management by promoting important results in the generation of organizational ambidexterity environments. Lin and McDonough (2014) indicate that these cognitive structures allows the solving of contradictions by enabling individuals to follow certain courses of action rather than avoid or deny these tensions between individual and organization. The results obtained enable the validation of firms as entities that shape the cognitive structures of individuals.

Another approach is focused on the behavioral as an element highlighted in studies distinguishing personality styles. Raisch et al. (2009) states that individuals who are oriented in exploration activities emphasizing creativity processes differ in personality compared with individuals who focus on prospecting activities, emphasizing process implementation and improvement.

Most studies on organizational ambidexterity start from the assumption that there is a certain homogeneity on an individual basis, not revealing how individuals influence the ability of firms to balance between exploration and exploitation activities. Acknowledging this, the study of Bonesso, Gerli and Scapolan (2014) addresses the issue of tension between exploration and exploitation, adopting a micro-level analysis. Unlike the vast literature on organizational ambidexterity investigating organizational solutions that enable companies to seek a balance between the two types of orientation, this study reflects on the relevance of individual perception about their role and about the expected actual behavior as an element of study the organizational ambidexterity still unexplored.

Turner, Swart and Maylor (2013) highlight the few studies conducted at the level of individual ambidexterity and little empirical evidence. The contribution of Mom, Van Den Bosch and Volberda, (2007, 2009) provides evidence that organizational ambidexterity can be achieved not only at the organizational level but also at the individual level. In this context, the definition of organizational ambidexterity for managers comprises the behavioral guidance that combines exploration and prospecting in a given period of time.

In ambidextrous firms, individuals face complex and challenges and it is expected that they can switch between those conflicting activities. For Mom et al. (2009) the formal structural mechanisms existing in firms is positively related to the mechanisms of formal structural and personal coordination of organizational ambidexterity evidenced by top managers.

Following this line of thought, Bonesso, Gerli and Scapolan (2014) report that the perception of individuals in situations of exploration or exploitation does not mean immediately that individuals find themselves facing an ambidexterity situation and that is important to understand how the formulation of the perception of individuals about their role and behavior is consistent or inconsistent. Another perspective is presented by Swart and Kinnie (2010) for whom individuals that play ambidextrous roles face tensions via different types of cognitive orientation required by the conflicting activities, at the organization level. In fact, several scholars have highlighted the importance of consistency/inconsistency between perceptions and demonstrated behavior and how it affects the individual satisfaction and work performance. This complex relationship between the role of individuals and their perceptions about what is expected and the behaviors adopted seems to open up a promising research field (Bonesso et al., 2014).

A number of research on the role of individuals have focused their attention primarily on the behavioral characteristics of managers. The study of Swart and Kinnie (2010) states that the tensions generated between contradictory activities of exploration and exploitation can lead to different types of cognitive orientation when the individual is placed before those activities. In this perspective, there is the possibility that the individual will experience cognitive dissonance processes. This dissonance, according to these scholars, begins when people make a behavior and then assess the significance of that behavior against a standard of judgment. The presence of this cognitive dissonance or the inconsistency between the perceptions and behavior can be psychologically uncomfortable to individuals, motivating the development of procedures to align these cognitions each other.

Another approach adopts a neurological perspective, arguing that individual ambidexterity is not a question of allocation of exploratory or exploitative orientation tasks but rather a question about the capacity of those who makes decisions direct their attention on different modes of cognitive functioning (Laureiro-Martínez, Brusoni and Zollo, 2010). Juxtaposing, the study of Jasmand, Blazevic and Ruyter (2012) shows that the motivational orientation of the individual facilitates ambidextrous behavior, especially if the individual interacts positively with individual assessment guidance due to a preference for critical comparison of alternative states, judging their relative value. Lin and McDonough (2014) illustrate that the cognitive styles have a positive impact on learning and organizational ambidexterity and the tension that arises from the exploitation and exploration begins with the presence of cognitive styles through information processing.

Another study, from Good and Michel (2014), has a cognitive perspective of individual ambidexterity but relates it to dynamic contexts able to challenge the cognitive ability of individuals to the level of exploitation and exploration. These contexts include different levels of complexity, constraints and personal experiences in dynamic organizational environments.

Other studies report other organizational factors to be considered alongside the personal characteristics when studying organizational ambidexterity at the individual level. The study of Jansen et al. (2009) report on the formal and informal mechanisms of integration of top management teams (for example, through the use of extrinsic and intrinsic rewards) and mechanisms of informal and formal organizational integration (for example, via internal communication), and examine how they mediate the relationship between the structural differentiation and organizational ambidexterity. Taylor and Helfat (2009) describe the important role played by middle managers in implementing organizational systems. Top management can use economic, structural, social and cognitive influences to enable middle management to carry out these activities. Another example is the study of Yang and Li (2011) that focus on the influence of environmental dynamism at the level of individual skills for exploratory and exploitative activities. Lubatkin et al. (2006) refer to behavioral integration as a mechanism of action between exploitation and exploration activities. Table 8.3 shows the main elements of context and structure relating to the balancing between individual and organization.

Table 8.3 Balancing between the individual and organization: relationship between variables presented and major contribution to the study of organizational ambidexterity

Study	Study variables	Main contribution	Elements for context and structure	Major research lines
Sirén et al. (2012)	Organizational learning, strategic knowledge	The strategic learning favors the exploration over exploitation to improve organizational performance.	• There are cognitive characteristics that play an important role in promoting the generation of organizational ambidexterity.	• Analyze the strategic dimensions of learning and its effects. • Analyze the impact of other characteristics of managers as personal networks.
Mom et al. (2007, 2009)	Ambidexterity orientation, flows of knowledge	The importance of knowledge flows and the impact of organizational factors on the orientation of ambidexterity.	• Firms shape the cognitive characteristics of the relevant individuals for ambidextrous behavior.	• Analyze how cognitive structures can create a context for promoting results for organizational ambidexterity at an individual level.
Li et al. (2014)	Domestic capital, foreign capital and environmental dynamism	Management relationships are the cause different types of innovation, reflecting the level of organizational ambidexterity.	• Individuals have the ability to influence the ability of firms to adopt certain guidelines of organizational ambidexterity.	• Analyze how the differences in the type and variety of individual experience of previous work may influence differently the ability to reconcile both exploratory and forward looking activities.
Lin & McDonough (2014); Cantarello, Martini & Nosella (2012)	Cognitive styles, learning mechanisms	The orientation for organizational ambidexterity begins with the presence of cognitive styles.	• Individual skills act as moderators of organizational ambidexterity guidance.	

Reference	Key concepts	Description	Notes
			• Analyze what factors may explain the different approaches taken in case studies.
Bonesso et al. (2014)	Ambidexterity guidance perception, learning orientation	It suggests that individual characteristics such as previous work experience and the skills profile has an impact on the different situations of individual ambidexterity.	• Existing structural mechanisms in firms for organizational ambidexterity helps top management to guide individual behavior.
Swart & Kinnie (2010)	Human capital, counseling for ambidextrous learning	Identifies learning guidelines, dominant knowledge assets and HR practices that support each learning orientation.	• The guidance for organizational ambidexterity in the individual level has a relationship with cognitive dissonance processes.
Laureiro-Martínez et al. (2010)	Ambidextrous organizational behavior and individual guidance for ambidexterity	Research in neuroscience, psychology and management can be combined to understand the fundamentals of management decision-making at the individual level.	• The dynamic contexts in firms serve as moderator for the individual ambidexterity guidance.
Jasmand et al. (2012)	Individual guidance for ambidexterity, motivational orientation and efficiency	The individual guidance to organizational ambidexterity has positive effects on the positive individual performance.	
Good & Michel (2014)	Individual ambidexterity, individual guidance for ambidexterity and cognitive flexibility	The results indicate a new combination of individual skills that can contribute to the guidance in individual ambidexterity.	
Lubatkin et al. (2006)	Behavioral integration, orientation to ambidexterity	SMEs behaviorally integrated by top management have shown greater ambidextrous orientation capacity and achieve higher levels of performance.	

(Continued)

Table 8.3 (Continued)

Study	Study variables	Main contribution	Elements for context and structure	Major research lines
Jansen et al. (2009)	Ambidexterity, structural differentiation, formal and informal integration, connectivity, functional interface	The direct effect of structural differentiation in organizational ambidexterity operates by top management and formal organizational interfaces and integration mechanisms.		
Yang & Li (2011)	Individual guidance for ambidexterity, environmental dynamism	It suggests the importance of considering the environmental dynamism and competitiveness as moderators in the individual orientation of organizational ambidexterity.		
Taylor & Helfat (2009)	Organizational structure, social, organizational cognition	The importance of middle managers in creating organizational ambidexterity connections in firms, key to the dynamic capabilities in technological transitions.		

Balancing between static ambidexterity and dynamic ambidexterity

Prior research has suggested that organizational ambidexterity can be considered as static or dynamic whether firms assume in the first case, certain configurations or, in the second case, switch between cycles of exploitation with exploration in a time sequence (Raisch et al. (2009).

Adopting this static conceptualization, Gibson and Birkinshaw (2004) suggest that firms become ambidextrous when they take certain settings on the context. According to these scholars, contextual ambidexterity differs from structural ambidexterity on two ways: first, organizational ambidexterity is achieved by establishing a set of systems that encourage individuals to make choices about their own alignment and adaptability and, in the second, organizational ambidexterity is achieved through the creation of organizational structures separately. In the perspective of these scholars, the concept of contextual ambidexterity is markedly conditioned by the role of top management in creating systems that facilitate the adoption of ambidexterity behaviors in the organization (see Table 8.4).

Previously, Tushman and O'Reilly (1996) had referred to the structural patterns in firms that evolve over time and favor incremental innovation occasionally interrupted by changes of a radical innovation kind. These settings occur in time, reflecting itself in firms, demonstrating that they have the capacity to reconstitute the adjustment to the new environment via the contextual influences of internal processes.

Studies about the contextual targeting and its relationship with the leadership are also examples of static conceptualization of organizational ambidexterity. Prieto-Pastor and Martin-Perez (2014) for example, suggested that the involvement of systems for human resources in large companies were significantly related to orientation to ambidexterity for employees, moderated by top management.

A particular approach on literature suggests that although the role of top management teams in firms have been studied in many aspects there is enough evidence on how managers can actually orchestrate exploration and exploitation in firms. Song and Chen (2014) argue, on the subject of organizational attributes, that these are indispensable for the functioning of firms and that their impact on them is related to the product innovation and market growth.

Other studies analyze the relationship between organizational ambidexterity and innovation and its structural setting in the organization. Blindenbach-Driessen and van den Endem (2014) investigated the effects of innovation units operating separately in industries and service companies in accordance with traditional paradigms of the discipline of management innovation, concluding that the units working separately improve the competence for organizational ambidexterity. A similar study conducted by He and Wong (2004) addressed the issue of organizational design and specific field of technological innovation and its context as a facilitating factor in the development of ambidextrous environments.

This static view of organizational ambidexterity comes next from the perspective of the contingency theory proposed by Ginsberg and Venkatraman (1985).

Table 8.4 Balancing between the static and dynamic ambidexterity: relationship between variables presented and major contribution to the study of organizational ambidexterity

Study	Study variables	Main contribution	Elements for context and structure	Major research lines
Gibson & Birkinshaw (2004)	Orientation for ambidexterity, organizational performance, organizational context	Contextual ambidexterity mediates the relationship between the characteristics of the organizational context and subsequent performance.	• Characteristics that occur in organizational structures separately (in the case of structural ambidexterity) and through a set of systems and incentives that drive individuals (if the contextual ambidexterity)	• Analyze the dynamic conditions in several business areas. • Analyze the high involvement HR practices and other important organizational factors in order to determine how the HRM affects the contextual conditions of firms.
Prieto-Pastor & Martin-Perez (2014)	High involvement work systems, individual ambidexterity, organizational learning	High involvement HR systems can develop ambidexterity environments encouraging employees to acquire ambidextrous behaviors.	• Structural patterns in firms evolve over time. • Incremental innovation periods are occasionally interrupted by rapid processes of radical innovation. • Organizational ambidexterity is strongly conditioned by contingent factors. • The market and the specific features determine firms.	• Analyze the variables that explain the relationship between the management of human resources of high involvement and the mediating effect of learning for organizational ambidexterity. • Analyze procedures conducive to product innovation. • Analyze potential with specific areas for trade-offs between research and exploitation.

Song & Chen (2014)	Formalization, risk taking, product innovation	Organizational structures geared to flexibility have significant impacts on product innovation capacity.	• Analyze information exchanges on small and medium enterprises.
Blindenbach-Driessen & Van den Ende (2014)	Exploration, exploitation and performance for ambidexterity	Exploitation and exploration activities benefit when working separately.	• Organizational capabilities are predominantly dynamic.
He & Wong (2004)	Organizational performance, ambidexterity guidance	There is a positive relationship between organizational ambidexterity, innovation strategies with the sales growth rate and the relative imbalance between innovation strategies is negatively related to the sales growth.	• Stability and change are opportunities to transcend the paradoxical relationship between exploitation and exploration. • Contextual and structural ambidexterity have themselves dynamic elements.
Zajac et al. (2000)	Strategic change, environmental and organizational contingencies, organizational resources	Strategic guidelines can be logically predicted from different contexts and organizational resources.	
Siggelkow & Levinthal (2003)	Organizational structures, performance scenarios, degree of decentralization	Interactions between organizational activities lead to better performance which underlines the importance of coordination of these interactions in firms.	

(Continued)

Table 8.4 (Continued)

Study	Study variables	Main contribution	Elements for context and structure	Major research lines
Sarkees et al. (2014)	Orientation for exploration and exploitation	The orientation for ambidexterity can not only change with time, but may also affect organizational capabilities on different time periods.		
Taylor & Helfat (2009)	Organizational structure, social, organizational cognition	The middle managers play an important role in creating ambidexterity connections in firms, key to the dynamic capabilities in technological transitions.		
Lavie & Rosenkopf (2006)	Orientation for ambidexterity organization dimension	There is a dynamic perspective on the balance between exploitation and exploration, adjusted over time and varying according to market contingencies.		
Uotila et al. (2009)	Market value, orientation for ambidexterity	The results show that environments characterized by low technological dynamism, are not characterized by balance between exploration and exploitation activities.		

| Hodgkinson et al. (2014) | Effective implementation and support organizational learning | The influence of middle management in the implementation of organizational environments of ambidexterity. |
| Kim et al. (2014) | Organizational structure, action plans, organizational size, operation strategy | The centralized style positively affects the strategy of firms. |

They suggest that the contingent character of general elements such as market structure, management characteristics, technology or organizational structure with the environment in which it operates underlines the static view of organizational ambidexterity. However, according to Zajac, Kraatz and Bresser (2000) firms have to continually reconfigure their activities due to the volatility of the markets where they operate. These scholars emphasize the construction of a dynamic approach to the industry as a way to predict the strategic fit and their performance implications (described as specific measures for the industry more generally as the organizational skills or the competitive environment). The modern contingency theory holds that organizational ambidexterity is essentially dynamic (Raisch et al., 2009).

Related to these aspects, the literature has suggested two paths for firms to relate with the environment and its evolution to the market (O'Reilly and Tushman, 2008). The first states that firms are adaptable and that they evolve in a balanced way using capabilities that are dynamic. The second indicates that companies are inert and the change takes place through an evolutionary process of variation–selection–retention. This perspective suggests that when environments are facing changes, inactions of firms are replaced with new shapes that best fit into this context of change. Following these scholars, the dynamic capabilities integrate both static elements and dynamic elements of organizational ambidexterity.

To survive and thrive, organizations must reconcile the stability, reliability and exploitation with change, innovation with exploration. Farjoun (2010) presents a dual view where stability and changes are fundamentally contradictory, but also mutually inclusive. This view proposes several ideas about stability and change and offers theoretical and pragmatic opportunities to dissolve and transcend the paradoxical relationship between exploitation and exploration, integrating both static elements such as dynamic organizations.

O'Reilly and Tushman (2008) had argued that some companies can adapt to markets due to the ability to exploit existing assets and positions and at the same time, explore new technologies and markets, configuring existing organizational resources as well as new opportunities. Under the tension between static and dynamic ambidexterity, difficulties arise when a company seeks to engage in exploitation activities to ensure its viability and at the same time devote sufficient resources to exploration activities to ensure its future viability. In these circumstances and under the right conditions, the scholars suggest that firms may be able to explore opportunities both in new markets as well as exploit their existing capacities, and that essentially involves top management. At this point, the top management can devise strategic processes to dynamically manage resources, allocating them intentionally and allowing businesses to reconfigure existing assets and learn new capabilities for exploration and exploitation.

Research refers to organizational ambidexterity as a synchronous search for both exploration and exploitation either through structural units in the organization or by individuals. However, Gupta, Smith and Shalley (2006) propose another way to accomplish organizational ambidexterity, called punctuated equilibrium. This mechanism can be translated to a time difference mode, rather than organization, where the cycles of operation and operation allows for a more viable approach than one simultaneous pursuit of the two, and interpreted as a dynamic capability that is manifested throughout time.

The explanation for this temporal sequence had already been suggested by Siggelkow and Levinthal (2003) in which, to create competitive advantage, firms need to find settings for activities, not only internally consistent but also adequate in function for the environment in which they operate. This challenge is particularly special, given the competitive landscape where new choices of activities aimed for performance are required. According to these scholars firms tend to engage in activities aimed at the balance between exploitation and exploration. This perspective is also shared by Lavie and Rosenkopf (2006) according to which companies need to balance their tendencies of exploration and exploitation temporally. The study of Taylor and Helfat (2009) suggests that organizational ambidexterity emerges from continuous alignment activities throughout the various stages of technological change in firms.

However, Ghemawat and Ricart Costa (1993) had pointed out that firms cannot simultaneously pursue exploration and exploitation. The tension between static and dynamic efficiency seems to be central to the strategy of the companies, since the structure of the company and its competitive strategy may affect the relationship between static and dynamic efficiency. Yet, another approach underscored the dynamic character of organizational ambidexterity through the observation of the way firms are efficient in the use of investment resources to build capacities of exploitation and exploration according to the competitive landscape (Sarkees, Hulland and Chatterjee, 2014). It suggests that the nature of the firms growth is related to the overall strength capabilities for exploration and exploitation and its resources can not only change with varying degrees over time, but also that resources can affect the company differently during alternating periods. The same conclusion is later confirmed by Uotila, Maula, Keil and Zahra (2009) in their study of 279 companies in the index ranking of Standard and Poor's 500, suggesting that firms, in order to get superior performance, are dependent on the balance between exploration and exploitation and its relationship with environmental conditions.

Raisch et al. (2009) are not clear how the organizational ambidexterity evolves over time. Siggelkow and Levinthal (2003) studied different organizational structures settings: centralized organization, where decisions are taken only at the enterprise level as a whole; and decentralized organization, where decisions are taken independently. The centralized and decentralized nature at the level of decision-making processes and subsequent integration of ambidextrous behavior in the organization was also contemplated in the study of Kim, Sting and Loch (2014). This study investigates the processes of formation of the strategy at a micro-level governing interactions between competing priorities, objectives and action plans. Other studies focus their attention on the dilemma between exploration and exploitation activities in organizational ambidexterity and suggest other levels of analysis. The study of Stadler, Rajwani and Karaba (2014) proposes a systematic analysis of structural solutions, behavioral, systemic and time indicated in the literature suggesting networks and as a means to explain how the solutions currently identified in the literature on organizational ambidexterity can be implemented and combined successfully. Table 8.4 shows the main elements of context and structure for the balance between static ambidexterity and dynamic ambidexterity.

Balancing between internal and external factors

The literature on organizational ambidexterity has identified a number of factors that contribute to a better understanding of the tensions between exploration and exploitation concerning their internal or external focus. According to Raisch et al. (2009) the research on this subject has integrated research areas as diverse as knowledge management and organizational learning, strategic alliances, partnerships or inter-organizational strategies.

Hjelmgren and Dubois (2013) report that businesses need, simultaneously, to exploit technological solutions while developing and exploring new solutions. The way a firm handles these issues depends on the way it has organized the interaction between different actors within the firm and with external partners. Their case study presents a company that combines the two elements of organizational ambidexterity (exploration and exploitation) through the interaction established with specific customers.

Other studies on organizational ambidexterity emphasize the way firms deal with the internal processes of exploration and prospecting, highlighting how it is achieved and developed through process of knowledge creation and organizational learning. For example, Sirén, Kohtamäki and Kuckertz (2012) present an empirical study conducted in 206 Finnish companies focused on software mediating the role of strategic learning between exploitation strategies and exploration strategies and their relationship to organizational performance. These scholars suggest that the learning process through their intra-organizational elements of dissemination, interpretation and application of strategic knowledge enables firms to capitalize benefits of both strategies in their relationship with performance. Swart and Kinnie (2010) sought to understand the relationship between the nature of knowledge assets, people management practices in firms and the types of organizational learning. The results achieved in their study suggest that people management approaches combined between exploratory and prospective learning may have a positive effect on organizational learning processes. Moreover, Benner and Tushman (2003) state that firms must learn to deal simultaneously with requirements of ambidextrous activities and for this purpose there should be internal architectures within the organization to maintain the contrasting benefits of experimentation and variability, i.e., the exploration of processes and exploration, strategically integrated by top management.

On the other hand, research on exploration underlines the importance of external knowledge acquisition. Puranam and Srikanth (2007) report that in acquisitions of small technology-based companies by large companies that are allowed to use existing knowledge as an input to their own innovation processes, leveraging existing innovation processes. Lin (2014) in an empirical study on Thai companies of electronic components sought to examine how the different strategies affect exploration and prospecting and how organizational ambidexterity affects performance after acquisition and merger processes. It was suggested that processes with a high degree of integration positively affect exploration and exploitation, reflecting the performance of the company and its ambidexterity capacity. Other studies on the inclusion of new technological capabilities, recombination technology resources, performance and innovation, the role of individuals in the perspective of information processing, human capital and entrepreneurial complementary assets found empirical evidence that exploration activities across organizational boundaries has more impact than exploration activities inside firms (Lehmann et al., 2011; Sears and Hoetker, 2014; Turner and Makhija, 2012).

Studies on access to external knowledge suggest that firms need to establish relational contexts characterized by a wide range of resources of other organizational actors so as to integrate to realize their potential (Bang and Esmark, 2009; Eklinder-Frick, Eriksson and Hallén, 2012).

Other studies reflect the tensions arising from the acquisition and integration of external knowledge in the organization. Studies on the absorptive capacity suggest that the processing of internal knowledge and integration of external knowledge are equally important to the development of firms to respond to market requirements. Harvey et al. (2014) in their empirical study of firms of the National Service of UK Health, examines how the internal and external contextual factors mediate organizational performance through the absorption capacity. The results suggest that the internal characteristics, including strategic priorities, information management processes, communication and orientation for learning have an impact on the organization's ability to successfully engage with external stakeholders and make use of knowledge available. The important study of Rothaermel and Alexander (2009) argues that the organizational and technological boundaries of a company are two important lines of demarcation when purchasing technology. These scholars, applying the perspective of organizational ambidexterity, raise the possibility that there is a curvilinear relationship between the outsourcing of technology and a firm's performance. In addition, they introduce an element of contingency by proposing that the absorption capacity of a company has a positive moderating effect on this relationship. The results show that organizational ambidexterity in these circumstances (external use of technology) requires that the company be able to resolve the exchanges that arise from internal combination and the use of external technology.

Based on the literature some aspects can be summarized as follows: first, organizational ambidexterity may depend on the company's ability to integrate internal or external sources of knowledge bases. Second, this ability depends on a combination of external mediation, based on the strategic interests and ability to internally absorb this knowledge. Finally, the organizational ambidexterity can be, externally, founded by social networks that define the internal and external relationships. Table 8.5 summarizes the main elements relevant to the context and structure as the main line of research.

Table 8.5 Balancing between internal and external factors: relationship between variables presented and major contribution to the study of organizational ambidexterity

Study	Study variables	Main contribution	Elements for context and structure	Major research lines
Hjelmgren & Dubois (2013)	Orientation for ambidexterity, customer orientation	The ways of organizing the interaction between organization and external environment are increasingly complex and require creative forms of orientation for organizational ambidexterity.	• The prospecting process and exploitation should be considered together because different actors within the company articulated in internal and external interaction.	• Analyze new forms of organization and interaction management intra-organizational and inter-organizational.
Sirén et al. (2012)	Organizational learning, strategic knowledge	The strategic learning favors the exploration over exploitation allowing both types of strategies to improve organizational performance.	• The processes of organizational learning and knowledge have an internal and external perspective.	• Analyze the resulting interaction of particular forms of organization, the central concerns of organizational actors.
Swart & Kinnie (2010)	Human capital, counseling for ambidextrous learning	Identifies learning guidelines, dominant knowledge assets and HR practices that support each learning orientation.	• Organizational learning has a positive relationship with the management approaches that manage the internal and external processes of knowledge.	• Analyze the limits of the process of using overlays and other formal coordination mechanisms to compensate for the discrete nature of organizational grouping options in acquisitions.
Puranam & Srikanth (2007)	Structural integration, acquisition of knowledge	The organizational measures to leverage existing knowledge may be incompatible with the need to leverage resources for continued innovation. Acquisition management practices that encourage the results of the leverage capacity of innovation tend to do so at the expense of reduced innovation leverage the knowledge, and vice versa.	• The external relationship processes of firms have an important component of knowledge generation.	

Author	Variables	Findings	Objectives
Li et al. (2014)	Internal social capital, foreign capital and environmental dynamism	Management relationships cause different types of innovation reflected in the level of organizational ambidexterity.	• The integration of external knowledge has a positive effect on prospecting and exploration activities in firms. • Access to external knowledge is characterized by the establishment of relationship contexts.	• Analyze the weight of precise measurements of the quality of intangible assets to shed light on the process of matching entrepreneurial companies and large companies as purchasers in mergers and acquisitions. • Analyze the micro environment of the relationship between capacity and performance from acquisitions.
Lehmann et al. (2011)	Specific intangible assets and human capital, organizational characteristics	The ability of participation in assets of a young high-tech company that is being reallocated through an acquisition significantly decreases the amount of intangible assets and complementary assets that are owned by the acquiring company.		
Sears & Hoetker (2014)	Technological capabilities	The value created from technological capabilities of the acquired companies varies due to the absorption capacity and the redundancy of knowledge.		
Turner & Makhija (2012)	Organizational structure, information processing	Individuals process information differently under the cognitive point of view.		
Stettner & Lavie (2014)	Performance difference, acquisition and alliance.	Exploring via externally oriented modes such as acquisitions or alliances enhances these firms' performance.		
Rothaermel & Alexandre (2009)	Organizational performance, industry characteristics	The highest levels of absorption capacity allows a company to capture more fully the benefits of technology.		

Conclusion

This review sought to revive the debates, tensions and dilemmas in the literature on organizational ambidexterity highlighting the main aspects related to the dichotomy structure and context. As proposed in the introduction, the four balancing classifications were explored for organizational ambidexterity according to the typology presented by Raisch et al. (2009). In organizational ambidexterity, context and structure are important in influencing actions. In this perspective, the concept of organizational ambidexterity arises mainly on the systems and organizational structures and, therefore, people management, activities, procedures and their outputs, organizational performance and innovative performance (Lubatkin, 2006;. Maletic et al., 2014; Mom et al., 2007).

In general, the literature refers to structural ambidexterity consisting of autonomously oriented structural units and contextual ambidexterity linked to work processes, systems and facilities necessary for the relationships exist. Thus, exploration and exploitation manifested in a complementary way reflecting on contexts and organizational structures where their characteristics are typified in each balancing presented in this research.

An element shown in this research reflects the literature finding about the growing interest in recent years on the subject of organizational ambidexterity. Multiple approaches in the literature help to support the idea that organizational ambidexterity environments can be obtained and relevant to management. In fact, this study makes it relevant to consider the idea (and why not the trend) that the concept of organizational ambidexterity can become a more prevalent concept in the management lexicon in general, since it includes elements that show a trend in the literature. This tendency is materialized and reflected through the mechanisms for organizational ambidexterity presented in this study.

To the question posed by O'Reilly and Tushman (2013) to know how organizational ambidexterity is achieved, this study helps to answer, typified by the presentation of a set of mechanisms relevant to context and to structure. These reflect different organizational realities to each other but realizing the activities of exploration and exploitation with consequences for management.

Research on organizational ambidexterity is broad and deep. Some final considerations regarding future research include refinement of the structure future research level, and context of how each of which becomes crucial for the development of others fields of research, in particular in the relationship between areas of different activities.

References

Adler, P.S., Goldoftas, B. and Levine, D.I. (1999) 'Flexibility versus efficiency? A case study of model changeovers in the toyota production system', *Organization Science*, 10(1): 43–68.

Alexiev, A.S., Jansen, J.J.P., Van den Bosch, F.A.J. and Volberda, H.W. (2010) 'Top management team advice seeking and exploratory innovation: The moderating role of TMT heterogeneity', *Journal of Management Studies*, 47(7): 1343–64.

Andriopoulos, C. and Lewis, M.W. (2009) 'Exploitation-exploration tensions and organizational ambidexterity: Managing paradoxes of innovation', *Organization Science*, 20(4): 696–717.

Bang, H. and Esmark, A. (2009) 'Good governance in network society: Reconfiguring the political from politics to policy', *Administrative Theory and Praxis*, 31(1): 7–37.

Benner, M.J. and Tushman, M.L. (2003) 'Exploitation, exploration, and process management: The productivity dilemma revisited', *Academy of management review*, 28(2): 238–56.

Birkinshaw, J. and Gupta, K. (2013) 'Clarifying the distinctive contribution of ambidexterity to the field of organization studies', *The Academy of Management Perspectives*, 27(4): 287–98.

Birkinshaw, J., Hood, N. and Jonsson, S. (1998) 'Building firm-specific advantages in multinational corporations: The role of subsidiary initiative', *Strategic Management Journal*, 19(3): 221–42.

Blindenbach-Driessen, F. and Van den Ende, J. (2014) 'The locus of innovation: The effect of a separate innovation unit on exploration, exploitation, and ambidexterity in manufacturing and service firms', *Journal of Product Innovation Management*, 31(5): 1089–105.

Bonesso, S., Gerli, F. and Scapolan, A. (2014) 'The individual side of ambidexterity: Do individuals' perceptions match actual behaviors in reconciling the exploration and exploitation trade-off?', *European Management Journal*, 32(3): 392–405.

Cantarello, S., Martini, A. and Nosella, A. (2012) 'A multi-level model for organizational ambidexterity in the search phase of the innovation process', *Creativity and Innovation Management*, 21(1): 28–48.

Cao, Q., Gedajlovic, E. and Zhang, H. (2009) 'Unpacking organizational ambidexterity: Dimensions, contingencies, and synergistic effects', *Organization Science*, 20(4): 781–96.

Chang, Y.-Y. and Hughes, M. (2012) 'Drivers of innovation ambidexterity in small-to medium-sized firms', *European Management Journal*, 30(1): 1–17.

Chebbi, H., Yahiaoui, D., Vrontis, D. and Thrassou, A. (2015) 'Building multiunit ambidextrous organizations – A transformative framework', *Human Resource Management*, 54(S1): s155–s177.

De Visser, M., de Weerd-Nederhof, P., Faems, D., Song, M., Van Looy, B. and Visscher, K. (2010) 'Structural ambidexterity in NPD processes: A firm-level assessment of the impact of differentiated structures on innovation performance', *Technovation*, 30(5): 291–99.

Eklinder-Frick, J., Eriksson, L.T. and Hallén, L. (2012) 'Effects of social capital on processes in a regional strategic network', *Industrial Marketing Management*, 41(5): 800–6.

Farjoun, M. (2010) 'Beyond dualism: Stability and change as a duality', *Academy of Management Review*, 35(2): 202–25.

Gassmann, O., Widenmayer, B. and Zeschky, M. (2012) 'Implementing radical innovation in the business : The role of transition modes in large firms', *R andD Management*, 42(2): 120–32.

Ghemawat, P. and Ricart Costa, J.E. (1993) 'The organizational tension between static and dynamic efficiency', *Strategic Management Journal*, 14(S2): 59–73.

Ghoshal, S. (1997) 'The individualized corporation: An interview with Sumantra Ghoshal', *European Management Journal*, 15(6): 625–32.

Gibson, C.B. and Birkinshaw, J. (2004) 'The antecedents, consequences, and mediating role of organizational ambidexterity', *Academy of Management Journal*, 47(2): 209–26.

Gilbert, C. (2005) 'Unbundling the structure of inertia: Resource versus routine rigidity', *Academy of Management Journal*, 48(5): 741–63.

Ginsberg, A. and Venkatraman, N. (1985) 'Contingency perspectives of organizational strategy: A critical review of the empirical research', *Academy of Management Review*, 10(3): 421–34.

Good, D. and Michel, E.J. (2014) 'Individual ambidexterity: Exploring and exploiting in dynamic contexts', *The Journal of Psychology*, 147(5): 435–53.

Groysberg, B. and Lee, L.E. (2009) 'Hiring stars and their colleagues: Exploration and exploitation in professional service firms', *Organization Science*, 20(4): 740–58.

Gupta, A.K., Smith, K.G. and Shalley, C.E. (2006) 'The interplay between exploration and exploitation', *Academy of Management Journal*, 49(4): 693–706.

Güttel, W.H., Konlechner, S.W. and Trede, J.K. (2015) 'Standardized individuality versus individualized standardization: The role of the context in structurally ambidextrous organizations', *Review of Managerial Science*, 9(2): 261–84.

Harvey, G., Jas, P., Walshe, K. and Skelcher, C. (2014) 'Analysing organisational context: Case studies on the contribution of absorptive capacity theory to understanding inter-organisational variation in performance improvement', *BMJ Quality and Safety*, bmjqs-2014.

He, Z.L. and Wong, P.K. (2004) 'Exploration vs. exploitation: An empirical test of the ambidexterity hypothesis', *Organization Science*, 15(4): 481–94.

Heinemeyer, M. and Amnuayskul, T. (2014) 'Innovation framework: How can departments learn from each other to increase innovativeness?' http://www.diva-portal.org/smash/get/diva2:731814/FULLTEXT01.pdf, accessed July 25, 2016.

Hill, S.A. and Birkinshaw, J. (2012) 'Ambidexterity and survival in corporate venture units', *Journal of Management*, 40(7): 1899–931.

Hjelmgren, D. and Dubois, A. (2013) 'Organising the interplay between exploitation and exploration: The case of interactive development of an information system', *Industrial Marketing Management*, 42(1): 96–105.

Hodgkinson, I.R., Ravishankar, M.N. and Aitken-Fischer, M. (2014) 'A resource-advantage perspective on the orchestration of ambidexterity', *The Service Industries Journal*, 34(15): 1234–52.

Jansen, J.J.P., Simsek, Z. and Cao, Q. (2012) 'Ambidexterity and performance in multiunit contexts: Cross-level moderating effects of structural and resource attributes', *Strategic Management Journal*, 1303(March): 1286–303.

Jansen, J.J.P., Tempelaar, M.P., Van den Bosch, F.A.J. and Volberda, H.W. (2009) 'Structural differentiation and ambidexterity: The mediating role of integration mechanisms', *Organization Science*, 20(4): 797–811.

Jasmand, C., Blazevic, V. and Ruyter, K. De. (2012) 'Generating sales while providing service: A study of customer service representatives' ambidextrous behavior', *Journal of Marketing*, 76(1): 20–37.

Kim, Y.H., Sting, F.J. and Loch, C.H. (2014) 'Top-down, bottom-up, or both? Toward an integrative perspective on operations strategy formation'. *Journal of Operations Management*, 32(7–8): 462–74.

Kostopoulos, K., Bozionelos, N. and Syrigos, E. (2015) 'Ambidexterity and Unit Performance: Intellectual Capital Antecedents and Cross-Level Moderating Effects of Human Resource Practices', *Human Resource Management*, 54(S1): s111-s132.

Laureiro-Martínez, D., Brusoni, S. and Zollo, M. (2010) 'The neuroscientific foundations of the exploration–exploitation dilemma', *Journal of Neuroscience, Psychology, and Economics*, 3(2): 95–115.

Lavie, D. and Rosenkopf, L. (2006) 'Balancing exploration and exploitation in alliance formation', *Academy of Management Journal*, 49(4): 797–818.

Lehmann, E.E., Braun, T.V. and Krispin, S. (2011) 'Entrepreneurial human capital, complementary assets, and takeover probability', *The Journal of Technology Transfer*, 37(5): 589–608.

Levinthal, D.A. and March, J.G. (1993) 'The myopia of learning', *Strategic Management Journal*, 14(S2): 95–112.

Li, C.R., Lin, C.J. and Huang, H.C. (2014) 'Top management team social capital, exploration-based innovation, and exploitation-based innovation in SMEs', *Technology Analysis and Strategic Management*, 26(1): 69–85.

Lin, H.E. and McDonough, E.F. (2014) 'Cognitive frames, learning mechanisms, and innovation ambidexterity', *Journal of Product Innovation Management*, 31: 170–88.

Lubatkin, M.H. (2006) 'Ambidexterity and performance in small-to medium-sized firms: The pivotal role of top management team behavioral integration', *Journal of Management*, 32(5): 646–72.

Lubatkin, M.H., Simsek, Z., Ling, Y. and Veiga, J.F. (2006) 'Ambidexterity and performance in small-to medium-sized firms: The pivotal role of top management team behavioral integration', *Journal of Management*, 32(5): 646–72.

Maletič, M., Maletič, D., Dahlgaard, J.J., Dahlgaard-Park, S.M. and Gomišček, B. (2014) 'Sustainability exploration and sustainability exploitation: From a literature review towards a conceptual framework', *Journal of Cleaner Production*, 79: 182–94.

Mihalache, O.R., Jansen, J.J.P., Van den Bosch, F.A.J. and Volberda, H.W. (2014) 'Top management team shared leadership and organizational ambidexterity: A moderated mediation framework', *Strategic Entrepreneurship Journal*, 8(2): 128–48.

Mom, T.J.M., Van Den Bosch, F.A.J. and Volberda, H.W. (2007) 'Investigating managers' exploration and exploitation activities: The influence of top-down, bottom-up, and horizontal knowledge inflows', *Journal of Management Studies*, 44(6): 910–31.

Mom, T.J.M., Van Den Bosch, F.a.J. and Volberda, H.W. (2009) 'Understanding variation in managers' ambidexterity: Investigating direct and interaction effects of formal structural and personal coordination mechanisms', *Organization Science*, 20(4): 812–28.

Nosella, A. (2014) 'Search practices in the early phase of the innovation process and ambidexterity: Testing a sample of high-tech companies', *Technology Analysis and Strategic Management*, 26(2): 135–53.

O'Cass, A., Heirati, N. and Ngo, L.V. (2014) 'Achieving new product success via the synchronization of exploration and exploitation across multiple levels and functional areas', *Industrial Marketing Management*, 43(5): 862–72.

O'Reilly, C.A. and Tushman, M.L. (2008) 'Ambidexterity as a dynamic capability: Resolving the innovator's dilemma', *Research in Organizational Behavior*, 28: 185–206.

O'Reilly, C.A. and Tushman, M.L. (2011) 'Organizational ambidexterity in action: How managers explore and exploit', *California Management Review*, 53(4): 5–22.

O'Reilly, C.A. and Tushman, M.L. (2013) 'Organizational ambidexterity: Past, present, and future', *The Academy of Management Perspectives*, 27(4): 324–38.

Patel, P.C., Messersmith, J.G. and Lepak, D.P. (2013) 'Walking the tightrope : An assessment of the relationship between high-performance work systems and organizational ambidexterity', *Academy of Management Journal*, 56(5): 1420–42.

Pellegrinelli, Murray-Webster, R. and Turner, N. (2014) 'Facilitating organizational ambidexterity through the complementary use of projects and programs', *International Journal of Project Management*, 33(1): 153–64.

Prieto-Pastor, I. and Martin-Perez, V. (2014) 'Does HRM generate ambidextrous employees for ambidextrous learning? The moderating role of management support', *The International Journal of Human Resource Management*, 26(5): 589–615.

Puranam, P. and Srikanth, K. (2007) 'What they know vs. what they do: How acquirers leverage technology acquisitions', *Strategic Management Journal*, 28(8): 805–25.

Raisch, S., Birkinshaw, J., Probst, G. and Tushman, M.L. (2009) 'Organizational ambidexterity: Balancing exploitation and exploration for sustained performance', *Organization science*, 20(4): 685–95.

Rothaermel, F.T. and Alexandre, M.T. (2009) 'Ambidexterity in technology sourcing: The moderating role of absorptive capacity', *Organization Science*, 20(4): 759–80.

Sarkees, M., Hulland, J. and Chatterjee, R. (2014) 'Investments in exploitation and exploration capabilities: Balance versus focus', *The Journal of Marketing Theory and Practice*, 22(1): 7–24.

Sears, J. and Hoetker, G. (2014) 'Technological overlap, technological capabilities, and resource recombination in technological acquisitions', *Strategic Management Journal*, 35(1): 48–67.

Siggelkow, N. and Levinthal, D.A. (2003) 'Temporarily divide to conquer: Centralized, decentralized, and reintegrated organizational approaches to exploration and adaptation', *Organization Science*, 14(6): 650–69.

Sirén, C. a., Kohtamäki, M. and Kuckertz, A. (2012) 'Exploration and exploitation strategies, profit performance, and the mediating role of strategic learning: Escaping the exploitation trap', *Strategic Entrepreneurship Journal*, 6(1): 18–41.

Song, M. and Chen, Y. (2014) 'Organizational attributes, market growth, and product innovation', *Journal of Product Innovation Management*, 31(6): 1312–29.

Stadler, C., Rajwani, T. and Karaba, F. (2014) 'Solutions to the exploration/exploitation dilemma: Networks as a new level of analysis', *International Journal of Management Reviews*, 16(2): 172–93.

Stettner, U. and Lavie, D. (2014) 'Ambidexterity under scrutiny: Exploration and exploitation via internal organization, alliances, and acquisitions', *Strategic Management Journal*, 35(13): 1903–29.

Sun, L.Y., Aryee, S. and Law, K.S. (2007) 'High-performance human resource practices, citizenship behavior, and organizational performance: A relational perspective', *Academy of Management Journal*, 50(3): 558–77.

Swart, J. and Kinnie, N. (2010) 'Organisational learning, knowledge assets and HR practices in professional service firms', *Human Resource Management Journal*, 20(1): 64–79.

Taylor, A. and Helfat, C.E. (2009) 'Organizational linkages for surviving technological change: Complementary assets, middle management, and ambidexterity', *Organization Science*, 20(4): 718–39.

Turner, K.L. and Makhija, M.V. (2012) 'The role of individuals in the information processing perspective', *Strategic Management Journal*, 33(6): 661–80.

Turner, N. and Lee-Kelley, L. (2012) 'Unpacking the theory on ambidexterity: An illustrative case on the managerial architectures, mechanisms and dynamics', *Management Learning*, 1350507612444074.

Turner, N., Swart, J. and Maylor, H. (2013) 'Mechanisms for managing ambidexterity: A review and research agenda', *International Journal of Management Reviews*, 15(3): 317–32.

Tushman, M.L. and O Reilly, C.A.I. (1996) 'Ambidextrous organizations : Managing evolutionary and revolutionary change', *California Management Review*, 38(4): 8.

Uotila, J., Maula, M., Keil, T. and Zahra, S.A. (2009) 'Exploration, exploitation, and financial performance: Analysis of S andP 500 corporations', *Strategic Management Journal*, 231(November 2008): 221–31.

Voss, G. B. and Voss, Z.G. (2012) 'Strategic ambidexterity in small and medium-sized enterprises: Implementing exploration and exploitation in product and market domains', *Organization Science*, 7039: 1–19.

Yang, T. and Li, C. (2011) 'Competence exploration and exploitation in new product development. Management', *Decision*, 49(9): 1444–70.

Zacher, H., Robinson, A.J. and Rosing, K. (2014) 'Ambidextrous leadership and employees' self-reported innovative performance: The role of exploration and exploitation behaviors', *The Journal of Creative Behavior*, 50(1): 24–46.

Zajac, E.J., Kraatz, M.S. and Bresser, R.K.F. (2000) 'Modeling the dynamics of strategic fit : A normative approach to strategic change', *Strategic Management Journal*, 453(august 1999): 429–53.

9 Learning to compete

Entrepreneurial roles exploiting knowledge spillovers

Ronald C. Beckett and *Gerard Berendsen*

Introduction

Entrepreneurship is about translating a vision into a reality, generally with limited resources, and overcoming obstacles along the way. It involves launching and evolving a new enterprise. The vision may or may not include ideas new to the world, but will be new in the context in which the enterprise operates, and there is some uncertainty about the viability of the new operation. Once established, the same mindset may facilitate growth of the enterprise. Whilst there is often an emphasis on the heroic individual, it takes a multidisciplinary team enacting a variety of roles to create and extract value.

Entrepreneurs tend to see the world differently, like Albert Szent-Gyorgyi (1937), Nobel prize winner, who offered the following thought: 'Discovery consists of seeing what everybody has seen, and thinking what nobody has thought.' For entrepreneurs their vision may be stimulated by technological or market knowledge spillovers, but this requires a capacity to appreciate the significance of what is observed – a matter of absorptive capacity. Drawing on a thematic analysis of 289 published articles, Lane, Koka and Pathak (2006:865) suggested the following definition of the absorptive capacity construct: 'Absorptive capacity is a firm's ability to utilize externally held knowledge through three sequential processes: (1) recognizing and understanding potentially valuable new knowledge outside the firm through exploratory learning, (2) assimilating valuable new knowledge through transformative learning, and (3) using the assimilated knowledge to create new knowledge and commercial outputs through exploitative learning.' In other words, becoming aware of new knowledge is not enough – it needs to be combined with other knowledge.

Creating conditions that support entrepreneurship as a strategic tool is the role of industry and government leaders. Established firms may need to nurture entrepreneurship as a strategic imperative to compete in changing environments, but to successfully do so requires particular employee and management competencies. Governments nurture entrepreneurship as a strategic imperative promoting regional development (e.g. Venkataraman, 2004). In researching public sector entrepreneurship, Bartlett and Dibben (2002) noted the need for a combined effort by a champion and a sponsor in facilitating initiatives in a local government setting, and that stakeholder considerations were different for internal and external-oriented initiatives.

This background and prior studies leads us to think about some generic roles that support entrepreneurship as a process (e.g. as viewed by Baron and Shane, 2008) that benefits from knowledge spillovers. Do we always need a champion and sponsor, an innovator and a broker? Are there other roles that need to be considered? What activities are associated with these roles and how do they interact?

These questions are also raised in a body of literature about innovation champions and intermediary enterprises, and we will start with a discussion of the literature. We will draw on observations from more than 60 case studies of innovative small and medium-sized enterprises (SMEs) assembled over a number of years in conjunction with academic colleagues, plus some personal experience with larger firms. We present descriptions of two spillover program examples along with a specific project initiated from each one. Observations from the literature and these cases facilitate a discussion of balancing exploration and exploitation initiatives to deliver value.

Some multidisciplinary viewpoints

The notion of aligning multiple functions does not seem reflected in the academic literature. Whilst there are elements of knowledge, innovation and technological change frequently associated with entrepreneurship, Bhupatiraju et al. (2012) observed from network analysis of a citation database covering each area that there was little cross-referencing. There are none-the-less some common elements such as obtaining advantage from the interplay of exploration and exploitation activities. Someone must champion the cause, and there needs to be some particular forms of sponsorship. There are structured multi-stage processes that support evolutionary value creation, and there are varying degrees and forms of 3rd party engagement. In the following review we consider what is common and what is different in generic roles supporting innovation, knowledge spillovers and entrepreneurship.

Innovation champions

It is recognised that without a champion who shows persistence, belief and commitment, an innovative idea may not realise its full potential (e.g. Schon, 1963). Coakes and Smith (2007) suggest (p77) 'Championing innovation must become a norm in organisations and not an episodic event that relies on happenstance and a strong-minded individual expending large amounts of effort.' Support for both an individual idea and the process of innovating is required. An Innovation Champion has been described as someone who links people passionate about their idea with others who can help them (e.g. Howell et al., 2005). Or it might be someone who more broadly supports the process of innovating by providing permissions and resources (e.g. Barsh et al., 2008). Some descriptors used by management researchers include: new product champion, user champion, technology champion, business innovator, project champion, gatekeeper, organizational change agent, organisational maverick, innovation midwife, broker, network facilitator, consultant, idea champion, innovation team, innovation ambassador, power champion, transformational leader, organisational buffer, senior management sponsor, and executive champion. Some organisations established with the express purpose of stimulating innovation may be seen as champions of the process of innovating (e.g. Howells, 2006). A study drawing on more than 60 Australian and Dutch case studies (Beckett and Berendsen, 2015) suggested this list of role descriptors could be represented in three meta-roles as follows.

The idea champion

What is ultimately seen as an innovation starts with an idea or an invention. The incorporation of an idea into a product or process or practice requires first an individual, then progressively more people to become enthusiastic about its potential. An idea champion may be the originator of the idea or someone who picks it up (Damanpour and Wischnevsky, 2006). As an idea evolves into a usable innovation, there may be handovers between idea champions along the way who promote and adapt its ability to satisfy unmet needs, passing the baton in the style of a relay race. The idea champion is continuously promoting/selling the idea to others.

The interaction champion

The interaction champion is seen as a champion of the innovation process and excels in bringing people, organizations and resources together, acting like a hub to make it all happen. Martin (2011) described how a catalyst role has been beneficially formalised in one firm. Catalysts might be an expert, but are more likely to be generalists. They distinguish themselves by being the go-to person for others, by committing time and effort to solving problems. Dalziel (2010) suggested that interaction can be supported by innovation intermediaries – external organizations or groups within organizations that work to facilitate innovation, either directly by enabling the innovativeness of one or more firms, or indirectly by enhancing the innovative capacity of regions, nations, or sectors. Howells (2006) studied the potential services offered by various kinds of innovation intermediary organisations, identifying ten functions and 28 sub-functions helping to discover, develop and deploy innovations. Not all functions were provided by a particular intermediary – there was a tendency towards specialisation. He made the point that intermediaries do not operate on a simple 'one-to-one-to-one' basis, but in more complex ways. Howells also noted that increasingly both the initiator of an innovation and potential users are engaging with intermediary organisations, who facilitate two-way flows.

The investment champion

This kind of champion frequently takes a strategic view, confirming innovation as an enterprise or regional necessity with top management support, establishing

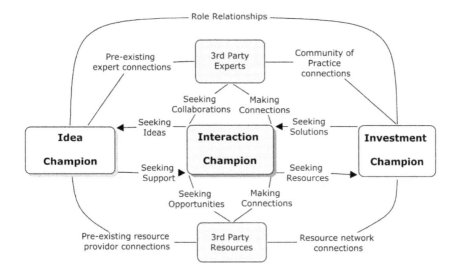

Figure 9.1 Generic innovation roles and some interactions between them

program credibility, understanding risks and finding ways to preserve budgets (Dong et al., 2009). A particular approach to innovation may need promotion at this level, e.g. open innovation (Chesborough and Crowther, 2006), business model innovation (Bucherer et al., 2012). An infrastructure champion may stimulate innovation by promoting a supportive culture, by establishing infrastructure like research and testing laboratories and by funding interaction champions. Governments may play this role to address perceived market failures (Martin and Scott, 2000). The infrastructure champion creates access to relevant resources and assets and coordinates the approach and processes in line with the desired strategy.

Beckett and Berendsen (2015) identified two additional roles supporting a project team in some, but not all cases:

- *3rd party experts* who may provide advice to any of the champions at some stage of development
- *3rd party resource providers* who may provide access to supplementary finance or to specialist infrastructure.

It was noted there could be direct two-way interactions between the different kinds of actors within a project context or external to it, some of which are illustrated in Figure 9.1.

Knowledge spillover champions

Knowledge spillovers may facilitate the enhancement of an established operation, solving a current problem, launching an innovation project or launching a new business enterprise. But how does this happen? As with innovation and entrepreneurship, there are activities exploring possibilities and exploiting opportunities associated with knowledge spillovers in a variety of contexts (e.g. Lavie et al., 2010). Large firms seeking new sources of competitive advantage from knowledge spillovers may change their strategies accordingly and leverage their market power. In a presentation on open innovation, the Phillips Company suggested that 'Innovation is 99% shared technology and 1% exclusive technology', and announced – the lab is our world but 'not invented here' of the past is compared with 'proudly found here' of today.

At the same time, small firms are seen as 'an important conduit for the spillover of knowledge from an incumbent organization creating that knowledge to a new organization, commercializing that knowledge through innovative activity' (Acs and Audretsh, 2010, p296). Kickul and Gundry (2002) studied the practices of 107 small business owners seeking sources of competitive advantage, finding that a prospector strategy orientation mediated the relationship between proactive personality and three types of innovations: innovative targeting processes, innovative organizational systems, and innovative boundary supports. Here the quest was for both ideas and improved practices.

Breschi and Lissoni (2001) had noted the need for a knowledge production function to be linked with a knowledge transmission function to facilitate knowledge transfer. This might be through the movement of people to share their tacit knowledge or via other means to share codified knowledge. In either case the recipient needed the absorptive capacity to benefit from the transfer, and there may be some time lags in the process. Inkpen and Tsang (2005) examined how social capital affected knowledge transfer, suggesting that structural, cognitive and relational dimensions influenced three types of network (intra-corporate, strategic alliance and industrial district) in different ways. Whilst structural elements varied, working towards common goals and the need for relational trust were common attributes.

As practitioners, the authors have observed knowledge spillovers at three organisational levels:

1   *At the project level.* First, where technology developed in one project can be used in another project, even if the first project was unsuccessful, and second where management lessons learned can be used in subsequent projects. In our observation the most effective facilitating mechanism is the interaction of people through progressive projects and project phases. Fershtmann and Gandal (2011) observed this effect in open source projects where social networks were a facilitating resource. Consistent with the observations of Bogers and Lhuilery (2011), we observe spillovers may come via a variety of project functional participants. First an R&D function may identify technology spillovers from 3rd party researchers. Second, manufacturing may contribute spillovers from supplier or competitors sources. Third, the marketing function may identify spillovers from customer or competitor sources. Ajmal and Koskinen (2008) observe that knowledge transfer in project-based organisations (e.g. in Construction and Defence sectors) could encounter a number of obstacles that may be minimised if an organisational culture supporting the creation, sharing and utilisation of knowledge is established.

2 *At the enterprise level.* Knowledge from one part of a large enterprise has been observed to spill over into another part. A study of 105 MNC subsidiaries by Yang et al. (2008) found that whilst inflows from a parent organisation might be expected, there were also beneficial outflows from the subsidiaries, providing the value of such outflows are appreciated by the parent. Tsai (2001) has observed that business unit innovation is influenced by the centrality of its position (subject to both internal and external knowledge flows) and its absorptive capacity. Knowledge may flow between enterprises from different forms of collaborative arrangement (e.g. benchmarking – Hyland and Beckett, 2002 or innovation networks – Sammarra and Biggiero, 2008). Multiple studies of best practice transfer suggest that inhibitors may be the absorptive capacity of the recipient firm, the extent to which knowledge sharing has been legitimised, and the matching of internal and external context (e.g. Szulanski, 1996). Spillovers of technological, market and/or managerial knowledge may occur, subject to what the participants are prepared to share via alliances. Success factors relating to the extent to which the firms are complementary, and the extent to which they may compete (e.g. Bouncken and Kraus, 2013) can influence what is shared and what can be utilised by the recipient enterprise.

3 *At the industry level.* There is a large body of literature relating to academia/government researcher–industry knowledge spillovers (e.g. Ponds, van Oort and Frenken, 2010) where matters of geographic proximity and broader professional networks influence the impact of spillovers on regional innovation. Such spillovers may be facilitated by intermediary organisations. One example is the Finnish organisation Spinverse that aims at 'accelerating innovation' by drawing on researcher and unwanted corporate intellectual property. At the end of 2015 it was claimed that 83 innovations resulted in start-up companies; that established companies adopted 29 innovations; and that 1000 new jobs had been created between 2009 and 2014. Technological spillovers between industry sectors may support recombinant innovation initiatives (e.g. Hargadon, 2003). The Danish Alexandra Institute is an example of an intermediary organisation working this way. Whilst it is a multidisciplinary organisation, its primary focus is on information technology applications. In broad terms, large-scale ICT technologies like satellite navigation and cloud computing are applied in non-ICT sectors, such as the agriculture sector, engaging with both industry and users. The re-use of generic business models initially developed in one industry sector but also utilised in another provides an example of a managerial spillover supporting strategic positioning. Take the case of the 'power by the hour' business model initiated by Rolls Royce (Smith, 2013). Instead of simply selling a major technologically complex item, it is leased by the user and paid for on a usage basis. The idea has been adopted by General Electric in both their power and medical technology businesses, and by Caterpiller in their mining technology business. Business models combine a customer value proposition with a means of delivering value and extracting value for the provider along the way. Spillover knowledge about markets and about operational processes

may facilitate the development of unique interpretations of particular opportunities in international markets (e.g. Filatotchev et al, 2009) or different industry sectors (e.g. George and Bock, 2011).

In summary, whilst the dominant narrative relates to technological knowledge spillovers, competitive advantage may be obtained from managerial and market knowledge spillovers. Firms seeking advantage from knowledge spillovers need to establish structures to explore possibilities (e.g. networking arrangements) and have the absorptive capacity to facilitate exploiting opportunities. Having a clear challenge or goal provides a focus for knowledge spillover activities, and trust facilitates knowledge sharing. The knowledge spillover literature implies key enabling roles may be characterised as:

- Prospector, searching for specific possibilities (e.g. Kickul and Gundry, 2002)
- Interpreter, conveying the significance of a spillover idea and helping others reinterpret it (e.g. Zahra and George, 2002),
- Mentor/facilitator nurturing a culture of knowledge sharing, supporting positive social interactions (e.g. Yang, 2007), and
- Champion, endorsing the utility of working with knowledge spillovers, investing in related processes and building trust from a position of influence (e.g. Inkpen, 1998).

Strategic entrepreneurship champions

Firms make strategic decisions about what kind of business to be in, e.g. manufacturing, retail, professional services, based on three considerations: accessible capabilities, accessible resources and perceived opportunities. The *entrepreneur* identifies and pursues opportunities and is able to create a vision of a future that is novel in some context and mobilises resources to achieve that vision. At the core of entrepreneurship is the notion of creating a stand-alone enterprise that establishes a new market niche or fills a gap in an existing market. Value creation may involve moving towards a sell-off or an IPO, it may involve global domination of a specific niche, or developing a platform for substantial growth.

Hitt et al. (2001, p479) have suggested 'Entrepreneurship involves identifying and exploiting entrepreneurial opportunities. However, to create the most value entrepreneurial firms also need to act strategically. This calls for an integration of entrepreneurial and strategic thinking.' Kuratko and Audretch (2009) note that strategic entrepreneurship may be framed in two contexts:

- Entrepreneurial strategy – (citing Morris et al., 2008, p194) 'A vision-directed, organisation-wide reliance on entrepreneurial behaviour that purposefully and continuously rejuvenates the organisation and shapes the scope of its operations through the recognition and exploitation of entrepreneurial opportunity'. It is not just a course of action to be pursued; rather it is more of a mindset.
- A strategy for entrepreneurship – concerns the need to develop a strategy for guiding particular entrepreneurial activities within the firm.

Van de Ven (1993) observed that from an infrastructure perspective there are interactions between institutional, resource endowment and proprietary functional roles and that success 'rests on orchestrating a highly uncertain journey by linking with numerous organisations and actors and *appropriating the competencies and resources relevant to developing and commercialising the innovation*' (p220).

Hayton and Kelley (2006) maintain that an entrepreneurial team collectively requires some generic competencies, defined in terms of:

* Knowledge – specialist core, multidisciplinary and organisational knowledge
* Skills – cognitive ability, creativity, analogic reasoning, influencing, transformational leadership, emotional intelligence and networking
* Personality – conscientiousness, openness to experience, confidence, credibility, risk tolerance.
* Tenacity and passion were required by all actors.

They characterised generic functional roles as:

* Innovating – involving opportunity recognition, defined as having the creative insight about particular knowledge and information combinations and what they can mean for users – and the company seeking to serve these customers.
* Brokering – accessing new sources of information and knowledge, transferring this knowledge and combining different sources, both existing and new.
* Championing – identifying with the project, and taking responsibility for its success and success is often dependent on champions.
* Sponsoring – helping entrepreneurs gain access to the resources they need for their ventures. They ensure there is legitimacy and support for the project and may also provide advice and guidance to the venture on how to best proceed. Higher-level sponsors can use their power and control over resources to get the support necessary for the projects they value. Sponsors differ from champions. While a champion identifies and selects projects deserving support, a sponsor ensures that resources become available.

Ireland et al. (2001) identified six contextual factors that collectively create firm wealth through entrepreneurship:

* Innovation – bringing novelty to the firm and to the marketplace, the centrality of the idea;
* Networks – bringing firms and networks together;
* Internationalisation – extending the firm/s reach and potential;
* Organisational learning – facilitating rapid transfer of knowledge;
* Top management teams and governance – mechanisms serving stakeholders;
* Growth – stimulating success and change in entrepreneurial ventures and through mergers/acquisitions.

The challenge is to establish an integrating operational space.

In considering structural arrangements, Wolcott and Lippitz (2007) suggested four scenarios that link the nature of organisational responsibility (ownership) for corporate entrepreneurship with responsibility for providing resources in a corporate entrepreneurship setting:

- The enabler – the firm provides funding and senior executive attention to prospective projects;
- The producer – the firm establishes and supports a full service group with a mandate for corporate entrepreneurship;
- The advocate – the firm strongly endorses corporate entrepreneurship, but business units provide primary funding;
- The opportunist – the firm has no deliberate approach to corporate entrepreneurship. Internal and external networks drive concept selection and resource allocation.

Thompson and Downing (2007) examined ways to identify and support entrepreneurs with potential in a corporate setting. Enabling roles were seen as talent spotting, counselling (to help people realise their potential), advising (about sources of knowledge and resources), training (imparting relevant knowledge), performance coaching (improving competence in business functions), mentoring (helping to redraw and reshape the bigger picture), and personal coaching (developing and enhancing individual capabilities).

The literature suggests a number of roles that support strategic entrepreneurship: talent spotter, entrepreneurial visionary, opportunist, enabler, advocate, producer, advisor, networker, investment custodian, resource allocator, innovator, broker, champion, and sponsor. Using the higher level structure described in the discussion of innovation champions, the following roles are suggested:

- Entrepreneurial Visionary – an opportunist able to 'sell' a clear vision of the end-game, using internal and external networks to facilitate its implementation.
- Entrepreneurship Champion – understands and facilitates the process of business-building and how to extract value from it. Includes talent-spotter, enabler, networker, broker and gatekeeper functions.
- Investment Champion – sponsors entrepreneurship as a strategic tool, establishes infrastructure, advocates for an opportunity, allocates resources, acts as an investment custodian for a variety of stakeholders.
- 3rd Party Expert – providing specialist business (e.g. legal, regulatory, market) and technological knowledge, personal and business mentoring services.
- 3rd Party Resource Provider – providing supplementary financial support (e.g. venture capital or government grants) or access to specialist infrastructure (e.g. business incubators, supply/logistics networks, development/testing facilities).

Innovation, knowledge spillover and entrepreneurship roles

The notion of enterprise generic roles is embedded in the business sector with titles like CEO, CFO and CTO, HRM Director, etc.; in filmmaking with titles like Cast, Director, Producer, and Screenwriter, and in sport with tiles like Club Manager, Player and Coach. It is hypothesised that if one of these requisite enterprise or team roles is not effectively enacted, the outcome can be sub-optimal. There is less clarity about generic roles supporting strategic entrepreneurship exploiting knowledge spillovers.

The recurring theme from the previous observations is that there needs to be someone enthusiastic about a particular proposal, someone who sponsors a proposal(s) in some way, and some process for achieving the desired outcome. The word 'champion' is used differently in the three literature streams considered earlier. A knowledge spillover champion was regarded as someone who invests in the process of opportunity identification. An innovation champion may be someone who promotes a particular idea, someone who facilitates the innovation process, or someone who supports and invests in innovation as a strategic tool. In the corporate entrepreneurship literature a champion is seen as someone identifying with a project that takes responsibility for its success. This may not be the person who first identifies the business opportunity.

A common thread in all three literatures is the need to explore possibilities and exploit opportunities. This leads us to suggest the need for two kinds of role – the first kind associated with opportunity identification and promotion, and the second kind associated with opportunity realisation. The outcome of combining this global view with the notion of meta-roles from our innovation studies leads to the encapsulation of five generic functional roles shown in Table 9.1.

Table 9.1 Five generic roles facilitating innovation, entrepreneurship and knowledge spillovers

Kind of role	Generic functional role
Opportunity identification and promotion core roles	Opportunity Explorer: including idea champion (innovation context), prospector (knowledge spillover context), entrepreneurial visionary (entrepreneurship context) variants
Opportunity realisation process core roles	Core role of Process Champion that may support multiple individual opportunities: including interaction champion (innovation context), interpreter (knowledge sharing context), entrepreneurship champion
	Core role of Investment Champion: (innovation and entrepreneurship contexts), champion (legitimising knowledge sharing in a knowledge diffusion context). These are process legitimisation, authority assignment and resource allocation roles.
Supporting roles that may facilitate exploration or exploitation activities	3rd party expert providing business and technology inputs in innovation and entrepreneurship contexts, intermediary organisations facilitating matchmaking in a knowledge spillover context
	3rd party resource providers giving access to financial assets, complementary physical assets and to specific intellectual property

Two illustrative examples

The following case studies provide examples of strategic entrepreneurship programs with a knowledge spillover orientation. Each program supported multiple initiatives, and each case describes one of those initiatives to give some program level and project level insights. The cases selected had been observed over a longer period of time (more than 4 years) and from that point of view provided a richer data set.

A Dutch case study

This case describes a strategic initiative stimulated through a Dutch regional collaboration, MAIN (Manufacturing & Innovation Network East Netherlands) in response to challenges from the globalisation of business. The regional network is supported by seven local network organisations that, in conjunction with their client firms developed the concept of pursuing innovative ideas through collaborative efforts, bringing together enterprises to both combine physical capabilities and stimulate knowledge spillovers. The entrepreneurs in this case had already established businesses they were seeking to sustain or grow. About 20 business cases were initially developed, each involving two or more firms. Support was sought from local, regional and national governments. A pilot program involving four business cases was launched in 2007. It was observed that a lead time of about 3 years was required, with an investment of the order of €250,000 and strong project management was required. Larger scale funding was subsequently negotiated through the combined contributions of a number government agencies. Program delays were experienced due to the 2008–2010 Global Financial Crisis as the firms struggled with cash flow difficulties, and a 3-year support program with a completion date in 2012 was established, subject to compliance with a framework of detailed rules. Sixteen business cases were initially supported, and grants provided to individual project groups included provision for project management, administration, pubic relations and knowledge transfer costs. Each business case was assigned an external moderator to mediate between the government agencies and the individual firms.

Whilst the broad focus of the business cases was on manufacturing excellence, particularly where a stand-alone product was to be developed, there was a need for additional knowledge, expertise and market access arrangements beyond that resident in the collaborating firms. The specific business case described below involved two firms that traditionally served different business sectors collaborating to develop a metal surface protection process that provided flow-on benefits to both firms.

The companies were Aeronamic, an aerospace specialist component manufacturer with operations in the Netherlands and Romania, and EmoTech, a Dutch designer, manufacturer and maintainer of industrial coating equipment. Some years before, the firms had been aware of each other in a different setting, and this facilitated development of a specific joint business initiative. The challenge was to economically apply semi-automated industrial powder coating technologies in the manufacture of light metal aerospace components in a high variety/low volume production environment. Chemical surface pre-treatment would be followed by powder coating and baking to yield a durable, lightweight protective coating without degrading the performance on the underlying metal.

Whilst both companies were successful innovators in their fields, they were inexperienced in collaborative ventures. A separate development operation was established, drawing team members from both firms, based on their expertise. There were cultural differences between the firms – one having a production orientation and the other a project management orientation, and each using different project management tools. Both a detailed project plan and a code of behaviour were agreed. It was observed that their successful implementation required mutual trust. It was also observed that in addition to having technical expertise, the team could benefit from the enactment of a variety of generic roles (such as resource investigator, coordinator, completer) as suggested by Belbin (1996). The DMAIC methodology (Define, Measure, Analyse, Improve, Control) was adopted to provide common understandings of what had to be done to progress the project and to deal with emergent issues. It was found that providing interim progress reports and documenting issues, whilst an additional effort, forced participants to stand back a little and reflect on the current position and future actions.

As has been observed in many projects involving new combinations of established technologies, there were different kinds of issues to be resolved – technical issues at each process step, system integration and budget issues. Whilst there was a risk assessment at the planning stage, there was little detail about how to confront the issues identified. Perseverance, remaining focused on the goal, and contributions by the external moderator helped to resolve such issues. The project was successfully completed. Aeronamic had established a novel facility, and could be regarded as a launch customer for new EmoTech technologies. One issue noted with the knowledge spillover scenario was that whatever is developed is difficult to patent, as the novelty is in the way existing elements are combined. This resulted in a 'trade secret' approach to IP protection, again emphasising the need for mutual trust.

An Australian case study

This case describes a strategic entrepreneurship program where Victorian (Australia) State Government Departments were invited to submit a 'challenge' for someone to develop a product/service needed by their client base or the community in general. It was based on a US Small Business Innovation Research program (see Audretsch, 2003) that has been operating successfully for some 30 years. The strategic intent was to deliver community value from the investment made by addressing a specific issue and delivering economic benefits by stimulating entrepreneurial firm growth. A structured process brought together non-traditional partners.

Departmental submissions were reviewed and a short list published seeking innovative solutions from Victorian SMEs. 'Challenge' Departments were declared to be the sponsor/champion at a project level and chaired a project control board related to their particular challenge. At the program level, the Minister for Innovation, Services and Small Business was declared to be the program sponsor, responsible for funding and the release of approved 'technology challenges'. The Minister's Department was responsible for program implementation. A number of challenges were funded through three stages, depending on the quality of the submission, its emergent practicality and the budget available. Following a pilot program, a broader range of challenges was issued in 2010, and another set in 2012. Some projects were into the deployment stage by 2014. The entrepreneurs in this case were a mix of people with ideas who wanted to establish a new business or people who wanted to expand a business they had launched.

At the Feasibility Study Project stage, up to $75,000 was available to help selected SMEs undertake a 3-month study into their proposed solution to a government challenge. Some submissions may have already passed this stage at the time of submission. Technology and commercialisation experts drawn from an independently established panel reviewed and assessed Feasibility Study reports, and provided expert advice to the Government when required. Accepted proposals were supported in a proof of concept program, and subsequently in a program supporting commercialisation. The commercialisation support program assisted Victorian technology businesses to establish global markets in conjunction with contracted partner organisations specialising in technology commercialisation. The commercialisation partner organisations provide a suite of targeted learning programs to assist SMEs to use and develop science and technology for export, growth and profit. Over the period 2010–2014 some 32 feasibility studies were completed, but only about half the proposals proceeded beyond this stage.

Collaboration was encouraged under the program. Lead SMEs could choose to collaborate with another business enterprise, a university or other publicly funded research institute. All collaborations had to be SME-led. The total contribution to the proof of concept project from collaboration partners could not exceed the value of 30 percent of the total project grant. Some projects went into the proof of concept stage slowly as firms took time to organise the requisite co-funding, whilst others had moved on to the commercialisation stage. As a part of the proof of concept, the Department issuing the challenge could assume the role of lead user, and experts putting the challenge could provide specialist advice during development. When products/services were developed, the government could become a lead customer, potentially helping in broader marketing of the product/service.

This is illustrated in the following project case where a challenge was put by the Royal Children's Hospital, Melbourne. The following information was drawn from publicly available documents and a videotaped interview with some project participants. The Hospital's Nutrition & Food Services provides nutrition care to over 150 infants daily. This includes sick and small neonates, and infants undergoing cardiac surgery with complex nutrition needs and feeding difficulties. The service uses up to 400 teats daily, and currently these often fail to meet the needs of infants with feeding difficulties. Teats had been found to produce flow rates varying by as much as 50 percent. The wrong flow rate makes it difficult for an infant learning to feed, but as the flow rate is highly sensitive to the force applied when teats and bottles are assembled, the appropriate teat for an infant can be very difficult to identify.

The solution developed by a design and development firm (APS Innovations) incorporated a teat form that has been anatomically designed to suit the needs of feeding infants. Development was carried out over a 4-year period in close collaboration with The Royal Children's Hospital, accessing anatomical scan data not previously available to designers, leading to provisional patents for both the anatomical shape and venting system. Beginning as a specialist services company to the plastics industry, APS Innovations has grown to be a company capable of developing products from a simple, single component right through to complex electro-mechanical devices. APS Innovations identified and sourced new non-toxic material, customised the teat form and developed a compatible feeding bottle to deliver reliable flow with the additional benefits of easy flow identification, recyclability and simpler functionality.

Drawing together people experienced in different fields during development identified some challenges that were not anticipated, leading to some applied research into the breathing/feeding process appropriate to premature babies and the use of non-traditional materials, and to some operational knowledge spillovers.

A spinoff company (Sepal Pty Ltd.) was established to manufacture and package the products in volume, consistent with regulatory requirements, with the Royal Children's Hospital as a launch customer. Whilst the government may be viewed as the investment champion in the early stages of development, the participating firms still had to find 50 percent of the total cash, with commercial finance channels supporting company growth. However the government-supported activities did help make the potential spinoff company 'investment-ready'.

Discussion

Observations from the cases

In both cases, some form of challenge had stimulated the strategic programs. In the Dutch case, the challenge was from the internationalisation of business that stimulated the exploration of new sources of competitive advantage through sharing complementary knowledge sets. In the Australian case, the challenge was finding cost-effective ways to stimulate regional entrepreneurship whilst delivering community benefits. In both cases there were clear goals. In both cases business plans had to be developed and critically reviewed. In both cases some form of joint investor/entrepreneur governance arrangement was established to help manage projects at the development stage. In both project examples there was a close link between end-users and technology developers. In the Dutch case a spinoff development team was established with a negotiated charter. In the Australian case a spinoff firm was launched following the development phase. The desired performance outcome in both cases was to deliver long-term benefits.

Utilising ideas presented in Table 9.1, we identified who was responsible for opportunity identification and for capturing value from it, and who provided support. Not all of the initial project proposals associated with our two illustrative case programs received government support, and some that received seed funding did not proceed to the next stage. Generally, they did not attract investment champion support in a competitive program environment.

We observed that individual actors could play different roles in different circumstances. There were roles played in establishing the programs described, roles played in the projects described, and roles played at different project stages. For example, the government employee who played an opportunity identification role in setting up the Australian program became a process champion engaged in its implementation. A government group who played an opportunity identification role during program roll-out became 3rd party experts, then acted as a different kind of champion as a lead user. At the program launch stage, the government saw itself as an investment champion, whereas the firms involved at the project level saw it as a 3rd party resource provider whose influence diminished with time as they initially had to provide a matching contribution, then more funding as the projects reached the commercial deployment stage.

We observed that the process champion exploitation role required the broadest set of capabilities and connections, similar to the broker function described by Hayton and Kelly (2006), and that a variety of internal and external actors could contribute to this role at different times. For example in the Dutch case, the founding industry network, the project SMEs and the funding program moderators all made contributions at some time, such as helping to make network connections.

From an exploration–exploitation interaction perspective, we suggest opportunity exploitation pathways may depend on the opportunity identification source as shown in Table 9.2.

Extracting value from spillovers

The strategic decision to extract value from knowledge spillovers requires action to identify candidate spillovers (e.g. through patent data mining), or to search for solutions to a current problem outside a traditional field or place (e.g. adopting Indian frugal innovation ideas). Our cases illustrated some other possibilities. The notion of cooperative entrepreneurship that brings enterprises with different knowledge bases together was described in the Dutch case. The notion of traditional user-developer cooperation is extended in the Australian case to bring people from different industry sectors together.

Table 9.2 Alternative opportunity sources and possible exploitation pathways

Opportunity identification source	Opportunity exploitation pathways
Knowledge spillover stimulates innovation or entrepreneurial action	Innovation may spawn a novel product, process, or organisational arrangement that adds value to enterprise operations, with novelty resulting from the way existing artefacts or organisational arrangements are combined rather than from something new to the world. An entrepreneur may pursue a niche opportunity in the original market space, a start-up business at a different time and place or an opportunity in a parallel market space.
Innovation stimulates knowledge spillover or entrepreneurship	Knowledge spillover from innovation may stimulate a search for applications of knowledge declared available for export or publicly broadcast by its creator(s), e.g. researchers seeking applications for their ideas Entrepreneurship may establish a high-tech start-up or expand a business combining innovative ideas with perceived opportunities
Entrepreneurial action stimulates knowledge spillover or innovation	Knowledge spillover from one business activity may highlight an opportunity for a non-competing enterprise or replication, e.g. through a franchising strategy Unmet needs identified by an entrepreneur may stimulate research and development of a new or improved product or process.

For extracting value from knowledge spillovers to become embedded in enterprise culture, responsibility for action needs to be assigned and a process put in place. Here we outline an approach taken by IBM as reported by Bjelland and Wood (2008).

Starting in 2001, IBM had established a practice of inviting all employees to participate in a 3-day online 'Jam' session exploring a challenge confronting the firm. Whether employees were working from home, at client premises or at globally disparate locations, all could contribute a post via IBM's intranet, and they could see other people's posts. There were about 52,000 posts from the 2001 session, and a form of data mining tool was used to encapsulate ideas for action. 2006 was the first time the focus was on accelerating the launch of new technologies. The 'Jam' involved 150,000 participants contributing 62,000 ideas, and $100 million in funding was provided to progress key ideas from the jam. Rather than emerging directly for the online posts, new visions emerged through a subsequent analysis process, as key concepts had to be discerned amongst a lot of background 'noise'. It was observed that people rarely built on each other's ideas online, and online moderation proved difficult.

The 'Jam' process may be viewed as a prospector strategy that involves establishing a goal/challenge which could include categories or subjects for discussion, building web sites supporting a range of focus areas, followed by a review of potential 'big ideas' by a large executive/professional team (interpreters). Four macro-themes that could be related to global trends were identified. Some related ideas were combined in major new initiatives

Ten new businesses were created as a result of the 2006 IBM 'Jam'. Some provided new directions for IBM research, some provided an enhanced platform for IBM's current business activities, and some were spunoff at an incubator stage. Some spinoffs were incorporated in an existing IBM operation as they developed into viable businesses and one was sold off. Another as put on hold as it was found the market was not ready for it.

'Jam' events may be run every year or two, and the tools may be utilised by others. IBM hosted an event for the Canadian Government in 2005 considering the challenges of urban sustainability. In 2013 the IBM 'Jam' considered how to create the best experience for IBM clients.

Wolpert (2002) described another IBM initiative called alphaWorks, where a 90-day trial version of new IBM software could be downloaded, leading to new ideas for development or commercialisation. He suggested that an even better (or complementary) idea was to establish an independent intermediary to facilitate the exchange of sensitive information. Tura and Bishop (2011) reported on an implementation of this concept that involves three phases: intention (to overcome a problem or capture an opportunity), opportunity (the identification of gaps) and connection (bringing together normally disconnected actors). This framework could describe the precursor activities in our illustrative Dutch case, where the network facilitators acted as intermediaries. The Australian government launched a variant of this idea to develop new ways of delivering foreign aid programs (DFAT, 2015).

Concluding remarks

We find it convenient to identify some generic roles in organisational design, e.g. CEO or CFO in business or Actor, Director and Producer in filmmaking. We have broad understandings about what is expected of incumbents and that if a role is not enacted, then things may not go smoothly. The literatures on innovation, knowledge spillovers and entrepreneurship describe the need to identify and promote opportunities, combined with an opportunity realisation process to exploit them. A recurring theme from previous observations was that someone needs to be enthusiastic about a particular proposal, some-one needs to sponsor the proposal in some way, and some process for achieving the desired outcome is needed.

Following a review of potential champion roles in the three literatures, combined with some of the authors' research and practitioner experience, we have framed five generic roles as detailed in Table 9.1. These are:

- An opportunity identification and promotion core role (e.g. entrepreneurial visionary)
- A process champion opportunity realisation core role (e.g. spill-over interpreter)

- An investment champion opportunity realisation core role (e.g. program sponsor)
- A 3rd party expert supporting role (e.g. research institution)
- A 3rd party resource provider supporting role (e.g. test facility)

We contend that if the three core roles are not enacted at each stage in the evolution of an idea or a business, then the outcomes will be sub-optimal, but who plays each role may differ between evolutionary stages.

In a small enterprise or a start-up company the core roles may be enacted by one or a few individuals with significant utilisation of the supporting roles. In our illustrative cases, particular actors took different roles at different stages of development. In a large firm such expertise and resources may be available internally or through internal contacts. In our cases, third party support was not always required. In a large firm each core role may be enacted by a specific individual or group. The process champion roles are the most complex and may be enacted by a physical or virtual team.

Knowledge spillovers may be sought in a new opportunity context or in seeking a solution to a problem. Our cases illustrated some other possibilities. The notion of cooperative entrepreneurship that brings enterprises with different knowledge bases together was described in the Dutch case. The notion of traditional user-developer cooperation is extended in the Australian case to bring people from different industry sectors together. In both cases, the identification of a major challenge to be met shaped the development of project proposals. It was noted in the literature that, whilst the dominant narrative relates to technological knowledge spillovers, competitive advantage may be obtained from managerial and market knowledge spillovers. Whatever the context, the stimulus of a grand challenge provides a link between exploring possibilities and exploiting opportunities.

Observations from our cases resonated with the exploration/exploitation balance model proposed by Lavie et al. (2010) which characterises antecedents that frame context and alternative ways of providing balance between potentially conflicting short-term and long-term perspectives. They consolidated twelve potential antecedents influence factors into three categories – the external environment, the particular organisation capabilities and the senior management team attitudes. We add the suggestion that the origin of an opportunity also conditions its value capture pathway (Table 9.2).

References

Acs, Z.J. and Audretsch, D.B. (2010). 'Knowledge spillover entrepreneurship', In Z.J. Acs and D.B. Audretsch (Eds) *Handbook of Entrepreneurship Research*, pp 273–301, New York, Springer.

Ajmal, M.M. and Koskinen, K.U. (2008) 'Knowledge transfer in project-based organizations: An organizational culture perspective', *Project Management Journal*, 39(1): 7–15.

Baron, R.A and Shane, S.A. (2008) *Entrepreneurship: A process perspective.* Thomson South-Western, Mason Ohio.

Barsh, J., Capozzi, M.M. and Davidson, J. (2008) 'Leadership and innovation', *McKinsey Quarterly*, 2008(1): 37–48.

Bartlett, D. and Dibben, P. (2002). 'Public sector innovation and entrepreneurship: Case studies from local government', *Local Government Studies*, 28(4): 107–21.

Beckett, R.C. and Berendsen, G. (2015). The complex innovation champion: Three meta-roles facilitating innovation. 6th International CINet Conference Pursuing Innovation Leadership, 13–15 September 2015, Stockholm, Sweden.

Bhupatiraju, S., Nomaler, Ö., Triulzi, G. and Verspagen, B. (2012) 'Knowledge flows–Analyzing the core literature of innovation, entrepreneurship and science and technology studies', *Research Policy*, 41(7): 1205–18.

Bjelland, O.M. and Wood, R.C. (2008) 'An inside view of IBM's' innovation Jam', *MIT Sloan Management Review*, 50(1): 32.

Bogers, M. and Lhuillery, S. (2011) 'A functional perspective on learning and innovation: Investigating the organization of absorptive capacity', *Industry and Innovation*, 18(6): 581–610.

Bouncken, R.B. and Kraus, S. (2013) 'Innovation in knowledge-intensive industries: The double-edged sword of coopetition', *Journal of Business Research*, 66(10): 2060–70.

Breschi, S. and Lissoni, F. (2001) 'Knowledge spillovers and local innovation systems: A critical survey', *Industrial and Corporate Change*, 10(4): 975–1005.

Chesbrough, H. and Crowther, A.K. (2006) 'Beyond high tech: Early adopters of open innovation in other industries', *R&D Management*, 36(3): 229–36.

Coakes, E. and Smith, P. (2007) 'Developing communities of innovation by identifying innovation champions', *The Learning Organization*, 14(1): 74–85

Dalziel, M. (2010) 'Why do innovation intermediaries exist', In *Proceedings of DRUID Summer Conference*, June, London, pp 16–18.

Damanpour, F. and Wischnevsky, J.D. (2006) 'Research on innovation in organizations: Distinguishing innovation-generating from innovation-adopting organizations', *Journal of Engineering Technology Management*, 23: 269–91

DFAT (2015) InnovationXchange: Catalysing and supporting innovation across the Australian aid program, https://innovationxchange.dfat.gov.au/, accessed January, 2016.

Dong, L., Neufeld, D. and Higgins, C. (2009) 'Top management support of enterprise systems implementations', *Journal of Information Technology*, 25: 55–80.

Fershtman, C. and Gandal, N. (2011) 'Direct and indirect knowledge spillovers: The 'social network' of open-source projects', *The RAND Journal of Economics*, 42(1): 70–91.

Filatotchev, I., Liu, X., Buck, T. and Wright, M. (2009) 'The export orientation and export performance of high-technology SMEs in emerging markets: The effects of knowledge transfer by returnee entrepreneurs', *Journal of International Business Studies*, 40(6): 1005–21.

George, G. and Bock, A.J. (2011) 'The business model in practice and its implications for entrepreneurship research', *Entrepreneurship Theory and Practice*, 35(1): 83–111.

Hargadon, A. (2003) 'Retooling R&D: Technology brokering and the pursuit of innovation', *Ivey Business Journal*, 68(2): 1–7.

Hayton, J.C. and Kelley, D.J. (2006) 'A competency-based framework for promoting corporate entrepreneurship', *Human Resource Management*, 45(3): 407–27.

Hitt, M.A., Ireland, R.D., Camp, S.M. and Sexton, D.L. (2001) 'Strategic entrepreneurship: Entrepreneurial strategies for wealth creation', *Strategic Management Journal*, 22(6–7): 479–91.

Howell, J.M., Shea, C.M. and Higgins, C.A. (2005) 'Champions of product innovations: Defining, developing, and validating a measure of champion behavior', *Journal of Business Venturing*, 20: 641–61.

Howells, J. (2006) 'Intermediation and the role of intermediaries in innovation', *Research Policy*, 35: 715–28.

Hyland, P. and Beckett, R. (2002) 'Learning to compete: The value of internal benchmarking', *Benchmarking: An International Journal*, 9(3): 293–304.

Inkpen, A.C. (1998) 'Learning and knowledge acquisition through international strategic alliances', *The Academy of Management Executive*, 12(4): 69–80.

Inkpen, A.C. and Tsang, E.W. (2005) 'Social capital, networks, and knowledge transfer. *Academy of Management Review*, 30(1): 146–65.

Ireland, R.D., Hitt, M.A., Camp, S.M. and Sexton, D.L. (2001) 'Integrating entrepreneurship and strategic management actions to create firm wealth', *The Academy of Management Executive*, 15(1): 49–63.

Kickul, J. and Gundry, L. (2002) 'Prospecting for strategic advantage: The proactive entrepreneurial personality and small firm innovation', *Journal of Small Business Management*, 40(2): 85–97.

Lane, P.J., Koka, B.R. and Pathak, S. (2006) 'The reification of absorptive capacity: A critical review and rejuvenation of the construct', *Academy of Management Review*, 31(4): 833–63.

Lavie, D., Stettner, U. and Tushman, M.L. (2010) 'Exploration and exploitation within and across organizations', *The Academy of Management Annals*, 4(1): 109–55.

Martin, R.L. (2011) 'The innovation catalysts', *Harvard Business Review*, http://hbr.org/2011/06/the-innovation-catalysts/ar/pr, accessed April 8, 2015

Martin, S. and Scott, J.T. (2000) 'The nature of innovation market failure and the design of public support for private innovation', *Research Policy*, 29(4): 437–47.

Morris, M.H., Kuratko, D.F. and Covin, J.G. (2008) *Corporate entrepreneurship & innovation*, Cengage Learning, United States.

Ponds, R., Van Oort, F. and Frenken, K. (2010) 'Innovation, spillovers and university–industry collaboration: An extended knowledge production function approach', *Journal of Economic Geography*, 10(2): 231–55.

Sammarra, A. and Biggiero, L. (2008) 'Heterogeneity and specificity of Inter-Firm knowledge flows in innovation networks', *Journal of Management Studies*, 45(4): 800–29.

Schon, D.A. (1963, March–April) 'Champions for radical new inventions', *Harvard Business Review*, 77–86.

Smith, D.J. (2013) 'Power-by-the-hour: The role of technology in reshaping business strategy at Rolls-Royce', *Technology Analysis & Strategic Management*, 25(8): 987–1007.

Szent- Györgyi, A. (1937) Oxidation, energy transfer, and vitamins. Nobel lecture, 11.

Szulanski, G. (1996) 'Exploring internal stickiness: Impediments to the transfer of best practice within the firm', *Strategic Management Journal*, 17(S2): 27–43.

Thompson, J. and Downing, R. (2007) 'The entrepreneur enabler: Identifying and supporting those with potential', *Journal of Small Business and Enterprise Development*, 14(3): 528–44.

Tsai, W. (2001) 'Knowledge transfer in intraorganizational networks: Effects of network position and absorptive capacity on business unit innovation and performance', *Academy of Management Journal*, 44(5): 996–1004.

Tura, B. and Bishop, C. (2011) 'An examination of an innovation intermediary organisation's methodology using case studies', In R.J. Howlett (Ed) *Innovation through Knowledge Transfer 2010*, pp 285–95, Berlin Heidelberg, Springer.

Van de Ven, H. (1993) 'The development of an infrastructure for entrepreneurship', *Journal of Business Venturing*, 8(3): 211–30.

Venkataraman, S. (2004) 'Regional transformation through technological entrepreneurship', *Journal of Business Venturing*, 19(1): 153–67.

Wolcott, R.C. and Lippitz, M.J. (2007). 'The four models of corporate entrepreneurship', *MIT Sloan Management Review*, 49(1): 75.

Wolpert, J.D. (2002) 'Breaking out of the innovation box', *Harvard Business Review*, 80(8): 76–83.

Yang, J.T. (2007) 'The impact of knowledge sharing on organizational learning and effectiveness', *Journal of Knowledge Management*, 11(2): 83–90.

Yang, Q., Mudambi, R. and Meyer, K.E. (2008) 'Conventional and reverse knowledge flows in multinational corporations', *Journal of Management*, 34(5): 882–902.

Zahra, S.A. and George, G. (2002) 'Absorptive capacity: A review, reconceptualization, and extension', *Academy of Management Review*, 27(2): 185–203.

Part III

Strategic and international knowledge

Part III

Strategic and
International Knowledge

10 Interconnectivity between academic organizations and established firms for a strategic and knowledge fostering purpose

An exploratory study in an emerging economy

Fernando Herrera, Maribel Guerrero and *David Urbano*

Introduction

The literature has traditionally explained the main reasons behind the development of innovation practices in enterprises as motivated by potential outcomes in terms of innovation performance (Hagedoorn, 1993), technological evolution (Rosenkopf and Nerkar, 2001), product introduction (Laursen and Salter, 2006), and the types of collaborations they engage in (Tsai and Wang, 2009). Boyd (1991) argues that enterprises collaborations aimed at exploiting/exploring opportunities in an existing/new market based on their internal strengths/weaknesses and external opportunities/threats in developed economies.

According to Gruber and Henkel (2006), the key innovation challenges that enterprises face are liabilities associated with their age and size. In this regard, small new enterprises typically start with few resources (e.g. personnel and financial). A lack of financial resources limits the ability of small new enterprises to withstand unfavorable business conditions and makes them vulnerable to even minor inefficiencies (Carson, 1985). Therefore, a growing number of enterprises are starting to implement innovation practices in which they employ both internal/external flows of knowledge in order to explore/exploit innovation in collaboration with several agents (Yamin and Otto, 2004). The ability to develop innovation practices depends on their strategies for innovation (exploratory or exploitative), which in turn determine the available stock of innovation sources (van de Vrande et al., 2009).

Within this context, universities play a significant role in entrepreneurial innovation processes (Audretsch, 2014), by providing fertile knowledge-intensive environments to support the exploration and exploitation of innovative and entrepreneurial ideas (Guerrero et al., 2014a, 2014b, 2015; Guerrero and Urbano, 2012; Urbano and Guerrero, 2013), especially in emerging economies, where governments have created subsidies to promote enterprise innovation through compulsory university partnerships as a strategy to stimulate regional economic development and the transition from an efficiency economy to an innovation economy.[1] One example is Mexico, where universities currently play a major role in the development of an innovation ecosystem, in the transition to a Knowledge Economy (Guerrero and Urbano, 2012). As a consequence, the university business model is also in a state of transition, whereby knowledge transfer and innovation processes are evolving into primarily innovation processes (Miller et al., 2014), with multiple stakeholders trying to exert an influence on the process (Alsos et al., 2011).

A few studies also recognize an opportunistic behavior in these collaborations (Perkmann and Walsh, 2007; van de Vrande et al., 2009). Nevertheless, there is little known about the purposes (innovation or strategic) that motivate enterprises to collaborate towards compulsory university-enterprise agreements. Based on these arguments, this chapter explores the interconnectivity between enterprise and university collaborations for innovation/strategic practices in an emerging economy. Using a sample of 10,200 Mexican enterprises in the 2012 Research and Technological Development Survey (ESIDET) collected by the Mexican National Institute of Statistics and Geography (INEGI), we propose a multinomial regression model to study the role of universities in relation to different innovation practices.

The chapter is organized as follows: Section 2 presents a review of the literature and the proposed conceptual model. Section 3 describes the methodological design, including data collection and statistical analysis. Section 4 presents the results obtained and discusses them in the light of previous studies. Finally, Section 5 contains the concluding remarks, including the limitations and implications of our study, and avenues for further research.

Highlighting the relevance between enterprise and university interconectivity

Enterprise-university collaboration for innovation practices encourages cooperation based on the first stage of generic knowledge (Belderbos et al., 2004; Bonaccorsi et al., 2013). Traditionally, this practice is aimed not only at supporting final product innovation but also at providing a new scientific and technological knowledge base oriented towards radical innovations (O'Connor and De Martino, 2006). Enterprises that lack R&D investment or public funding, qualified personnel, and technological capabilities are more likely to explore innovation practices with universities rather than collaborate with other partners (e.g. purposive inflows of knowledge). However, the interest for this type of collaboration could vary in emerging economies. Starting from the assumption that basic research evolves independently from, but often drives, technological developments, many policymakers have begun to commit to public research. In a scenario, policymakers have encouraged universities to embrace the cause of innovation and technology commercialization (Cohen et al., 2002). In response to the widespread view that public research is too distant from industry in most sectors, they have called on universities and government R&D labs to make their science and engineering more relevant to industry's needs (Cohen et al., 2002, p. 2).

In many developed countries, collaboration is subsidized by public policy programs that provide resources for projects involving universities and enterprises; for example, the European Commission framework programmes (Caloghirou et al., 2001); federally-funded schemes such as the Advanced Technology Program in the US (Hall et al., 2001); funding instruments provided by research councils and government departments in the UK (Howells et al., 1998); federal university-industry projects in Germany (Almus and Czarnitzki, 2003); among others. Many empirical studies have estimated the effect of public R&D subsidies aimed at promoting R&D activities and cooperation (Segarra-Blasco and Arauzo-Carod, 2008), and have concluded that enterprises with access to such public subsidies tend to cooperate with one another (Cassiman and Veugelers, 2002). In line with these ideas, Astrom et al. (2008) have defended the important role of public subsidies in supporting all types of collaboration, but in emerging economies, where the compulsory character of enterprise-university partnerships for access to subsidies allows for an effective exchange of knowledge, this type of collaboration is the most widespread (Boschma, 2005).

One positive outcome of R&D cooperation agreements between universities and enterprises is an increase in innovation practices oriented to develop products, process or both (Perkmann and Walsh, 2007). There is evidence to support the existence of long-standing partnerships between universities and enterprises, and the fact that universities continue to aggressively seek industrial sponsorship. Although government subsidies and grants create strong administrative burdens for companies, as government support is considered to be highly inflexible, since it does not allow to change partners and the programs cannot end before a given date (van de Vrande et al., 2009). In this scenario, we believe that enterprises tend to access government subsidies with university partnerships when they provide them the resources that they need to develop both radical/incremental innovations, in other words, the development of new product lines, substituting current products, improving product quality, entering into new markets, and improving the production process. Based on these arguments, we proposed the following hypothesis:

Hypothesis 1: In emerging economies (as the Mexican one), the access to government subsidies with compulsory university partnerships is greater when the enterprise's innovation purpose is to develop mixed innovations rather than only to develop product or process innovations.

One of the main criticisms of the dynamic capabilities concept is that these capabilities are difficult to measure empirically, and the same is true for underlying operational processes such as innovation practices (Eisenhardt and Martin, 2000; Ambrosini et al., 2009). The strategic characteristics may represent the capabilities that enterprises require to grow and survive, based on their objectives

(Easterby-Smith et al., 2009; Narayanan et al., 2009). Access to external sources of innovation allows (new/established) enterprises to overcome internal barriers (Pisano, 1990), as collaboration practices are important sources of competitive advantage (Cohen and Levinthal, 1990; Nieto and Santamaría, 2007). In this regard, Belderbos et al. (2004) argue that any type of cooperation implies a decision to choose the type of partner when the enterprise requires knowledge for the innovation process (scientific), or when it exhibits faster technological and product development (commercial or intrapreneurial) or when it is looking for a source of competitive advantage to have long-lasting effects on firm performance (mixed).

Even though a number of empirical studies have found a positive impact of engaging in R&D cooperation on innovation performance (Klomp and van Leeuwen, 2001), other studies have obtained ambiguous results (Hall, 2005). An explanation is a substantial heterogeneity in the determinants to establish R&D collaborations with different partners and their impact on innovation performance (Hall and Lerner, 2010). It could be related to the measures used to analyze performance of the enterprise incentives to cooperate such as a high-growth orientation (Van Leeuwen and Klomp, 2001; Hall and Maffioli, 2008). The OECD-Eurostat Manual on Business Demography Statistics (2007) defines a high-growth enterprise as an enterprise with an average annualized growth greater than 20 percent per annum, over a 3-year period, and with ten or more employees at the beginning of the observation period. Growth is thus measured by the number of employees and by turnover. Extant empirical studies have evidenced that the innovations performance of high-growth enterprises is strongly supported by their collaboration with universities and public research centers because they look for more technologies and disrupt innovations (Audretsch, 2012; Delmar et al., 2003; Friar and Meyer, 2003; Moreno and Casillas, 2007). Based on these arguments, we proposed the following hypothesis:

Hypothesis 2: In emerging economies (as the Mexican one), the access to government subsidies with compulsory university partnerships is greater when high growth enterprises are oriented to develop mixed innovations rather than only to develop product or process innovations.

Methodology

The dataset used contains enterprise-level data from the 2012 Research and Technological Development Survey (ESIDET, Encuesta sobre Investigación y Desarrollo Tecnológico). This database was created by the Mexican National Institute of Statistics and Geography (INEGI) to enhance the statistical information on enterprise innovation activities. The sample is composed of the 10,167 enterprises that responded to the survey, and no distinctions are made between innovative and non-innovative ventures (Fritsch and Lukas, 2001). This may give rise to biased results, as shown in previous studies (Bayona et al., 2001).

Dependent variables

In order to analyze the importance of interconnectivity between universities and enterprises for knowledge purposes, we explored their partnerships in innovation processes (Yamin and Otto, 2004; Nieto and Santamaría, 2007). More concretely, we create a categorical dependent variable that has four innovation categories: (0) no innovation; (i) innovation in products; (ii) innovation in process; and (iii) mixed innovation (products and process). The enterprises' strategic profiles, and, on the basis of the criteria to identify high-growth (Audretsch, 2012; OECD, 2007),[2] we tested the model with two sub-samples: (i) enterprises that did not grow by more than 20 percent in either total sales or personnel during 2011–2012 (9,546 enterprises), and (ii) enterprises that grew by more than 20 percent in terms of both total sales and personnel during 2011–2012 (599 enterprises).

Independent variables

In emergent economies, a traditional way to support innovation and reinforce the interconnectivity between enterprises and universities is via public subsidies, and Mexico is not an exception. In line with Cohen et al. (2002), Czarnitzki et al., (2007), and Perkmann and Walsh (2007), our main independent variables take into consideration the relevance of access to public subsidies for innovation practices, whether these subsidies require compulsory university partnerships (GOB support with universities) or not (Gob support individually). Interestingly, the 2012 ESIDET survey includes a list of public innovation support programs, and this allows us to build our main independent variables according to the number of subsidies received from the government.

Control variables

Almost all types of enterprises face innovation challenges – financial limitations, management issues, risks, lack of experience, and fierce competition from large competitors – (Aldrich and Auster, 1986; Thompson, 1999). More specifically, Christensen (1997) and Storey (1991) have stated that the growth and survival of enterprises are associated with the entrepreneurs' characteristics (education, age, motivation, etc.), the company's strategy (market, technological, exporting, competition, etc.), and its structure (resources, age, size, sector, location, ownership, etc.). Based on the data available for this study, we used control variables related to certain structural characteristics. First, the enterprise's age determines its products' life cycle and the barriers it faces. There is evidence to suggest a positive relationship between young ventures and innovation practices (Cohen and Keppler, 1996). For this reason, we included a dummy variable that controls whether or not young firms, less than 5 years old, developed innovation practices (Less than 5 years old). Second, following Gruber and Henkel (2006) and Barge-Gil (2010), we introduced the availability of innovation resources: the investment in R&D expressed in pesos and the number of qualified personnel. Third, we included the enterprise size, measured as the number of employees and expressed in logarithms (Size), as there is a substantial body of evidence to suggest scale economies in the innovation production function (Stephan, 2012) and an increased availability and access to critical resources (Gooding and Wagner III, 1985). Fourth, Galende and de la Fuente (2003) have shown that exports and internationalization have a positive significant effect on collaboration agreements. Therefore, we also controlled the ventures' export activities (Exports), measured by means of a dummy variable, where 1 represents those enterprises that have exported and 0 those that have not. Fifth, Wadhwa et al. (2011) have found a positive relationship between enterprises that are a part of a company group and collaboration practices (Company group), and we created a binary variable that takes a value of 1 if the enterprise is a part of a company and a value 0 if it is a single-unit enterprise. Sixth, we used a binary variable (Technological sector) to account for the different propensities to innovate across technological sectors. Finally, we controlled the location, including the entrepreneurial density of the state where the enterprises developed their economic activities.

Statistical model

On the basis of previous studies (Barge-Gil, 2010; Gruber and Henkel, 2006), we used a multinomial logistic regression model with a categorical dependent variable that has four innovation categories followed by a set of control variables. We estimated the multinomial logistic model (Greene, 1992).[3] Table 10.1 shows the main descriptive analysis for all the variables.

During 2011 and 2012, only 9 percent of the Mexican enterprises surveyed implemented collaborative innovation practices. By contrast, in a developed

Table 10.1 Descriptive statistics

Variables	Entire sample [n = 10,200]			
	Min	Max	Mean	SD
Gob support (Universities)	0	7	0.068	0.381
Gob support (individually)	0	14	0.134	0.503
HGE_Total sales > 20%	0	1	0.224	0.417
HGE_Personnel > 20%	0	1	0.111	0.315
Less than 5 years old	0	1	0.084	0.278
R&D investment	0	2900867	1823.610	38.203
Number of qualified personnel	0	0.533	0.002	0.016
Size	0	5.168.93	2037.704	0.700
Exports	0	1	0.273	0.445
Company group	0	1	0.282	0.450
Number of establishments	1	2.427.00	5.578	4.693
Technological sector	0	1	0.215	0.411
Entrepreneurial density	0.007	0.126	0.047	0.036

economy like Spain's, on the basis of a similar sample of enterprises, the percentage of innovative collaborating enterprises is about 35 percent (Segarra-Blasco and Arauzo-Carod, 2008; Barge-Gil 2010).

Interconectity between Mexican enterprises and Mexican universities to achieve innovation and strategic purposes

Table 10.2 presents the main results obtained from the multinomial regression model that analyzes the enterprise–universities partnership in the development of innovation practices. Concretely, results show that enterprises collaborate compulsory with universities to access government subsidies when they have the purpose of develop new products (1.01; p < 0.001), improve processes (1.19; p < 0.001), and in mixed innovations (1.20; p < 0.001). These results are interesting because the purpose of developing a processes are higher than that of new products for enterprises located in developed economies (Bayona et al., 2001; Segarra-Blasco and Arauzo-Carod, 2008; Barge-Gil 2010). A possible explanation is that we are not using the traditional measure of university–enterprise collaboration

Table 10.2 Multinomial regression analysis for innovation purposes

Determinants	All sample								
	Product innovation vs. no innovation			Process innovation vs. no innovation			Mixed innovation vs. no innovation		
	Coef.	*S.E.*	*P>|z|*	*Coef.*	*S.E.*	*P>|z|*	*Coef.*	*S.E.*	*P>|z|*
Gob support with universities	1.01	0.12	***	1.19	0.12	***	1.20	0.16	***
Gob support with others	0.14	0.13		0.11	0.16		-0.06	0.18	
R&D investment	0.00	0.00		0.00	0.00		0.00	0.00	
Qualified personnel	1.23	0.29	***	1.22	0.31	***	7.74	0.41	*
Size	0.07	0.09		0.21	0.08	**	0.34	0.14	**
Exportations	0.01	0.00	***	0.00	0.00	*	0.00	0.00	**
Company group	0.24	0.14	**	0.15	0.13		0.41	0.21	*
Number of establishments	0.00	0.00	**	0.00	0.00	*	0.00	0.00	*
Technological sectors	1.28	0.12	***	0.71	0.12	***	0.53	0.21	**
GDP10	-1.08	0.78		-1.15	0.80		-1.80	0.15	
Density14	2.53	0.15	*	-1.45	0.30		3.86	0.15	**
< 5 years	-0.20	0.20		-0.24	0.24		-0.10	0.41	
Const	-3.94	0.20	***	-4.19	0.20	***	-5.35	0.35	***

Observations 10200; Wald chi2 439.06; Prob > chi2 ***; Pseudo R2 0.1000; Log pseudo likelihood −34.324.

Level of statistical significance: ***p ≤ 0.000, ** p ≤ 0.05, †p ≤ 0.10.

adopted in extant empirical studies. In addition, we found a positive influence of qualified personnel, being part of a company group and involved in technological sectors on each type of innovation practice. Interestingly, enterprises are more likely to develop mixed innovation when they are located in regions with more density than others located in regions with less density. Intuitively, it could show us that mixed innovations would be an opportunity to survive and be competitive in the market. Based on these results, we support H1 that states that in emerging economies, the access to government subsidies with compulsory university partnerships is greater when the enterprise's innovation purpose is to develop mixed innovations rather than only to develop product or process innovations.

Table 10.3 presents the main results obtained from the multinomial regression model that analyzes the enterprise–universities partnership to achieve strategic purposes. Results show that high-growth enterprises (previous year growth more than 20 percent both in sales and employees) using compulsory collaboration with universities to access government subsidies when they have the purpose of develop new products (1.29; $p < 0.001$), improve processes (1.53; $p < 0.001$), and in mixed innovations (2.71; $p < 0.001$). However, the effect of university – enterprise collaboration on product innovation (0.87; $p < 0.001$), innovation

Table 10.3a Multinomial regression analysis for strategic purposes

Determinants	Enterprises' grow profile: sales > 20% & employees > 20% t – 1								
	Product innovation vs. no innovation			Process innovation vs. no innovation			Mixed innovation vs. no innovation		
	Coef.	*S.E.*	*P>|z|*	*Coef.*	*S.E.*	*P>|z|*	*Coef.*	*S.E.*	*P>|z|*
Gob support with universities	1.29	0.41	***	1.53	0.39	***	2.71	0.86	***
Gob support with others	-0.28	0.39		-0.14	0.33		-3.43	1.48	**
R&D investment	0.00	0.00	**	0.00	0.00	*	0.00	0.00	**
Qualified personnel	1.41	0.59	**	2.30	1.75		1.15	0.62	*
Size	-0.80	0.69		0.07	0.39		0.82	1.20	
Exportations	-0.01	0.02		-0.01	0.01		0.01	0.02	
Company group	0.73	0.71		-0.04	0.57		0.94	1.09	
Number of establishments	0.01	0.00	*	-0.00	0.01		0.02	0.01	**
Technological sectors	1.50	0.64	**	-0.02	0.45		1.25	0.96	
GDP10	2.76	1.82		-0.42	0.28		-2.25	0.93	
Density14	1.09	0.68		0.12	0.69		4.82	1.09	
< 5 years	0.62	0.52		-0.71	0.81		0.99	1.31	
Const	-3.55	1.22	***	-3.85	0.88	***	-6.49	4.17	

Observations 599; Wald chi2 164.95; Prob > chi2 ***; Pseudo R2 0.311; Log pseudo likelihood –18.676

Table 10.3b Multinomial regression analysis for strategic purposes

Determinants	Enterprises' grow profile: sales < 20% & employees < 20% t – 1								
	Product innovation vs. no innovation			Process innovation vs. no innovation			Mixed innovation vs. no innovation		
	Coef.	*S.E.*	*P>|z|*	*Coef.*	*S.E.*	*P>|z|*	*Coef.*	*S.E.*	*P>|z|*
Gob support with universities	0.87	0.15	***	1.08	0.15	***	1.18	0.22	***
Gob support with others	0.09	0.20		0.00	0.23		–0.21	0.27	
R&D investment	0.00	0.00	*	0.00	0.00	*	0.00	0.00	*
Qualified personnel	1.27	0.37	***	0.98	0.36	***	0.93	0.45	**
Size	0.05	0.12		0.12	0.11		0.07	0.18	
Exportations	–0.01	0.00	***	0.00	0.00		0.00	0.00	*
Company group	0.13	0.17		0.08	0.17		0.26	0.26	
Number of establishments	0.01	0.00	**	0.00	0.00	**	0.00	0.00	*
Technological sectors	1.16	0.15	***	0.63	0.15	***	0.36	0.28	
GDP10	–0.53	0.99		–1.16	0.11		0.29	0.14	
Density14	1.62	0.18		–2.66	0.39		3.92	0.18	**
< 5 years	–0.70	0.35	*	–0.14	0.32		–1.48	0.10	
Const	–4.08	0.25	***	–4.24	0.25	***	–5.03	0.42	***

Observations 9546; Wald chi2 482.60; Prob > chi2 ***; Pseudo R2 0.1320; Log pseudo likelihood –21.958

Level of statistical significance: ***p ≤ 0.000, **p ≤ 0.05, † p ≤ 0.10.

process (1.083; p < 0.001), and mixed innovations (1.18; p < 0.001) is lower when the enterprises do not have a high-growth orientation. It is aligned with previous studies that have explored the patterns of high-growth vs. non-high-growth enterprises. Based on these arguments, we support H2 that states that in emerging economies, the access to government subsidies with compulsory university partnerships is greater when high-growth enterprises are oriented to develop mixed innovations rather than only to develop product or process innovations.

Conclusions and implications

During the last few decades, the contribution of universities to innovation and entrepreneurial processes has changed the perception of the different actors involved in the innovation system. This scenario has been created by the natural evolution of the activities of universities, which have created fertile environments for identifying, creating, and exploring opportunities (Kirby et al., 2011), and have also benefited from government initiatives based on subsidy programs designed to promote innovation (Cohen et al., 2002). As a consequence, in both developed and developing economies, public research has been oriented to industry's needs and public resources have been conditioned by the new rules of the game whereby universities contribute to social and economic development (Grimaldi et al., 2011). However, in emerging economies, university transformation is slow because there is not a strong base to build upon and obtain high-quality research outcomes, while enterprises interested in partnerships usually face challenges in terms of communication, expectations and agreements. In this scenario, this paper contributes to a better understanding of the interconnectivity of universities and enterprises for innovation and strategic purposes in emerging economies. In the light of previous studies, our results confirm that Mexican enterprises collaborate with universities to access government subsidies for the development of mixed innovations (H1) and this relationship is higher when those enterprises have a high growth orientation (H2).

This study has several limitations that, nonetheless, provide good opportunities for future research. The first limitation is related to the database used. As a result of the INEGI's confidentiality rules, we did not have access to all the variables and their treatment/analysis was limited by the statistical resources available. Future research requires an in-depth exploration of university–enterprise–government links via longitudinal analyses that allow for a follow-up of innovation/strategic purposes. Nevertheless, the number of innovative enterprises is lower than in developed economies, and so is the number of enterprises that collaborate with universities through access to governmental subsidies. Several implications for the main actors involved in the Mexican innovation system emerge from our study. For policymakers, the study presents the key determinants of enterprises' participation in collaborative innovation models. However, the focus of the intervention, using public funds, is normally small and medium enterprises. These kinds of conditions demand the creation of special policy to stimulate SME´s participation inside the innovation networks and bring support for enterprises which are not yet high-growth firms. For enterprise managers, this study offers insights about the best mechanisms and practices for innovation in collaboration with external public and private partners. For university managers, the entrepreneurial university model is a good example to follow in their transformation processes.

Acknowledgment

The authors acknowledge the support received by the Mexican National Institute of Statistics and Geography (INEGI) to access the databases in its installations (Micro-data Laboratory). Fernando Herrera acknowledges the PhD scholarship and support from the Tecnológico de Monterrey (ITESM). Maribel Guerrero acknowledges the financial support from Santander Universidades (Iberoamerica Scholarship for Young Researchers). David Urbano acknowledges the financial support from projects ECO2013–44027-P (Spanish Ministry of Economy & Competitiveness) and 2014-SGR-1626 (Economy & Knowledge Department – Catalan Government).

Notes

1 Compulsory collaboration encourages enterprises and universities to collaborate and create innovation networks supporting R&D, technology transfer and adopt innovation though critical mass of experts and participants working together in a certain knowledge area. With policy interventions targeted at individual firms, policymakers are increasingly supporting the formation of innovation networks such as R&D consortia, networks of excellence, and university–industry partnerships. Recently, behavioral additionality analyze and capture particular kinds of behavioral changes induced by policy interventions, such as 'network additionality', intended as the ability of public funding instruments to increase networking and cooperation (Rossi et al., 2016).

2 In our study, we used a proxy for this concept because we only had information available from the previous and the current year.

3 This analysis used data management in STATA 9.0.

References

Aldrich, H.E. and Auster, E.R. (1986) 'Even dwarfs started small: Liabilities of age and size and their strategic implications', *Research in Organizational Behavior*, 8: 165–98.

Almus, M. and Czarnitzki, D. (2003) 'The effects of public R&D subsidies on firms innovation activities: The case of eastern Germany', *Journal of Business and Economic Statistics*, 21(2): 226–36.

Alsos, G.A., Hytti, U. and Ljunggren, E. (2011) 'Stakeholder theory approach to technology incubators', *International Journal of Entrepreneurial Behaviour and Research*, 17: 607–25.

Ambrosini, V., Bowman, C. and Collier, N. (2009) 'Dynamic capabilities: An exploration of how firms renew their resource base', *British Journal of Management*, 20(1): S9–S24.

Astrom, T., Eriksson, M.L., Niklasson, L. and Arnold, E. (2008) *International Comparison of Five Institute Systems*, Forsknings-og Innovationsstyrelsen, Denmark.

Audretsch, D. (2012) Determinants of High-Growth Entrepreneurship Report prepared for the OECD/DBA International Workshop on High-growth firms: Local policies and local determinants, Copenhagen, March 28, 2012.

Audretsch, D. (2014) 'From the entrepreneurial university to the university for the entrepreneurial society', *Journal of Technology Transfer*, 39(3): 313–21.

Barge-Gil, A. (2010) 'Cooperation-based innovators and peripheral cooperators: An empirical analysis of their characteristics and behavior', *Technovation*, 30(3): 195–206.

Bayona, C., García-Marco, T. and Huerta, E. (2001) 'Firms' motivations for cooperative R&D: An empirical analysis of Spanish firms', *Research Policy*, 30: 1289–1307.

Belderbos, R., Carree, M. and Lokshin, B. (2004) 'Cooperative R&D and firm performance', *Research Policy*, 33(10): 1477–92.

Bonaccorsi, A., Colombo, M.G., Guerini, M. and Rossi-Lamastra, C. (2013) 'University specialization and new firm creation across industries', *Small Business Economics*, 41(4): 837–63.

Boschma, R. (2005) 'Proximity and innovation: A critical assessment', *Regional Studies*, 39(1): 61–74.

Boyd, B.K. (1991) 'Strategic planning and financial performance: A meta-analytic review', *Journal of Management Studies*, 28(4): 353–74.

Caloghirou, Y., Tsakanikas, A. and Vonortas, N.S. (2001) 'University-industry cooperation in the context of the European framework programmes', *Journal of Technology Transfer*, 26(1–2): 153–61

Carson, D.J. (1985) 'The evolution of marketing in small firms', *European Journal of Marketing*, 19: 7–16.

Cassiman, B. and Veugelers, R. (2002) 'R&D cooperation and spillovers: Some empirical evidence from Belgium', *The American Economic Review*, 92(4): 1169–84.

Christensen, C.M. (1997) *The innovator's dilemma: When new technologies cause great firms to fail*, Harvard Business School Press, Boston.

Cohen, W.M. and Klepper, S. (1996) 'A reprise of size and R & D', *The Economic Journal*, 106(437): 925–51.

Cohen, W.M. and Levinthal, D.A. (1990) 'Absorptive capacity: A new perspective on learning and innovation', *Administrative Science Quarterly*, 35(1): 128–52.

Cohen, W.M., Nelson, R.R. and Walsh, J.P. (2002) 'Links and impacts: The influence of public research on industrial R&D', *Management Science*, 48(1): 1–23.

Czarnitzki, D., Ebersberger, B. and A. Fier. (2007) 'The relationship between R&D collaboration, subsidies and R&D performance: Empirical evidence from Finland and Germany', *Journal of Applied Econometrics*, 22(7): 1347–66.

Delmar, F., Davidsson, P. and Gartner, W.B. (2003) 'Arriving at the high-growth firm', *Journal of Business Venturing*, 182: 189–216.

Easterby-Smith, M., Lyles, M.A. and Peteraf, M.A. (2009) 'Dynamic capabilities: Current debates and future directions', *British Journal of Management*, 20(s1): S1–S8.

Eisenhardt, K. and Martin, J. (2000) 'Dynamic capabilities: What are they?', *Strategic Management Journal*, 21: 1105–21.

Friar, J.H. and Meyer, M.H. (2003) 'Entrepreneurship and start-ups in the Boston region: Factors differentiating high-growth ventures from micro-ventures', *Small Business Economics*, 212: 145–52.

Fritsch, M. and Lukas, R. (2001) 'Who cooperates on R&D?', *Research Policy*, 30(2): 297–312.

Galende, J. and de la Fuente, J.M. (2003) 'Internal factors determining a firm's innovative behaviour', *Research Policy*, 32(5): 715–36.

Gooding, R.Z. and Wagner III, J.A. (1985) 'A meta-analytic review of the relationship between size and performance: The productivity and efficiency of organizations and their subunits', *Administrative Science Quarterly*, 30(4): 462–81.

Greene, W. (1992) *Econometric analysis*, Macmillan, New York.

Grimaldi, R., Kenney, M., Siegel, D.S. and Wright, M. (2011) '30 years after Bayh-Dole: reassessing academic entrepreneurship', *Research Policy*, 40(8): 1045–57.

Gruber, M. and Henkel, J. (2006) 'New ventures based on open innovation–An empirical analysis of start-up firms in embedded Linux', *International Journal of Technology Management*, 33(4): 356–72.

Guerrero, M., Cunningham, J.A. and Urbano, D. (2015) 'Economic impact of entrepreneurial universities' activities: An exploratory study of the United Kingdom', *Research Policy*, 44(3): 748–64.

Guerrero, M. and Urbano, D. (2012) 'The development of an entrepreneurial university', *Journal of Technology Transfer*, 37(1): 43–74.

Guerrero, M., Urbano, D., Cunningham, J. and Organ, D. (2014[a]) 'Entrepreneurial universities in two European regions: A case study comparison', *The Journal of Technology Transfer*, 39(3): 415–34.

Guerrero, M., Urbano, D. and Gajón, E. (2014b) 'The internal pathways that condition university entrepreneurship in Latin America: An institutional approach', In Sherry Hoskinson and Donald Kuratko (Eds) *Innovative Pathways for University Entrepreneurship in the 21st Century*, pp 89–118, Advances in the Study of Entrepreneurship, Innovation, Emerald, United Kingdom.

Hagedoorn, J. (1993) 'Understanding the rationale of strategic technology partnering: Interorganizational modes of cooperation and sectorial differences', *Strategic Management Journal*, 14(5): 371–85.

Hall, B.H. (2005) 'The financing of innovation', In S. Shane (Ed) *The Handbook of Technology and Innovation Management*, pp 409–30, Wiley, United Kingdom.

Hall, B.H. and Lerner, J. (2010) 'The financing of R&D and innovation', *Handbook of the Economics of Innovation*, 1: 609–39.

Hall, B.H., Link, A.N. and Scott, J.T. (2001) 'Barriers inhibiting industry from partnering with universities: Evidence from the advanced technology program,' *Journal of Technology Transfer*, 26(1–2): 87–98.

Hall, B.H. and Maffioli, A. (2008) 'Evaluating the impact of technology development funds in emerging economies: Evidence from Latin America', *The European Journal of Development Research*, 202: 172–98.

Ho wells, J., Nedeva, M. and Georghiou, L. (1998) Industry-academic links in the UK, Higher Education Funding Council for England, Bristol.

Kirby, D.A., Guerrero, M. and Urbano, D. (2011) 'Making universities more entrepreneurial: Development of a model', *Canadian Journal of Administrative Sciences*, 28(3): 302–16.

Klomp, L. and van Leeuwen, G. (2001) 'Linking innovation and firm performance: A new approach', *International Journal of the Economics of Business*, 8(3): 343–64

Laursen, K. and Salter, A. (2006) 'Open for innovation: The role of openness in explaining innovation performance among UK manufacturing firms', *Strategic Management Journal*, 27(2): 131–50

Miller, K., McAdam, M. and McAdam, R. (2014) 'The changing university business model: A stakeholder perspective', *R&D Management*, 44(3): 265–87.

Narayanan, V.K., Colwell, K. and Douglas, F.L. (2009) 'Building organizational platforms in the pharmaceutical industry: A process perspective on the development of dynamic capabilities', *British Journal of Management*, 20(s1): S25–S40.

Nieto, M.J. and Santamaria L. (2007) The importance of diverse collaborative networks for the novelty of product innovation. *Technovation*, 27(6): 367–77.

O'Connor G.C. and De Martino, R. (2006) 'Organizing for radical innovation: An exploratory study of the structural aspects of RI management systems in large established firms', *Journal of Product Innovation Management*, 23(6): 475–97.

OECD (2007) *Eurostat-OECD manual on business demography statistics*, OECD, Paris.

Perkmann, M. and Walsh, K. (2007) 'University–industry relationships and open innovation: Towards a research agenda', *International Journal of Management Reviews*, 9(4): 259–80.

Pisano, G.P. (1990) 'The R&D boundaries of the firm: An empirical analysis', *Administrative Science Quarterly*, 153–76.

Rosenkopf, L. and Nerkar, A. (2001) 'Beyond local search: boundary-spanning, exploration, and impact in the optical disk industry', *Strategic Management Journal*, 22(4): 287–306.

Rossi, F., Caloffi, A. and Russo, M. (2016) 'Networked by design: Can policy requirements influence organisations´ networking behaviour?', *Technological Forecasting & Social Science*, 105: 203–14.

Segarra-Blasco, A. and Arauzo-Carod, J.M. (2008) 'Sources of innovation and industry–university interaction: Evidence from Spanish firms', *Research Policy*, 37(8): 1283–95.

Stephan, P.E. (2012) *How economics shapes science*, Harvard University Press, Cambridge, MA, USA.

Storey, D.J. (1991) 'The birth of new firms – does unemployment matter? A review of the evidence', *Small Business Economics*, 3(3): 167–78.

Thompson, J.L. (1999) 'A strategic perspective of entrepreneurship', *International Journal of Entrepreneurial Behavior & Research*, 5(6): 279–96.

Tsai, K.H. and Wang J.C. (2009) 'External technology sourcing and innovation performance in LMT sectors: An analysis based on the Taiwanese technological innovation survey', *Research Policy*, 38(3): 518–26.

Urbano, D. and Guerrero, M. (2013) 'Entrepreneurial universities socioeconomic impacts of academic entrepreneurship in a European region', *Economic Development Quarterly*, 27(1): 40–55.

Van de Vrande, V., De Jong, J.P., Vanhaverbeke, W. and De Rochemont, M. (2009) 'Open innovation in SMEs: Trends, motives and management challenges', *Technovation*, 29(6): 423–37.

van Leeuwen, G. and Klomp, L. (2001) On the contribution of innovation to multifactor productivity growth, Paper Presented at the Eindhoven Centre for Innovation Studies ECIS Conference, September 20–23, 2001

Wadhwa, A., Freitas, I.M.B. and Sarkar, M.B. (2011) The paradox of being open: External technology sourcing and knowledge protection. In paper presented at the DIME Final Conference (Vol. 6, p. 8).

Yamin, M. and Otto, J. (2004) 'Patterns of knowledge flows and MNE innovative performance', *Journal of International Management*, 10: 239–58.

11 International knowledge transfer from Kodak to ITRI

A strategic alliance learning perspective

Frank Shiu, Connie Zheng and Mei-chih Hu

Introduction

International knowledge transfer between strategic alliance partners has been much discussed in the literature, with reference to how organizations learn from their partners and develop new competencies through their collaborative efforts (Simonin, 2004; Inkpen and Tsang, 2007; Schildt et al., 2012). However, the process by which strategic alliance partners manage and transfer knowledge, and what impact of such knowledge transfer on collaborative outcome and performance is less known (Castro, 2015). Using the case study of strategic knowledge transfer from the then nearly bankrupt Kodak (USA) to Taiwan's Industrial Technology Research Institute (subsequently as ITRI), we intend to examine this process, supported by the strategic learning framework proposed by Simonin (2004) and further developed by Schildt et al. (2012) for inter-organizational learning in the international business setting.

According to Simonin (2004), 'the heart of the learning process in alliances is knowledge-specific, partner-specific (at the level of the knowledge seeker, knowledge provider, and their inter-relationship), and context-specific variables' (p. 409). Various facets of the learning process would include: learning intent, learning capacity, organizational culture, size (knowledge-seeker level); partner protectiveness (knowledge-holder level); tacitness and knowledge ambiguity (knowledge level); and context (such as alliance form and competitive environment). A strategic partnership between the dwindling Kodak and Taiwan's ITRI represents a unique case study to examine the relationship between and among these alliance learning variables.

On one hand, Kodak was a large global company focusing on producing soft films, yet with the development of digital camera, Kodak needed to reposition itself and seek opportunity to transfer and sell its advanced technology and capability. On the other hand, Taiwan's ITRI has been very successful in transfering the RCA semiconductor technology from the USA, and led the transformation of Taiwan's semiconductor industry and creation of many enterprises since the 1990s. As the semiconductor industry is mature, ITRI now has a vision of leading the electronic paper technology to create new industries and small firms in Taiwan. Kodak apparently possessed the technology and know-how to develop such new products. Thus, strategic alliance for knowledge transfer was formed in 2006. During the period of 2006–2014, Kodak transferred 217 patents, 14 authorized patents, and five sets of machines. The Display Technology Centre (DTC) of ITRI subsequently liaised with three international organizations and five domestic firms to further research, develop and refine the production of different types of electronic papers. The electronic paper industry is predicted to be a new and another big industry, similar to the earlier semiconductor industry, which will attract many entrepreneurs setting up small and medium sized firms around Taiwan and the greater China region. The technology of electronic paper is considered as the key bridge to bring Taiwan's existing FPD (flat panel display) industry into another stage of novel flexible display for the future.

The implication of the current investigation is two-fold. One is to provide additional empirical evidence and explain the process of international knowledge transfer between strategic alliance partners. Second is to encourage the sunset industries and firms with high-tech components and technical/technological capabilities in the Western developed countries to seek strategic partners especially in the less developed nations so as to utilize their technology and know-how to build new industries and firms for the future.

The remaining chapter is thus outlined as follows. Section 2 explains the strategic alliance learning framework as a theoretical underpinning of the current study. Section 3 outlines the longitudinal case study to explain the complex process whereby the international knowledge transfer from Kodak to ITRI took place in the period of 2006–2014. Section 4 evaluates this knowledge transfer process and illustrates key learning success and hindrance factors for international knowledge transfer. Concluding marks are made in Section 5.

The strategic alliance learning framework

According to Inkpen and Tsang (2007), existing organizational research has helped develop an understanding of alliances, learning and knowledge transfer. However, much remains to be done to more fully understand the complexities and dynamics of alliance learning process. Alliance learning is defined by Kim and Inkpen (2005) as a two-stage process in which firms get access to external knowledge, internalize what they have accessed, and increase firm capabilities (p. 315). Kale and Singh (2007) further argue that an alliance learning is in fact a multifaceted and interrelated process that requires 'articulation, codification, sharing, and internalization of alliance management know-how' in order achieve a firm's overall alliance success (p. 981).

The general understanding is that strategic alliances offer many benefits, such as operating efficiencies, risk and uncertainty reduction. Mostly, alliances provide an ideal platform for organizational learning, giving the alliance and partner firms' access to new knowledge (see Inkpen and Tsang, 2007, p. 479–480). Unlike other organizational learning contexts, the formation of an alliance helps organizations learn with and from their partners through executing 'shared tasks, mutual interdependence and problem solving, and observation of alliance activities and outcomes' (Inkpen and Tsang, 2007, p. 480). In addition, different skills, knowledge, and strategic complementarities of two or more organizations can be leveraged through alliance. Thus, alliance has now been commonly used as a strategic tool for acquiring knowledge and developing capabilities not only in the domestic setting but also largely among international joint-ventured business (Schildt et al., 2012; Garud et al., 2013; Castro, 2015).

There are four types of alliance learning. Inkpen and Tsang (2007) classified the first three learning types, that is, 1) learning about alliance management; 2) learning about an alliance partner; and 3) learning with an alliance partner as 'partner learning from a strategic-alliance experience' (p. 481), which are relatively easy and straight forward. In contrast, the fourth type of learning from an alliance partner can be complex and dynamic as it involves a collaborative process; and this type is the focus of the current case analysis with involvement of ITRI learning and acquiring technology and knowledge from its partner, Kodak. Consequently, in analyzing the case, knowledge, partner and context-specific perspectives must be understood (Simonin, 2004; Inkpen and Tsang, 2007; Kale and Singh, 2007; Schildt et al., 2012).

In developing an international knowledge transfer model, Simonin (2004) argued that the antecedents of successful alliance learning include measuring knowledge characteristics (e.g. knowledge ambiguity and tacitness), learning partner characteristics (i.e. learning intent, learning capability, organizational culture and size, partner protectiveness and relationship factors), and context-specific variables that cover alliance form and competitive environment (p. 409). The model has been further extended by Schildt et al. (2012) to encompass timing and assessing the different levels of learning partner's absorptive capacity during different stages of knowledge transfer, which are applicable to the current longitudinal study of Kodak-ITRI knowledge transfer over an almost 10-year period (2006–2015).

The integrated model is depicted in Figure 11.1, which covers key factors influencing the alliance learning. In the remaining section, we will detail each component of alliance learning to illustrate the dynamics of international knowledge transfer process.

Knowledge characteristics

Learning in strategic alliances involves the creation, transfer and absorption of knowledge. While there are different ways of classifying knowledge, the most common distinction is between tacit and explicit knowledge (Simonin 2004; Inkpen and Tsang, 2007). Tacit knowledge is defined by Inkpen and Tsang (2007) as 'unarticulated, highly personal, and difficult to communicate', and explicit knowledge can be 'codified and transmittable in formal, systematic language' (p. 486). However, in many cases of international knowledge transfer, it is harder to distinguish between tacit and explicit knowledge (Inkpen and Dinur, 1998). More often, ambiguity of knowledge exists, hindering the success of knowledge transfer. Simonin (2004) defines 'knowledge ambiguity' as a 'lack

Timeline

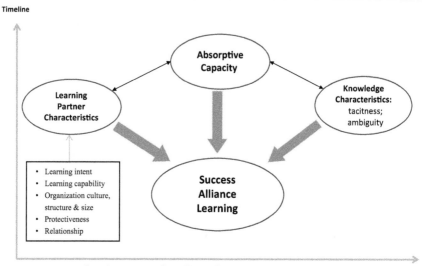

Changing Contexts (i.e. alliance forms, competitive environment)

Figure 11.1 Integrated strategic alliance learning model

of understanding of the logical linkages between actions and outcomes, inputs and outputs, and causes and effects that are related to technological or process know-how' (p. 413). Empirical evidence has shown that ambiguity had a negative impact on knowledge transfer (Simonin, 1999). In a case of the high-tech knowledge transfer, tacit knowledge is hard to value and ambiguity plays a negative role in the process of knowledge transfer between strategic alliance partners. Consequently, the learning partners tend to focus more on easily transferable (and less valuable) explicit knowledge than on tacit and ambiguity knowledge (Inkpen and Dinur, 1998; Inkpen and Wang, 2006). Tacit knowledge tends to be more valuable, acting as vehicles for creativity and innovation when positive collaboration and teamwork among staff of partner organizations are being built in the process of knowledge exchange and transfer.

To manage more valuable tacit knowledge and overcome knowledge ambiguity, it is suggested that interpersonal connection, good relationships and communication channels should be built between learning partners to articulate, codify, share and internalize knowledge (Kale and Singh, 2007; Schildt et al., 2012). This aspect is likely associated with learning partners' characteristics discussed next.

Learning partners characteristics

Simonin (2004) argues that motivation to learn is one of the major determinants of individual learning (p. 409). In the context of interorganizational strategic alliance, the same motivation, desire and will of an organization to learn from its partner applies (see also Tsang, 2002). The intent to learn, in the international business setting, refers to 'the level of desire and will of the parent (firm) with respect to learning from the joint venturing experience' (Tsang, 2002, p. 839). Thus, the knowledge seeker in the international knowledge transfer process must have a strong sense of need to learn and desire to internalize its joint-ventured partner's skills and competencies (Inkpen and Tsang, 2007).

In addition to the learning intent, an attitude of receptivity, that is, the readiness of the learning partner to appreciate and receive the knowledge brought in by the teaching partner (Tsang, Nguyen and Erramilli, 2004), would help a firm develop mechanisms and make accommodations for learning activities. Hamel (1991) suggested that generating an attitude of receptivity among operating employees depended largely on whether the firm entered the alliance as a latecomer or as a laggard. In the former case, employees were motivated to learn and to close the gap of skills with the teaching partner. Taiwan is regarded as one of latecomers of the East Asian countries block with reference to technology catch-up (Matthews 2002; Hu, 2008). Thus it is likely that ITRI based in Taiwan would have a strong motivation to learn from Kodak based in the technologically more advanced USA. In contrast, if a firm has come to think of itself as a laggard, its employees are likely to heavily rely on the teaching partner (Inkpen and Tsang, 2007). Their corresponding attitude to learn would largely depend on the level of organizational capability and capacity for learning, and also to the different stages of knowledge development of the learning partner. The latter is associated with 'absorptive capacity', which is originally defined by Cohen and Levinthal (1990) as the ability of a firm 'to recognize the value of new external knowledge, assimilate it and apply it to commercial ends' (128). Some features of laggardness may also exhibit in ITRI as it is the largest R&D organization in Taiwan (see Section 3), possessing some degree of absorptive capacity and knowledge complementarities with Kodak.

The level of absorptive capability is determined by a number of factors. First, as noted in the seminal work by Cohen and Levinthal (1990), the role of prior knowledge is important to build learning capacity, as the nature of knowledge is cumulative and path dependent. Second, investments in R&D help create a diverse knowledge base that would enhance an organization's ability to absorb knowledge from a wide variety of external sources (Schildt et al., 2012). Third, industry nature, organizational structure, culture and size also contribute to absorptive capability. For instance, Schildt et al. (2012) documented the research findings and showed that the similarity of technological areas (measured either in terms of patenting or product market domains) and structure and culture (measured through formalization, centralization and compensations practices) help companies acquire and exploit knowledge from one another (p. 1156). Fourth, absorptive capacity tends to increase over time when the developed organizational routines and processes may help support the acquisition and assimilation of knowledge (Schildt et al., 2012). For example, Doz (1996) argued that effective interactions tend to require effective organizational routines and trust, which takes time for partners to develop. Therefore, in the early stage of strategic alliance, absorptive capacity may be low, whilst it may gradually increase when learning partners build mutual trust and facilitating routines for knowledge transfer.

Simonin (2004) further classified these organizational routines and mechanisms into three distinct groups, which are believed to help facilitate knowledge transfer in strategic alliance. They are: 1) resource-based learning capacity (LC); 2) incentive-based LC; and 3) cognitive-based LC. *Resource-based LC* corresponds to the commitment of both human and tangible support assets. This must contain two elements: one is to involve sufficient personnel in the alliance driven by an investment outlook, not cost consideration (Pucik, 1988); second is to involve key personnel of both management and operational staff in the venture to drive the learning process. In particular, Inkpen (1996) suggested that the top management's leadership commitment is vitally important, as even if there is intent to learn, the required resources may not be forthcoming due to a lack of top management commitment. Therefore, organizational leaders should play the role of architect and catalyst in the learning process and initiate linkages between parent and alliance strategies. Next to human resources, support assets in the form of information processing, logistic, financial and communications capabilities are necessary to help acquire, process, store and diffuse relevant information and knowledge components. It is predicted by Simonin (2004) that with a higher level of resource-based LC, the more successful knowledge transfer would incur.

Incentive-based LC corresponds to the earlier mentioned organizational routines and processes that help 'clarify individual expectations and duties, and steer learning activities in non-ambiguous ways' (Simonin, 2004, p. 411). There are two specific elements related to this type of LC: one is the presence of an actual reward system to appropriately reward staff in strategic alliance for what they learn; the other is to have a clear learning agenda. The main aim of such a mechanism is to reduce uncertainty and ambiguity in the process of knowledge transfer. It is also most likely that a higher level of incentive-based LC, the higher the level of knowledge transfer (Simonin, 2004).

Cognitive-based LC captures general attitudes and beliefs towards learning prevailing in the organization. Similar to an attitude of receptivity mentioned earlier, cognitive-based LC refers to individuals ready to unveil their own 'blind spots', which is 'skill incompetence', and recognize the existence of cognitive impediments to learning (Simonin, 2004). Once the needs for learning are established, it is easier to take the teaching of their partners. Hence, successful knowledge transfer could result.

Based on Simonin (2004), if an organization has a higher level of learning intent, it is possible that it also has a higher level of resource-based, incentive-based and cognitive-based LC. Thus, learning intent is closely linked to absorptive capacity, as shown in Figure 11.1 with two-way interactive arrows pointing at both ends.

The ability of a firm to learn through joint ventures depends not only on its own absorptive capacity, but also on the willingness of its partner to fully cooperate. In other words, the degree of protectiveness that the teaching partner desires, vis-à-vis its knowledge base, is a determinant of the potential for learning (Inkpen and Tsang, 2007). In the context of a strategic alliance, the teaching partner has to commit not only physical assets, but more importantly, the training and support required to make the transfer of knowledge a success (Teece, 1977).

Protecting knowledge from an alliance partner may lead to negative outcomes of knowledge transfer. Baughn et al. (1997) argued that a firm's inattentiveness to the learning potential of its partners as well as its over-reliance on structural and contractual means of protection often fail to effectively regulate the flow of skills to a partner. Norman's (2002) survey of US firms found that firms are more protective when the capabilities they contribute to the alliance are highly tacit and core, when their partners have a strong learning intent, and when the firm and its partner have highly similar resources. In general, Simonin (2004) found that partner protectiveness had a significant direct effect on knowledge transfer. However, negative impact of protectiveness may be mediated by close interpersonal relationship and effective teamwork. As argued by Kale, Singh and Perlmutter (2000), when firms build relational capital in conjunction with an integrative approach to managing conflict, they are able to achieve both learning and knowledge protection objectives simultaneously.

So far we have discussed various factors relating to knowledge characteristics and learning partner characteristics with two additional elements: timing and absorptive capacity, which could have impacted on the success of international knowledge transfer under the umbrella of the strategic alliance learning framework initially proposed by Simonin (2004). Effective knowledge transfer is also largely influenced by contextual factors, such as what types of alliance forms taken by learning partners, under which competitive environment and industry that learning partners are operating. Although organizational culture, structure and size were discussed with reference to the learning partner characteristics, national culture and language of communications are regarded as contextual issues that could also affect international knowledge transfer (Simonin, 2004). These dimensions as context-specific variables are explained next.

Context-specific variables

There are several alliance forms, such as equity joint ventures, minority equity relationships, licensing agreements and an array of non-equity contractual arrangements, including collaborative R&D, coproduction agreements, technology sharing and shared marketing and distribution deals (Inkpen and Tsang, 2007). With reference to Kodak-ITRI alliance form, there is no formal equity joint venture, but largely, licensing agreements were used in the early stage of collaboration, and non-equity contractual arrangements via collaborative R&D and technology sharing were subsequently applied (See Table 11.1).

A typical situation in alliances with strong learning objectives is that cooperation is preferable because the sought-after skills and capabilities are too costly to develop internally. Forming an alliance can also provide an opportunity to acquire highly tacit knowledge (Inkpen and Tsang, 2007). As elaborated next, if

Table 11.1 The process, people and performance of Kodak-ITRI international knowledge transfer (IKT)

Timeline	Events & appointment of key personnel	Corresponding IKT factors	Performance outputs
Prior to 2006	ITRI (Industrial Technology Research Institute) was the local knowledge leader in topics such as materials, process, equipment and system. Research in these areas focused on flat panel display on glass substrates prepared for emerging and growing display industry in Taiwan.	Specific and explicit knowledge areas; some level of absorptive capacity	
January, 2006	DTC (Display Technology Center) was established to integrate all display programs of ITRI. Dr. Jyuo-Min Shyu, Vice President of ITRI was the Interim DTC General Director.	Resource-based LC with leadership commitment to IKT	
July, 2006	Dr. Janglin Chen, who had previously worked at Kodak (USA) as Chief Technology Officer (CTO) for more than 24 years, was recruited as DTC General Director	Resource-based LC, with competent personnel appointed	
February – March, 2007	Dr. Chen led one team to visit Kodak to discuss the content of KT; subsequently Kodak also sent staff to visit DTC in Taiwan to discuss the feasibility of KT.	Incentive-based LC; Building interpersonal relationship	
April, 2007	The evaluating team consisting of experts from different departments of ITRI was formed for the task of KT. They provided perspectives on marketing, technology, application, IP, funding and legal issues.	Resource- and incentive-based based LC	
April, 2007	Dr. Jack Chang, earlier retired from Kodak as Vice President and Head of R&D department, was brought into ITRI as the external consultant of DTC. He visited and advised on details of KT on an ongoing basis.	Resource-based LC	
May, 2007	After 2 months' feasibility study, Dr. Chen led the team to visit Kodak (USA) to discuss the detailed contractual agreement on KT.		
July, 2007	Experts from different departments of ITRI, including finance, contract, IP, technology transfer, laboratory and operation were formed as an advisory board to monitor the speed of KT.	Resource-based LC	
August, 2007	The contractual agreement of KT was signed on 31 August, including transferring of 217 patents, 5 sets of equipment and related documents.		

September, 2007	The KT team consisting of 18 experts from Kodak with knowledge in the areas of MCL (Material and Chemistry Laboratory), EOL (Electro-Optical Laboratory), and DTC transferred roll-to-roll cholesteric liquid crystal display (ChLCD) technology came to ITRI for two weeks from 6 to 21 September.	
October, 2007	The equipment removed from Kodak (USA) was successfully set up inside Building 15 of DTC.	
December, 2007	In 90 days after signing of KT agreement, the 6'monochrome display with resolution 30 dpi was successfully created and presented	1st new product emerged
January, 2008	The longest flexible display based on the technology transferred from Kodak with dimension of 300 cm long and 24 cm wide was presented.	2nd new product presented
May, 2008	The 13.5', monochrome, 30 dpi resolution bi-stable ChLCD was demonstrated by the method of rolling writing with its advantage of having no limitation of displaying the length for a large size of display applications.	3rd product created
June, 2008	The continuous type bi-stable display technology was received the 'Gold Panel Awards' from Industrial Development Bureau of MOEA (Ministry of Economic Affairs) of Taiwan.	
January, 2009	Finished industrial collaboration project with 4 material companies in Taiwan for key materials of flexible ChLCD.	
January, 2009	Signed sub-contract with National Sun Yat-Sen University on topic of encapsulation ChLC.	
May, 2009	A4 size, multi-color, 75 dpi resolution flexible display has been demonstrated for applications of signage and price tag.	4th product created
June, 2009	Finished industrial collaboration project with 5 equipment companies in Taiwan for key process of flexible ChLCD.	
November, 2009	Large size (240 mm wide and 3000 mm long) flexible display with resolution of 300 dpi has been shown by method of thermal printing.	5th product emerged
January, 2010	Finished Industrial collaboration project with 1 manufacturing company in Taiwan for Roll-to-Roll coating process of flexible ChLCD.	

(*Continued*)

Table 11.1 (Continued)

Timeline	Events & appointment of key personnel	Corresponding IKT factors	Performance outputs
January, 2010	Cooperated with a system integration company to demonstrate conceptual product of flexible clock in the CES show.		
April, 2010	Demonstrated 300 cm long e-paper in the FINTECH Show in Japan.		6th product emerged
June, 2010	A4 size multi-color signage with resolution 75 dpi shown in Taipei Optical Show.		7th product emerged
October, 2010	Flexible ChLCD with trade mark named 'i2Rrewritable e-paper' has received the R&D 100 Awards and the Wall Street Journal TIA Awards in USA.		
December, 2011	The 'i2R rewritable e-paper' received the National Industrial Innovation Award from MOEA.		
July, 2012	The 'i2R e-Paper' received the Outstanding Research Silver Award of ITRI.		
November, 2012	The application of e-ticket by i2R e-paper has been demonstrated with different colors (blue, red, and purple), resolution 300 dpi and durability of 300 times rewriting.		8th product created
October, 2013	Signed contract and IP licensing with Taiwan's system integration company (GoDex) for the application of e-ticket.		
July, 2014	The spin-off project has been started and led by the deputy general director, Dr. Lai Cheng Cheng, for the plan of marketing, product design, business model and financial arrangement.		
October, 2015	The start-up company named 'i2R Technology' led by Dr. Chen, was spun-off from DTC and located in the incubation center of ITRI.		

the knowledge is tacit, it may be acquirable only by close observation and interactions with the owners/managers of the tacit knowledge. Thus, an alliance may provide access to this knowledge. In the context of Kodak-ITRI collaboration, both explicit and tacit knowledge is present, thus, intensive personnel exchange and training is required to facilitate the alliance form for collaborative R&D and technology sharing.

As argued by Osborn and Hagedoorn (1997), national culture may serve as either support or hindrance to successful technology transfer. Arguably, if learning in domestic alliances is complicated, it will be more so in the case of international alliances where geographic distance and cultural differences generate additional difficulties and challenges for managers (Osborn and Hagedoorn, 1997, p. 270). In a learning context, culture influences how people process, interpret and make use of a body of knowledge. Thus, complications may arise when knowledge is transferred across dissimilar cultures (Bhagat et al., 2002). In the context of international joint ventures, Child and Rodrigues (1996) argued that if the perceived cultural distance is great, that is dissimilar to a greater extent, knowledge transfer is likely to be impeded. Lyles and Salk (1996) maintained that cultural misunderstandings among managers in international joint ventures hinder flows of information and learning. Therefore, greater national cultural differences would moderate the effectiveness of cross-border knowledge transfer. To overcome this cultural distance, appointment of personnel with similar cultural backgrounds in the process of knowledge transfer is often recommended (Makela et al., 2012).

Closely related to cultural differences is the issue of language differences. Effective communication is a precondition for learning. Villinger (1996) found that language difficulties were the most frequently cited barrier to successful learning by both local and expatriate managers, followed by problems due to pronounced differences in cultures and systems, mentalities and ways of thinking. Even with the help of interpreters, a communication barrier existed between local and expatriate managers when they could not accurately translate ideas (Tsang, 2001). To overcome this issue of language differences, staff who are bilingual (e.g. speaking and understanding both English and Chinese in the case of Kodak-ITRI) should be selected to participate in the knowledge transfer process.

In addition to alliance form, cultural and language issues, other alliance contextual factors, such as alliance industry, the competitive environment and the linkages between the focal alliance and a larger knowledge network, can also impact on the learning process (Inkpen and Tsang, 2007, p. 506). These contextual factors will be explained in more details with reference to the longitudinal case study of Kodak-ITRI collaboration in the next section.

Research method – a longitudinal case study

We adopt a case study approach by looking at the chronology of Kodak-ITRI collaboration in the period from 2005 until present day. Table 11.1 outlines the key activities of collaboration and outcomes of such collaboration, especially for the receiving partner, ITRI. The benefits of collaboration for Kodak as the partner of teaching and transfusion of knowledge would include its economic reap of selling 217 patents, 14 authorized patents and 5 sets of machines, which would be obsolete without this type of international transfer. Thus the focus of the analysis would be more on how ITRI has utilized knowledge from Kodak to further research and develop new products and leverage industry linkage to facilitate the incubation of new enterprises throughout Taiwan.

Profile of ITRI

Industrial Technology Research Institute (ITRI) was found in Taiwan in 1973. It is a non-profit research and development (R&D) organization engaging in applied research and technical services. Since its establishment, ITRI has played a vital role in transforming Taiwan's economy from a labor-intensive industry to a high-tech industry (www.itri.org.tw/eng/index.aspx). The key success of ITRI is its ability to home-breed some well-known, high-tech companies in Taiwan, such as those leaders in the semiconductor industry, TSMC and UMC – the two largest semiconductor manufacturers.

ITRI currently employs 5,579 personnel, including 1,320 who hold PhDs and 3,024 with master's degrees. ITRI has also taken the role of nurturing Taiwan's emerging industries. It focuses on six major research areas: information and communication, electronics and optoelectronics, biomedical technology and device, green energy and environment, material and chemical, and mechanical and systems (ITRI, 2015). The institute has a mission of serving as a pioneer for industries by strengthening its capabilities of multidisciplinary innovation and cooperation with international partners all over the world.

Prior to the collaboration with Kodak, ITRI had been reconstructed into three major groups of organizations: Core Laboratory, Focus Centre and Linkage Centre. Under the Focus Centre, there were five key centres: Display Technology Centre, Photovoltaics Technology Centre, Cloud Computing Technology Centre, Medical Device Technology Centre and Identification and Safety Technology Centre. It was the Display Technology Centre that has enabled the integration of display projects in different units of ITRI and made it possible to actively collaborate with international partners, such as Kodak.

A retrospective study

In order to observe the complex process by which knowledge transfer from Kodak to ITRI took place, a longitudinal study approach was used. The logic of applying the longitudinal study approach is that it helps study developmental trends across the life span of knowledge transfer process in the current case. Often longitudinal studies allow researchers to distinguish short from long-term phenomena. There are several types of longitudinal study, one of which is a retrospective study that could help researchers look back in time, examine the events already taken place and identify key factors contributing to generating multiple outcomes in the complex evolving process.

Often the retrospective study is used in medical research to counter against the prospective study that may be expensive to conduct and need to involve a longer period of time to collect data with large cohorts (Doran et al., 2012). The retrospective study takes shorter time on a smaller scale but is useful to examine the inter-related factors that might have contributed to achieving multiple results. This is more or less the phenomena in the international knowledge transfer process, whereby multifaceted and alliance learning characteristics could make distinct and/or complementary contributions to achieving multiple performance outcomes.

Multiple performance outcomes with reference to ITRI success in knowledge transfer rest in five main areas: 1) number of patents transferred from the teaching partner (Kodak), 2) number of patents generated by the receiving partner (ITRI); 3) number of new products created; 4) number of new enterprises incubated; and 5) number of awards received (see Table 11.1).

In the next section, our aims are to evaluate the case through the lens of historical events, and endeavor to identify the factors that would have contributed to achieving the performance outcomes of knowledge transfer and management in the case of ITRI-Kodak cooperation.

Evaluation and discussion of the case study

Examining the key events in light of the strategic alliance learning framework proposed by Simonin (2004), it is found that three main learning characteristics, *aka* knowledge, learner and context, were clearly exhibited in the case of the Kodak-ITRI knowledge transfer process. In particular, there appear to be some knowledge complementarities between Kodak and ITRI. Prior to the collaboration, ITRI had been very successful in leading Taiwan's transformation in the semi-conductor industry. The organization had its own R&D capabilities, especially in the areas of materials, process, equipment and systems that provided the bolsters to develop flat panel display, which facilitated the transfer of Roll-to-Roll cholesteric liquid crystal display (ChLCD) from Kodak in the subsequent strategic alliance.

Explicit knowledge in this case refers to 217 patents and 5 sets of equipment and related documents transferred from Kodak after signing off the contractual agreement on 31 August 2007. Although tacit knowledge was not clearly indicated via examining the historical events, it could be argued that several times of staff exchange visits; appointment of key personnel such as Dr. Janglin Chen who had previously worked in Kodak as Chief Technology Officer (CTO) for more than 24 years; regular advice provided by former Kodak Vice President and Head of R&D department Dr Jack Chang; and internal working of expert teams consisting of finance, contract IP, technology transfer, laboratory and operation, have all carried the character of 'tacit knowledge'. These activities also helped reduce knowledge ambiguity, leading to the success of knowledge transfer (Simonin 2004; Inkpen and Wang, 2006).

From the learning partner's perspective, it can be found that ITRI as a knowledge receiver had a strong learning intent. Despite ITRI being the local knowledge leader, there was some catch-up work to do with reference to the display technology. Moreover, at the time of collaboration, Taiwan's semi-conductor manufacturing firms had become the world leading industry with mature structure and supply chain. The flat panel display industry in Taiwan had also become another mature business then. There was an urgent need to develop new industry and new enterprises so as to sustain Taiwan's economic development. Kodak's coating technology and knowledge was believed to serve as a springboard to help Taiwan develop an emerging electronic papers industry and flexible display industry, which were seen to be the pathway for transform-ing Taiwan's industrial landscape in modern times. Thus the degree of intent and attitude to learn for ITRI was high, leading to the success of knowledge transfer.

The intent to learn was clearly complemented by the resource-based learning capacity (LC), though the incentive-based and cognitive-based LC were less evi-dent in examining the historical events. First, the appointment of Vice-President of ITRI, Dr. Jyuo-Min Shyu as the Interim DTC General Director, initially dem-onstrated a strong top management commitment to the international knowledge transfer project. This was subsequently backed up by the appointment of former Kodak executive Dr. Chen as DTC General Director. Support staff from differ-ent departments of ITRI, i.e. marketing, technology, application, IP, funding and legal issues, were present to drive the learning process of the entire organization of ITRI. Whilst the top management commitment helped ensure the sufficient financial resources to acquire necessary patents from Kodak, support teams with skills in information processing, logistic, legal, financial, marketing and commu-nications guaranteed the successful acquisition, processing, storage and diffu-sion of relevant information and knowledge component (Inkpen, 1996; Simonin, 2004). Thus, it is believed that ITRI's strong resource-based LC helped the suc-cess of knowledge transfer from Kodak.

However, the incentive-based LC built around the reward system to compen-sate staff in strategic alliance was not explicitly shown, though some forms of external awards to the organization (not to individual staff) were present. For instance, ITRI had received the 'Gold Panel Awards' from the Ministry of Eco-nomic Affairs (MOEA) of Taiwan in June 2008; and flexible ChICD or 'i2R rewritable e-paper' received the R&D 100 Awards and the Wall Street Journal TIA Awards in 2010 and the National Innovation Awards from MOEA in 2011. Internal human resource (HR) motivation and incentive reward system might be mandate, less likely recorded as significant historical events in Table 11.1. But these systems, together with employees' response to the HR policies and prac-tices as a way to indicate the cognitive-based learning capacity, are important to formulate the organizational routines and mechanisms that may facilitate future creativity and innovation. These aspects should be further investigated in future studies.

Apart from strong learning intent and high level of resource-based learning capacity, successful international knowledge transfer from Kodak to ITRI was also related to the patent protection via structural and contractual means. For instance, Taiwan has a relatively well-institutionalized IP protection law (Sun, 1997; StudyinTaiwan, 2015). In addition, the contractual agreement was signed to ensure subsequent collaboration in research and development. However, knowledge protectiveness of Kodak as the knowledge deliverer was mediated by close interpersonal relationship, especially at the leadership level, and effective teamwork built by ITRI-Kodak staff via training programs and exchange visits. Thus it appears that powerful relational capitals with strong IP protection enabled both parties to achieve learning and knowledge protection objectives simultaneously (Kale et al., 2000).

It is noticed that the appointment of key personnel with bilingual ability (i.e. speaking both English and Chinese) and prior working experience in USA and Taiwan in the current case helped overcome cultural and language issues often present in the international knowledge transfer process.

It is also noted that different stages of knowledge transfer may induce different levels of absorptive capability. There appear to be three stages of knowledge transfer in the current case. In the early stage (Jan 2006-Dec 2007) before the first new product emerged, ITRI's absorptive capability might be strong in the area of recognizing the value of Kodak's knowledge in display technology, but the ability to apply this knowledge to commercial ends was weak. In the second stage (Jan 2008-Jan 2011), the level of ITRI's absorptive capability was the highest. While still collaborating with Kodak, ITRI actively worked with 3 universities and 15 domestic companies, and commercialized their collaborative research outputs with creating and marketing several new products. ITRI's absorptive capability with reference to its collaboration with Kodak decreased, because the formal strategic alliance relationship ended in 2011. However, several industrial collaboration projects from the Kodak-ITRI knowledge transfer have been operating before 2014, and one spin-off company has been established even up to October 2015 while this paper was formulated. Therefore, as argued by Schildt et al. (2012), when the technological areas measured by the number of patents and product market domains of the learning partners start to divert, it is the time to break up the strategic alliance. At this stage, ITRI moved away from relying on Kodak's coating technology, and was able to take lead and become itself the knowledge diffuser, especially to industry, or help incubated relevant enterprises in the area of e-paper technology.

Figure 11.2 summarizes the key learning variables in light of the strategic alliance learning framework developed by Simonin (2004) and Schildt et al. (2012). Sustained knowledge transfer and management will lead to strong entrepreneurship and product innovation, helping Taiwan lead the e-paper industry in the region for future.

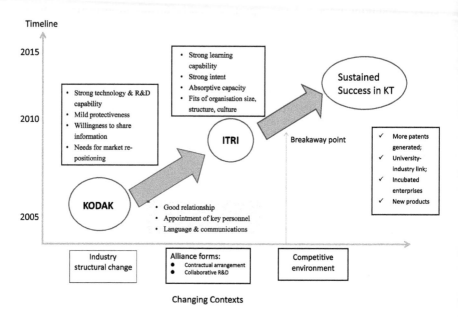

Figure 11.2 Key factors influencing Kodak-ITRI knowledge transfer

Conclusion

Using the strategic alliance learning framework, the current case study identified key factors contributing to the learning success in the dynamic international knowledge transfer process. These factors cover knowledge complementarities, top management commitment, strong learning intent and high level of learning capability (LC), especially in the aspect of resource-based LC of the receiving partner (ITRI) and strong IP protection accompanying with low level of tacit knowledge protectiveness from the teaching partner (Kodak). In addition, good interpersonal relationships and strong collaborative teamwork between two parties have also assisted the smooth transfer process. As a result of appointment of key personnel with bilingual ability and cross-cultural competency, cultural barriers and language communication often regarded as key challenges to international knowledge transfer (Lyles and Salk, 1996; Bhagat et al., 2002) were not an issue in the current case study.

There are several limitations contained in the current case study, nonetheless. First, the results generated from a single case study examining the knowledge transfer process from Kodak to ITRI obviously are not generalizeable. More case studies in future could be collected to further verify the strategic learning model as initially proposed by Simonin (2004) and extended in the current study. Second, the historical events tend to focus on those significant and spotlight activities, neglecting normal organizational routines and tasks that might also contribute to learning effectiveness. For instance in the current study, we were not able to examine the aspects of incentive-based and cognitive-based learning capability as they were not recorded in the chronological events. It is important in future studies to examine how organizational routines and mechanisms such as human resource (HR) reward and compensation policies and practices help in learning and knowledge management process. Following the second point, third, the current case tends to focus more on organizational level of awards, neglecting to reward individual achievements in the knowledge transfer process. Because organizational creativity and innovation would largely come from individual employees, we are left to question: what are some key incentive HR policies and practices that could motivate employees? Future studies should look at this aspect, together with examination of employees' response to these policies, i.e. developing cognitive-based learning capability to facilitate organizational knowledge transfer and management across borders. Lastly, a retrospective study approach was sufficient to examine the inter-related factors that might have contributed to multiple performance outcomes. However, because of displaying sequential activities in light of historical events, it is difficult to examine the actual cause-effect relationship between learning variables and multiple performance outcomes. Collecting quantitative data might help overcome this issue in future studies.

Despite the limitations, the current case study provides additional empirical evidence and explains key variables affecting the strategic alliance learning process in light of international knowledge transfer between strategic alliance partners. The findings would encourage the sunset industries and firms with high-tech components and technical/technological capabilities in the advanced economies to seek strategic partners especially in the less developed nations so as to utilize their technology and know-how to build new industries and firms for future.

References

Baughn, C., Denekamp, J.G., Stevens, J.H. and Osborn, R.N. (1997) 'Protecting intellectual capital in international alliances', *Journal of World Business*, 32: 103–17.

Bhagat, R.S., Kedia, B.L., Harveston, P.D. and Triandis, H.C. (2002) 'Cultural variations in the cross-border transfer of organizational knowledge: An integrative framework', *Academy of Management Review*, 27: 204–21.

Castro, L. (2015) Strategizing across boundaries: Revisiting knowledge brokering activities in French innovation clusters, *Journal of Knowledge Management*, 19(5): 1048–68.

Child, J. and Rodrigues, S. (1996) 'The role of social identity in the international transfer of knowledge through joint ventures', In S.R. Clegg and G. Palmer (Eds) *The Politics of Management Knowledge*, pp 46–68, London, Sage.

Cohen, W.M. and Levinthal, D.A. (1990) 'Absorptive capacity: A new perspective on learning and innovation', *Administrative Science Quarterly*, 35: 128–52.

Doran, T., Kontopantelis, E., Fullwood, C., Lester, H., Valderas, J.M., and Campbell, S. (2012) 'Exempting dissenting patients from pay for performance schemes: Retrospective analysis of exception reporting in the UK Quality and Outcomes Framework', *British Medical Journal*, 344: e2405.

Doz, Y.L. (1996) 'The evolution of cooperation in strategic alliance: Initial conditions or learning processes', *Strategic Management Journal*, 17: 55–83.

Garud, R., Tuertscher, P. and Van De Ven, A.D. (2013) 'Perspective on innovation process', *The Academy of Management Annals*, 7(1): 755–819.

Hamel, G. (1991) 'Competition for competence and inter-partner learning within international strategic alliances', *Strategic Management Journal*, 12: 83–104.

Hu, M.C. (2008) 'Knowledge flows and innovation capability: The patenting trajectory of Taiwan's thin film transistor-liquid crystal display industry', *Technological Forecasting & Social Change*, 75: 1423–38.

Inkpen, A.C. (1996) 'Creating knowledge through collaboration', *California Management Review*, 39(1): 123–40.

Inkpen, A.C. and Dinur, A. (1998) 'Knowledge management processes and international joint ventures', *Organization Science*, 9: 454–68.

Inkpen, A.C. and Tsang, E.W.K. (2007) 'Learning and strategic alliances", *The Academy of Management Annals*, 1: 479–511.

Inkpen, A.C. and Wang, P. (2006) 'The China-Singapore Suzhou industrial park: A knowledge transfer network', *Journal of Management Studies*, 43: 779–811.

ITRI (2015) https://www.itri.org.tw/eng/Content/Messagess/contents.aspx?Site ID=1&MmmID=617731521661672477, accessed December 20, 2015

Kale, P. and Singh, H. (2007) 'Building firm capabilities through learning: The role of the alliance learning process in alliance capability and firm-level alliance success', *Strategic Management Journal*, 28: 981–1000.

Kale, P., Singh, H. and Perlmutter, H. (2000) 'Learning and protection of proprietary assets in strategic alliances: Building relational capital', *Strategic Management Journal*, 21: 217–37.

Kim, C.S. and Inkpen, A.C. (2005) 'Cross-border R&D alliances, absorptive capacity and technology learning', *Journal of International Management*, 11: 313–29.

Lyles, M.A. and Salk, J.E. (1996) 'Knowledge acquisition from foreign parents in international joint ventures: An empirical examination in the Hungarian context', *Journal of International Business Studies*, 27: 877–903.

Makela, K., Andersson, U. and Seppala, T. (2012) 'Interpersonal similarity and knowledge sharing within multinational organizations', *International Business Review*, 21: 439–51.

Matthews, J. (2002) 'Competitive advantages of the latecomer firm: A resource-based account of industrial catch-up strategies', *Asia Pacific Journal of Management*, 19: 467–88.

Norman, P.M. (2002) 'Protecting knowledge in strategic alliances: Resource and relational characteristics'. *Journal of High Technology Management Research*, 13: 177–203.

Osborn, R.N. and Hagedoorn, J. (1997) 'The institutionalization and evolutionary dynamics of interorganizational alliances and networks', *Academy of Management Journal*, 40: 261–78.

Pucik, V. (1988) 'Strategic alliances, organizational learning, and competitive advantage: The HRM agenda', *Human Resource Management*, 27: 77–93.

Schildt, H., Keil, T. and Maula, M. (2012) 'The temporal effects of relative and firm-level absorptive capacity on interorganizational learning', *Strategic Management Journal*, 33: 1154–73.

Simonin, B.L. (1999) 'Ambiguity and the process of knowledge transfer in strategic alliances', *Strategic Management Journal*, 20: 595–623.

Simonin, B.L. (2004) 'An empirical investigation of the process of knowledge transfer in international strategic alliances', *Journal of International Business Studies*, 35: 407–27.

StudyinTaiwan (2015) Comprehensive IP Protection, http://www.studyintaiwan. org/living_ip_protection.html, accessed January 12, 2015.

Sun, A.Y. (1997) From pirate king to jungle king: Transformation of Taiwan's intellectual property protection, http://apli.org/ftp/taiwanipr.pdf, accessed January 12, 2016

Teece, D.J. (1977) 'Technology transfer by multinational firms: The resource cost of transferring technological know-how', *Economic Journal*, 87: 242–61.

Tsang, E.W.K. (2001) 'Managerial learning in foreign-invested enterprises of China', *Management International Review*, 41: 29–51.

Tsang, E.W.K. (2002) 'Acquiring knowledge by foreign partners from international joint ventures in a transition economy: Learning-by-doing and learning myopia', *Strategic Management Journal*, 23: 835–54.

Tsang, E.W.K., Nguyen, D.T. and Erramilli, M.K. (2004) 'Knowledge acquisition and performance of international joint ventures in a transition economy', *Journal of International Marketing*, 12(2): 82–103.

Villinger, R. (1996) 'Post-acquisition managerial learning in Central East Europe', *Organization Studies*, 17: 181–206.

12 Heterogeneous professional identities as an intra-sectoral knowledge filter

Daniel Feser and *Till Proeger*

Introduction

Innovation has been identified as the predominant driver for the development of global, national and regional economies (Jensen et al., 2007). The role of innovative activities has been pioneered in the endogenous growth theory, which has integrated knowledge into theoretical growth models (Romer, 1986, 1994). A broad strand of publications has subsequently emerged, operationalizing knowledge spillover as an explanation concerning how knowledge drives growth (e.g. Acs et al., 2012; Agarwal et al., 2007).

On the level of individual firms, the intra-firm innovative capacity has been highlighted as a major determinant of competitiveness (Vega-Jurado et al., 2008). In this context, the occurrence of knowledge spillovers is explained as a strategic decision to find arbitrage opportunities and is conceptualized in the knowledge spillover theory of entrepreneurship (KSTE). Audretsch's (1995) seminal paper on the KSTE has described the contribution of small and medium-sized companies to the innovative capacity of economies. Critical accounts on the KSTE have suggested that no automatic spillover of knowledge occurs, but rather that specific managerial decisions determine the extent of knowledge sharing by firms (Acs et al., 2013; Braunerhjelm et al., 2010). The observation of differences in the occurrence of sectoral and regional knowledge spillover has created a strand of literature focusing on the barriers for knowledge spillover by introducing the analytical framework of knowledge filter (Acs et al., 2004).

Our study furthers the aspect of knowledge filters within the KSTE to broaden our understanding of knowledge filters as a barrier to successful knowledge spillovers, which could reduce regional and national innovativeness. Accordingly, we conducted a series of 17 semi-structured interviews with experts from the market for energy efficiency consultants (EEC).[1] The sector is dynamic and has recently developed following government interventions to improve energy efficiency in the residential sector. The use of innovative technologies is imperative in this sector and novel insight is regularly produced. However, the spillover of expert knowledge among sectoral firms has been described as highly deficient (Feser and Proeger, 2015). We use this case study to illustrate an important aspect of the KSTE, namely the role of different professional backgrounds and identities in fostering or impeding knowledge spillovers in innovative sectors.

We show that entrepreneurs in the respective sector have very different professional backgrounds, which provides us with an explanation for the lack of knowledge spillovers. Firms in the EEC sector have been founded by architects, engineers and members of different crafts. Thus, while they provide a similar service and constitute a common professional sector, their professional training, ethics and identities substantially diverge. This leads to distrust and in many cases dissociations among the respective entrepreneurs and firms, which in turn precludes knowledge spillovers. The diversity of backgrounds within the sector thus cannot be exploited as innovative potential, but rather precludes innovative cooperation. We analyze this situation based upon the broad literature on the role of particular identities provided in the field of behavioral economics in recent years. Experimental research has shown that common identities are crucial in sustaining human cooperation over time. Thus, initiating and nurturing common identities among economic actors is a strong prerequisite for cooperative norms. Establishing a sectoral 'social fabric' that includes a common professional understanding and sectoral identity can thus be seen as an important investment in sectoral knowledge spillovers. These insights are used to formulate concise policy implications that can help to establish common sectoral identities and thus reduce the knowledge filter of heterogeneous professional backgrounds. Specifically, we propose establishing sectoral networks and professional associations as well as common training courses intended to establish a 'common ground' for firms in the respective sector.

The remainder of this study is structured as follows. We review the literature relevant to our approach in section two, followed by the methodological section in section three, which features a description of our sample. In section four, the results on the role of heterogeneity on expert markets are analyzed and connected to behavioral insight, before section five concludes.

Literature review

Our contribution draws upon three distinct strands of literature. First, we build upon the literature that constitutes the KSTE, which has furthered our understanding of the role of knowledge for companies (Acs et al., 2009a; Audretsch et al., 2006; Audretsch and Keilbach, 2007). The KSTE has primarily focused on testing different aspects of the theory empirically (Acs et al., 2009b; Agarwal and Shah, 2014; Audretsch and Keilbach, 2008; Audretsch and Lehmann, 2005), whereby the effective use of knowledge has been identified as the key determinant for sustaining competitive advantages in companies.

Second, we draw on studies aiming to operationalize knowledge spillovers, whereby different empirical measures have been used thus far. One approach has been to use codified knowledge, primarily by counting the number of patents and other forms of registered intellectual property rights (Acs et al., 2002; Plummer and Acs, 2014). Other measures include the change of employees (Agarwal and Shah, 2014), the creation of start-ups using knowledge provided by universities (Acosta et al., 2011; Audretsch et al., 2005) and research institutions (Cappelli et al., 2014). Most recently, it has been suggested to use entrepreneurial creativity (Audretsch and Belitski, 2013) and the entrepreneurial activities of employees (Stam, 2013) to explain the commercialization of new knowledge. Overall, while different factors have been suggested as driving knowledge spillovers, the main result remains that the degree of sectoral knowledge intensity is the main determinant of knowledge spillovers.

Third, and most relevant, we build upon studies investigating the effectiveness of knowledge spillovers between sectors and companies, for which Acs et al. (2004) have introduced the concept of knowledge filters, thus describing the barriers of transformation from new to commercialized knowledge. The literature builds upon the observation that companies decide not to commercialize their entire knowledge (Hayter, 2013). While knowledge filters have been analyzed at the regional (Acs et al., 2009a; Acs and Plummer, 2005), institutional (Stenholm et al., 2013) and individual (Guerrero and Urbano, 2014) level, the heterogeneity of market participants has not yet been discussed as a potential knowledge filter. Therefore, we extend the existing literature in two distinct domains: first, by showing the impact of firms' heterogeneity on the occurrence of knowledge spillovers using case studies; and second, by providing insights from behavioral economics to explain cooperative behavior within heterogeneous groups.

Data and methodology

To date, only preliminary results on experts' behavior within the KSTE have been presented and the concept of knowledge filter remains at an early stage. Therefore, an exploratory approach using case studies (Eisenhardt, 1989; Eisenhardt and Graebner, 2007) is used in this study to further develop the initial understanding of the impact of intra-sectoral heterogeneity on knowledge spillovers. Qualitative and semi-qualitative approaches have been used to explore the field of EECs (Gram-Hanssen et al., 2007; Muench et al., 2014; Virkki-Hatakka et al., 2013) due to the lack of quantitative material and the dynamically changing political framework, which influences the development of the EEC sector. Consequently, we refrain from explicitly formulating and testing a hypothesis for our case studies (Edmondson and McManus, 2007); rather, we will focus on improving the general understanding of heterogeneity on knowledge spillover using the grounded theory (Corbin and Strauss, 2008; Glaser and Strauss, 2008).

We developed a questionnaire based upon common approaches in the social sciences that initially provided open questions to avoid biasing interviewees' answers, followed by more precise literature-based questions. Drawing upon Muench et al. (2014), the questionnaire was structured as follows. We grouped questions into three sections: definition, barriers and recommendations. In the first part, due to the scarce literature and existing variety of definition of EECs and its service, the interviewee's understanding of his job definition was discussed. Regarding barriers, the interviewees were asked about problems concerning the sectoral developments, with reference to the customer, the political framework and other relevant stakeholders. The interviews concluded with recommendations for the policy-makers regarding an optimal intra-sectoral development.

The interviews were carried out face-to-face or via phone between February and July 2015, with an interview length from 40 to 70 minutes. To reduce socially desirable response patterns, full anonymity was assured to the interviewees. Subsequently, the results of the transcriptions of the documents were compared with public accessible documents such as online publication and press releases to ensure their validity.[2]

The sample was analyzed using Mayring's (2004) content analysis method, which concentrates on the condensation of the relevant material. In the beginning, we conducted open coding with the collection of all relevant content concerning our research question. Subsequently, the categories and (in the case of several factors) sub-categories were ordered according to specific topics. Additionally, the reviewed literature was used to categorize the aforementioned coding. To assure the quality of our analysis, we further conducted a cross-case analysis to compare the internal validity of the content. The content of the interviews was discussed between the authors, redefining critical coding with new categories.

The selection of experts for our sample follows the requirements of the grounded theory (Glaser, 1965; Glaser and Strauss, 2008). We chose the interviewees to fulfill theoretical saturation, thus selecting experts who represent the heterogeneous perspectives on the EEC market. Starting with gatekeeper from the craft chamber and the EEC associations, experts were recommended who fully represented the heterogeneity within the field. Consequently, our sample of 17 experts from the EEC sector includes individuals with a technical background as well as legal and administrative specialists. The interviewees were sorted into the 'Research and Education', 'EEC' and 'Political and Professional Association' groups. The first group had expertise regarding details about the certification and training of the EECs with architectural, engineering and crafts backgrounds. The second group contained the market participants themselves, while the third group comprised experts on the political framework and market interventions, as well as the funding mechanisms in the EEC market. Table 12.1 summarizes our sample and the respective professional backgrounds of the interviewees.

Table 12.1 Overview of the sample

Stakeholder code	Research and education	EEC	Political and professional association	Professional background
#A	X			Architecture
#B	X			Engineering
#C	X			Crafts
#D	X			State Regulator
#E		x		Crafts
#F		x		Crafts
#G		x		Engineering
#H		x		Architecture
#I		x		Architecture
#J			x	Regional Energy Agency
#K			x	National Energy Agency
#L			x	Innovation Support Coordination
#M			x	Innovation Support Bank
#N			x	EEC Journal
#O			x	Architect Professional Association
#P			x	EEC Association
#Q			x	EEC Association
Total	**4**	**5**	**8**	**17**

In the next section, our results concerning the role of heterogeneity in the EEC market are presented, highlighting its impact on knowledge spillovers, which is further elaborated in three case studies.

The role of heterogeneity on an expert market

The term 'Energy Efficiency Consultant' (EEC) is not regulated in terms of copyright in Germany and thus it can be used by any person. The heterogeneity of the EEC sector is only limited through a regulatory intervention of the federal government restricting the firms that are eligible to award the official energy performance certificates (EPCs) and apply for federal retrofit subsidies. In this regulation, the access is restricted to EECs with a background in architecture, engineering and the crafts. Nevertheless, the educational level of these groups varies between a completed traineeship with additional certified courses and university graduations. Similarly, the knowledge intensity of the firms is fairly heterogeneous due to the technological complexity of conducting energy efficiency measures in residences and the firms' differentiated specialization.

In the KSTE, heterogeneity of firms is recognized as an opportunity for creativity, resulting in innovative knowledge (Audretsch and Belitski, 2013). Identifying the possibility to receive knowledge spillover from diverse sources, it appears ideal to find arbitrage possibilities for commercializing innovative knowledge. Nevertheless, the willingness to cooperate with other companies on a heterogeneous market needs to be taken into account. In the EEC sector, the separation according to the educational background – university graduates and traineeship from the craft chamber – resulted in two different professional organizations responsible for the lobbying and training of EECs, which potentially has a detrimental impact on knowledge spillovers.

This problem is elaborated in the presentation of our results using the interviewees' descriptions of the effects of heterogeneous actors on knowledge spillover in their sector. The heterogeneity is based upon the entrepreneurs' educational backgrounds, which determines the sub-groups' professional identities. This initial heterogeneity on the EEC market is further deepened by common meetings and sectoral professional terminology of the different sub-groups, which substantially affects the transferability and thus the value of sub-group-specific knowledge. We identify the heterogeneous educational backgrounds as being path-dependent, emphasizing that cooperation only occurs within groups of similar educational backgrounds as potential drivers for knowledge spillover processes in the EEC sector. We exemplify this issue using three cases studies on entrepreneurial decisions from our sample, thereby emphasizing the relevance of groups' professional identities for explaining the occurrence of knowledge spillovers.

Identity based upon educational background

Although the architectural, engineering and crafts sector have similar perspectives on retrofit, education within the sectors in Germany substantially varies, both qualitatively and quantitatively. The architectural and engineering sector comprises theoretically trained university graduates, while the crafts sector conducts an applied training, with mostly long-term trainings and traineeships. The sectors are organized in different chambers with mandatory membership of the companies. The chambers conduct the sector-specific training, meaning that there are different EEC trainings for the different sectors.

It is also important to keep in mind that the EEC market is a free access market, with no established organizing institutions regulating market entry. However, the government uses a top-down approach to establish quality standards by limiting the access for granting subsidies. The market for EECs has swiftly developed during the past two decades, growing from a niche market towards a market with a considerable size with more than 13,000 experts listed on an official website in 2015.[3] Driven by the political will to conduct policy interventions that lead to a reduction in energy consumption, the building sector has been granted substantial subsidies for EECs to consult primarily private homeowners.

The traineeship for EEC is organized in educational institutions, which can be accessed by all professions related to the housing and building sector. However, each sub-sector also offers their own traineeships, while the experts are allowed to take part in any of the EEC courses. Consequently, the interviewees stated that the training is mostly completed in courses given by their sub-sectors' educational institution since EECs are familiar with the institutions, given that they also organized the trainings in their old professions. There is no standardized curriculum for the EEC training courses; thus, the content and the quality strongly vary along with the educational institutions. Furthermore, there is a variation in terms of the hours per course required to conduct publicly subsidized retrofit, ranging from 70 to 400 hours. Once the certificate is received, the EECs are required to regularly participate in training courses to keep up with technological developments and maintain certification to apply for subsidies. Again, the selection of courses is free for all the EECs, although in reality the respondents considered attending a training course that is not given by their sub-sectoral institution as an exception.

The impact of the different professional identities can also be understood from the structure of the companies. The architectural and engineering EECs largely concentrate exclusively on EEC, while EECs with crafts background often have additional building companies and only offer EEC as an additional service. This results in different perspectives concerning the way in which EEC should be conducted, thus contributing to the heterogeneity in the sector.

Overall, while the trainings for becoming an EEC expert conducting publicly certified measures can be attended by a large group of professions, the experts tend to receive their EEC training from an institution close to their original profession. Therefore, it can be stated that the professional identity formed during their initial training is reinforced during the additional training to become an EEC expert and further during the subsequent courses required to uphold the certification to apply for public subsidies. Consequently, there are strongly diverging professional identities and approaches to conducting EEC, which stiffen over time and create barriers to communication among the different professions on the market. These diverging path dependencies have distinct effects on the individual behavior within the EEC sector.

Experts' behavior on the market

The creation of strong identities based upon the professional background has led to path dependencies of specialization in the EEC market and distrust among the different expert groups. Both trends are not visible to customers due to the credence good properties on the EEC market yet they preclude innovative cooperation and knowledge spillovers.

Due to information asymmetries on the EEC market, the experts have little information about their competitors or potential cooperation partners and their view of other market participants is dominated by negative stereotypes. The interviewees described the mutual trust among market participants as being excessively low, specifically regarding different professional backgrounds. The mistrust is expressed with stereotypes, which are constructed by previous misbehavior of members of other sub-sectors. For instance, the experts with architectural and engineering backgrounds complain about competitors with crafts backgrounds, perceiving that they have a narrow-minded perspective on EEC services. The same respondents claim that craftsmen are unable to consult the homeowner appropriately owing to a lack of EEC-specific knowledge. Therefore, crafts EECs are considered as impartial based upon the assumption that craftsmen are biased towards crafts-related technologies. Thus, some of the interviewees mentioned the painters' example – painters always propose to fix the insulation regardless of the economic efficiency – while others underlined that companies that offer heating services mostly recommend new radiation systems as the only energy efficient method for the customer.

By contrast, the interviewees with a crafts background voice strong concerns about the behavior of architectural and engineering EECs. In the interviews, mistrust is expressed about the lack of close-to-the-market knowledge of professionals from the engineering and architectural field. Interviewees with crafts backgrounds criticize EECs with a university degree as not responding to economic efficiency since their only interest is to maximize the output of the planning budget, while low-cost solutions are not offered to the customers.

The lack of trust leads to an excessively low willingness for cooperation among the EECs, with different educational backgrounds suspecting that the respective other sectors tend to offer low-quality services. This distrust is also observable when looking at the regulatory framework of the EEC market. The professional organizations of the architectural and engineering EECs succeeded in excluding the craftsmen from subsidy programs to gain a competitive advantage for their clients. This form of rent-seeking was fought by the craftsmens' professional organization in cooperation with the crafts chambers. This resulted in a revision of the regulation, which again granted craftsmen equal access to the retrofit subsidies. Consequently, the mistrust on the EEC market affects the behavior of the market participants, not only on the educational and individual level but also on the political level.

Case studies on knowledge spillover and sectoral heterogeneity

The relevance of knowledge for EECs and knowledge transfers to homeowners has been unanimously confirmed by the interviewees, particularly due to the technical complexities connected to retrofit in the housing sector. Placing an emphasis on the opportunities for knowledge spillover, the respondents delineated a diverse picture about knowledge processes in the same sector due to EECs belonging to sub-groups with architectural, engineering and craftsmen backgrounds. Therefore, we have selected three different cases showing the diversity of the sample to offer a clearer picture of the impact of heterogeneity. Focusing on the educational background and knowledge sources, our first case – henceforth denominated #F – is a chimney sweeper established in the craft sector, where knowledge spillover is only observable among colleagues. The second case study – henceforth #H – deals with an EEC with an architectural background, selected owing to his/her regular interaction with university graduates, whereas contact with non-university graduate EECs only happens in an unplanned manner and has little impact on #H's use of knowledge. Finally, in study #G, a university graduate engineer is engaged in the professional organization of the crafts business – despite his educational background – and orients his knowledge processes at the crafts sub-sector.

Part-time crafts EEC – case study #F

Respondent #F owns a chimney sweeper company and offers the EEC service only in addition to his other services. Furthermore, only 20 percent of the turnaround is created from energy consulting-related activities, while the chimney sweeping is the main business area. Due to regional monopoly structures in the chimney sweeping sector, the access is viable for potential customers of retrofit services. #F's business predominantly offers low-tech and low-cost solutions based upon lower volumes of subsidies. The training of interviewee #F took place at the regional crafts chamber, where #F continues to take most of the additional training courses.

Knowledge spillover is the key factor for #F's ability to offer the service at the current state of the art of knowledge. In particular, the part-time occasion of offering EEC consulting demands #F to rely on external sources of information about technology and market developments. Therefore, technical knowledge in codified form is acquired in advanced courses where new knowledge is provided. Additionally, #F receives and distributes tacit knowledge, such as information about the market situation, the interaction with customers and the expectations about future business development on an informal level, mostly with colleagues and acquaintances with a crafts background.

Interestingly, new knowledge is mostly transmitted via chimney sweeper colleagues operating their companies under similar conditions and also offering EEC as an additional service. To become an EEC, the chimney sweeper association advertised courses among its members at the crafts chamber, suggesting the opportunity for them to increase their services basis. Taking into consideration the lack of experts with experience in retrofit and access to residential houses, chimney sweepers were strongly encouraged by crafts chambers to participate in the EEC training. Additionally, the knowledge processes are discussed within the group of chimney sweepers. In particular, the search for codified and tacit knowledge sources and the selection of educational institutions were discussed among colleagues.

Other EECs – especially with architectural and engineering backgrounds – are hardly met since there are no common meeting points and activities. #F mostly concentrates on low-cost retrofit measures without the need to cooperate with other professionals. Nevertheless, #F has debated with his colleagues the possibility of participating in EEC courses offered at the university, although these deliberations are currently rejected and postponed owing to uncertainty about the qualifications required to participate.

Interviewee #F uses knowledge spillover to commercialize his knowledge, which is connected with his/her willingness to exchange knowledge with other craftsmen on an informal level. By contrast, the exchange with EECs of higher education is practically non-existent and in the rare situations that it takes place it rather creates additional uncertainty for #F. Hence, #F does not perceive the limited use of knowledge as a disadvantage, since the additional service only plays only a minor role in his/her entrepreneurial decisions.

Graduate EEC – case study #H

In the case of #H, the interviewee studied architecture at the university and did not need to undertake many courses, since he started his business before stricter regulatory prerequisites were established. EEC #H participates in the training courses that take place at the university. The business model focuses on retrofit activities with mostly energy-specific and large projects. Besides the EEC activities – which are often connected to his profession as an architect – #H voluntarily participates in public low-cost programs, which partially result in EEC contracts.

In this case, #H considers tacit knowledge as more important than formal qualifications since codified knowledge has been taught extensively in architectural studies. Additional long-term working experience led the respondent to the conclusion that the knowledge-collecting process is 'almost' completed, while the certification courses hardly offer any extra profit. Furthermore, #H's business model includes a competitive advantage with fulfilling the formal standards to obtain the permission to receive a particular fund that craft companies cannot receive. Furthermore, the cooperation with craftsmen is described as a top-down relation whereby craftsmen need explanations to improve the retrofit activities achieving better energy-saving potential. The knowledge flow is interrupted due to #H's perception of a one-way communicative path.

The heterogeneity of the stakeholder on the EEC market influences #H's behavior and has consequences for the impact of knowledge spillover on his/her company. Therefore, #H treats colleagues with architectural background as equals. On this level, knowledge is exchanged and new knowledge is integrated in the business model, influencing strategic decisions. Especially tacit knowledge such as experience with customer relationships and advertisement of the EEC services is discussed with business partners and colleagues. Knowledge from the crafts sector is not evaluated as equally valuable in comparison to their own knowledge base. Thus, there is an apparent knowledge gap between architectural and craftsmen knowledge, whereby the respondents avoid reciprocal knowledge exchange. Spillover among the sub-sectors appears thus limited to a minimum. The interviewee's success can be explained by the use of knowledge in the sub-sector, particularly when dealing with public subsidy regulations and the commercialization of the innovative knowledge. However, the successful exchange of innovative concepts across sub-sectors does not play a role in the respective business model.

Changing identity – case study #G

In our final case – case #G – the university graduate in electronic engineering turned his/her business selling photovoltaic systems into an EEC. Therefore, the entire professional training took place at an engineering academy. Since that time, #G works as an independent EEC offering his/her services to a broad range of customers, from homeowners to housing companies. Additionally, the interviewee participates as an active member at the crafts professional organization including his/her involvement in the member board, organizing and taking part in events aimed at EECs with crafts background.

The sectoral identification of #G is orientated towards the crafts sub-sector. For example, during the interview, the respondent #G uses the stereotype of the German 'craftsmen' as a role model describing the advantages of craftsmen services, although #G is not originally assigned to the crafts sector. In comparison to the other interviewees with a crafts background, #G more strongly emphasizes the identity of craftsmen and defends the quality offered by crafts businesses. This has consequences for #G's knowledge organization and commercialization of new knowledge, which is strongly dependent on the professional crafts organization. #G cooperates not only on an informal and formal level, but also gives courses for new members of the knowledge network, teaching about retrofit activities and the regulatory framework. The reason behind the implementation of these courses is the perception of quality problems on the EEC market and mistrust in EECs originating from other sectors. The trust in the own colleagues and the good quality of the knowledge that they offer in the courses is considered more valuable than insights from external experts and institutions. Furthermore, informal cooperation with EECs is valued higher within the own sectoral and network boundaries and is seen as easier due to more detailed information about the other EECs' behavior and the long-term relationship established within a small-sized knowledge network.

In contrast to the previously described cases of professional identity, #G undertook a change from his/her group identity – the educational background of engineering, where #G received initial training through studies and work experience – to his/her current identity. Although the educational background would lead to an engineering identity in the EEC market, changes in profession led to the perception of belonging to the crafts group. This has the effect that the knowledge formation and knowledge spillover mostly takes place for #G in the surrounding of crafts companies. Therefore, #G is familiar with different perspectives on the EEC sector, while – similar to the two previous cases – the knowledge spillovers are limited to one sub-sector.

Intra-sectoral cooperation and social identity

The results of our interviews indicate that path dependencies following the professional training of experts lead to strongly heterogeneous professional identities, which preclude cooperation and knowledge spillovers. Mutual distrust thus leads to widespread adverse sentiments towards experts with different professional backgrounds, entailing a refusal to initiate cooperation that could lead to intra-sectoral knowledge exchanges.

On a more general level, the issue of dysfunctional knowledge spillovers in our case can be understood as following from in-group norms precluding cooperative behavior with different groups who themselves have established specific in-group norms. Research in behavioral economics has extensively studied this specific setting, most prominently by considering social dilemmas and the determinants for contributions to public goods (see Chaudhuri, 2011 for a review). Behavioral investigations in this line of research have studied various determinants of individuals' willingness to engage in costly cooperation with other persons, even if the outcome is unknown beforehand.

It can be considered a well-established result that group identity can play a major role in the successful provision and maintaining of contributions to public goods, i.e. to interpersonal cooperation. On the one hand, groups in competitive settings have been shown to develop strong intra-group norms, which lead to less altruism and cooperativeness towards other groups. Thus, groups in market settings behave more selfishly and uncooperatively than individuals in similar settings (Charness and Sutter, 2012; Kugler et al., 2012). We would suggest that this finding resonates well with the current situation on the EEC market as described by the interviewees. On the other hand, the establishment of in-group norms among participants succeeds in fostering cooperation and contributions when compared to participants deciding anonymously (Chen and Chen, 2011; Solow and Kirkwood, 2002). A number of different mechanisms for creating group identities have been proposed, including discussing common interests, solving simple problems as a team or merely being assigned a team symbol or color (see e.g. Eckel and Grossman, 2005). Although these mechanisms are fairly simple, they lead to substantial increases in cooperation and can be considered a core driver for cooperative behavior in economic domains (Chen and Li, 2009).

Therefore, we suggest that different professional identities serving as a knowledge filter should be interpreted as groups in a competitive situation with a low willingness to cooperate. Without a policy intervention to change the behavioral patterns connected to this situation, no increase in cooperation and thus knowledge spillover can be expected. Accordingly, efforts should be engaged to consider how to create a new professional identity that effectively overlaps the previous sub-sectoral identities and thus creates common ground and trust for the respective firms to reduce the knowledge filter.

Conclusion: consequences for innovation policy

In this study, we have contributed an investigation of a specific knowledge filter to the KSTE. We suggest that professional identities can serve as powerful filters preventing knowledge spillovers by spreading distrust and adverse sentiments among different sub-sectors of a given market. Using a broad sample of interviews with German EECs with different professional backgrounds, we have described the disciplinary perspectives, identities and their consequences on the market. This has led us to argue that the diverse identities lead to a competitive in-group situation, in which each group avoids cooperation with other groups and refrains from contributing to common institutions and cooperative approaches. Drawing on behavioral economics, we suggest that social identity can be the key to overcoming the uncooperative situation in the market investigated. A broad strand of literature has focused on the initiation and maintenance of contributions to cooperation, giving potential starting points for public interventions to change the market outcomes in terms of knowledge spillovers.

Our basic result from the interviews conducted with experts from different sub-sectors is that there are no automatic spillovers of knowledge; rather, certain prerequisites are necessary for sectoral spillovers to happen. Among the substantial knowledge filters is the non-existence of common professional identities, which foster trust and reduce transaction costs for cooperation. Governments interested in fostering knowledge spillovers in specific sectors should thus foster the creation of overarching professional organization (similar to craft chambers) for the respective sectors. These chambers should be required to conduct both the initial professional training and further continued education. Rather than having individual sub-sectors carrying further their own perspectives and disciplinary knowledge, all sub-sectors of the respective field should conduct the training jointly.

This would lead to a stronger mixture of different professions during the training courses, in turn prompting interdisciplinary exchanges and the creation of a common professional terminology, i.e. a specific language of the respective field that is understandable across the field. The introduction of this common professional jargon coincides with a common knowledge basis within the field, which can substantially reduce the personal frictions and transaction costs for future cooperation.

Building common institutions – and thus stepwise introducing a common language – will foster the creation of a common identity that exceeds the previous professional identities acquired during the initial training of the respective experts. While this process will very likely take a considerable amount of time, it has the potential to create a 'social fabric' among the members of a previously unconnected sector, enabling cooperation and knowledge spillovers in the future. Accordingly, we suggest that the creation of common institutions and training courses can substantially reduce the issue of heterogeneous professional identities as a knowledge filter.

While we would suggest that these policy implications hold for numerous sectors characterized by similar knowledge filters, our explorative analysis is of course limited in scope. A more comprehensive analysis would require a broader sample of businesses, sectors and regions, from which further qualitative and quantitative evidence on expert markets should be collected. This would enable establishing broader evidence on the issue of heterogeneous professional identities as a knowledge filter. Moreover, the sector investigated in this study is characterized by strong public interventions and subsidy programs have a substantial influence on the market's development. Further studies should focus on markets less affected by public policies and investigate whether the issue of heterogeneous identities has a lesser influence in these situations. This approach could be fruitfully connected to the experimental and theoretical literature on expert behavior in markets with asymmetric information (see e.g. Dulleck et al., 2011; Dulleck and Kerschbamer, 2006).

Acknowledgement

Financial support for conducting the interviews from the iENG project (grant number 03EK3517A), funded by the Federal Ministry of Education and Research, is gratefully acknowledged.

Notes

1 EECs offer an expert service particularly used by private homeowners to support customers at the retrofit to reduce households' energy consumption. The homeowners are confronted with two different types of information asymmetries. On the one hand, the homeowners face information asymmetries about the quality of retrofit, caused by the complexity of applied technological measures, since there is uncertainty about building companies' behavior at the retrofit and ex-post rebound effects from the changing energy consumption behavior of the homeowner. On the other hand, the behavior of the EECs is affected by information barriers due to difficulties in evaluating experts' intention and behavior, specifically when it comes to fraudulent actions. In a study using the same sample of expert interviews, the credence goods characteristics of the services provided on the EEC market and the impact on knowledge spillover are discussed (Feser and Proeger 2015).

2 In one case, recording the interview was not possible due to technical problems. To assure the quality, an extensive memo was written down following the interview.

3 The list is accessible at www.energie-effizienz-experten.de.

References

Acosta, M., Coronado, D. and Flores, E. (2011) 'University spillovers and new business location in high-technology sectors: Spanish evidence', *Small Business Economics*, 36(3): 365–76.

Acs, Z.J., Anselin, L. and Varga, A. (2002) 'Patents and innovation counts as measures of regional production of new knowledge', *Research Policy*, 31(7): 1069–85.

Acs, Z.J., Audretsch, D.B., Braunerhjelm, P. and Carlsson, B. (2004) *The missing link: The knowledge filter and endogenous growth* (discussion paper), Center, Stockholm.

Acs, Z.J., Audretsch, D.B., Braunerhjelm, P. and Carlsson, B. (2012) 'Growth and entrepreneurship', *Small Business Economics*, 39(2): 289–300.

Acs, Z.J., Audretsch, D.B. and Lehmann, E.E. (2013) 'The knowledge spillover theory of entrepreneurship', *Small Business Economics*, 41(4): 757–74.

Acs, Z.J., Braunerhjelm, P., Audretsch, D.B. and Carlsson, B. (2009a) 'The knowledge spillover theory of entrepreneurship', *Small Business Economics*, 32(1): 15–30.

Acs, Z.J. and Plummer, L.A. (2005) 'Penetrating the "knowledge filter" in regional economies', *The Annals of Regional Science*, 39(3): 439–56.

Acs, Z.J., Plummer, L.A. and Sutter, R. (2009b) 'Penetrating the knowledge filter in "rust belt" economies', *The Annals of Regional Science*, 43(4): 989–1012.

Agarwal, R., Audretsch, D. and Sarkar, M.B. (2007) 'The process of creative construction: Knowledge spillovers, entrepreneurship, and economic growth', *Strategic Entrepreneurship Journal*, 1(3–4): 263–86.

Agarwal, R. and Shah, S.K. (2014) 'Knowledge sources of entrepreneurship: Firm formation by academic, user and employee innovators', *Research Policy*, 43(7): 1109–33.

Audretsch, D.B. (1995) *Innovation and industry evolution*, MIT Press, Cambridge, MA.

Audretsch, D.B. and Belitski, M. (2013) 'The missing pillar: The creativity theory of knowledge spillover entrepreneurship', *Small Business Economics*, 41(4): 819–36.

Audretsch, D.B. and Keilbach, M. (2007) 'The theory of knowledge spillover entrepreneurship', *Journal of Management Studies*, 44(7): 1243–54.

Audretsch, D.B. and Keilbach, M. (2008) 'Resolving the knowledge paradox: Knowledge-spillover entrepreneurship and economic growth', *Research Policy*, 37(10): 1697–1705.

Audretsch, D.B., Keilbach, M. and Lehmann, E.E. (eds). (2006) *Entrepreneurship and economic growth*, Oxford University Press, Oxford.

Audretsch, D.B. and Lehmann, E.E. (2005) 'Does the knowledge Spillover theory of entrepreneurship hold for regions?', *Research Policy*, 34(8): 1191–202.

Audretsch, D.B., Lehmann, E.E. and Warning, S. (2005) 'University spillovers and new firm location', *Research Policy*, 34(7): 1113–22.

Braunerhjelm, P., Acs, Z.J., Audretsch, D.B. and Carlsson, B. (2010) 'The missing link: Knowledge diffusion and entrepreneurship in endogenous growth', *Small Business Economics*, 34(2): 105–25.

Cappelli, R., Czarnitzki, D. and Kraft, K. (2014) 'Sources of spillovers for imitation and innovation', *Research Policy*, 43(1): 115–20.

Charness, G. and Sutter, M. (2012) 'Groups make better self-interested decisions', *Journal of Economic Perspectives*, 26(3): 157–76.

Chaudhuri, A. (2011) 'Sustaining cooperation in laboratory public goods experiments: A selective survey of the literature', *Experimental Economics*, 14(1): 47–83.

Chen, R. and Chen, Y. (2011) 'The potential of social identity for equilibrium selection', *American Economic Review*, 101(6): 2562–89.

Chen, Y. and Li, S.X. (2009) 'Group identity and social preferences', *American Economic Review*, 99(1): 431–57.

Corbin, J.M. and Strauss, A.L. (2008) *Basics of qualitative research: Techniques and procedures for developing grounded theory* (3rd ed). Sage Publications, Los Angeles, Calif.

Dulleck, U. and Kerschbamer, R. (2006) 'On doctors, mechanics and computer specialists: The Economics of credence goods', *Journal of Economic Literature*, 44(1): 5–42.

Dulleck, U., Kerschbamer, R. and Sutter, M. (2011) 'The economics of credence goods: An experiment on the role of liability, verifiability, reputation, and competition', *American Economic Review*, 101(2): 526–55.

Eckel, C.C. and Grossman, P.J. (2005) 'Managing diversity by creating team identity', *Journal of Economic Behavior & Organization*, 58(3): 371–92.

Edmondson, A.C. and McManus, S.E. (2007) 'Methodological fit in management field research', *The Academy of Management Review*, 32(4): 1155–79.

Eisenhardt, K. (1989) 'Theories from case study research', *The Academy of Management Review*, 14(4): 532–50.

Eisenhardt, K. and Graebner, M.E. (2007) 'Theory building from cases: Opportunities and challenges', *Academy of Management Journal*, 50(1): 25–32.

Feser, D. and Proeger, T. (2015) 'Asymmetric information as a barrier to knowledge spillovers in expert markets', *cege Discussion Papers* (259).

Glaser, B.G. (1965) 'The constant comparative method of qualitative analysis', *Social Problems*, 12(4): 436–45.

Glaser, B.G. and Strauss, A.L. (2008) *The discovery of grounded theory: Strategies for qualitative research*, Recording for the Blind & Dyslexic, Princeton, NJ.

Gram-Hanssen, K., Bartiaux, F., Jensen, O.M. and Cantaert, M. (2007) 'Do homeowners use energy labels? A comparison between Denmark and Belgium', *Energy Policy*, 35(5): 2879–88.

Guerrero, M. and Urbano, D. (2014) 'Academics' start-up intentions and knowledge filters: An individual perspective of the knowledge spillover theory of entrepreneurship', *Small Business Economics*, 43(1): 57–74.

Hayter, C.S. (2013) 'Conceptualizing knowledge-based entrepreneurship networks: Perspectives from the literature', *Small Business Economics*, 41(4): 899–911.

Jensen, M.B., Johnson, B., Lorenz, E. and Lundvall, B.Å. (2007) 'Forms of knowledge and modes of innovation', *Research Policy*, 36(5): 680–93.

Kugler, T., Kausel, E.E. and Kocher, M.G. (2012) 'Are groups more rational than individuals? A review of interactive decision making in groups', *Wiley Interdisciplinary Reviews. Cognitive Science*, 3(4): 471–82.

Mayring, P., 2004. 'Qualitative content analysis', In U. Flick, E. Kardoff, I. von, Steinke (Eds) *A Companion to Qualitative Research*, vol. 1, pp 266–69, London, Sage.

Muench, S., Thuss, S. and Guenther, E. (2014) 'What hampers energy system transformations? The case of smart grids', *Energy Policy*, 73: 80–92.

Plummer, L.A. and Acs, Z.J. (2014) 'Localized competition in the knowledge spillover theory of entrepreneurship', *Journal of Business Venturing*, 29(1): 121–36.

Romer, P.M. (1986) 'Retruns and long-run growth', *Journal of Political Economy*, 94(5): 1002–37.

Romer, P.M. (1994) 'The origins of endogenous growth', *Journal of Economic Perspectives*, 8(1): 3–22.

Solow, J.L. and Kirkwood, N. (2002) 'Group identity and gender in public goods experiments', *Journal of Economic Behavior & Organization*, 48(4): 403–12.

Stam, E. (2013) 'Knowledge and entrepreneurial employees: A country-level analysis', *Small Business Economics*, 41(4): 887–98.

Stenholm, P., Acs, Z.J. and Wuebker, R. (2013) 'Exploring country-level institutional arrangements on the rate and type of entrepreneurial activity', *Journal of Business Venturing*, 28(1): 176–93.

Vega-Jurado, J., Gutiérrez-Gracia, A., Fernández de Lucio, I. and Manjarrés-Henríquez, L. (2008) 'The effect of external and internal factors on firms' product innovation', *Research Policy*, 37(4): 616–32.

Virkki-Hatakka, T., Luoranen, M. and Ikävalko, M. (2013) 'Differences in perception: How the experts look at energy efficiency (findings from a Finnish survey)', *Energy Policy*, 60: 499–508.

13 From knowledge to innovation
A review on the evolution of the absorptive capacity concept

Dennis Lyth Frederiksen and *Alexander Brem*

Introduction

The aim of this paper is to chronicle the development of the concept of absorptive capacity as first defined and described by Wesley M. Cohen and Daniel A. Levinthal in their 1990 article *Absorptive Capacity: A New Perspective on Learning and Innovation* (Cohen and Levinthal, 1990). As this concept quickly approaches a quarter of a century since its introduction, it is bound to have seen changes in one way or another and in the following sections we shall attempt to give an overview of its evolution through the years. How has it been adapted and used? In what way does it exist in use today – if at all?

Looking at just the raw number of citations this article has received, it is quickly clear that the concept was indeed used and certainly still is today. The interesting question however is the form it is in, and how it transformed to adapt to this changing world we live in. Has globalization had an impact? What about the continuing explosive developments in not only the semiconductor industry – mentioned quite a few times in the original article – but also in the general consumer electronics market? Can a concept described without equations and a slew of hard numbers survive repeated contact with an ever-changing reality?

First, we will present a general background on the concept to allow perspective and comparisons to later adoptions. This will exclusively be based on the original article. Next, the use of the term will be quantified through various online databases. Doing so will allow us to roughly gauge both the popularity of the original article as well as the concept itself. With hopefully a firm foundation and a quantitative perspective, the last section will explore more qualitative changes through a limited review of papers on the topic in the immediate years following the appearance of the paper and continuing until today.

Absorptive capacity

To begin the brief background into the concept of absorptive capacity, the initial definition ought to be given. From the original article we find the following:

> *Absorptive capacity: The ability of a firm to recognize the value of new, external information, assimilate it, and apply it to commercial ends.*
> (Adapted) (Cohen and Levinthal, 1990, p. 128)

In other words – or more precisely our words – absorptive capacity is essentially an umbrella term for a firm's ability to learn something new and apply it to succeed in the marketplace. We can in more practical terms think of this idea as a description of how efficiently a firm can take a piece of information, say a technical breakthrough or key insight into demographics, view it in the perspective of the firm's existing knowledge base and capabilities, and finally try to combine the two into a single foundation from which new products can originate.

The central theme in their article revolves around how absorptive capacity is improved, which the authors argue is based on the firms existing knowledge. The central idea here is that to efficiently acquire new information and utilize it – essentially assimilate in the terminology above – you must have some understanding in a related area. This arises from the way we as individuals learn. Everything new we are exposed to is automatically put in relation to something we already know and are familiar with. It is this notion that Cohen and Levinthal extend to a view of the firm as a learning entity. An entity is not just the sum of all individuals working within it, but also – as absorptive capacity too pertains to information exploitation – the addition of the collective as a whole finding a way to commercialize this newfound knowledge. These specific aspects are what the authors refer to as distinctly organizational. They further discuss the interfaces between which information sharing happens, and how these not only face the outside environment, but also play a significant part in how information travels throughout an organization consisting of many individual departments – again containing many individuals. Figure 13.1 depicts the model of absorptive capacity and R&D incentives.

Absorptive capacity in the original article finds its link to a measureable firm characteristic in R&D budgets, which the authors continue on to do an empirical analysis of based on data from 351 firms in 151 lines of business. They make the observation that the process of doing R&D itself helps build a foundation of

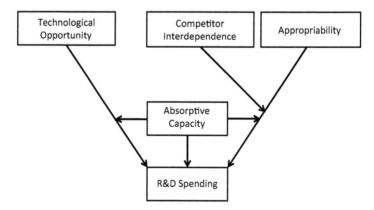

Figure 13.1 Model of absorptive capacity and R&D incentives (Cohen and Levinthal, 1990)

knowledge, which again improves absorptive capacity, further increasing the ability to acquire new knowledge. Here it is important to note that this is the *ability*, not motivation, to acquire new knowledge. Of course, such may itself originate from the ease with which knowledge is exploited – absorptive capacity – and thus we have a feedback loop. The exact opposite scenario naturally exists too. Here a company fails to exploit a set of new information, which then impacts the managerial motivation to spend resources acquiring new information going forward, which again makes new undertakings even more likely to fail.

Cohen and Levinthal also co-authored a paper in 1989 with absorptive capacity as the subject (Cohen and Levinthal, 1989). Their 1990 paper appears however to supersede it, and the earlier paper does not add significantly to the foundation. The two authors complete the trilogy on absorptive capacity with their final collaborative writing effort in 1994. Here they 'develop a stylized model in which we focus exclusively on firms' decisions to invest in their absorptive capacities' (Cohen and Levinthal, 1994, p. 227). No essential additions are made to the core concept explained here.

An attempt at bibliometrics

In order to gauge the popularity of the original article and the concept of absorptive capacity, Google Scholar has been used to collect an overview of the number of its database entities that have cited the article over the years. Google Scholar indexes not only scientific papers, but many different sources such as books, technical reports, patents and more (Google, 2016). While not all the sources are equally relevant in this specific case, the database still ought to give a decent general impression of the measure in question.

The process went as follows: The original article was found on Google Scholar. Using the feature 'cited by' a new search was made of all sources found to cite the original. The additional search term 'absorptive capacity' was added – quotes included – in an attempt to root out anything not directly related. Finally, in successive steps the search was limited to a specific year, from 1991 to 2013, and the number of results noted down for each.

In the full period – from 1991 to 2013 – Google Scholar produces a total of 16,300 results. It is clear from Figure 13.2 that the general popularity of the paper – and likely the concept of absorptive capacity – has risen quite consistently since publication and introduction in 1990. While, as stated above, the results probably include a fair number of erroneous and irrelevant results, the graph produced in Figure 13.2 does at least give the impression of a field still in development. Looking at the popularity of these citing papers themselves did not reveal any patterns or tendencies of interest. The 50 most popular papers – as deemed so by their number of citations – were compared in both absolute and relative terms (citations per year) versus the year of publication to further attempt to gauge general popularity, the idea being that if the subject gained popularity the relative number of citations a paper on the subject reaches should increase.

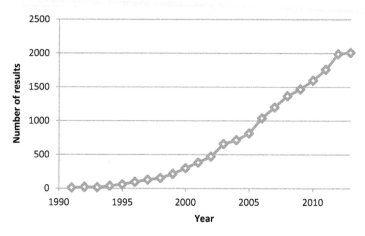

Figure 13.2 Number of Google Scholar search results on cited papers

Defining selection criteria

Let us now look at the qualitative side. To select from the many papers on the subject, a set of selection criteria were set up. This was done to produce a representative and limited set of material for the analysis that could realistically be worked through while still giving a good overview of the subject. The criteria were the following:

- Must cite the original article *Absorptive Capacity: A New Perspective on Learning and Innovation*
- Must contain the exact phrase 'absorptive capacity'

Passing these two criteria it

- Must either be one of the ten most cited overall (Web of Science), or
- Must be the most cited in a given year from 1992 to 2013 (Google Scholar)

Web of Science (Thomson Reuters, 2016) was used as the initial database to find the top 10 most-cited papers. These were then vetted for relevance by requiring 'absorptive capacity' to appear in the *main* text, not just the references. This eliminated one of the ten. No distinction was made between review and non-review papers. To further help create a basis for an evolving understanding of absorptive capacity, the years not represented in the top 10 were filled out using Google Scholar. In a process similar to that for gauging general popularity detailed above, the feature 'cited by' was used to create a list of the most popular citing papers. Again the search term 'absorptive capacity' was added, quotes included. The search was then in turn narrowed down to the specific years in question.

The first step of the 10 most cited covered 5 years and so an additional 17 papers were found in the second step yielding a total of 26 papers for use in the following analysis (as mentioned – one of the top 10 most cited was eliminated due to lack of relevance). Additionally, a review paper from 2014 was included to have input from the newest writings as well. While this process of selection is undoubtedly only one of many potential options, we believe it has produced a good variety of papers able to cover the desired topic. The full list of all 27 papers – this number excluding the three by Cohen and Levinthal – can be found in Table 13.1.

Table 13.1 The selected papers and their sources

Title	Author(s)	Year of publication	Source
Toward a knowledge-based theory of the firm	(Grant, 1996)	1996	Web of Science
The relational view: cooperative strategy and sources of interorganizational competitive advantage	(Dyer and Singh, 1998)	1998	Web of Science
Interorganizational collaboration and the locus of innovation: networks of learning in biotechnology	(Powel et al., 1996)	1996	Web of Science
Exploring internal stickiness: impediments to the transfer of best practice within the firm	(Szulanski, 1996)	1996	Web of Science
Absorptive capacity: a review, reconceptualization, and extension	(Zahra and George, 2002)	2002	Web of Science
Deliberate learning and the evolution of dynamic capabilities	(Zollo and Winter, 2002)	2002	Web of Science
Relative absorptive capacity and interorganizational learning	(Lane and Lubatkin, 1998)	1998	Web of Science
Strategic networks	(Gulati et al., 2000)	2000	Web of Science
'Sticky Information' and the locus of problem solving implications for innovation	(von Hippel, 1994)	1994	Web of Science
A practice-centered model of organizational renewal through product innovation	(Dougherty, 1992)	1992	Google Scholar
The nature of organizational search in high technology markets	(Weiss and Heide, 1993)	1993	Google Scholar
International expansion strategy of Japanese firms: capability building through sequential entry	(Chang, 1995)	1995	Google Scholar

(Continued)

Table 13.1 (Continued)

Title	Author(s)	Year of publication	Source
Regional innovation systems: institutional and organisational dimensions	(Cooke et al., 1997)	1997	Google Scholar
Ambiguity and the process of knowledge transfer in strategic alliances	(Simonin, 1999)	1999	Google Scholar
Knowledge transfer in intraorganizational networks: effects of network position and absorptive capacity on business unit innovation and performance	(Tsai, 2001)	2001	Google Scholar
Network structure and knowledge transfer: the effects of cohesion and range	(Reagans and McEvily, 2003)	2003	Google Scholar
Network structure and the diffusion of knowledge	(Cowana and Jonard, 2004)	2004	Google Scholar
Managing potential and realized absorptive capacity: how do organizational antecedents matter?	(Jansen et al., 2005)	2005	Google Scholar
The reification of absorptive capacity: a critical review and rejuvenation of the construct	(Lane et al., 2006)	2006	Google Scholar
Absorptive capacity: valuing a reconceptualization	(Todorova and Durisin, 2007)	2007	Google Scholar
Inter- and intra-organizational knowledge transfer: a meta-analytic review and assessment of its antecedents and consequences	(van Wijk et al., 2008)	2008	Google Scholar
Absorptive capacity, environmental turbulence, and the complementarity of organizational learning processes	(Lichtenthaler, 2009)	2009	Google Scholar
The future of open innovation	(Gassmann et al., 2010)	2010	Google Scholar
Smart cities in Europe	(Caragliu et al., 2011)	2011	Google Scholar
Absorptive capacity and information systems research: review, synthesis, and directions for future research	(Roberts et al., 2012)	2012	Google Scholar
Towards an open R&D system: internal R&D investment, external knowledge acquisition and innovative performance	(Berchicci, 2013)	2013	Google Scholar
Knowing, power and materiality: a critical review and reconceptualization of absorptive capacity	(Marabelli and Newell, 2014)	2014	(Additional Review Paper)

The evolution of absorptive capacity

It is now time to delve into the selected material in order to chronicle the evolution of absorptive capacity during this first quarter century of its life. We begin with a paper by Dougherty (1992) and an attempt to put absorptive capacity, and other constructs detailing learning and knowledge acquisition, into a practice-centered approach. Dougherty comments on, if not outright criticizes, the literature on knowledge and learning as being 'vast and confusing' and for the presented practical model uses – amongst others – the paper by Cohen and Levinthal and the idea of absorptive capacity as it is 'based on extensive summaries of the literature' (Dougherty, 1992, p. 79). A quite different application of the concept is found in the paper by Weiss and Heide (1993), where it is applied to a subset of presented and tested hypotheses on buyer behavior. The authors predict – based on the suggestion by Cohen and Levinthal that 'a lack of experience results in a decreased ability to perceive differentiated patterns in market information' (Weiss and Heide, 1993, p. 230) – that an inexperienced buyer will tend to deem the market more technologically heterogeneous than an experienced one. This is disproven by their research findings. They do not speculate as to how the result may change the original view of the issue in relation to an organization. While Cohen and Levinthal (1990) do argue that the absorptive capacity of an organization is more than just the sum of that of its individuals, it is still interesting as the finding by Weiss and Heide (1993) is not just a slight adjustment, but a complete contradiction. Perhaps such is more likely to show itself at the organizational level?

Also discussing this separation between the individual and the collective is a paper by Grant (1996). This is also the most cited of the ones selected. With a view of the firm as knowledge based, Grant argues the opinion of '. . . the firm as integrating the specialist knowledge resident in individuals into goods and services' (Grant, 1996, p. 120) and puts more emphasis on the individual than Cohen and Levinthal do. We thus get closer to a perspective of the collective being exactly the sum of its parts, rather than more, and the organization holds little to no knowledge itself. From the same year we find the fourth most cited in the selection, a paper by Szulanski (1996). Here, absorptive capacity is once again brought down on the level of the individual to explain how knowledge and best practices travel within an organization. Through empirical evidence Szulanski finds it to be a major factor in making the transfer of knowledge happen. While the general thinking behind this application appears sound and in tune with Cohen and Levinthal, it is clearly not used as defined earlier – '*Absorptive capacity: The ability of a firm to. . . .*'

What can be considered a subsection of absorptive capacity is applied by Dyer and Singh (1998) in their paper on cooperative strategy and sources of interorganizational competitive advantage. This is the second most cited paper in the selection. They develop the notion of partner-specific absorptive capacity that 'refers to the idea that a firm has developed the ability to recognize and assimilate valuable knowledge from a particular alliance partner' (Dyer and Singh, 1998,

p. 665). Thus, we can in some ways look at firms as individuals in a larger network of firms involved in a collaboration effort and extend the notion of the overall absorptive capacity of an alliance as yet again made up of that of its individual members. From this macro view Dyer and Singh zoom all the way down to interpersonal relationships between employees from different firms of the alliance. Partner specific absorptive capacity is here illustrated as knowledge one firm or employee has on who in a participating firm can solve their problem, assist them in design, etc. They also more formally describe this as 'the extent to which partners have developed interaction routines that maximize the frequency and intensity of sociotechnical interactions' (Dyer and Singh, 1998, p. 665). In line with the general thinking behind absorptive capacity, the ability of this initial firm or employee to apply the acquired insight is then dependent on what they term 'overlapping knowledge bases' (Dyer and Singh, 1998, p. 665). Empirical evidence on the combination of absorptive capacity and networks is also presented in a paper by Tsai (2001). As with the original paper by Cohen and Levinthal, R&D intensity (R&D expenditures divided by sales) is used as the measure of absorptive capacity. Based on the results, Tsai goes on to suggest that investments in expanding the network go hand in hand with R&D intensity, the reasoning being that the now available knowledge coming in from the network resources will go untapped or even unnoticed without adequate absorptive capacity.

In the first review paper of the selection, Zahra and George (2002) examine the concept a little over 10 years after its introduction. They note the growing use of it, but also state that it remains difficult to study due to 'the ambiguity and diversity of its definitions, components, antecedents, and outcomes' (Zahra and George, 2002, p. 185). We believe that even the limited look this analysis has given so far fits fairly well with that view. Being more than just a review paper, Zahra and George go on to extend the original concept with what they title 'potential and realized absorptive capacity'. These distinctions are defined as compromising knowledge acquisition and assimilation capabilities, and knowledge transformation and exploitation respectively. They further go on to 'recognize ACAP as a dynamic capability that influences the nature and sustainability of a firm's competitive advantage' (Zahra and George, 2002, p. 185). This is the first mention of dynamic capabilities in relation to absorptive capacity among the selected papers, although it does appear quite easy to link the two. As defined by Teece et al. (1997), dynamic capabilities are 'the firm's ability to integrate, build, and reconfigure internal and external competences to address rapidly changing environments' (Teece et al., 1997, p. 516). One key difference between the two appears to lie in whether the recognition of the knowledge – or competences – is a distinct part itself. We believe it is accurate enough for this purpose to equate knowledge and competences here. Were the two definitions of absorptive capacity and dynamic capabilities pictured as a Venn diagram, we would surely see a large overlap. In fact, we went ahead and made that illustration (Figure 13.3). Note that knowledge has been changed to information to fit with the original definition of absorptive capacity cited earlier.

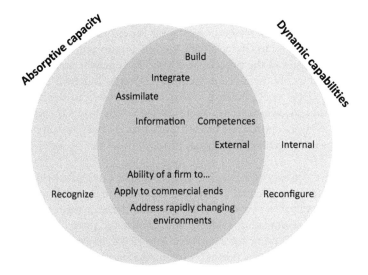

Figure 13.3 Venn diagram, absorptive capacity and dynamic capabilities

To connect the two, as Zahra and George do, appears a safe bet. Exactly how the concepts should be arranged, perhaps one the superset of the other, is not immediately clear from a brief overview of related papers on the subject. At least ever-changing definitions and expressed opinions do not indicate a consensus. Maybe these various concepts trying to explain and characterize competitive advantage are looking for an advantage of their own to fight the fierce battles on the journal pages.

Letting this tangent lie, we continue on to 2005, where Jansen et al. investigate what preexisting factors influence the now-split version of absorptive capacity: potential (acquisition and assimilation) and realized (transformation and exploitation) (Jansen et al., 2005). Through empirical research at a multi-unit European firm in the financial sector they find coordination capabilities – cross-functional interfaces, participation in decision making and job rotation – primarily affect potential absorptive capacity, and socialization capabilities – connectedness and socialization tactics – primarily affect realized absorptive capacity. The authors argue that these two aspects of absorptive capacity and the factors now found contributing to them, will help explain why 'organizational units may differ in their ability to manage levels of potential and realized absorptive capacity; follow different developmental paths; and differ in their ability to create value from their absorptive capacity' (Jansen et al., 2005, p. 1009). This generally appears to be a sound addition to the original concept, and, as the authors note, should facilitate a greater understanding of differences in performance levels found even within the same organization.

A serious critique of not the concept of absorptive capacity, but rather the research surrounding it is found in a review paper by Lane et al. (2006). Through a very substantial literature review of 289 papers on absorptive capacity the authors argue that the literature has led to a reification of the concept. They define reification as 'the outcome of the process by which we forget the authorship of ideas and theories, objectify them (turn them into things), and then forget that we have done so' (Lane et al., 2006, p. 835). This, according to the authors, gives rise to the problem of inaccurate, uncritical use of the original concept, which accumulates as layers upon layers of such work that are built on top one another. In an attempt to rejuvenate the original concept, they offer up a new definition:

> Absorptive capacity is a firm's ability to utilize externally held knowledge through three sequential processes: (1) recognizing and understanding potentially valuable new knowledge out-side the firm through exploratory learning, (2) assimilating valuable new knowledge through transformative learning, and (3) using the assimilated knowledge to create new knowledge and commercial outputs through exploitative learning.
>
> (Lane et al., 2006, p. 856)

Of course the immediate difference from the original that springs to mind is the length. More words means the opportunity to further narrow and focus, while avoiding potentially vague phrasing. And that is largely what the new definition achieves. The *ability* is segregated into three distinct processes that add description to the three main keywords from the original: recognize, assimilate and commercialize. It would have suited the paper to have included a clear description of what the authors associate with the three learning methods mentioned – exploratory, transformative and exploitative – but alas, we will have to do without.

Leaving the navel gazing behind, we move to an example of absorptive capacity in the wild. In a paper on open innovation by Gassmann et al. (2010), examples of how the importance of absorptive capacity has reached large corporations are given. These include Apple, Microsoft and SAP, with the latter two apparently having opened research divisions at university campuses to 'increase their absorptive capacity for outside-in innovation processes' (Gassmann et al., 2010, p. 215). Such an example draws parallels all the way back to the talks about creating and sustaining an adequate interface between the 'units' containing diverse knowledge.

And finally we get to the last paper in this analysis and fittingly it is also the most recently published of the selected. Again part review, part reconceptualization, the paper by Marabelli and Newell (2014) attempts to add a new facet to absorptive capacity – power. The authors argue that viewing knowledge as just possessed by individuals and being transferable leaves out the important aspect of power and how it impacts the absorptive capacity. A model is developed that 'describes how the interaction between knowledge and knowing involving human and material actors (and power-over and power-to), produces (more or less) capacity to absorb external knowledge' (Marabelli and Newell, 2014, p. 495). This perspective is certainly interesting and does add elements not previously found in the other papers here presented on absorptive capacity. The idea of knowledge itself has not been investigated to such a degree in relation to absorptive capacity as Marabelli and Newell here do, and adding the power facet will probably be a first step in exploring this avenue in greater detail.

Conclusion

In this paper we have sought to chronicle the evolution of absorptive capacity as defined by Cohen and Levinthal (1990). Through an initial introduction to the concept, the ideas and theory behind the foundation were set up for comparison to later changes. Following this, a cautious step into the field of bibliometrics produced evidence to suggest a still increasing interest in absorptive capacity – the number of yearly citations of the original article has been steadily increasing since its publication. While the accuracy of the absolute figures found is not likely to survive intense scrutiny, the general tendency appears unquestionable. Next, a set of criteria for selecting the papers were then set up before the papers chosen to highlight the evolution of absorptive capacity were introduced. We believe this overview has shown absorptive capacity to be a highly active topic of research, with the original definition remaining largely intact. With redefinitions and additions having been attempted multiple times, the common factor in all of them is the original, still standing here 25 years after its inception. This largely speaks to the sound foundation upon which Cohen and Levinthal built the original concept and the relative ease with which it can be understood. Clearly the contention regarding where it should head next – of which we have presented only a small portion – must speak to some passion or need for the concept. There also appears to be a decent breadth in the types of areas the concept has been applied to and – at least according to the respective authors – it was found worthwhile to produce related output and adding additional important perspectives. While making guesses about the future is no doubt extremely difficult, we do think the previous 25 years of history with absorptive capacity makes the next 25 years look quite promising for it as well.

References

Berchicci, L. (2013) 'Towards an open R&D system: Internal R&D investment, external knowledge acquisition and innovative performance', *Research Policy*, 42(1): 117–27.

Chang, S.J. (1995) 'International expansion strategy of Japanese firms: Capability building through sequential entry', *The Academy of Management Journal*, 38(2): 383–407.

Cohen, W.M. and Levinthal, D.A. (1989) 'Innovation and learning: The two faces of R&D', *The Economic Journal*, 99(397): 569–96.

Cohen, W.M. and Levinthal, D.A. (1990) 'Absorptive capacity: A new perspective on learning and innovation', *Administrative Science Quarterly*, 35(1): 128–52.

Cohen, W.M. and Levinthal, D.A. (1994) 'Fortune favors the prepared firm', *Management Science*, 40(2): 227–51.

Dougherty, D. (1992) 'A practice-centered model of organizational renewal through product innovation', *Strategic Management Journal*, 13: 77–92.

Dyer, J.H. and Singh, H. (1998) 'The relational view: Cooperative strategy and sources of interorganizational competitive advantage', *The Academy of Management Review*, 23(4): 660–79.

Gassmann, O., Enkel, E. and Chesbrough, H. (2010) 'The future of open innovation', *R&D Management*, 40(3): 213–21.

Google, 2016. *Google Scholar*, https://scholar.google.com/intl/en/scholar/about.html accessed March 14, 2016.

Grant, R.M. (1996) 'Toward a knowledge-based theory of the firm', *Strategic Management Journal*, 17: 109–22.

Jansen, J.J.P., Van Den Bosch, F.A.J. and Volberda, H.W. (2005) 'Managing potential and realized absorptive capacity: How do organizational antecedents matter?', *The Academy of Management Journal*, 48(6): 999–015.

Lane, P.J., Koka, B.R. and Pathak, S. (2006) 'The reification of absorptive capacity: A critical review and rejuvenation of the construct', *The Academy of Management Review*, 31(4): 833–63.

Lichtenthaler, U. (2009) 'Absorptive capacity, environmental turbulence, and the complementarity of organizational learning processes', *Academy of Management Journal*, 52(4): 822–46. (Retracted by author.)

Marabelli, M. and Newell, S. (2014) 'Knowing, power and materiality: A critical review and reconceptualization of absorptive capacity', *International Journal of Management Reviews*, 16(4): 479–99.

Simonin, B.L. (1999) 'Ambiguity and the process of knowledge transfer in strategic alliances', *Strategic Management Journal*, 20(7): 595–623.

Szulanski, G. (1996) 'Exploring internal stickiness: impediments to the transfer of best practice within the firm', *Strategic Management Journal*, 17: 27–43.

Teece, D.J., Pisano, G. and Shuen, A. (1997) 'Dynamic capabilities and strategic management', *Strategic Management Journal*, 18(7): 509–33.

Thomson Reuters, 2016. *Web of Science*, https://webofknowledge.com/ accessed March 14, 2016.

Tsai, W. (2001) 'Knowledge transfer in intraorganizational networks: Effects of network position and absorptive capacity on business unit innovation and performance', *The Academy of Management Journal*, 44(5): 996–1004.

von Hippel, E. (1994) 'Sticky information' and the locus of problem solving: Implications for innovation', *Management Science*, 40(4): 429–39.

Weiss, A.M. and Heide, J.B. (1993) 'The nature of organizational search in high technology markets', *Journal of Marketing Research*, 30(2): 220–33.

Zahra, S.A. and George, G. (2002) 'Absorptive capacity: A review, reconceptualization, and extension', *The Academy of Management Review*, 27(2): 185–203.

14 Knowledge spillovers and innovation spaces in Australia

*Paul K. Couchman, Andrew O'Loughlin,
Ian McLoughlin and Vanessa Ratten*

Introduction

The literature on innovation spaces stresses the importance of knowledge spillovers, particularly local forms that explain the geographic agglomeration of clusters. Local knowledge spillovers are knowledge externalities bounded by geographic region, which foster the flow of information (Ko and Liu, 2015). This enables firms in a region access to knowledge sources and depositories, which may have unintended consequences. Knowledge is often seen as a non-rival production asset so the geographic position of firms can help create positive externalities and lead to economic gain (Zahra, 2015). More importantly, local knowledge spillovers can facilitate further innovation efforts to induce market change. This is evident in countries like Australia, which, despite its large land mass, has the majority of its major regional and urban cities clustered along the eastern coastline.

In his seminal contribution to innovation policy debates in Australia, West (2001) examined how successful national innovation systems are built. He argued that Australia's national innovation system had developed critical gaps since Federation, which occurred on 1 January 1901, in particular. '. . . in its ability to mobilize resources, its system for allocating investment to innovation, and – most significantly – its institutions for managing the risk of science-based innovation' (West, 2001, p. 42). His conclusion was that the nation was not in a good position to build a knowledge-based economy. From the perspective of an economist this may seem to be an incisive analysis. However, we suggest that from the knowledge spillover theory of management and organisation, it overlooks not only the historical dimension of why the Australian economy has developed in the way that it has, but also the political and symbolic dimensions that shapes how it will develop into the future. In this chapter, we seek to put the 'political' back into the 'economy', and in so doing pursue a perspective which hitherto has been poorly developed in the study of innovation and its management.

We argue that innovation and associated government policy is essentially political in so far as the actors so engaged 'exert control, influence, or power over each other' (Lindblom, 1980, p. 28) in order to pursue interests and achieve desired ends. The political processes involve the deployment of symbols, including language, in the 'play of power' and investigation of the symbolic in politics – and as we will show the politics and management of innovation – can help us understand how we got to where we are now and how we are likely to proceed into the future. We therefore draw on political theory (Edelman, 2001; Burke, 1966), organisational discourse theory (Grant, Keenoy and Oswick, 1998) and the ideas of 'cultural pragmatics' and 'performance' (e.g. Alexander, 2004) to address the symbolic dimension of innovation policy, a perspective similar in intent to that proposed by Cavalli (2007) for the study of the innovation process itself. We have also drawn inspiration from a long-established tradition that has focused on the symbolic dimensions of management and organisational behaviour (e.g. Brown, 1994; Kamoche, 1995; Pfeffer, 1981; Zajac and Westphal, 1995; Westphal and Zajac, 1998).

To illustrate the utility of the perspective, we examine one element of contemporary innovation policy and practice, i.e. attempts at fostering innovation at sub-national levels in regions and localities through the designation of defined spaces – 'precincts' and 'corridors' – in terms of their presumed or prospective capacity to become locales of innovation. Such spaces take many forms and can be found in most developed economies, (e.g. the six 'Science Cities' in the UK, the California Innovation Corridor in the USA, the Hsinchu Technology District in Taiwan, the One-North Science Habitat in Singapore, and the Atlantic Technology Corridor in Ireland). We argue that the designation of these spaces and what is in them cannot be understood in purely economic terms. Rather we suggest that what is particularly interesting about such spaces is that they require considerable acts of imagination to bring them into being where symbolic and discursive practices play a key role in generating meaning and, in Alexander's terms 're-fusing' social performances in a 'convincing and effective' rather than 'artificial and contrived' manner (Alexander, 2004, p. 529). We discuss how such practices can be seen as the means through which otherwise disparate phenomena might, in principal, be *tied together* in a 'ritual-like' way (Alexander, 2004, p. 529). The political nature of such projects means of course that both process and outcomes are often messy, indeterminate and unpredictable. While the rhetoric and associated political performance will strive to create a *future perfect* (Pitsis et al., 2003), the outcomes are likely to be more complex as interests and agendas combine in the uncertain arenas of translation and enrolment. Ultimately, the rhetoric and performance of key actors may not be able to tie things together as intended and thereby make it far more difficult for intentions to be realized.

We explore the recent discourse in Australia associated with policies seeking to create localised innovation spaces within urban corridors and precincts. In so doing we depart from conventional approaches by addressing the symbolic rather than the instrumental dimension of innovation policy. We draw upon political theory concerned with rhetoric and more recent organizational studies concerns with discourse to analyse the rhetoric of actors engaged in these initiatives. Two local examples are examined of discourse seeking to construct arguments for and representations of such spaces within the broader context of the national system of innovation. Although the examples represent different stages in the process, the rhetoric of both has similar elements, including locating the local within the global 'knowledge economy', the central role of 'entrepreneurial universities' as wellsprings of innovation, the proximity of disparate actors leading to commercialisable knowledge flows, and expectations of resulting clustering effects. We conclude that, whilst such discourses present compelling visions, they seem to struggle to 'tie things together' and deliver on that vision. We conclude by offering some observations on the strength and weaknesses of taking and stressing the more symbolic dimensions of innovation.

Localised innovation spaces and innovation policy in Australia

Since the late-20th century, innovation policy makers and researchers in the field of innovation studies have become increasingly interested in sub-national innovation systems, notably those of cities and regions (e.g. OECD, 2001; Scott and Harding, 2007). In the global *knowledge economy* the paradox is that *local* places have taken on an increased economic significance, and as Porter (1998, p. 78) has suggested '. . . enduring competitive advantages in a global economy lie increasingly in local things – knowledge, relationships, motivation – that distant rivals cannot match'. Within this emergent context of *glocalisation* (Robertson, 1992; Wellman, 2002; Swyngedouw, 2004) are policy initiatives which seek to promote localised (i.e. sub-regional) innovation. Such initiatives involve public sector actors, from governments at different levels within nation–states, demarcating local spaces as sites of innovation. These spaces tend to be geographically expansive (they include urban corridors, districts and even cities) and they encompass localised sites such as zones, parks and precincts. A common theme is that within these localised spaces innovation systems will evolve from the *wellspring* of university research, which is then created, transferred and transformed by industry.

A central premise of these localised innovation policies is that, if the panoply of actors engaged in the creation, application and commercialisation of knowledge can be brought into geographical proximity, the resulting processes of interaction and exchange will assist a dynamic, innovative and expanding cluster to develop. The material manifestation of the resulting virtuous circle within this cluster will, it is envisaged, be new venture start-ups, in-flows of investment and firms, job creation and other knock-on effects throughout the local economy (Koh, Koh and Tschang, 2005). There is, however, a growing body of evidence, which suggests that such policies may not achieve the desired innovation activity and thereby deliver the anticipated benefits. For example, Bakouros, Mordas and Varsakelis (2002) contend that innovation corridors, science parks and innovation clusters tend not to be major sources of technological development, and the geographical proximity of a university within a space seems to have little, if any, impact on technology transfer to industry. They argue that many of the synergies expected to occur through association among collocated organizations simply do not occur. This argument is consonant with the view that proximity itself does not necessarily make interaction easier to create an *innovative milieu* (Coenen, Moodysson and Asheim, 2004; Larrson and Malmberg, 1999).

Although government interest in science and technology can be traced back to the earliest days of the European colonisation of Australia, it was not until the late-1960s that governments, notably the Commonwealth Government (which has taken a lead role), began to engage with an explicit policy focusing on scientific discovery and its application. While *science and technology* policy developed over the subsequent two decades (with an increasing focus on the fostering of technology development in industry), it was not until the mid-1980s that there was specific reference to innovation – specifically technological innovation – in the policy arena (Timpson and Rudder, 2005). Gregory (1993), in reviewing Australia's national innovation system of the late-1980s, observed four main weaknesses: a low level of expenditure on science and technology, a high level of public sector involvement in the funding and conduct of R&D, a low level of business R&D, and a very high dependence on foreign technology. Under the influence of various government policies, some of these features were to change during the 1990s, notably business expenditure on R&D increased from a very low base as did business funding of university R&D, while government expenditure on public sector research agencies declined and their performance was eclipsed by university-based research (Garrett-Jones, 2007).

From the mid-1990s various discussions surrounding innovation policy had begun to develop, which culminated in an Innovation Summit sponsored jointly by the Commonwealth Government and the Business Council of Australia. This resulted in a landmark policy statement in 2001, *Backing Australia's Ability: An Innovation Plan for the Future*, which introduced a range of purportedly new support measures for innovation. Two themes emerging from this policy perspective (described as generally following 'a strongly neo-liberal approach to science and technology, but one tempered by political pragmatism', Garrett-Jones, 2007, p. 44) were the need for greater cross-sector collaboration, specifically between universities and businesses, and the need for greater commercialisation of research, especially that generated within the public sector (Krishna, 2005; Harman, 2010). In spite of these policy developments, concerns about the level of innovation in the Australian economy persisted (Stern and Gans, 2003; Scott-Kemmis, 2004; Johnston, 2009). Garrett-Jones has argued that the State-based innovation systems and innovation policies have simply marked time since the mid-1990s (Garrett-Jones, 2007, p. 65), and the national innovation system has even been described as broken (West, 2001, p.38).

A change of the Commonwealth Government in December 2007 brought a significant change of direction in innovation policy at that level. This was illustrated in a speech by the then responsible minister (Carr, 2009):

> Because social democrats understand that people have lives outside the marketplace, we also understand that no reform program – no innovation agenda – can be complete if it serves only economic objectives. Our kind of innovation must always have a social, cultural and political dimension as well.

Innovation appeared to become a 'catch-all term' in this new rhetoric, with wider application to broader economic and social objectives. This was underwritten by a policy blueprint, *Powering Ideas – An Innovation Agenda for the 21st Century*, in which innovation was harnessed to a social democrat agenda '. . . to create a better Australia – a fairer, richer, healthier and greener Australia that can meet the challenges and grasp the opportunities of the twenty-first century' (Commonwealth of Australia, 2009, p. 1). What was seemingly being sought under this new broader focus was a 'stronger' innovation system, to be achieved through selected policy elements, including the focusing of efforts on National Innovation Priorities, measures aimed at ensuring a viable national research capacity, and the fostering of collaboration among research performers and research users.

Whether such an approach will address the problems identified in a low tier innovation economy such as Australia (Stern and Gans, 2003) and deliver on the ambitious socio-economic agenda of the Commonwealth Government is something that remains to be seen. However, our reason for outlining this policy shift is that it provides the background context for two examples of attempts to develop localised innovation spaces, which involve the building of more effective links between universities and businesses to achieve knowledge transfer for commercial and other benefits. In general, such initiatives are an evolution of an older discourse concerned with emulating the success of *high technology breeding grounds* such as Silicon Valley through the creation of science or technology parks (e.g. Goldstein and Luger, 1990; Vedovello, 1997; Link and Scott, 2011). Although the notion of such parks persists, the newer rhetoric and performance arguably differs significantly in that it seeks to make an explicit link to broader social and cultural agendas as part of localised economic development or regeneration.

Constructing innovation spaces: symbolism and political discourse

The field of innovation studies has, to date, largely focused on the instrumental dimension of innovation policy, taking policy initiatives at face value and assessing them in terms of their success, and has overlooked the symbolic dimensions of the political processes involved. We depart from convention in this field by seeking to document and interpret the discourse and social actions associated with the phenomenon, thereby contributing to an understanding of observable developments in this area. The approach adopted has been inspired by Murray Edelman's work on the symbolic nature of politics (Edelman, 1964, 1971, 1977, 2001). His core argument is that political action, through the construction of political symbols, misinforms the public and fosters an '*uncritical acceptance of conventional assumptions*' (Edelman, 1964, p. 126) rendering constituents passive and subject to manipulation.

Given the limitations of Edelman's poorly theorised and essentially polemical analysis of political language (Arnhart, 1985; Fenster, 2005), we rather adopted Kenneth Burke's conceptualisation of rhetoric as 'the use of language as a symbolic means of inducing cooperation in beings that by nature respond to symbols' (Burke, 1950, p. 25). Rhetoric thus construed encompasses language and other human action. It is also a symbolic behaviour that seeks to define situations for all involved and induce cooperation (the very essence of political acts), although it may fail to do so. Like Edelman, Burke focused on the symbolic nature of communication (Burke, 1966), and he argued that it is through a society's symbolic systems that social reality is constructed for individuals, specifically what we understand of the world beyond our immediate experience is the result of '. . . a clutter of symbols about the past combined with whatever things we know mainly through maps, magazines, newspapers, and the like about the present . . . [that is] a construct of our symbol systems' (Burke, 1966, p. 5).

According to Burke, language is constitutive of reality and this is consonant with interpretive approaches to the study of organizational discourse (Heracleous and Hendry, 2000) which focus on the use of language to construct meaning and establish a collective identity for organizational members. The study of discourse has emerged as a key new area in management and organisational research in the last decade, as noted by Oswick and colleagues:

> . . . the study of discourse is emerging as one of the primary means of analysing complex organizational phenomena and engaging with the dynamic, and often illusive, features of organizing.
>
> (Oswick, Keenoy and Grant, 2000, p. 1115)

Where discourse can be defined as:

> . . . a set of interrelated texts that, along with the related practices of text production, dissemination and reception, bring an object or an idea into being. . . . Discourses . . . help to constitute a material reality by producing 'identities, contexts, objects of value, and correct procedures' . . . which lead to particular practices through the way they shape what can be said and who can say it.
>
> (Hardy, Lawrence and Grant, 2005, p. 60)

Here the term discourse encompasses spoken and written text, as well as other text-related artefacts. In the examples we explore below this includes all forms of speech acts and text produced by the actors engaged in the creation of localised innovation spaces and its broader socio-economic context. In analysing this discourse, the authors adopt a multi-dimensional view (Fairclough, 1992, 1995; van Dijk, 1997) that explores (i) the language in use (i.e. the form and content of the texts), (ii) the discursive practices of text production and interpretation and (iii) the social context within which the discourse occurs and which shapes it. In other words, the approach aims to explore '. . . who uses language, how, why and when' (van Dijk, 1997, p. 2).

In this approach, discourse can be seen as strategic resource in the political processes surrounding the creation of phenomenon such as localised innovation spaces but this involves an inter-relationship between the actors' situated actions and their associated discourse:

> . . . it is possible for individuals to engage in discursive activity and to access different discourses to generate new meanings that help – or hinder – the enactment of particular strategies. However, such use of discourse is not infinitely pliable. Strategic actors cannot simply produce a discourse to suit their immediate needs and, instead, must locate their discursive activities within a meaningful context if they are to shape and construct action. As a result, a complex relationship emerges as the activities of actors shape discourses, while those discourses also shape the actions of those actors.
>
> (Hardy, Palmer and Phillip, 2000, p. 1228)

Two key elements of this approach are that, first, strategic discourses seek to construct a particular understanding of a situation that aligns with the goals and actions of the strategic actor and, second, it is possible for some actors to speak and act in this discourse while others remain unheard and are therefore rendered invisible. In what follows, we focus on the rhetoric of specific actors pursuing their interests and agendas in relation to the conceptualisation, promotion and formation of localised innovations spaces. In this process they seek to enroll other actors in this discourse and in order to realise their strategic objectives. This activity is akin to what Alexander refers to as social performance:

> Cultural performance is the social process by which actors, individually or in concert, display for others the meaning of their social situation. This meaning may or may not be one to which they themselves subjectively adhere; it is the meaning that they, as social actors, consciously or unconsciously wish to have others believe. In order for their display to be effective, actors must offer a plausible performance, one that leads those to whom their actions and gestures are directed to accept their motives and explanations as a reasonable account . . . Successful performance depends on the ability to convince others that one's performance is true, with all the ambiguities that the notion of aesthetic truth implies.
>
> (Alexander, 2004 p. 529–530)

Such insights notwithstanding this is a field of research that is 'still under theoretical refinement and elaboration' (Rogers, 2009, p. 835). For example, there are no widely accepted methods of analysing rhetorical statements (Haslett, 1987) which might then be deployed to analyse the symbolic and discursive dimensions of innovation and innovation policy. To address this we have developed a framework derived from Burke and Gusfield (1989). This approach was based on Burke's Pentad, of Act, Scene, Motives, Agency and Agent, which he developed/used. We have combined this with Kahane and Cavender's (1997) investigation of logic and rhetoric; Cognition, Persuasion, Tone, Slant and Weasel Words (See Table 14.1).

Table 14.1 Constructing the discourse analysis framework

Burke and Gusfield (1989)		Kahane and Cavender (1997)	
Act (What)	Participants' acts are based on context rules and structures – What happened?	Cognition (Facts)	These statements focus on the emotional attributes of the discourse – Are the facts +/– in their assessment?
Scene (Where)	Focuses on the situation and where the activity takes place – Where is the act happening?	Persuasion (Syntax)	Indicates the attitudes, desires and beliefs present in the discourse – What is the use of language?
Agent (Who)	Identifies the individual actors and their reasons for acting and being part of the scene – Who is involved and why?	Tone (Tone)	Searches for statements that deal with how the discourse is developed through expression – How are feelings managed?
Agency (How)	Explains how the agents world is structured through language and symbols – How do the agents act?	Slant (Context)	Centres on the presentation of the argument (deductive, inductive, questionable analogy/cause/ sample/fallacy – How is the argument presented?
Purpose (Why)	Highlights the motives that guide an agents responses – What do the agents want and why?	Weasel Words (Clarity)	Concerned with the discourses' level of clarity – Is the meaning beyond what has been specified?

By treating Burke's Pentad and the Kahane and Cavender categories of logic and rhetoric as two dimensions of discourse we are able to develop a framework for the analysis of rhetorical statements (see Table 14.2). The purpose of this framework is to identify semiotic strategies employed by the various actors in order to achieve specific objectives. So, for example, innovation corridors are often established in order for industry to achieve greater economies of scale, networking, association, and also reduce research costs. The rhetorical incon-sistency is that governments often broaden the term innovation to encompass a wider social and political agenda which, as highlighted by Edelman (2001) and Linton (2009), creates problems of perspective, as well as diluting the role of the

Table14.2 The discourse analysis framework

Discourse actions	Facts	Syntax	Tone	Context	Clarity
What	What is the context of the discourse?	What is the focus of the beliefs held in the discourse?	What feelings are being expressed in the discourse?	What argument is presented in the discourse?	What is the meaning of the discourse?
Where	Where does the discourse take place?	In what ways are the beliefs about the location constructed?	What feelings are held about the location?	In what ways does the location influence the discourse?	Is the location clear?
Who	Who is involved in the discourse?	Which actors hold which beliefs in the discourse?	Which symbols and expressions are used?	Which actors have constructed the argument?	Do the agents express themselves clearly within the discourse?
How	How are the facts in the discourse presented?	How are the beliefs in the discourse presented?	How are feelings managed within the discourse?	How is the argument presented?	How clear is the discourse?
Why	Why are the facts presented this way?	Why are the beliefs presented this way?	Why are feelings presented this way?	Why is the argument constructed like this?	Why are the agents seeking this and is it clear?

actors and agents who participate in the scene. The danger here is that innovation becomes a *symbolic catch-all* which has little or no real meaning for the wider population, universities and/or industry as a whole, and as Gordon et al., (2009) point out, may undermine trust over the longer term.

The framework also acts as a focusing device, facilitating a cross-case comparison of the strategies employed in a single, or across multiple discourses. So, for example, when using the framework it is possible to examine the underpinnings of the discourse across a broad range of actions taken, as well as identify which actors are central to the discourse.

To show how this approach can help us understand developments and outcomes in innovation policy, and overcome the limitations of more narrow instrumentalist approaches, we now apply it to the two selected illustrative examples. We make no claims that these are fully developed case studies, following more rigorous research methods such as those advocated by Yin (1993) and de Vaus (2001). Rather they are illustrative accounts based on publically available information and whose purpose is to demonstrate how the analytical framework might be deployed and with what insights. The two examples are therefore offered as a basis for identifying where further in-depth analysis might be best undertaken, rather than constituting that analysis in themselves.

Applying the framework: two illustrative cases

Both of the examples we examine are sustained policy initiatives, pursued by actors within and outside of government, who deploy both symbolic and material resources, and are focused on fostering technological innovation within a designated locality. They involve the demarcation of a space by a particular actor or consortium of actors for a specific purpose, into which other actors are invited to participate. The two cases provide a contrast between the earliest stages of these initiatives (case one) and a more mature stage (case two, wherein the policy had been in existence for some years), a contrast in terms of location (specifically, established industrialised-urban versus rapidly-developing coastal hinterland), and each had a distinctive constellation of actors and associated performances as the initiatives have developed. We explore each of these using the discourse analysis framework we propose as a focusing device to identify the key themes and symbols that come to the fore in the associated discourses.

The symbolic construction of 'corridors' and 'precincts' in South East Melbourne

The origins of the idea of a South East Melbourne Innovation Precinct (SEMIP; originally this was called a 'corridor', e.g. Monash University, 2009, but as plans unfolded 'precinct' became the preferred term) lay in what appears to be an attempt to create a *triple helix* partnership between government, knowledge producing institutions, and business (Etzkowitz and Leydesdorff, 2000). The partners include the state government, local government, Monash University and the CSIRO working with industry, represented by three industry bodies.[1] The partnership is new – it was officially launched in October 2009 – and is still embryonic. Attempts by the partners to construct definitions of what SEMIP is and is not are therefore of particular interest since, to accomplish this, key symbolic resources need to be evoked to create a meaningful basis for the discourse to develop.

A key aspect of this performance is that in symbolic terms the partners are not dealing in what may be considered to be 'virgin territory'. Many of the component elements that might be deemed necessary to establish the innovation 'precinct', 'corridor' or for that matter 'innovation eco-system' are, as is often pointed by actors themselves, already there. Published SEMIP documents emphasise that the locality is accessible to Melbourne's CBD (25 kilometers southeast) and, in searching for some notion of the boundaries involved, map these to the existing jurisdictions of four local government areas (the suburban cities of Greater Dandenong, Kingston, Knox, and Monash within the

Melbourne metropolitan area). This serves a clear purpose in allowing the discourse to then speak authoritatively about what of relevance to the project is contained within these boundaries. We are informed in a promotional brochure (SEMIP, 2011), for example, that the area so bounded, 'covers 40 per cent of Victoria's manufacturing activities and over 56,000 registered businesses'. It encompasses a 'broad range of industry sectors including manufacturing, retail, property and business services, and scientific and engineering services'. More generally, the area is focused on the 'high-end growth sectors of chemicals, polymers, machinery and equipment manufacture, and applications in transport, health, construction and the environment'. Also located within the space embraced by the precinct are the Australian Synchrotron,[2] a major site of the Australian Government's public research agency the Commonwealth Scientific and Industrial Research Organization (CSIRO), and the largest campus of Australia's largest university, Monash University. The precinct, we are informed, forms the top end of a broader area that has been labelled the 'South East Melbourne Growth Corridor', earmarked in Victorian State strategic growth plans as a centre of population growth.

These images of a precinct as a space conveniently bounded by local administrative boundaries within which are most of the things one might possibly need to start an innovation ecosystem can be found in a publically available document (SEMIP, 2011). It is immediately noticeable that the language of the document draws upon metaphors from the physical world, the purpose of the precinct being to '*connect*', '*accelerate*', '*excite*' and '*energize*' innovative activity within the precinct. There is a strong sense that what is to be joined-up in human and organizational terms in order to accomplish this innovative activity is presented as physical in character, as something that can be brought together as if by the same means as bringing together *physical* entities. Interestingly, the graphics in the document focus on the *doing of science and engineering*, and provide little sense of the broader social and economic context of the precinct or any of its cultural, historical or political aspects.

Nevertheless, the vision is bold:

> Melbourne's South East has an ambitious goal based on the region's key strengths and acknowledged potential: to become internationally recognized as 'the innovation business and knowledge capital of the Asia Pacific.
>
> (SEMIP, 2009, p. 2)

However, at present, this vision and the potential to realize it are not being effectively mobilised. Whilst the area bounded by the putative precinct encompasses publically-funded R&D organizations (CSIRO and Monash University) and a concentration of technology and knowledge-based businesses, many of these business operate in isolation, they rely on relatively few suppliers or customers to generate ideas for product or service improvements, and they appear to be unaware of knowledge sources or discoveries elsewhere that could help improve competitiveness (SEMIP, 2009, p. 2).

The performative challenge in articulating the SEMIP concept is to try to take an existing cluster of knowledge-based activities and resources seemingly relevant to the innovation agenda and process, and to develop a model of value added through linking these elements together in a geographically bounded entity. As such it is claimed that the precinct:

> . . . will expand upon existing regional and innovation capabilities and networks by implementing initiatives that improve interactions between businesses and between businesses and researchers, provide streamlined access to business innovation services, and build a sense of place that fosters entrepreneurial culture and attracts people to invest, work and live in the region.
>
> (SEMIP, 2009, p. 2)

The strategy document identifies three key themes in bringing all of this about with specific objectives and initiatives to achieve these objectives. For example, the first theme focuses on increasing the possibilities for knowledge-sharing, cooperative problem-solving and open innovation. To achieve this, connections and interactions between precinct stakeholders have to be increased, early stage interactions between private and public R&D increased, and companies and public research bodies encouraged to share non-competitive IP and technologies. One early initiative aimed at achieving these objectives has been the introduction of 'knowledge clubs', which are intended to bring key precinct stakeholders together (SEMIP, 2009).

A further theme focuses on *accelerating business innovation* by providing a means of improving the performance of existing businesses, an attractive infrastructure to attract new knowledge-based business to the region and to open up publically funded technological and human-resources in the support of such business innovation. A variety of measures are proposed ranging from an *innovation portal*, secondments of public sector researchers to industry, and coordinated investment strategies to attract new business to the region.

A final theme speaks to the idea that precincts are no longer just about co-location of different technological resources or of technological resources with business support and prospective access to publically generated knowledge. Here attention is given to the broader non-technical and economic issues of creating a culture of social belonging and collectivity. In this theme the objectives are to do such things as foster an entrepreneurial culture, align education and training to business growth and support infrastructural development with a community as well as business perspective. Amongst the initiatives intended to accomplish such objectives are a high-level business and government forum, which is intended to influence planning and foster engagement between business and education.

One of the interesting things about this narrative is how far and in what ways it will appear as 'convincing and effective' to stakeholders who are set on existing trajectories defined more specifically by their own interests rather than those of a collaborative partnership. Even where the need for partnerships and collaboration is recognised as necessary, it cannot be assumed that such acceptance will readily translate into the internal assimilation of a new discourse and its associated meanings. For example, much has been written in policy and academic discourse about the future role of universities as knowledge-producing institutions more connected to the world around them (Kitson et al., 2009). Indeed for some this *entrepreneurial* model is the blueprint for any aspirational institution of higher learning (Tuchman, 2009). The kinds of knowledge-production suggested in concepts of precincts imply the seamless internal assimilation of new approaches to knowledge production, or at least new reasons for producing knowledge. However, in the 'organised anarchy' of the academy it is unlikely that a consensual reading of new texts about the future role and purpose of the university will be a naturally occurring phenomenon. In other words such exhortations may instead appear at best 'artificial and contrived'.

The Gold Coast's Pacific Innovation Corridor (GCPIC)

The Gold Coast is a strip of increasingly urbanised land in South-Eastern Queensland, bordered in the west by the Great Dividing Range and in the east by the Pacific Ocean, through which runs a major north-south transport route. The Gold Coast has developed only relatively recently to become Australia's sixth largest city. It has experienced rapid population growth over the past 10 years, which has placed enormous pressure on the local infrastructure of business and domestic services. It has a large proportion of retirees in its population, and its economy has been dominated by tourism. However, there are signs of limited economic diversification, and this is being pursued by two levels of government in a state where the public sector has long played a major role in the economy.

The Queensland State Government has a stake in the economic development of the Gold Coast. Its approach has been informed by the *Smart State* strategy, which was introduced by the newly elected State Labor Government in 1998 as an attempt to foster a broader-based and more innovation-focused economy. As the then Premier proudly proclaimed when launching the second phase of the strategy:

> . . . we focused on broadening the economy from just a rocks and crops culture to create new industries and make traditional industries smarter'. . . . And to sustain the standard of living in the State: 'Continue to innovate or stagnate. That is the stark choice facing all Queenslanders as the 21st century starts revealing new challenges . . .
>
> (Beattie and Loukakis, 2005)

A central underlying theme of the strategy is that Australia has become a knowledge-based economy and so R&D, innovation and key enabling technologies (notably Information Technology and Biotechnology) play an increasingly important role in this. For the future economic development of Queensland there was seen to be a '*need to move up the value chain in terms of the agriculture and mining industries and to diversify from these traditional industrial bases*' (DEST, 2003,

p. viii). The main goals of the strategy were to: (1) develop an R&D infrastructure as a basis for higher levels of innovation in the State's economy; (2) install a state-of-the-art information and communication technology infrastructure to enable global connectivity for all economic actors; (3) encourage the supply of angel and venture capital required for the commercialisation of new products and processes; and (4) foster collaborative linkages between public sector research performers and research users in industry.

The Gold Coast City Council (by population the second largest local body in Australia) has been committed to economic diversification since the mid-1980s. The Council's stated vision for the City emphasises the *'quality, diversity and sustainability of its lifestyle, economy and environment'* and envisions that the City be seen as *'Australia's most desirable place to live and favourite place to visit'* (Gold Coast City Council, 2007). A key element of the Council's approach to realising this vision, and the responsibility of its Economic Development and Major Projects Directorate, is the diversification and strengthening of the local economy *'ensuring that the city's economic base is robust, broad and able to service future growth and community needs. . . .'* To this end, an Economic Development Strategy promotes a vision for the city which emphasises its attractiveness as a place to live, to work and to do business (or as one Council slogan has put it: *'Have it all – innovation city'*), with an image of a city that is *'no longer considered solely as a holiday destination'* and where *'industry will be diverse and highly export oriented providing quality, well-paid and sustainable jobs'* (Gold Coast City Council, 2007).

To realise this vision of a highly prosperous city, and to facilitate the creation of conditions necessary for economic development and diversification, the strategy has identified eight fundamentals, which were seen as essential for enabling a shift from a tourism-based and regional servicing economy to that of a globally focused exporter, whereby businesses would leverage regional knowledge to add value in the global marketplace. These fundamentals include such concepts as *learning city* (acknowledging a key tenet of a knowledge-based economy), *innovation city* (recognising that innovation is about generating new ideas and successfully commercialising them), *creative city* (based on the belief that '. . . creativity is fundamental for the quality of life of individuals, communities and economies' (Gold Coast City Council, 2007)), and international connections (seen as an important determinant of a city's economic success in a globalised environment). Nine key industries have been identified as crucial for the future competitiveness of the local economy: the creative industries (notably the film production industry), food processing (including food and wine-based tourism), education, environment, health and medical, ICT, sport and tourism. An Economic Action Agenda aims to facilitate the development of industry clusters, support existing industry associations, promote networking and help form partnerships, promote training opportunities to develop the skills base and strengthen an export focus within industry.

Another central element of the Gold Coast Economic Development Strategy has been the designation of a *Pacific Innovation Corridor '. . . one of the Gold Coast*

City Council's signature economic development projects that encapsulates the vision for transforming Gold Coast City into a globally connected innovation, human capital and technology hot spot and knowledge economy' which comprises ten precincts spread along the north-south axis. It is within each of these precincts that the Council aims to foster the development of industry clusters '. . . *characterised by a critical mass of similar and related firms, and by the intensity of knowledge, R&D, innovation and extensive inter-firm and international interaction'* and to ensure that the centres are serviced by a state-of-the-art telecommunications infrastructure (Gold Coast City Council, 2007). The GCPIC Precincts are tracts of commercial or industrial land within a defined locality, and are supposedly centred on existing anchor organizations. The GCPIC project aims to enhance the economic specialisations, thereby facilitating the creation of the desired clusters based on the key growth industries at each of the centres.

The origins of the GCPIC date back to 1998, and it was originally associated with the installation of a broadband telecommunications infrastructure. A strategic alliance was formed in 1999 between a systems integrator, Boeing Australia, and a telecommunications network developer, Power Tel, to deliver a telecommunications network that would enable the Pacific Innovation Corridor concept. The resulting collaboration, involving the Queensland State Government, the Gold Coast City Council and the Boeing/Power Tel strategic alliance, was initiated in March 2000 and the network was officially launched in November of that year. A key benefit of this, it was claimed, was that it would attract knowledge-based industries and firms to help diversify the local economy.

By 2005, however, with the telecommunications infrastructure in place, the emphasis of the Corridor initiative (from the perspective of the Council) was on the ten centres within the corridor. The telecommunications network had been relegated to the role of supporting infrastructure linking the centres and the organizations within them, and but one element of a vision that saw the Gold Coast transformed into '*a globally connected innovation, technology and knowledge economy hotspot'*.

While some industry clusters have emerged on the Gold Coast (for example, based on the marine industry at Coomera and the IT industry at Robina), the grandiose rhetoric of the GCPIC project remains just that. The achievements of the Gold Coast City Council on this project have been modest to date, as would be expected given the constraints faced by a local government body and the relatively small dedicated workforce within the Directorate (the GCPIC team has five staff), and this is recognised in the Council's Economic Development Strategy wherein it is acknowledged that the Council can only facilitate and lead the process of economic development.

So far there is little evidence of the Pacific Innovation Corridor being anything other than a promotional label, consistent with the Smart State narrative, for local real estate and business development, and claims of higher levels of innovation in the local economy cannot be substantiated. However, the local universities (three of which – Bond, Griffith and Southern Cross – are represented on the Business Gold Coast Advisory Board) have become increasingly central to the Corridor vision and have benefited from the associated public funding. A Gold Coast Innovation Centre (funded by the State Government, Griffith University and the Council) has been established at Griffith's Southport Campus as a business technology incubator facility to facilitate the successful development of knowledge-based industries in Queensland by providing valuable mentoring and support to entrepreneurs. It is currently incubating eight businesses, three physically located in the Centre and five as *virtual* incubatees.

Comparing SEMIP and GCPIC

Having investigated the two cases, the question arises as to whether there are any similarities and/or differences in the various narratives. The various themes that emerge from the analysis centre on five particular aspects of the discourse (Table 14.3).

It is evident, for example, from the analysis that the *Facts* are driven by the symbolic nature of the discourse, which includes images of university, government and industry operating in a helical framework, whereby innovation is pulled from the universities into the commercial domain. Similarly the *Context* within which the discourse takes place employs various forms; deductive reasoning and

Table 14.3 Cross-case comparison of the SEMIP and GCPIC discourse

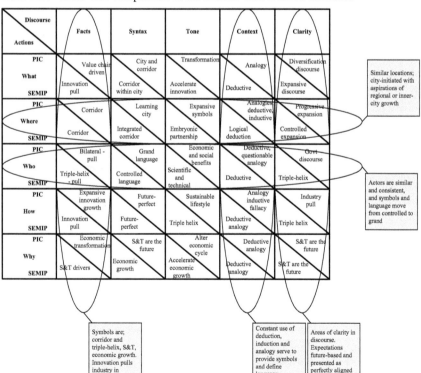

analogy are the primary representations. Questionable analogy and fallacy are driven by symbols (such as, global centre), which are difficult to reconcile with reality. In terms of the *Clarity* the narratives are consistent and centre on expansion and partnerships for SEMIP and progressive expansion and diversification for GCPIC. The *Where* aspects of each discourse are also generally consistent (the location and the beliefs underpinning the discourse), although some of the terminology may change. So, for example, while GCPIC focuses on city hubs linked via a corridor, the city metaphor does not change much, merely the descriptor (learning, creative, knowledge). An area of slight inconsistency involves the *Who* component. The actors in each discourse appear to be many and varied, and while SEMIP focuses on the triple helix as an expression of partnership, in reality various levels of government are driving the discourse, which one would expect to find at SEMIP, as it is relatively new, but not necessarily at the GCPIC, which is a mature project. As has been pointed out previously, within the GCPIC, while government is supporting the university sector, industry remains, for whatever reason, absent from the discussion.

Discussion

We have sought to depart from conventional approaches to innovation studies and introduce a perspective that focuses upon the discourse associated with innovation policy initiatives. We have addressed the symbolic dimensions of innovation policy and practice, where our focus is on the symbolic and communicative dimensions of the behaviour of the actors in the innovation process. The assumption is that organisational and institutional failures with regard to innovation can be attributed to failures in the way the actors attend to these aspects of the innovation process. The chapter has explored this in the context of recent attempts to establish localised innovation spaces and places. Such initiatives go beyond the idea of science parks and the simple collocation of actors and facilities to far reaching notions involving the creation of translational research and supporting socio-economic and cultural environments, where it is the quality of the human and social interaction that is seen as the key source of innovation. Available research evidence suggests that these projects often do not yield to their intended results.

In each case, a set of actors, notably local bodies, universities and industry representatives, seek to establish localised innovation spaces within demarcated areas. The sub-national government actors pursue economic diversification and development within their territories and, while the universities seek to establish relevance and gain access to further funding and resources, it is evident from the research that the industry partners remain ambivalent. In an Australian context these actions are carried out within a broader milieu framed by the innovation policy of the Commonwealth Government with its emphasis on national research priorities, cross-sector collaboration, the transfer of knowledge from public to private sectors, and the commercialisation of locally generated knowledge. While the examples contrast, in that they represent different stages in the establishment of localised innovation spaces and different initial conditions in the spaces to be colonised, the discourse around both does have similar elements. For example, the locally-focused initiatives resonate with the creative setting arguments of writers such as Florida (2002, 2008), and are aimed at achieving economic, social and even cultural transformation; the emergent globalised *knowledge economy*, with innovation as its driving force, is invoked in both instances as a major rationale for local action; the university is positioned as central to these spaces as a creator and disseminator of usable knowledge that will become the wellspring of innovation; reflecting the role of the *entrepreneurial university* (Etzkowitz, 2003), and the changing *triple helix* of government–university–industry relationships, (Eztkowitz and Leydesdorff, 2000).

Both of these visions represent valid academic contributions to this discourse, which purports to document and theorise observable changes; knowledge is depicted as flowing from centres of creation in universities to centres of commercial exploitation in businesses and university spin-offs (innovation push); geographical proximity within the demarcated space is seen as a basis for clustering different types of economic actors among which relationships will form as the actors rub shoulders together and channels for the flow of knowledge and economic resources will develop (innovations pull); and, above all, the expectation of a snowballing effect whereby the space becomes more attractive to key actors in the knowledge economy, including entrepreneurs, venture capitalists and other investors, innovative firms, and knowledge workers with the requisite skills.

Evidence from the research clearly points towards two discourses that have a specific modality, which is encoded in a particular way for different audiences. For example, the idea of a triple helix is a regular theme and symbol that appears within each narrative; the government, university and industry locked in a constant spiral with relationship links being developed at each turn (Etzkovitz, 2002). In approaching these cases from the perspective of Burke (1950) and Edelman (2001) it is evident that, while each discourse seeks to provide a vision of a happy union and partnership, the reality is somewhat different and many of the triple helix's relationships are more often the subject of *inaccurate assumptions* and therefore remain as little more than political motivated *myths*.

The research into innovation spaces has highlighted a number of important issues, and the authors have identified a corresponding dilemma, in that the implications of this study have important ramifications for a number of actors involved in the discourse, namely; Government, which operates on three levels in Australia (Commonwealth, State and Council); university actors, who both compete and collaborate, and are also subject to both Commonwealth and State regulation; and finally industry, which comprises international, inter-state and local actors. The question remains: how then should these actors navigate these complex narratives?

It is evident from the research that the number of actors involved with Australian innovations spaces moves beyond Etzkovitz's simplistic vision of the triple helix, and shows that innovation spaces within Australia are layered and multidimensional. This means that the discourse has a variety of threads, each of which needs to be carefully unpacked. In addition, our analysis illustrates that, while each case is based on a variety of rhetorical arguments, statements and symbols (for example, the triple helix, deductive and inductive logic and analogy), as Kahane and Cavender (1997) point out, semiotic contradictions add an extra dimension that actors need to be aware of when trying to navigate the discourse. For example, SEMIP is focused on attracting more scientific and technological orientated businesses into a space that is currently dominated by medium sized low-tech and service businesses (Victorian Government, 2010). Why is this aspect of the discourse important? It is because grandiose visions and statements may not actually match the reality, and in the case of SEMIP may take many years to attain some semblance of the vision that is being created.

The creation of *innovation* spaces (realisation) in Australia is founded upon a mistaken belief that innovation will be stimulated simply through wider association. Etzkovitz and Klofsten (2005) point out that there is a need to also create what are identified as *knowledge* (vision) and, most importantly, *consensus* (distillation) spaces. Evidence from this study suggests that at SEMIP and GCPIC there has been a tendency to rush from vision to realisation, without any serious distillation taking place. Making sure that ideas, visions and symbols are refined prior to engaging in any discourse, is very likely to assist the actors in overcoming the problem of sub-optimal outcomes.

Conclusions

This discourse we have identified constitutes a compelling vision. As Wray (2009) argues the new focus on the territorial dimension presents the possibility of a broader concept of innovation in so far as new actors, organisations and institutions are brought into the process. This in turn highlights the need for, and the importance of, new frameworks for the governance of the innovation process. As a result, attention is drawn to the new capacities and capabilities required to make innovation happen. These might include such things as leadership in partnerships, building collaborative innovation teams across organisational boundaries and an emphasis on the open and potentially user-led and community-led innovation. The public responsibility in this is particularly emphasised, for example in providing opportunities for improving human and social capital in the territory through skills development, nurturing the public understanding of science, and the promotion of educational programs to support scientific and technological careers. Clearly this discourse is a long way from that of science parks, with their emphasis on technology transfer and business incubation. However, if it exists at present, the examples given here are indicative of this, it is in the *future perfect* mode (Pitsis et al., 2003), specifically, a vision of what might be. In practice, it is questionable as to how far the would-be partners and participants might share such a vision, either together or within their respective organisational and institutional boundaries. In this sense, the component elements – or at least some of them – appear to be there. But what is the nature and what are the properties of the discourse that will tie them together? Recently, Donofrio, IBM Fellow and eminent former IBM employee, summarized this issue at the level of the Australian innovation system as follows:

> . . . we do not have an innovation system. We have research systems, we have business systems, but we do not have a shared agenda for innovation linking universities and research institutes, businesses and industry, and government. It is perhaps, therefore, not surprising that we find we have collocations, not collaborations; we have building blocks but not yet the exploitation of those synergies that could and should emerge.
>
> (Donofrio, 2009, p. 5)

At present, it is suggested that the actors are struggling with the interpretative and symbolic dimensions of this task, as the case studies clearly illustrate. Future research needs to further examine the role of innovation spaces in Australia by also comparing other growing regions that have a similar innovation strategy as evidenced in the Gold Coast. Examples are the Ballarat and Geelong regions in Victoria, which are supported by universities and research infrastructure. It would be interesting to see how additional elements of the helix approach, including sustainability, are becoming central to these growing innovation regions. More data and information from a longitudinal perspective would help to understand the role of regional governments in promoting innovation corridors. Given Australia's position in Asia it would be helpful to further research how knowledge spillovers in regional areas are then transformed into urban business ventures. This is especially evident in the farm industry with dairy companies innovating based on food technology, which is then exported to Asia.

Notes

1 These are, as a founding partner, the Small Technologies Cluster, a cross-sector body providing innovation services and facilities for micro-, nano- and bioresearch. More recently added to the membership are SEMMA (South East Melbourne Manufacturing Alliance) and SEBN (South East Business Network). Also part of the membership is Southern Health.
2 The Australian Synchrotron was officially opened in July 2007. It is the largest stand-alone piece of scientific infrastructure in the Southern Hemisphere and one of only 44 similar facilities globally. The Synchrotron is a source of highly intense light ranging from infrared to hard x-rays that can be used for a wide variety of research purposes.

References

Alexander, J.C. (2004) 'Cultural pragmatics: Social performance between ritual and strategy', *Sociological Theory*, 22(4): 527–73.

Arnhart, L. (1985) 'Murray Edelman, political symbolism, and the incoherence of political science', *The Political Science Reviewer*, 15: 185–213.

Bakouros, Y.L, Mardas, D.C. and Varsakelis, N.C. (2002) 'Science park, a high tech fantasy? An analysis of the science parks of Greece', *Technovation*, 22: 123–8.

Beattie, P. and Loukakis, A. (2005) *Making a Difference: Reflections on life, leadership and politics*, HarperCollins, New York.

Brown, A.D. (1994) 'Politics, symbolic action and myth making in pursuit of legitimacy', *Organization Studies*, 15: 861–78.

Burke, K. (1950) *A rhetoric of motives*, University of California Press, Berkeley, CA.

Burke, K. (1966) *Language as symbolic action: Essays on life, literature, and method*, University of California Press, Berkeley, CA.

Burke, K. and Gusfield, J.R. (1989) *On symbols and society*, University of Chicago Press, Chicago.

Carr, K. (2009) 'Innovation and social democracy underpin successful societies', Speech to the John Curtin Institute of Public Policy, Perth, http://www.atse.org.au/index.php?sectionid=1349 accessed February 10, 2010.

Cavalli, N. (2007) 'The symbolic dimension of innovation processes', *American Behavioral Scientist*, 50: 958–69.

Coenen, L., Moodysson, J. and Asheim, B.T. (2004) 'Nodes, networks and proximities: On the knowledge dynamics of the Medicon Valley Biotech Cluster', *European Planning Studies*, 12(7): 1003–18.

Commonwealth of Australia (2009) *Powering ideas*, Commonwealth of Australia, Canberra.

Department of Education Science and Technology (DEST) (2003) *The contribution of the states and the territories to Australia's science and innovation system*, DEST, Canberra.

De Vaus, D. (2001) *Research design in social research*, Sage, London.

Department of Innovation and Technology Research (2008) *Submission to the review of the national innovation system: Overall data and analysis*, DIITR, Melbourne, Australia.

Dodgson, M. (2008) *Content analysis of submissions by Leximancer*, University of Queensland, Brisbane, Australia.

Donfrio, N. (2009) cited in 'Precincts people and places – forging new partnerships', Proceedings from an International Symposium Convened by the University of Queensland and the PACE Precinct Initiative, July 24–25, 2009, Brisbane.

Edelman, M. (1964) *The symbolic uses of politics*, University of Illinois Press, Chicago, ILL.

Edelman, M. (1971) *Politics as symbolic action: Mass arousal and quiescence*, Markham, Chicago, ILL.

Edelman, M. (1977) *Political language: Words that succeed and policies that fail*, Academic Press, New York.

Edelman, M.J. (2001) *The politics of misinformation*, Cambridge University Press, Cambridge.

Etzkowitz, H. (2002) *The triple helix of university-industry-government: Implications for policy and evaluation*, Working Paper 2002-11 Science Policy Institute, Stockholm.

Etzkowitz, H. (2003) 'Research groups as quasi-firms: The invention of the entrepreneurial university', *Research Policy*, 32: 109–21.

Etzkowitz, H. and Klofsten, M. (2005) 'The innovating region: Toward a theory of knowledge-based regional development', *R&D Management*, 35(3): 243–55.

Etzkowitz, H. and Leydesdorff, L. (2000) 'The dynamics of innovation: From national systems and mode 2 to a Triple Helix of university-industry-government relations', *Research Policy*, 29: 109–23.

Fairclough, N. (1992) *Discourse and social change*, Polity, Cambridge.

Fairclough, N. (1995) *Critical discourse analysis: Papers in the critical study of language*, Longman, London.

Fenster, M. (2005) 'Murray Edelman, polemicist of public ignorance', *Critical Review*, 17(3): 367–91.

Florida, R. (2002) *The rise of the creative class and how it's transforming work, leisure and everyday life*, Basic Books, New York.

Florida, R. (2008) *Who's your city?* Basic Books, New York.

Garrett-Jones, S. (2007) 'Marking time? The evolution of the Australian national innovation system, 1996–2005', In T. Turpin and V.V. Krishna (Eds) *Science, Technology Policy and the Diffusion of Knowledge*, pp 34–69, Cheltenham, Edward Elgar.

Gold Coast City Council (2007) *Gold coast 2010 economic development strategy action plan*, Gold Coast City Council, Gold Coast.

Goldstein, H.A. and Luger, M.I. (1990) 'Science/technology parks and regional development theory', *Economic Development Quarterly*, 4(1): 64–78.

Gordon, R., Kornberger, M. and Clegg, S.R. (2009) 'Power, rationality and legitimacy in public organisations', *Public Administration*, 87(1): 15–34.

Grant, D., Keenoy, T. and Oswick, C. (1998) *Discourse + Organization*, Sage, London.

Gregory, R. (1993) 'The Australian innovation system', In R.R Nelson (Ed) *National Innovation Systems: A Comparative Analysis*, pp 324–352, New York, Oxford University Press.

Hardy, C., Lawrence, T.B. and Grant, D. (2005) 'Discourse and collaboration: The role of conversations and collective identity', *Academy of Management Review*, 30(1): 58–77.

Hardy, C., Palmer, I. and Phillips, N. (2000) 'Discourse as a strategic resource', *Human Relations*, 53(9): 1227–48.

Harman, G. (2010) 'Australian university research commercialisation: Perceptions of technology transfer specialists and science and technology academics', *Journal of Higher Education Policy and Management*, 32(1): 69–83.

Haslett, B. (1987) *Communication, strategic action in context*, Routledge, London.

Heracleous, L. and Hendry, J. (2000) 'Discourse and the study of organization: Toward a structurational perspective', *Human Relations*, 53(10): 1251–86.

Johnston, R. (2009) 'Innovation: Have we got it right yet?' Speech to the John Curtin Institute of Public Policy, Perth, http://www.atse.org.au/index.php?sectionid=1316 accessed February 10, 2010.

Kahane, H. and Cavender, N. (1997) *Logic and contemporary rhetoric*, Wadsworth Publishing Co Ltd., London

Kamoche, K. (1995) 'Rhetoric, ritualism, and totemism in human resource management', *Human Relations*, 48: 367–85.

Kitson, M., Howells, J., Braham, R. and Westlake, S. (2009) *The connected university: Driving recovery and growth in the UK economy*, NESTA Research Report, London.

Ko, W.W. and Liu, G. (2015) 'Understanding the process of knowledge spillovers: Learning to become social enterprises', *Strategic Entrepreneurship Journal*, 9: 263–85.

Koh, F.C.C., Koh, W.T.H. and Tschang, F.T. (2005) 'An analytical framework for Science parks and technology districts with an application in Singapore', *Journal of Business Venturing*, 20: 217–9.

Krishna, V.V. (2005) *Changing structure of public research systems in Australia: Institutions converging towards new science based innovation*, University of Western Sydney, Sydney.

Larrson, S and Malmburg, A. (1999) 'Innovations, competitiveness and local embeddedness: a study of machinery producers in Sweden', *Geografiska*, 81B: 1–18.

Lindblom, C.E. (1980) *The policy-making process*, Prentice-Hall, Englewood Cliffs, NJ.

Link, A.N. and Scott, J.T. (2011) Public goods, public gains: Calculating the social benefits of public R&D. Oxford University Press, Oxford.

Linton, J.D. (2009) 'De-babelizing the language of innovation', *Technovation*, 29: 729–37.

Organisation for Economic Cooperation and Development (OECD) (2001) *Cities and regions in the new learning economy*, OECD, Paris.

Oswick, C., Keenoy, T.W. and Grant, D. (2000) 'Discourse, organizations and organizing: Concepts, objects and subjects', *Human Relations*, 53(9): 1115–23.

Pfeffer, J. (1981) 'Management as symbolic action: The creation and maintenance of organizational paradigms', In L.L. Cummings and B.M. Strwa (Eds) *Research in Organizational Behavior*, Volume 3, pp 1–52, Greenwich, CT, JAI Press.

Pitsis, T.S., Clegg, S.R., Marosszeky, M. and Rura-Polley, T. (2003) 'Constructing the Olympic Dream: A future perfect strategy of project management', *Organization Science*, 14(5): 574–90.

Porter, M.E. (1998) 'Clusters and the new economics of competition', *Harvard Business Review*, 76: 77–90.

Robertson, R. (1992) *Globalization: Social theory and global culture*, Sage, London.

Rogers, J. (2009)' From "civilian power" to "global power": Explicating the European union's "grand strategy" through the articulation of discourse theory', *Journal of Common Market Studies*, 47(4): 831–62.

Scott, A. and Harding, A. (2007) 'Introduction: Universities, relevance and scale', In A. Harding, A. Scott, S. Laske and C. Burtscher (Eds) *Bright Satanic Mills: Universities, Regional Development and the Knowledge Economy*, pp 1–25, Ashgate, Aldershot.

Scott-Kemmis, D. (2004) 'The Australian innovation system: A scorecard', *Australian Chief Executive*, July: 29–35.

South East Melbourne Innovation Project (2009) *Energising the South East Melbourne innovation precinct*, Strategic Plan Summary 2009–2011, Monash University, Melbourne.

Stern, S. and Gans, J. (2003) *Assessing Australia's innovative capacity in the 21st century*, Australian Institute for Commercialization, Melbourne.

Swyngedouw, E. (2004) 'Globalisation or glocalisation? Networks, territories and rescaling', *Cambridge Review of International Affairs*, 17(1): 25–48.

Timpson, M. and Rudder, N. (2005) 'Governing innovation policy: The Australian experience', In *Governance of Innovation Systems: Volume 2 Case Studies in Innovation Policy*, pp 307–33, OECD, Paris.

Tuchman, G. (2009) *Wannabe U: Inside the corporate university*, Chicago University Press, Chicago, ILL.

van Dijk, T.A. (1997) 'The study of discourse', In T.A. van Dijk (Ed) *Discourse as structure and process*, pp 1–35, London, Sage.

Vedovello, C. (1997) 'Science parks and university-industry interaction: geographical proximity between the agents as a driving force', *Technovation*, 17(9): 491–531.

Victorian Government (2010) *The innovation state: Building a competitive and innovative Victorian economy*, Victorian Government, Melbourne, Australia.

Wellman, B. (2002) 'Little boxes, glocalization, and networked individualism', In M. Tanabe, P. van den Besselaar and T. Ishida (Eds) *Digital Cities II: Computational and Sociological Approaches*, pp 10–26, Berlin, Springer-Verlag.

West, J. (2001) 'The mystery of innovation: Aligning the triangle of technology, institutions and organisation', *Australian Journal of Management*, 26(Special Issue): 22–43.

Westphal, J.D. and Zajac, E.J. (1998) 'The symbolic management of stockholders: Corporate governance reforms and shareholder reactions', *Administrative Science Quarterly*, 43: 127–53.

Wray (2009) 'Science fiction? A critical examination of the UK Science City agenda', Newcastle University Business School, Newcastle-upon-Tyne.

Yin, R.K. (1993) *Case study research – Design and methods*, Second edition, Sage, Thousand Oaks, CA.

Zahra, S. (2015) 'Corporate entrepreneurship as knowledge creation and conversion: The role of entrepreneurial hubs', *Small Business Economics*, 44: 727–35.

Zajac, E.J. and Westphal, J.D. (1995) 'Accounting for the explanations of CEO compensation: Substance and symbolism', *Administrative Science Quarterly*, 40: 283–308.

Conclusion

15 Future research directions for knowledge spillovers and strategic entrepreneurship

Vanessa Ratten, Léo-Paul Dana
and *João J. Ferreira*

Introduction

Knowledge spillovers are an important way to encourage innovation, reconfigure strategies and enhance productivity. They also act as a source of entrepreneurship that allows firms to create strategies to enter new markets and exceed growth estimates. This chapter highlights future research suggestions that show how knowledge spillovers involve a variety of different types of knowledge, which are linked to strategic entrepreneurship activities. It also explains the role of knowledge spillovers in accumulating, converting and sharing information, enabling firms to build better strategies for international expansion.

Our agenda for future research suggests paying more attention to the processes by which knowledge spillovers becomes strategic entrepreneurship. To encourage more research into knowledge spillovers using strategic entrepreneurship, we extend the current definition of knowledge spillovers to focus more on strategic opportunities: knowledge spillovers involve the use of both internal and external knowledge for strategic benefits impacting the entrepreneurial development of business action transforming innovation into creative pursuits. We consider it important to focus on the creativity aspects of knowledge spillovers as it impacts value creation and global competitiveness especially for knowledge intensive business services. This expanded definition also allows for the study of strategic entrepreneurship utilizing creativity and innovation management paradigms.

The strategic view focuses on the competitiveness of international environments, such as resources and capabilities determining entrepreneurial opportunities. This means that future research should pay increased attention to the strategic features of knowledge spillovers. We also consider it important for more research to take an international approach to knowledge spillovers beyond the simple notion of location decisions impacting regional entrepreneurship. Research should explicate the features of international knowledge spillovers and how culture influences entrepreneurial opportunities. This correlates with Welter's (2011) contextual view of entrepreneurial opportunities. Inspired by the chapters included in this book, we proceed to suggest potential avenues for further research. We propose a number of directions that knowledge spillovers and strategic entrepreneurship may take.

The purpose of this chapter is to address the gap in the current literature about knowledge spillovers and strategic entrepreneurship. We first establish the importance of the knowledge spillover theory of entrepreneurship and then propose some suggestions for future research. This chapter advances that knowledge spillovers are important for encouraging strategic types of entrepreneurship being developed and converted into business ideas. It begins by discussing the importance of knowledge spillovers for the study of strategic entrepreneurship. The chapter then discusses emerging perspectives of knowledge spillovers and the dynamic nature of their development. After discussing the current thinking about knowledge spillovers, we focus on future directions for research in terms of focusing on strategic entrepreneurship. The chapter concludes by identifying several promising research avenues that contribute to the knowledge spillover theory of entrepreneurship and strategic management.

Knowledge spillovers: a broad overview

The role of knowledge spillovers is pervasive, enabling managers and entrepreneurs to build better linkages in the entrepreneurial economy. Knowledge spillovers are the foundation for entrepreneurship and a strategic weapon in the global marketplace. Huggins and Thompson (2015:110) define knowledge as 'information that changes something or somebody, either by becoming grounds for action or by making an organization capable of different or more effective action'. Nonaka and Takeuchi (1995) highlight how knowledge is the most important driver of the modern economy because of its scientific and dynamic application. There are two main types of knowledge that are evident in a spillover context: explicit and tacit. Explicit knowledge is information that can be codified through written or oral communication (Drucker, 1989). This means that sometimes explicit knowledge is in a symbolic form that can be translated by individuals. The other main type of knowledge is tacit, which is harder to describe as it incorporates experience and expertise embedded in an individual. The best way to understand tacit knowledge is that it is the competence, skills and talent residing in an individual (Huggins and Thompson, 2015).

Knowledge was previously considered a public good before the emergence of the information and communication industry made it crucial for global competitiveness (Antonelli, 2008). The role of knowledge in society has changed to be more combinatorial, as it is the result of complex economic systems (Mattes, 2012). It is hard to explain tacit knowledge, which has made it a key factor in the geography of innovation and the existence of entrepreneurial clusters (Asheim and Gertler, 2005). Explicit knowledge is considered less important than tacit knowledge as a source of global competitiveness due to it being easier to transfer and explain (Bathelt et al., 2004). Knowledge can be spilled over through a sticky or leaky process (Huggins and Thompson, 2015). Sticky knowledge is hard to move due to its association with its originator. This makes it usually tied to individuals or firms linked to its development (Brown and Duguid, 2000). Leaky knowledge is easier to access as it is considered the undesirable flow to external parties.

Ko and Lim (2015:264) states 'knowledge is a critical resource for business success because it is closely related to the development of organizations intellectual advantage, especially in tacit form'. Tacit knowledge is hard to communicate due to it being embedded in networks and routines (Acs et al., 2009). This has meant that tacit forms of knowledge integrate routines that involve task oriented know-how (Nelson and Winter, 1982). As the codification or formalization of tacit knowledge is difficult it leads to it being usually inimitable and hard to replicate. Due to these reasons tacit knowledge is key for organizations' competitiveness and spillovers are a way to obtain it. A way tacit knowledge is obtained is via interaction with knowledge holders within both external and internal networks (Ko and Liu, 2015).

Knowledge spillovers involve the flow of knowledge from entity to another. Hence, they emphasize externalities from the formation of knowledge to the benefits from the spillover to knowledge receiver (Audretsch and Lehmann, 2006). This means that the creator of knowledge may not always receive the benefits of the ideation and creative process. The key difference between knowledge spillovers and knowledge transfer is that it does not always involve cross-entity compensation because of the exchanging of knowledge (Ko and Liu, 2015). This links to research about entrepreneurial bricolage that suggests innovation is often the result of recombining knowledge. Sometimes knowledge is created with the distinct purpose of being able to share it with others. This often occurs by public institutions such as universities who want to share knowledge (Agarwal et al., 2010). In many cases, knowledge is only valuable after it has been acquired by others who can turn it into an innovation (Ko and Liu, 2015). This is due to the view of knowledge being free and for the public good (Audretsch and Keilbach, 2004).

Knowledge spillovers are the byproduct of knowledge coming from innovation activities in other firms (Gilbert et al., 2008). The spillovers can be direct or indirect depending on the type of knowledge transferred from one party to another (Audretsch, 1998). As knowledge is an elusive concept the evaluation of knowledge spillovers is difficult, as it is hard to determine when it occurs in a business setting. Some types of knowledge spillovers are more valued than others due to their business implications. Brown and Duguid (2000) discuss how with technological knowledge spillovers firms can obtain information about corporate activities that would otherwise be hard to collect. Technological knowledge spillovers that represent new and novel knowledge are highly valued due to the strategic nature of the technology industry.

Knowledge creation can occur in a number of ways including sharing of ideas, integrating information systems and learning by doing (Zahra, 2015). These occurrences enable knowledge spillovers to be accessed through a number of sources including personal contacts, industry networks and business communities (Maula et al., 2013). There are different types of knowledge spillovers that allow a firm to sustain entrepreneurial programs. Often additional knowledge spillovers will serve as an input to future strategies. The interpretation of knowledge will enrich the process of entrepreneurship within a firm setting. As knowledge can be fragmented individuals need to integrate it to give it meaning to a firm.

Agenda for future research

Knowledge spillovers as a creation process for strategic entrepreneurship

Knowledge spillovers in the context of strategic entrepreneurship provide a way to contribute to the competitiveness of a firm. Strategic entrepreneurship activities typically develop over time depending on the importance of the knowledge spillover. In each part of the strategic entrepreneurship process, firms share and test their ideas with the aim of integrating appropriate knowledge. Part of this involves firms creating new and extending knowledge. This process is important as it enables firms to convert knowledge and introduce novel ideas into a firm (Narayanan et al., 2009). This is an important component of strategic entrepreneurship as the facilitation of knowledge spillovers. Some of the key benefits of strategic entrepreneurship are a consequence of informal knowledge spilled over by other firms. Zahra (2015:728) states that 'knowledge, in particular, is an important asset in today's global economy, it is the fuel of innovation and discovery that renews companies and their operations'.

The consideration of strategic entrepreneurship as a key source of knowledge is important in the context of spillovers. This helps us address future research issues that will address this question: Why are knowledge spillovers important to the strategic development of entrepreneurial firms? The use of knowledge spillovers is a primary source of innovation creation, and this requires the entrepreneurial management of several processes. A firm's extended network plays a key role in developing knowledge spillovers that help increase strategic entrepreneurial projects.

The knowledge spillovers impacting strategic entrepreneurship are complex depending on the process in which the knowledge was conceived. The content of knowledge will impact firm activities, which are based on the integration of different skill sets. Knowledge is essential in entrepreneurship as it is the basis of variety in a firms operations and strategic initiatives (Zahra, 2015). Zahra (2015:730) states that 'strategy – whether domestic or global – centers on creating and exploiting this heterogeneity to create distinctive products, innovative business models, and well-protected and lucrative market spaces'.

Theoretical issues

The knowledge spillover theory of entrepreneurship has received considerable attention in terms of its contribution to literature. Despite this support of the theory as being important for entrepreneurs, more work is required to validate the theory in new contexts. We suggest that areas of further research look at the theory in the context of emerging technologies, especially in terms of biomedicine and health sciences. This is due to the theory being premised more on economic geography rather than the scientific application to multidisciplinary areas incorporating the wealth sector. This would offer exciting new theoretical avenues for expanding the knowledge spillover theory of entrepreneurship to other disciplines. As prior studies point out, there is a lack of general consensus about how to define knowledge spillovers. To address this research gap, future research should explain in more detail how different types of knowledge are spilled over and what they mean for entrepreneurs. This could be done by analyzing a wide range of knowledge spillovers to capture longitudinally how the transfer takes place.

As most studies focus on a single industry there is opportunity for future research to compare different situations to see how the knowledge spillover is conducted. The concept of knowledge spillovers is fundamental to entrepreneurship and, as such, can afford multiple opportunities to discover the connection between innovation and other theories that relate to knowledge. This opens the door for more sophisticated theoretical models of the knowledge spillover process, linking innovation-based models with emerging theory. New research can also consider learning outcomes, knowledge intensive business services and effectuation. More research is needed at capturing at the methodological level samples of knowledge spillovers to identify the causal effect of the entrepreneurial process. Researchers should attempt to triangulate findings about knowledge spillovers using multi-method approaches.

The role of context

Research on knowledge spillovers can make significant progress by training to improve the understanding underpinning the entrepreneurial behavior. By assessing the role of knowledge spillovers on strategic entrepreneurship, more research is needed on how entrepreneurial ventures are formed based on learning activity. This will shed light on the formation and spread of knowledge spillovers to see how intention changes to behavior. This will help entrepreneurial managers gain a better understanding of how human decision making occurs via knowledge spillovers.

Little research exists on the potential causal link between some contextual variables (past knowledge exposure, knowledge contexts, spillover methods, firm's personnel profiles, available resources, etc.) and the impact of knowledge spillovers on strategic entrepreneurship. Questions still remain about how the process of knowledge spillovers affects strategic entrepreneurship. How does the type of knowledge spillover (tacit, explicit, sticky, leaky) affect entrepreneurship? How do knowledge spillovers emerge and influence different forms of entrepreneurship? How do the contents of knowledge spillovers impact the strategies of firms? Research could probe into these research questions relating to the reciprocal relationships between knowledge spillovers and strategic entrepreneurship. This could include examining the quality of the entrepreneurial learning from knowledge spillovers and the development of core competences for regional innovation. Scholars should seek to conduct studies with more in-depth case studies about knowledge spillovers, then compare them in different contexts. Concerning future research about entrepreneurship education using knowledge spillovers as a factor, studies could include the type of knowledge as control group. Studies about the type of knowledge should include measures at both the pre- and post-spillover stage.

The context of knowledge spillovers is important in impacting strategic entrepreneurship. This is supported by Welter (2011:165) who stated that 'there is growing recognition in entrepreneurship research that economic behavior can be better understood within its historical, temporal, institutional, spatial and social context'. The historical context means that some firms learn that they receive more effective knowledge spillovers from certain individuals, partners and locations. The temporal context means that in fast-changing industries like the technology sector the flow of knowledge spillovers is important for competitiveness. The institutional context influences the role of knowledge spillovers due to the laws, regulations and policies affecting entrepreneurship (Welter and Smallbone, 2012). Both formal and informal institutions are crucial for the dynamic impact of knowledge spillovers in the community. These institutions incorporate cultural factors that may differ depending on environmental conditions. Institutions can directly and indirectly affect entrepreneurship due to their impact on employment and new venture rates. The spatial context of knowledge spillovers includes looking at the role of regions and countries. Much of the economic geography literature has focused on the location of firms, industries and clusters in promoting regional innovation (Linan et al., 2011). For this reason, the spatial context is important in determining how industrial communities affect knowledge spillovers. The social context is becoming more important as it links the non-profit and research sectors to the business applications of knowledge spillovers.

As some innovations are created for social reasons, knowledge spillovers can occur for altruistic reasons. Researchers could study the impact of social goals on knowledge spillovers to see the changes in firm attitudes towards entrepreneurship. Researchers could also evaluate the role of social policies on knowledge spillovers. Studying social reasons knowledge might be spilled over might also be possible to see the effect of regional policy on strategic entrepreneurship. This assessment could contribute to strengthening the link between social innovation, knowledge management research and entrepreneurship policy. In addition, new research about social linkages to knowledge spillovers could be a useful addition to the literature.

The knowledge spillover and then intention-behavior link

In strategic entrepreneurship research, an urgent need exists to investigate the link between intention to utilize and behavioral outcomes from knowledge spillovers. The importance of looking at the intention–behavior link in entrepreneurship research is emphasized by Bird (1992) who stated that there are many interrelated processes that are weaving together to form entrepreneurial ventures. This means that it takes time for the effect of knowledge spillovers to be felt depending on the entrepreneur's intention behind the use of knowledge.

The synchronization of activities also helps to form entrepreneurial patterns that emerge from knowledge spillovers. Fayolle and Linan (2014:665) state 'knowledge of the mechanisms and the temporalities that affect how entrepreneurial intentions lead to behaviors is still poor'. This creates opportunities for researchers using time series or panel studies to focus on the intention–behavior link in the knowledge spillover realm. This helps create new research ideas about how firms intend to locate and communicate with potential knowledge spillover partners.

Entrepreneurship researchers should apply different theoretical frameworks to the study of knowledge spillovers and the intention–behavior link. As most theories about behavior come from the psychology field, it would be useful to follow this tradition by applying social cognitive theory to knowledge spillovers. The role of social cognitive theory on technological innovations is a future research avenue that could be applied to knowledge spillovers. This would provide support for most of the current theoretical frameworks that use economic geography to evaluate knowledge spillovers. By utilizing social cognitive theory, it would provide support for the view that internal and external environmental factors affect behavior. Other theories such as action–theory or implementation–intention utilize knowledge and self-efficacy to evaluate proposed behaviors. Researchers should integrate social cognitive theory to the study of the intention–behavior link between knowledge spillovers and strategic entrepreneurship.

Measuring knowledge spillovers

Most research on knowledge spillovers examines them by focusing on horizontal and vertical differences. Horizontal spillovers occur when the knowledge is spread and received by firms in the same industry. Sometimes horizontal spillovers are referred to as inter-industry spillovers due to the recognition that firms usually get knowledge by association with others in the same field. Vertical or intra-industry spillovers occur between firms in different industries. This occurs when business activities in the value chain are shared amongst firms allowing them to access knowledge from other sources.

The non-measurability of knowledge spillovers means that capturing it in an explicit form is difficult for researchers. New measures of knowledge spillovers are needed that have more accurate recordings of the innovation that occurs. Future research could look at the quality of knowledge spillovers to see how a firm gathers external information during the entrepreneurship process. There is a difficulty in measuring knowledge spillovers, which requires further research attention. Particularly with international networks, the knowledge received and utilized may differ depending on the source but also the regulations that govern its usage. The role of knowledge spillovers has recently been highlighted by international regulatory bodies spending more time on intellectual capital and patent protection. This has been apparent in the smartphone industry with the regulation of knowledge spillovers becoming a political issue.

Knowledge flows are invisible, hard to track and difficult to measure (Krugman, 1991).

More research is needed on finding better ways to measure knowledge spillovers. At the moment most research about knowledge spillovers use proxies based on proximity or technological distance. Proximity is utilized in knowledge spillovers because geographical distance between firms helps encourage the receiving and sharing of information (Anselin et al., 1997). This means that location is a core element of existing knowledge spillover research but due to the increased usage of telecommunications the traditional definition of location being geographically based may need to change. Technological distance is similar to proximity but it focuses on research areas or clusters that encourage knowledge spillovers. As Mohnen (1997) points out there are numerous ways to measure spillovers due to the complexity of research and development in technology firms.

Strategic perspective of the knowledge spillover theory of entrepreneurship

This book was premised by an interest in understanding the role that knowledge spillovers play in strategic entrepreneurship. While many articles, books and policies have analyzed the effects of knowledge spillovers, few sources have integrated the strategic perspective into the knowledge spillover theory of entrepreneurship. Some of the chapters in this book have examined knowledge spillovers from regional and industry settings, but this could be combined with future research activity. In this research book, we observed that knowledge spillovers differ at the firm, regional and international level. It would be useful to compare these levels by obtaining a sample of firms at different stages of the knowledge spillover process. This could be combined by examining the varying perspectives of knowledge spillovers at alternative positions in an organization. Employees, supervisors and entrepreneurs evaluate knowledge spillovers by the impact they have on their jobs or firm positions in the marketplace. Future research could try to understand the effect that leadership innovation has on the positive effect of knowledge spillovers on strategic entrepreneurship. As a consequence, entrepreneurs can more easily establish who they should form an exchange with in order to obtain knowledge spillovers. This could include more research focusing on the negotiation of partnership agreements to see how knowledge spillovers are assessed in order to take into account the knowledge being transferred.

In this book, we have analyzed knowledge spillovers by taking into account a broad definition of how firms learn. It would be interesting to observe how firms learn by establishing relationships in the marketplace. Following the knowledge spillover literature, we have assumed that firms learn by doing, and the more knowledge that is spilled over the more they learn. This means that it would be intriguing for future research to look more into the experiential learning process especially with emerging technologies that are transforming the marketplace. We propose a future research line in the study of knowledge spillovers in investigating knowledge from different disciplines that have been largely ignored in the literature. As most research has focused on high technology industries, a fruitful research avenue would be to focus on the non-profit or social sector to see the role of knowledge spillovers by volunteers into profit-orientated firms. In addition, new industries such as the arts and sports sectors could be studied to see the role of non-profits and the knowledge spilled over into the professional sport sector.

Experiential knowledge spillovers

Knowledge is acquired based on experiences and situations that individuals encounter in their lives. We might study social psychology to find out more about the knowledge spillover process. This would enable a better understanding of how knowledge is stored and organized based on social psychology principles based on experiential spillovers. It would also allow us to go beyond entrepreneurship and knowledge management theory to find the determinants of the complex process of knowledge to help understand the business applications. Potential questions of interest might be: How does social psychology impact knowledge spillovers? What kind of social situations impact the discovery of knowledge spillovers?

There is a vague understanding of knowledge as it is rarely explained in terms of its definitions. Knowledge continually evolves because of its dynamic nature and integrative role in society. The evolution of knowledge depends on the ability and willingness to understand information. A broad definition of knowledge is that it involves all abilities and cognitions used to understand and make decisions about information. This means that knowledge is a tool that can be used consciously or unconsciously by an individual. The impact of knowledge depends on the context and time in which it is accessed, which affects the process of spillovers.

Knowledge can be acquired in a variety of ways, including experiential or objective ways (Diez-Vial and Fernandez-Olmos, 2014). Experiential knowledge is learning through experience and is typically learning by doing (Johanson and Vahlne, 1977). For entrepreneurship, experiential knowledge is an essential part of the venture process and helps distinguish successful businesses. The key focus of experiential knowledge is that it involves how to do something (Kogut and Zander, 1992). This is important for firms but is often tacit and difficult to obtain. Objective knowledge involves the collection of information through reports, websites or research (Diez-Vial and Fernandez-Olmos, 2014).

Diez-Vial and Fernandez-Olmos (2015:71) highlights how 'firms in science and technology parks benefit from knowledge spillovers that can be a consequence of research, ideas and experience stemming from universities or research centres . . . as well as from co-located firms such as providers, clients or socially-related firms'. This enables the recipient of a knowledge spillover to be the individuals or firms that adopt newly generated knowledge accessed through internal or external sources. Knowledge recipients need to have the capacity to utilize knowledge and be able to learn new processes (Cohen and Levinthal, 1990). This may occur through cognitive capacities that enable the learning of new knowledge. Firms often seek external knowledge through indirect market mechanisms like knowledge spillovers (Alcacer and Chung, 2007). These indirect flows of knowledge can occur by serendipity or informal arrangements. The transfer of knowledge is usually tacit, meaning it requires frequent interactions from firms involved in the process.

International context of knowledge spillovers

There are several areas of research that remain. The international context, especially in the context of increasing computing power, needs further examination. There may be other mechanisms apart from spillovers that are more effective for accessing knowledge and location choice might be less relevant due to the increasing amount of electronic information. As Alcacer and Chung (2007) point out there are idiosyncrasies of innovation systems that affect knowledge spillovers. Especially in the United States there exists an entrepreneurial culture fostering knowledge spillovers, which may be different due to the cultural conditions in other countries. This gives rise for further inquiries from international comparisons about the role of culture on knowledge spillovers and strategic entrepreneurship. Other mechanisms apart from location might benefit from additional scrutiny in the international context.

The development of knowledge spillovers is constructed based on local and foreign environments that influence market opportunities. Future research needs to acknowledge an international opportunity about creating knowledge from information collected in a multiple country context rather than a single partner approach. Mainela et al. (2014:12) states that 'researchers need to be able to collect data and analyze the ways in which the entrepreneurial mind arranges the pieces of information, relates them to one another and thereby creates a new knowledge structure, an international opportunity'. This is particularly important in the context of developed countries but also emerging countries, which are transforming their economic systems as a result of knowledge spillovers.

More research that explores culture and the way individuals receive knowledge spillovers would enhance our understanding of the process. A logical next step would be to cross-culturally compare the transmitting and receiving of knowledge spillovers. Overall, our book highlights knowledge spillover differences in how firms pursue strategic entrepreneurship. International strategies for firms in knowledge industries are becoming more apparent in the need to maximize the use of potential spillovers. Research that explores the nexus between knowledge spillovers and strategic entrepreneurship are important for enhancing our understanding in this fertile research area.

The role of collocation in knowledge spillovers is important to understanding the link between collaboration and location in strategic entrepreneurship. Alcacer and Chung (2007) highlight how collocation benefits a firm's competitive position in an industry. Our book has supported the idea that the role of collocation is changing as more communication is done via the internet and there is less dependence on face-to-face interactions. Firms may choose to locate in regions closer to family or friends rather than for business reasons. By looking at firms' strategies around location it will be interesting for future research to see how location takes on a different meaning.

Knowledge-based innovation and spillovers

The main sources of knowledge spillovers are industry, academia and government (Alcacer and Chung, 2007). Industry or private sources produce more appropriable knowledge due to their practical applicability. Academia and government sources are public depositories of knowledge that contain more theoretical forms that can be commercialized when combined with private sources. The shift towards a knowledge economy has meant firms focus more on innovation for their competitiveness. This requires more careful consideration about the role of knowledge-based innovation on environmental uncertainty. This book has important implications for firms, entrepreneurs and policy makers. Our book has demonstrated how firms contribute to knowledge-based innovation and global competitiveness.

We highlight in the book the intriguing issue of whether knowledge spillovers are a good thing in terms of their potential entrepreneurial applications. Most current research focuses on the positive benefits of knowledge spillovers but in addition to the advantages of innovation there may be disadvantages to societal well-being. This is evident in the increased number of people working from home and telecommunicating instead of the past usage of offices as a way to interact with other members of a firm. This increasing isolation of knowledge workers may mean that spillovers are occurring more through online networking rather than the traditional past forms of communication. An open question for future research is: Are knowledge spillovers and strategic entrepreneurship a positive or negative for society? A related area worth investigation is the use of different types of knowledge spillovers for societal advancement.

Conclusion

This book has analyzed how knowledge spillovers can increase entrepreneurship by strategically assimilating and exploiting knowledge. In the book, we observed how there are a number of ways firms utilize knowledge spillovers from the type, context and involvement with partners. The results of the book chapters indicate that knowledge spillovers can have a positive influence on strategic entrepreneurship by increasing innovation and development. We examined in the book chapters how firms utilize knowledge spillovers by contributing to innovative business activity. In this sense, the spillover of knowledge by firms succeeds in international markets by acting as innovation depositories.

This book makes several important contributions to the literature about knowledge spillovers. First, we extend the current thinking about the role of firms' strategies to innovation performance. By doing so we seek to develop a better understanding of the strategies organizations use to improve the processes they use to acquire and utilize knowledge spillovers. Second, we identify the positive and negative elements of knowledge spillovers in different country contexts. As little prior research has paid attention to emerging economies, we utilize different economic stages of development to see the various approaches to knowledge spillovers. This will help us to gain a better understanding of the contextual factors affecting the process of knowledge spillovers. It will also allow a more comprehensive framework to develop that includes knowledge spillovers at different stages of economic development. Third, we highlight the interplay between receiving and sending knowledge to see how it impacts entrepreneurial strategies for organizations. By doing so, we show how entrepreneurship is developed from knowledge spillovers, depending on the strategies utilized by organizations. Finally, we add to the literature about knowledge spillovers by exploring it in both the profit and non-profit sectors. This helps future research integrate existing research with social organizations that are shifting to more profit-orientated strategies.

This book adds to the existing literature about knowledge spillovers by including a number of chapters from different industry and contextual situations. The purpose of these chapters is to develop ideas and thoughts around knowledge spillovers in order to suggest new directions for future research. The evolution of the literature on knowledge spillovers is a good example of integrating economic geography, regional development and knowledge management with entrepreneurship theory. The move in the knowledge spillover literature to shift more into the entrepreneurship realm has coincided with the increased interest about innovation clusters.

Knowledge spillovers are a crucial area of research within the field of strategic entrepreneurship. The ongoing importance of knowledge spillovers is shown in the number of citations papers about this topic receive in the literature. This is partly due to the increased significance of the knowledge economy to society and the growing role technology plays in everyday lives. Research about knowledge spillovers continues to attract the attention of policy makers, whose role is to leverage competitive advantage to generate better regional performance. As new knowledge emerges more questions arise about the spillover effect to regions and more broadly the integration of the process into regional activity. Therefore, more research is necessary to contribute to our understanding about the dynamic nature of knowledge spillovers. It is hoped the chapters in this research book will extend current thinking about knowledge spillovers from a strategic entrepreneurship point of view. We look forward to contributing to the continued debate about the effectiveness of knowledge spillovers in the global economy.

References

Acs, Z.J., Braunerhjelm, P., Audretsch, D.B. and Carlsson, B. (2009) 'The knowledge spillover theory of entrepreneurship', *Small Business Economics*, 32(1): 15–30.
Agarwal, R., Audretsch, D.B. and Sarkar, M.B. (2010) 'Knowledge spillovers and strategic entrepreneruship', *Strategic Entrepreneurship Journal*, 4(4): 271–83.

Alcacer, J. and Chung, W. (2007) 'Location strategies and knowledge spillovers', *Management Science*, 53(5): 760–76.

Anselin, L., Varga, A. and Acs, Z. (1997) 'Local geographic spillovers between university research and high technology innovations', *Journal of Urban Economics*, 42(3): 422–48.

Antonelli, C. (2008) *Localised technological change: Towards the economics of complexity*, London, Routledge.

Asheim, B. and Gertler, M. (2005) 'The geography of innovation: Regional innovation systems', In J. Fagerberg, C. Mowery and R.R. Nelson (Eds) *The Oxford Handbook of Innovation*, pp 291–317, Oxford, Oxford University Press.

Audretsch, D.B. (1998) 'Agglomeration and the location of innovative activity', *Oxford Review of Economic Policy*, 14(2): 18–29.

Audretsch, D.B. and Keilbach, M. (2004) 'Does entrepreneurship matter?', *Entrepreneurship Theory and Practice*, 28: 419–30.

Audretsch, D.B. and Lehmann, E. (2006) 'Entrepreneurial access and absorption of knowledge spillovers: Strategic board and managerial composition for competitive advantage', *Journal of Small Business Management*, 44(2): 155–66.

Bathelt, H., Malmberg, A. and Maskell, P. (2004) 'Clusters and knowledge: Local buzz, global pipelines and the process of knowledge creation', *Progress in Human Geography*, 28(1): 31–56.

Bird, B. (1992) 'The operation of intentions in time: The emergence of the new venture', *Entrepreneurship Theory and Practice*, 17(1): 11–20.

Brown, J.S. and Duguid, P. (2000) *The social life of information*. Boston, Harvard Business School Press.

Cohen, W.M. and Levinthal, D.A. (1990) 'Absorptive capacity: A new perspective on learning and innovation', *Administrative Science Quarterly*, 35(1): 128–52.

Diez-Vial, I. and Fernandez-Olmos, M. (2014) 'How do local knowledge spillovers and experience affect export performance', *European Planning Studies*, 22(1): 143–63.

Diez-Vial, I. and Fernandez-Olmos, M. (2015) 'Knowledge spillovers in science and technology parks: How can firms benefit most?', *The Journal of Technology Transfer*, 40(1): 70–84.

Drucker, P.F. (1989) *The new realities: In government and politics/in economics and business/in society and world view*, New York, Harper and Row.

Fayolle, A. and Linan, F. (2014) 'The future of research on entrepreneurial intentions', *Journal of Business Research*, 67: 663–66.

Gilbert, B.A., Mc Dougall-Covin, P.P. and Audretsch, D. (2008) 'Clusters, knowledge spillovers and new venture performance: An empirical examination', *Journal of Business Venturing*, 23: 405–22.

Huggins, R. and Thompson, P. (2015) 'Entrepreneurship, innovation and regional growth: A network theory', *Small Business Economics*, 45: 103–28.

Johanson, J. and Vahlne, J.E. (1977) 'The internationalization process of the firm- a model of knowledge development and increasing foreign market commitments', *Journal of International Business Studies*, 8(1): 23–32.

Ko, W.W. and Liu, G. (2015) 'Understanding the process of knowledge spillovers: Learning to become social enterprises', *Strategic Entrepreneurship Journal*, 9: 263–85.

Kogut, B. and Zander, U. (1992) 'Knowledge of the firm, combinative capabilities, and the replication of technology', *Organization Science*, 3(3): 383–97.

Krugman, P. (1991) *Geography and trade*, MIT Press, Cambridge.

Linan, F., Urbano, D. and Guerrero, M. (2011) 'Regional variations in entrepreneurial cognitions: Start-up intentions of university students in Spain', *Entrepreneurship and Regional Development*, 23(3&4): 187–215.

Mainela, T. Puhakka, V. and Servais, P. (2014) 'The concept of international opportunity in international entrepreneurship: A review and a research agenda', *International Journal of Management Reviews*, 16: 105–29.

Mattes, J. (2012) 'Dimensions of proximity and knowledge bases: Innovation between spatial and non-spatial factors', *Regional Studies*, 46(8): 1085–99.

Maula, M., Keil, T. and Zahra, S. (2013) 'Top management's attention to discontinuous technological change: Corporate venture capital as an alert mechanism', *Organization Science*, 24(3): 926–47.

Mohnen, P. (1997) 'Introduction: Input-Output analysis of interindustry R&D spillovers', *Economic Systems Research*, 9(1): 3–8.

Narayanan, V., Yang, Y. and Zahra, S. (2009) 'Corporate venturing and value creation: A review and proposed framework', *Research Policy*, 38:58–76.

Nelson, R.R. and Winter, S.G. (1982) *An evolutionary theory of economic change*, Cambridge, MA, Belknap Press.

Nonaka, I. and Takeuchi, H. (1995) *The knowledge-creating company: How Japanese companies create the dynamics of innovation*, Oxford, Oxford University Press.

Welter, F. (2011) 'Contextualizing entrepreneurship: Conceptual challenges and ways forward', *Entrepreneurship Theory and Practice*, 35: 165–84.

Welter, F. and Smallbone, D. (2012) 'Institutional perspectives on entrepreneurship', In D. Hjorth (Ed) *Handbook on organizational entrepreneurship*, pp 64–78, Cheltenham, Edward Elgar Publishing.

Zahra, S. (2015) 'Corporate entrepreneurship as knowledge creation and conversion: The role of entrepreneurial hubs', *Small Business Economics*, 44: 727–35.

Index

Page numbers in *italics* refer to figures and tables.

For Product Safety Concerns and Information please contact our EU
representative GPSR@taylorandfrancis.com
Taylor & Francis Verlag GmbH, Kaufingerstraße 24, 80331 München, Germany